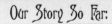

Our Story So Far:

Far, far away in the land of Spooner, terrible, cruel Sorcerers enslave defenseless Parsoners with their evil enchantments, and only one man can end the darkness! Well, actually, there are three men and two women. And those five are kinda helped by a goddess, her magical knights, and past generations of warriors. But still, you get the point—the odds are against justice in this wicked wizard world, where spirit-stealing spellcasters and nefarious necromancers are out to oppress the innocent.

In the last volume our heroes faced Sirus, a winged disciple of Lord Sacher with a soft spot in his heart for Daughter. However, it was only because of Daughter's urging for a truce that the battle came to a peaceful conclusion, in which their feathery foe willingly surrendered his Platina stone. Next, after taking a break from action to enter a local village's cooking contest, the gang faced down a wave of ninja assassins, as well as Kengyu Kiba, a fearsome guardian spirit. Marron stepped up to the challenge, and after Mille gave him the legendary Hamato Blade, his seemingly indestructible foe was defeated. But as the Hunters begin the last stretch of their journey to face Lord Sacher, one final challenge remains for Gateau...

CONTENTS

36 SEASIDE DAYS IN THE SPRINGTIME OF YOUTH

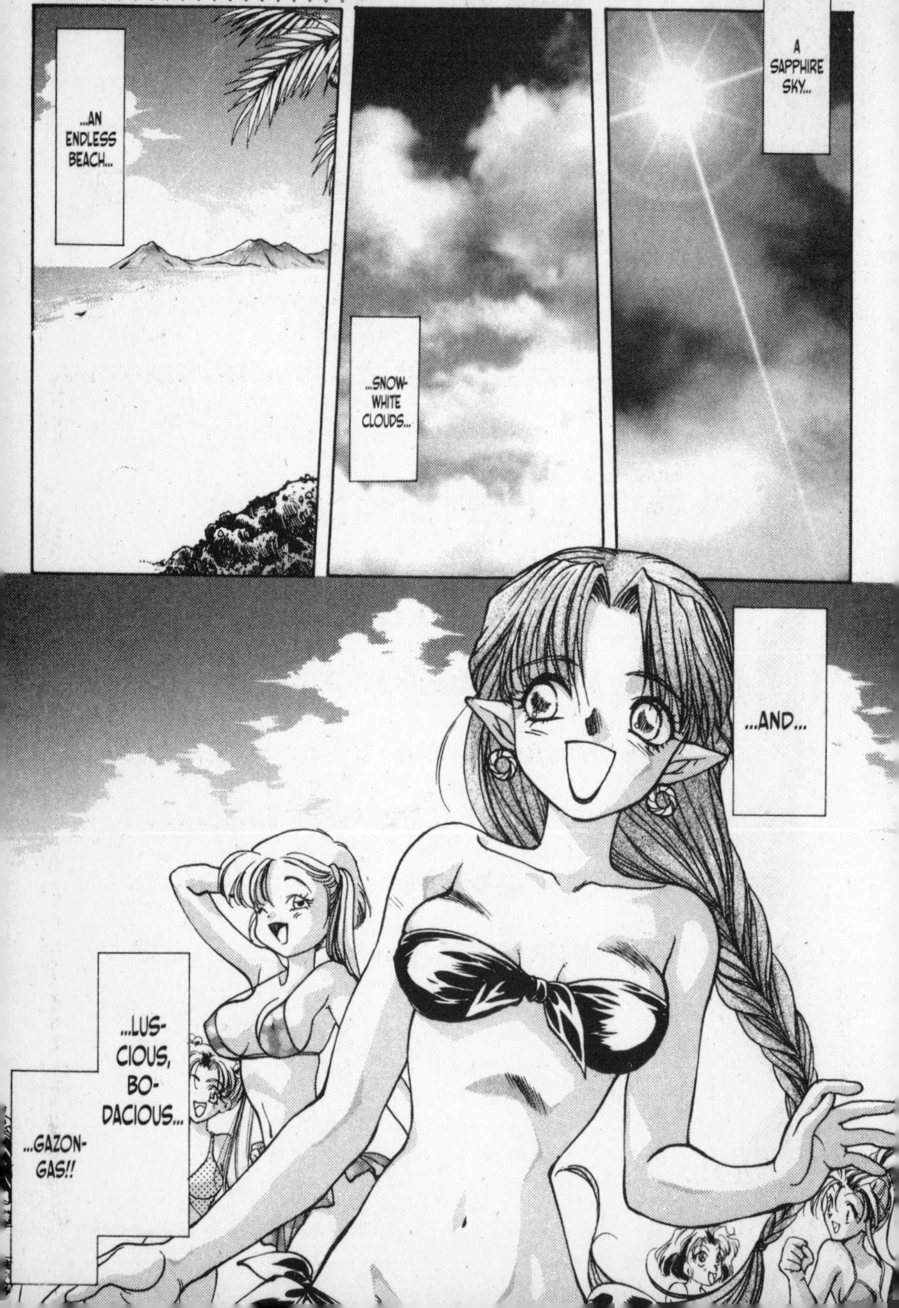
A SAPPHIRE SKY...
...SNOW-WHITE CLOUDS...
...AN ENDLESS BEACH...
...AND...
...LUS-CIOUS, BO-DACIOUS...
...GAZON-GAS!!

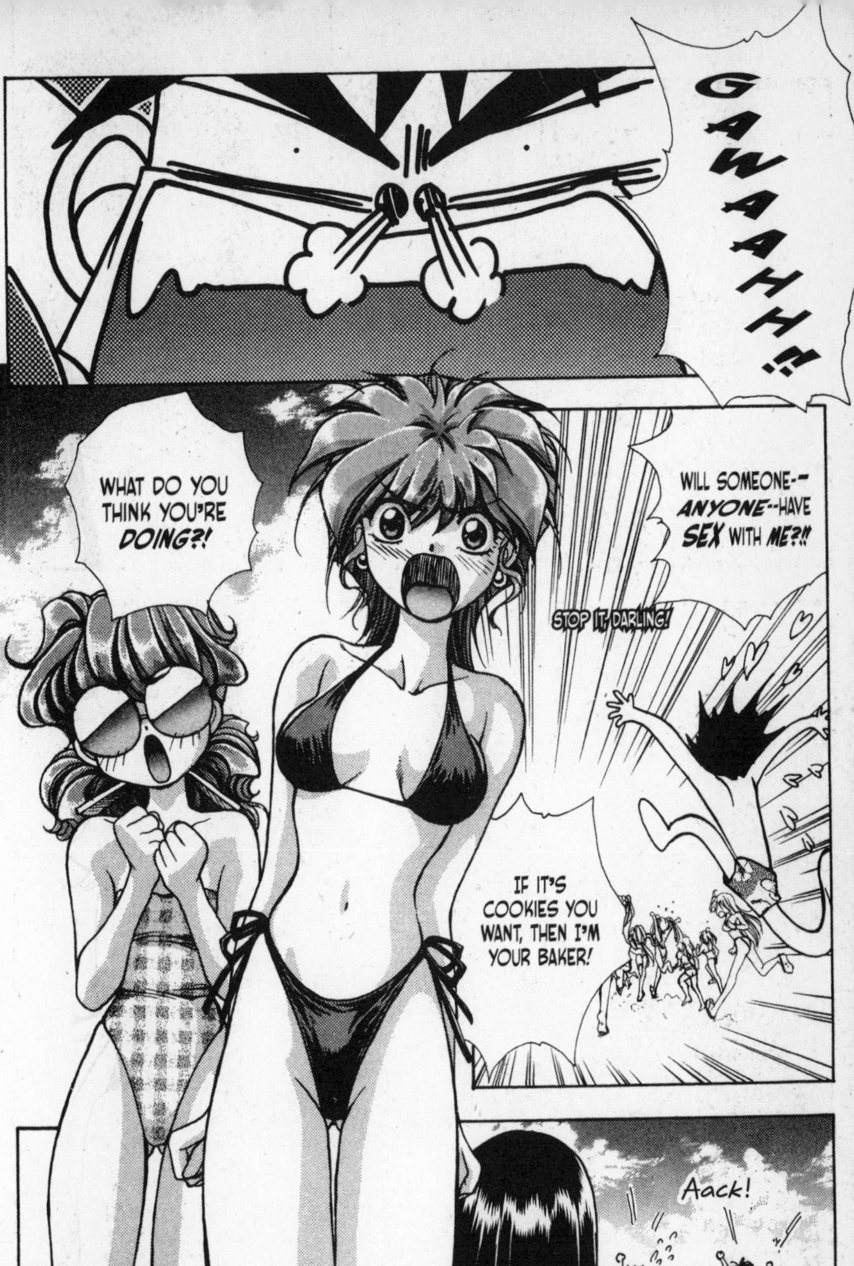
GAWAAHH?!!
WILL SOMEONE--ANYONE--HAVE SEX WITH ME?!!
STOP IT, DARLING!
IF IT'S COOKIES YOU WANT, THEN I'M YOUR BAKER!
WHAT DO YOU THINK YOU'RE DOING?!
Aack!

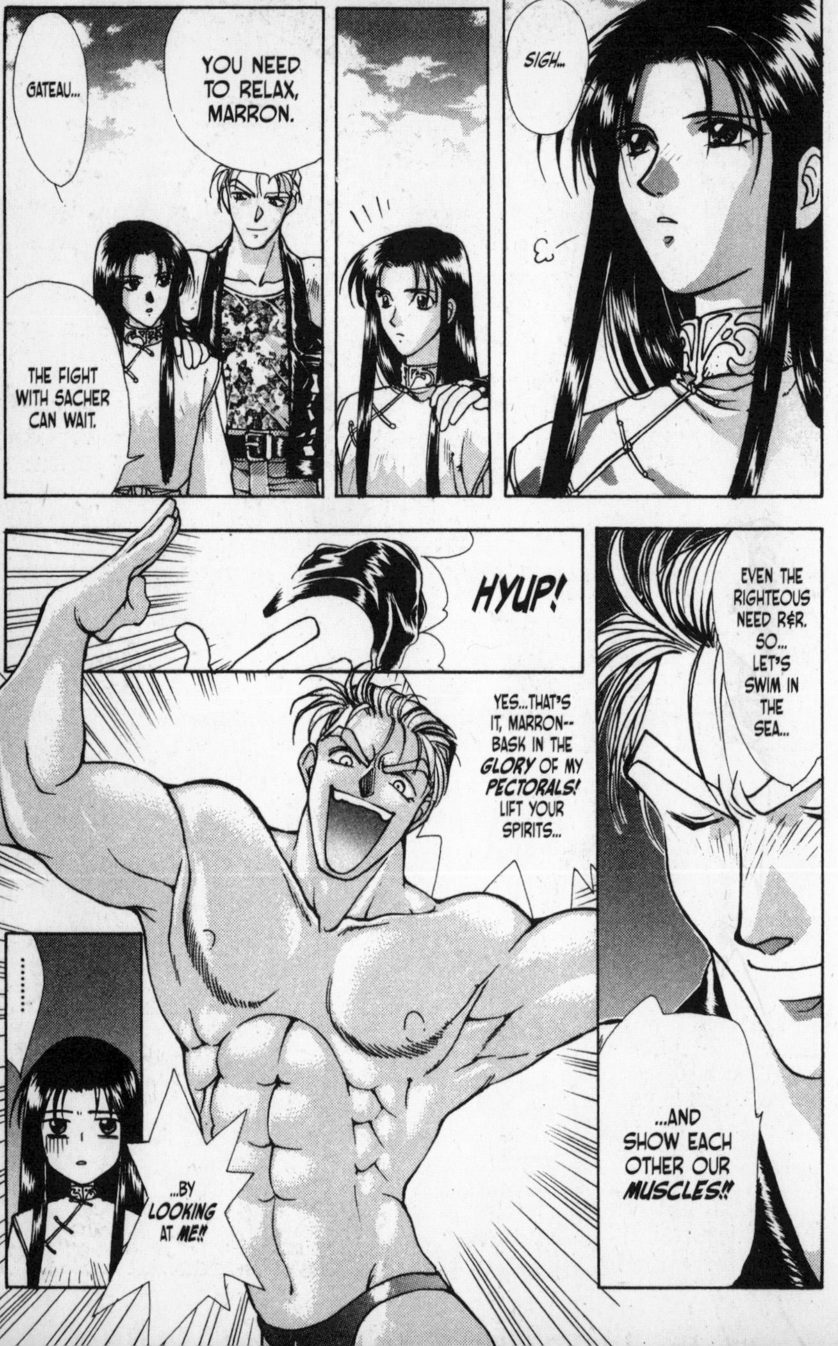
SIGH...
YOU NEED TO RELAX, MARRON.
GATEAU...
THE FIGHT WITH SACHER CAN WAIT.
EVEN THE RIGHTEOUS NEED R&R. SO... LET'S SWIM IN THE SEA...
...AND SHOW EACH OTHER OUR MUSCLES!!
HYUP!
YES...THAT'S IT, MARRON-- BASK IN THE GLORY OF MY PECTORALS! LIFT YOUR SPIRITS...
...BY LOOKING AT ME!!
....

Yeek! Yeek! Miss! Darling! Look at mee!

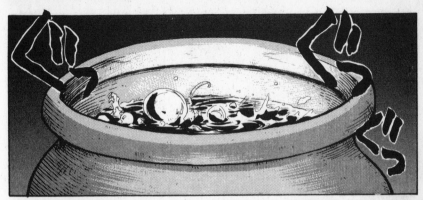

AACK!!

NYEH HEH HEH HEH...

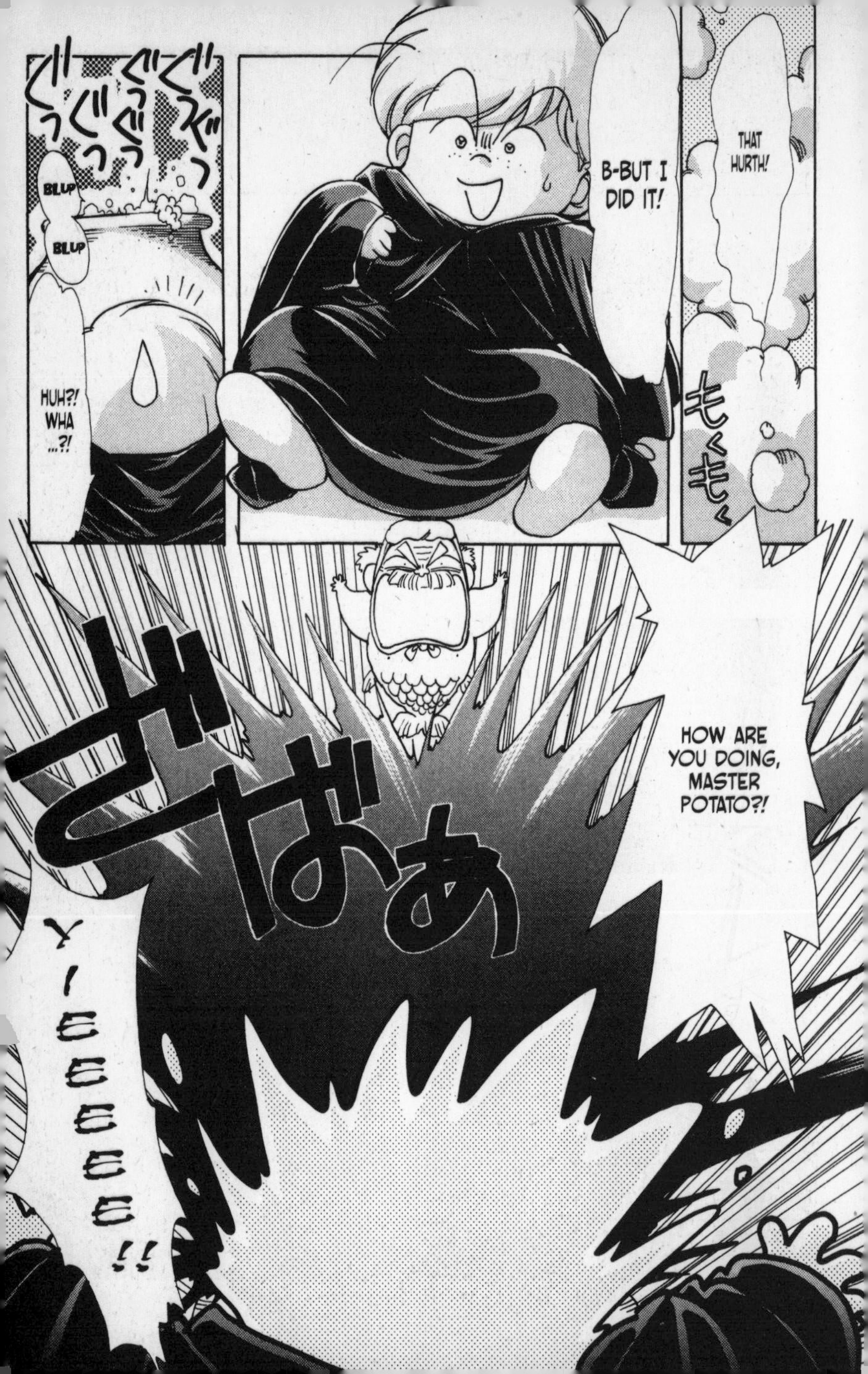
THAT HURTH!
もくもく
B-BUT I DID IT!
ぐつぐつ
BLUP
BLUP
HUH?! WHA ...?!
HOW ARE YOU DOING, MASTER POTATO?!
ざばあ
YIEEEEEE!!

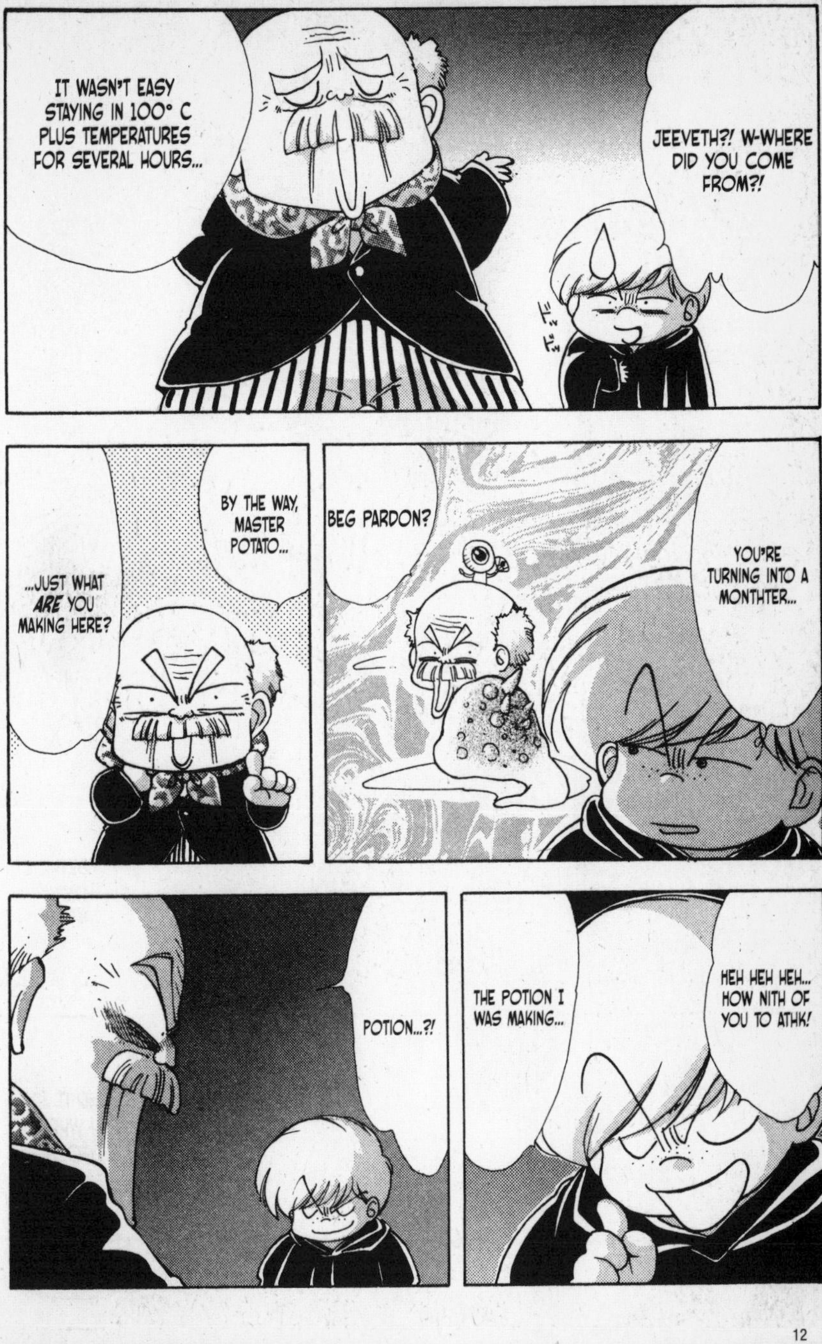
JEEVETH?! W-WHERE DID YOU COME FROM?!
IT WASN'T EASY STAYING IN 100° C PLUS TEMPERATURES FOR SEVERAL HOURS...
YOU'RE TURNING INTO A MONTHTER...
BEG PARDON?
BY THE WAY, MASTER POTATO...
...JUST WHAT ***ARE*** YOU MAKING HERE?
HEH HEH HEH... HOW NITH OF YOU TO ATHK!
THE POTION I WAS MAKING...
POTION...?!

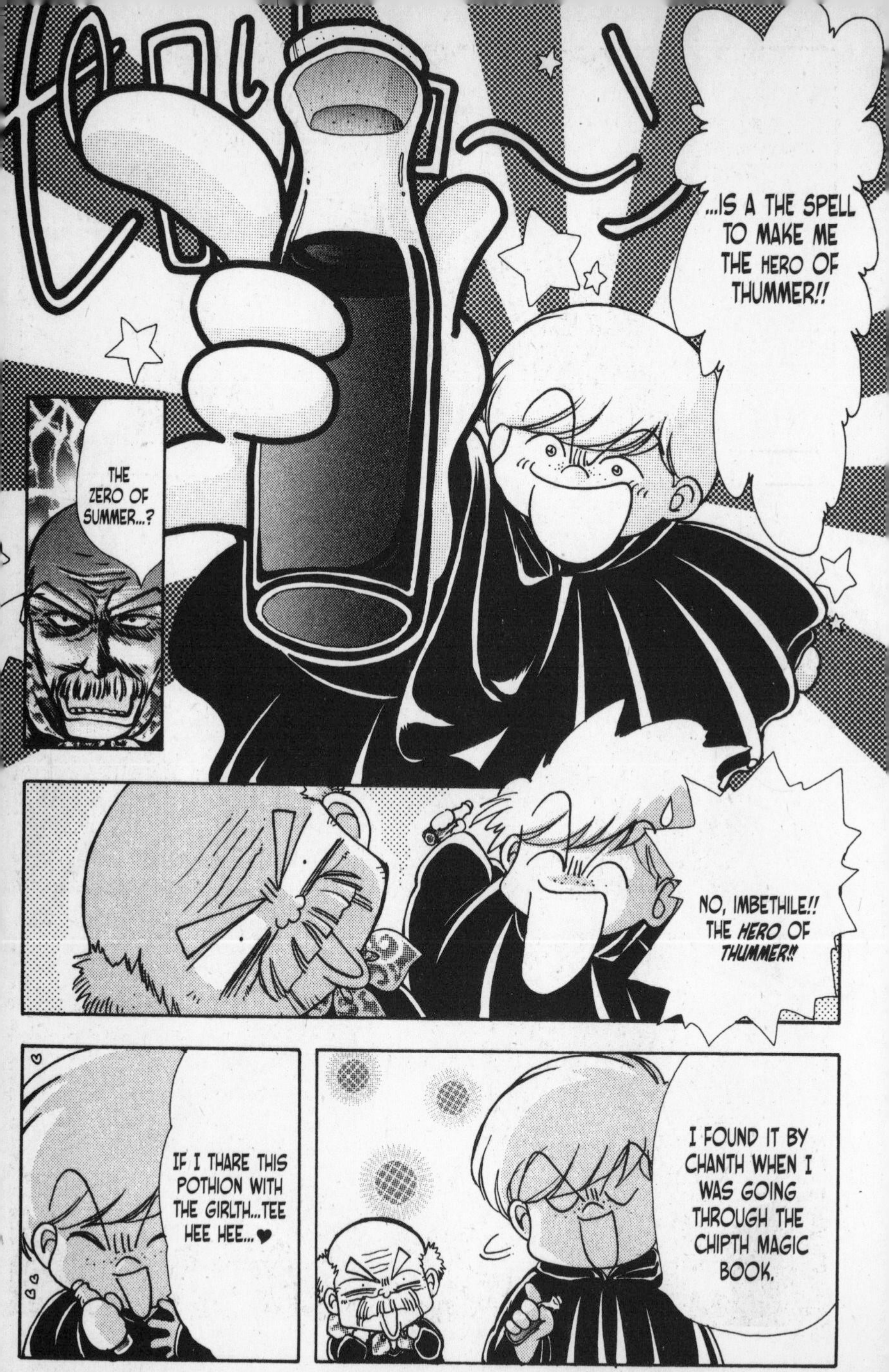
...IS A THE SPELL TO MAKE ME THE HERO OF THUMMER!!
THE ZERO OF SUMMER...?
NO, IMBETHILE!! THE *HERO* OF *THUMMER!!*
I FOUND IT BY CHANTH WHEN I WAS GOING THROUGH THE CHIPTH MAGIC BOOK.
IF I THARE THIS POTHION WITH THE GIRLTH...TEE HEE HEE...♥

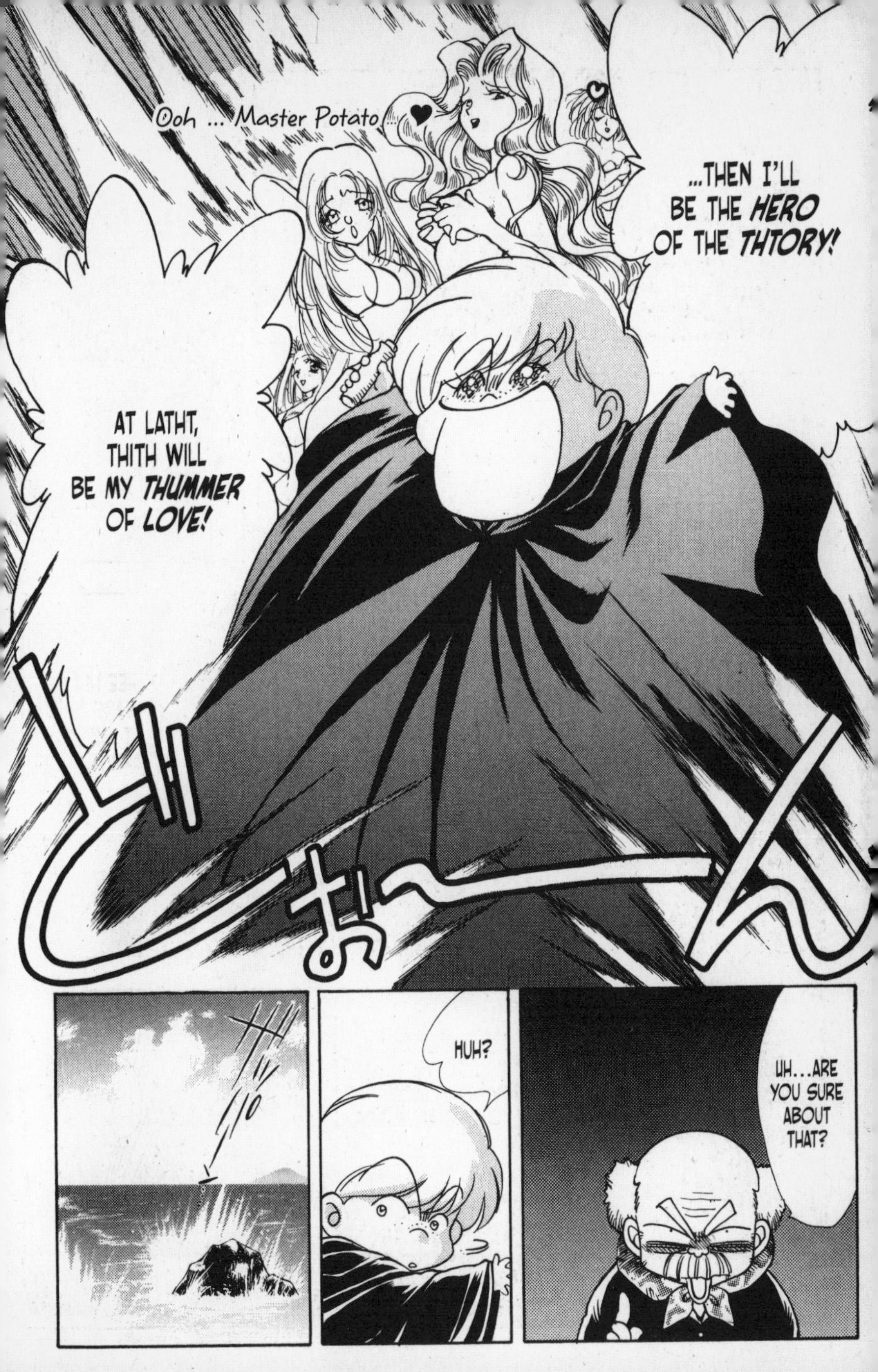
Ooh ... Master Potato ...
...THEN I'LL BE THE *HERO* OF THE *THTORY!*
AT LATHT, THITH WILL BE MY *THUMMER* OF *LOVE!*
どお〜ん
UH...ARE YOU SURE ABOUT THAT?
HUH?

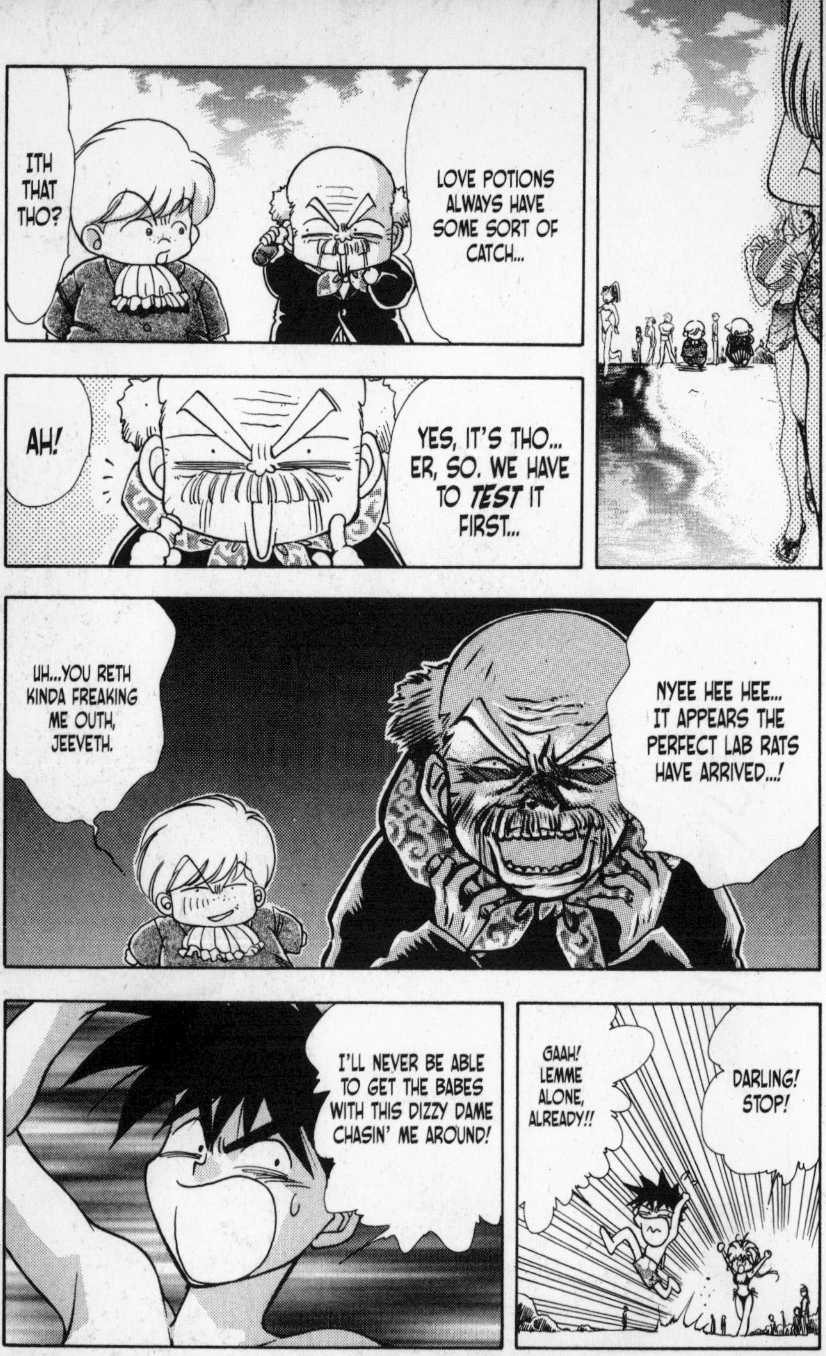
LOVE POTIONS ALWAYS HAVE SOME SORT OF CATCH...
ITH THAT THO?
YES, IT'S THO... ER, SO. WE HAVE TO *TEST* IT FIRST...
AH!
NYEE HEE HEE... IT APPEARS THE PERFECT LAB RATS HAVE ARRIVED...!
UH...YOU RETH KINDA FREAKING ME OUTH, JEEVETH.
DARLING! STOP!
GAAH! LEMME ALONE, ALREADY!!
I'LL NEVER BE ABLE TO GET THE BABES WITH THIS DIZZY DAME CHASIN' ME AROUND!

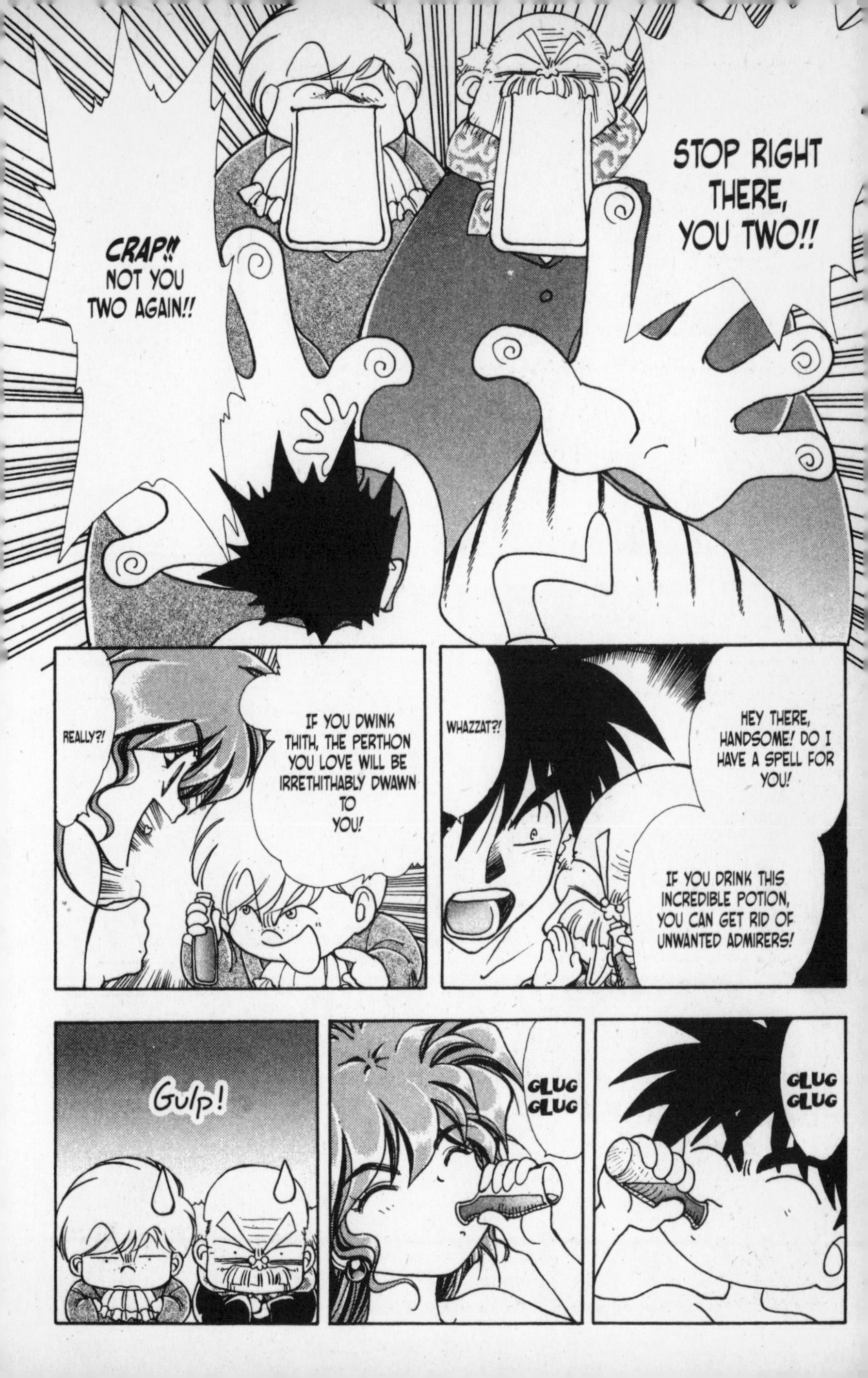

STOP RIGHT THERE, YOU TWO!!
CRAP!! NOT YOU TWO AGAIN!!
HEY THERE, HANDSOME! DO I HAVE A SPELL FOR YOU!
WHAZZAT?!
IF YOU DRINK THIS INCREDIBLE POTION, YOU CAN GET RID OF UNWANTED ADMIRERS!
IF YOU DWINK THITH, THE PERTHON YOU LOVE WILL BE IRRETHITHABLY DWAWN TO YOU!
REALLY?!
GLUG GLUG
GLUG GLUG
Gulp!

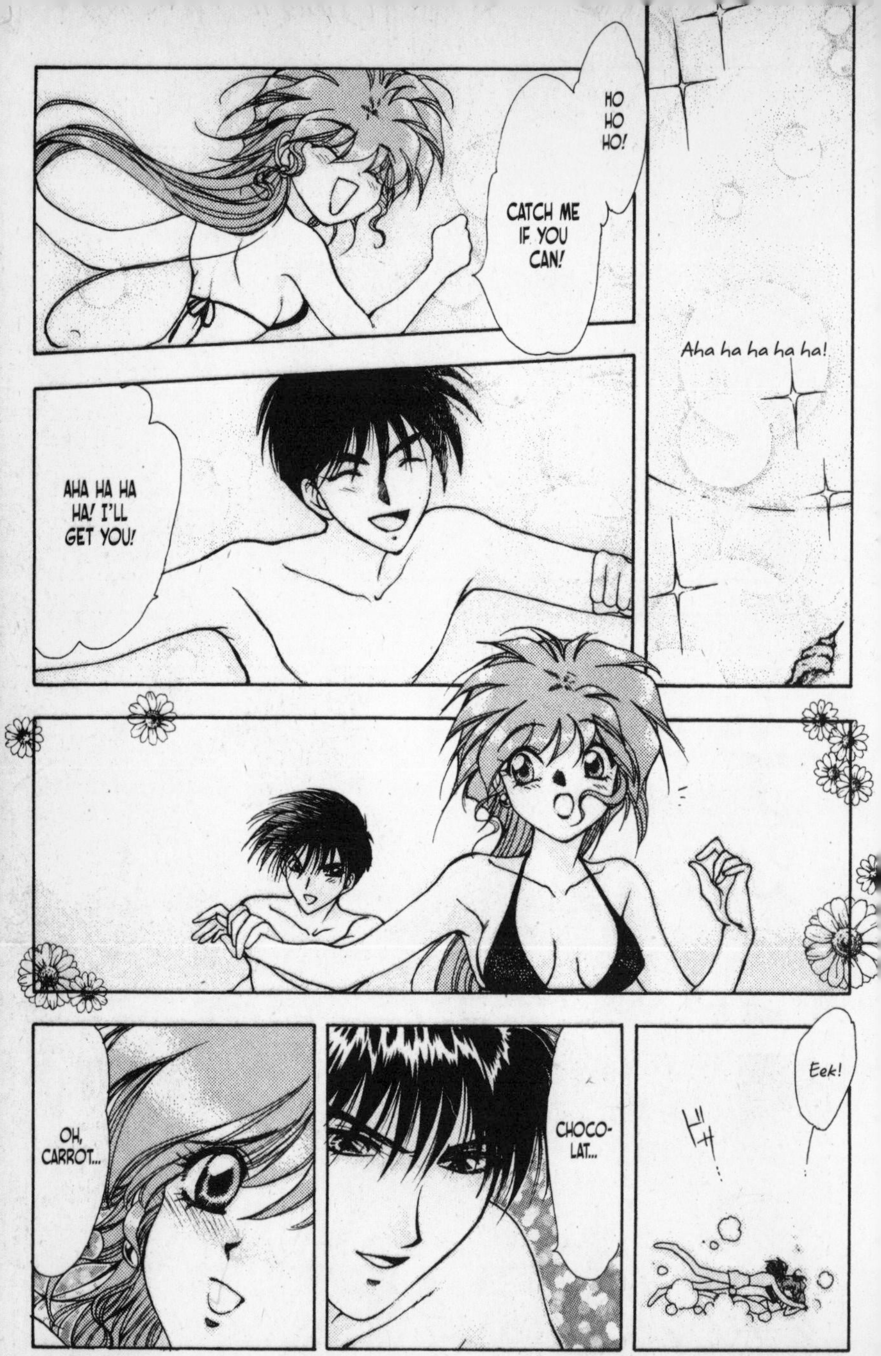
Aha ha ha ha ha!
HO HO HO!
CATCH ME IF YOU CAN!
AHA HA HA HA! I'LL GET YOU!
Eek!
CHOCO-LAT...
OH, CARROT...

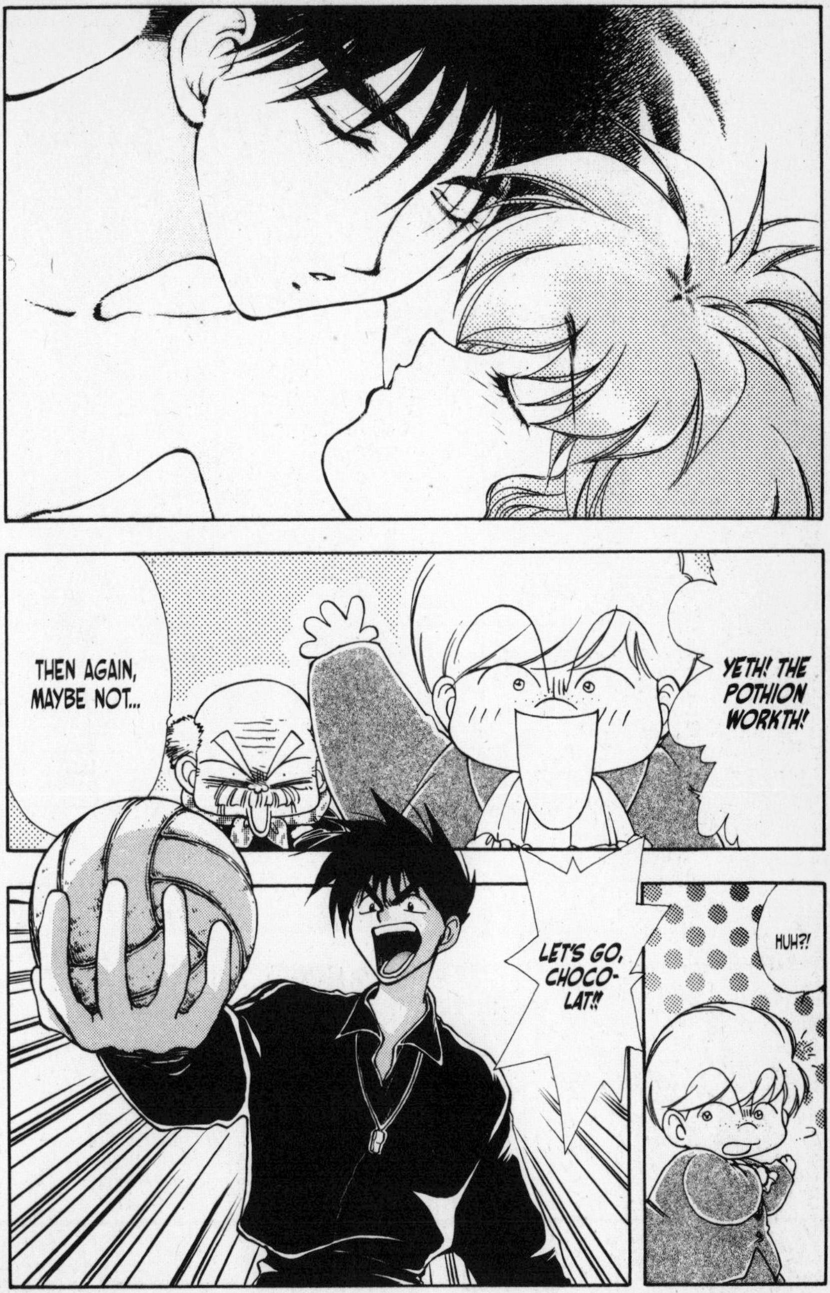
YETH! THE POTHION WORKTH!
THEN AGAIN, MAYBE NOT...
HUH?!
LET'S GO, CHOCO-LAT!!

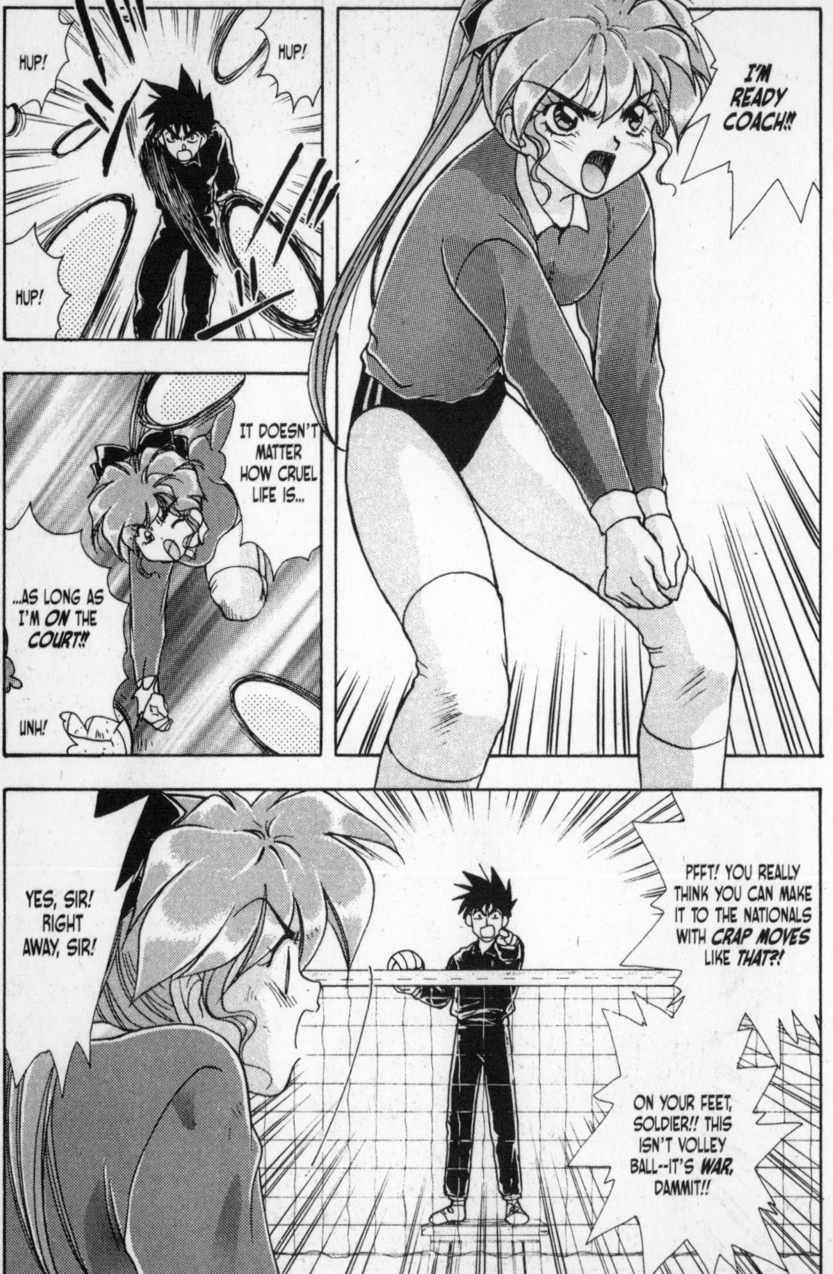
I'M READY COACH!!
HUP!
HUP!
HUP!
IT DOESN'T MATTER HOW CRUEL LIFE IS...
...AS LONG AS I'M ON THE COURT!!
UNH!
PFFT! YOU REALLY THINK YOU CAN MAKE IT TO THE NATIONALS WITH CRAP MOVES LIKE THAT?!
ON YOUR FEET, SOLDIER!! THIS ISN'T VOLLEY BALL--IT'S WAR, DAMMIT!!
YES, SIR! RIGHT AWAY, SIR!

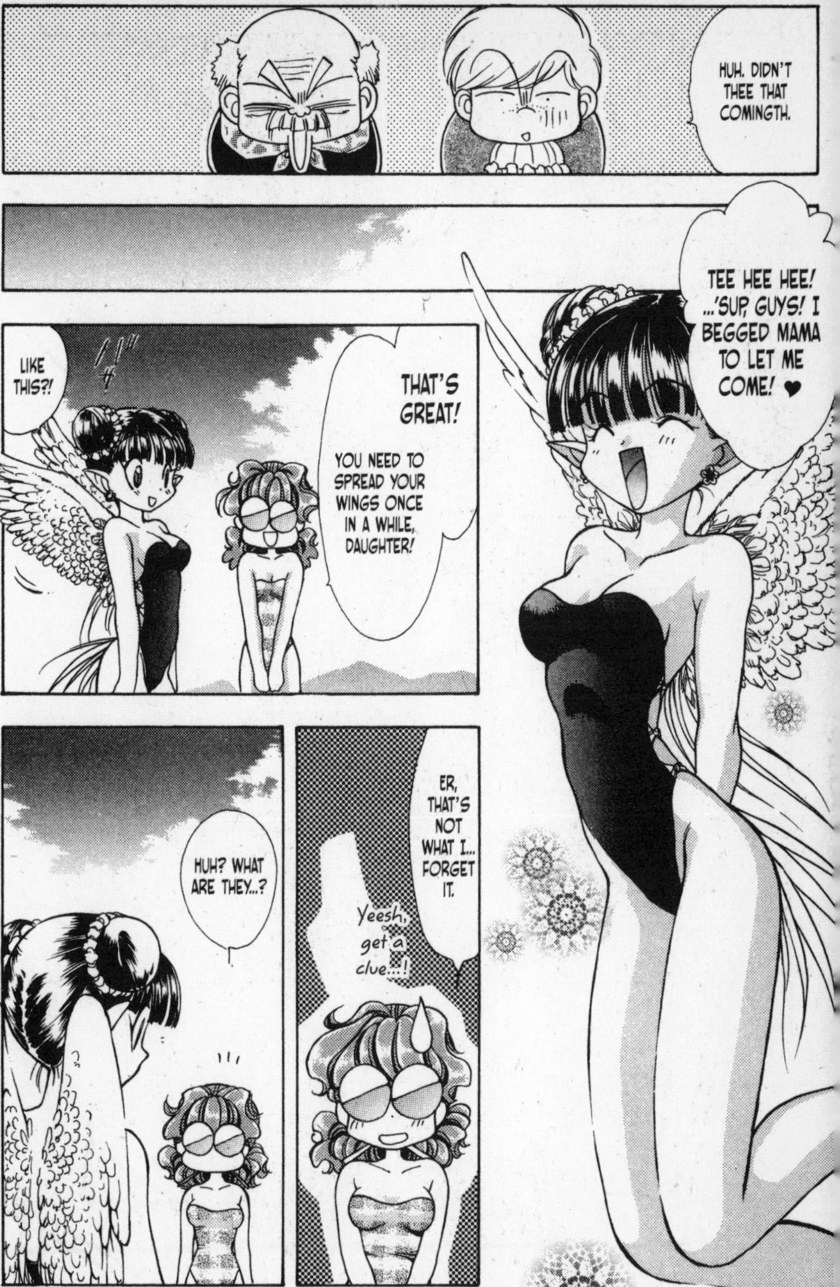
HUH. DIDN'T THEE THAT COMINGTH.
TEE HEE HEE! ...'SUP, GUYS! I BEGGED MAMA TO LET ME COME! ♥
THAT'S GREAT!
YOU NEED TO SPREAD YOUR WINGS ONCE IN A WHILE, DAUGHTER!
LIKE THIS?!
ER, THAT'S NOT WHAT I... FORGET IT.
Yeesh, get a clue...!
HUH? WHAT ARE THEY...?

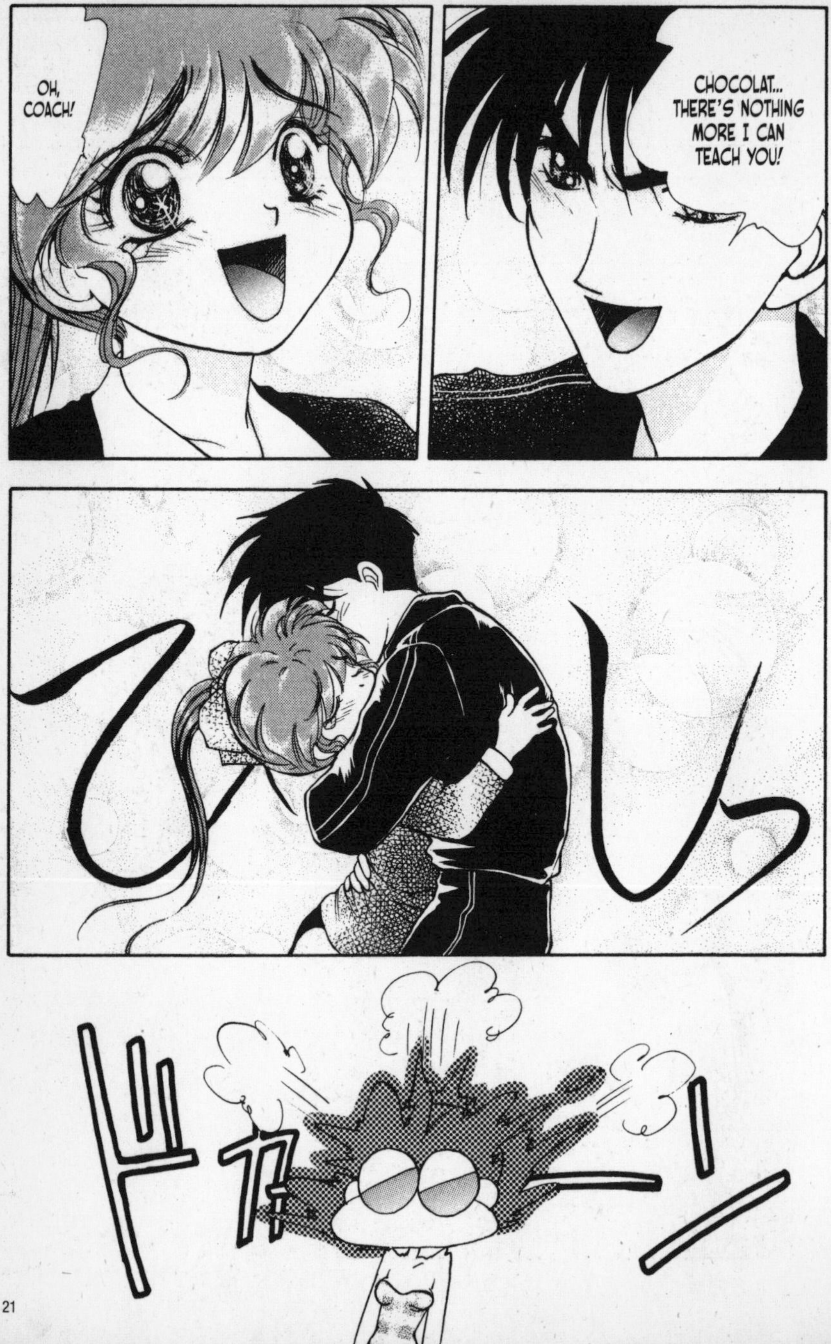
CHOCOLAT... THERE'S NOTHING MORE I CAN TEACH YOU!
OH, COACH!

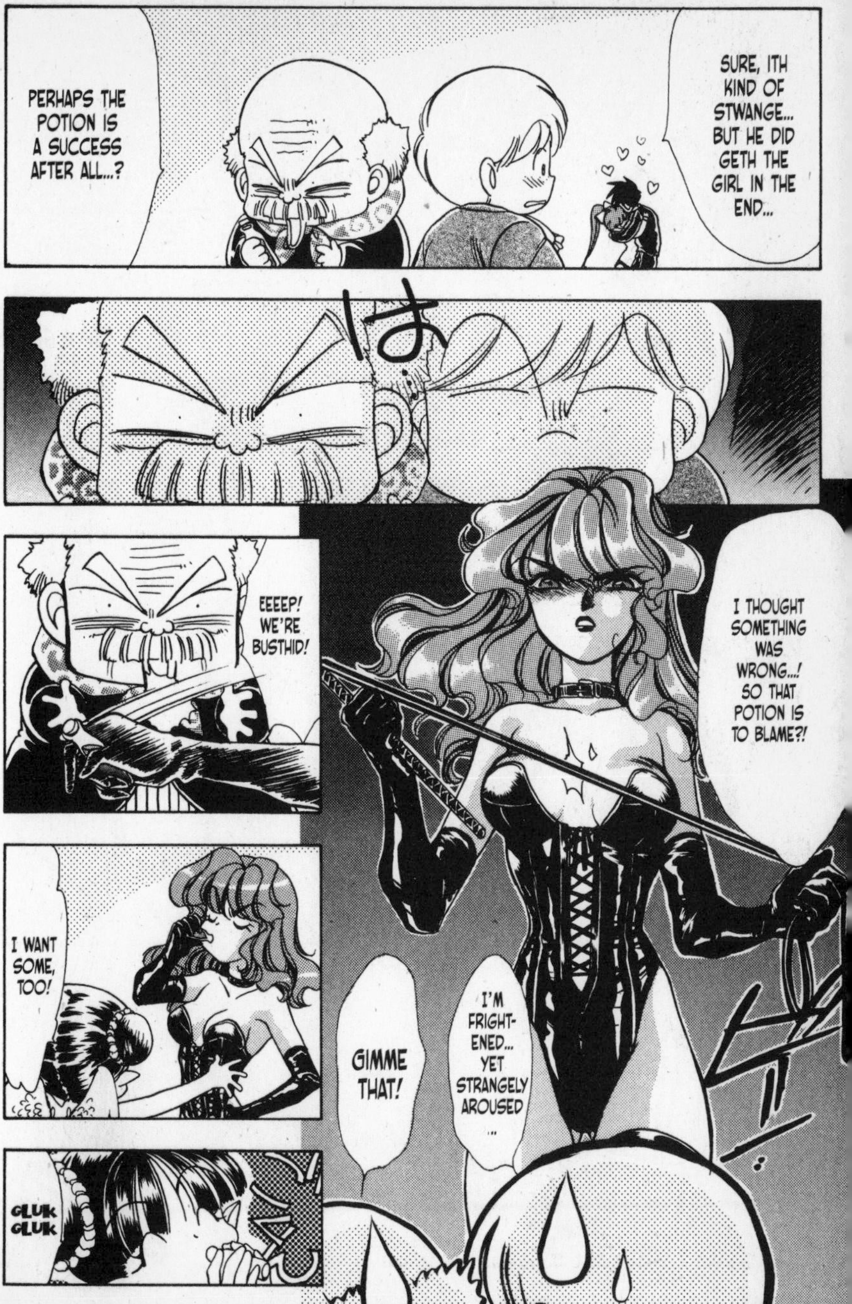
SURE, ITH KIND OF STWANGE... BUT HE DID GETH THE GIRL IN THE END...
PERHAPS THE POTION IS A SUCCESS AFTER ALL...?
は
I THOUGHT SOMETHING WAS WRONG...! SO THAT POTION IS TO BLAME?!
I'M FRIGHT-ENED... YET STRANGELY AROUSED...
GIMME THAT!
EEEEP! WE'RE BUSTHID!
I WANT SOME, TOO!
GLUK GLUK

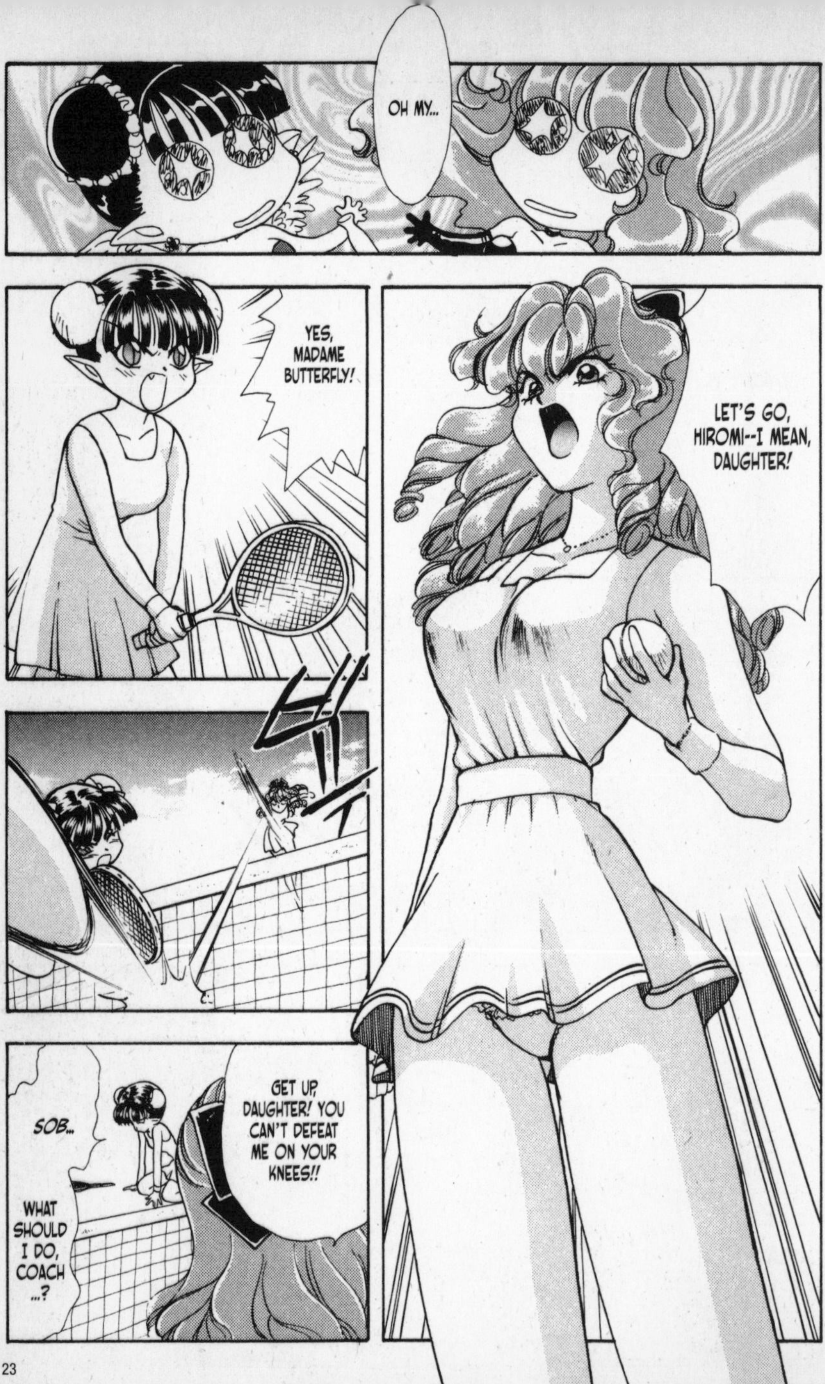
OH MY...
LET'S GO, HIROMI--I MEAN, DAUGHTER!
YES, MADAME BUTTERFLY!
GET UP, DAUGHTER! YOU CAN'T DEFEAT ME ON YOUR KNEES!!
SOB...
WHAT SHOULD I DO, COACH ...?

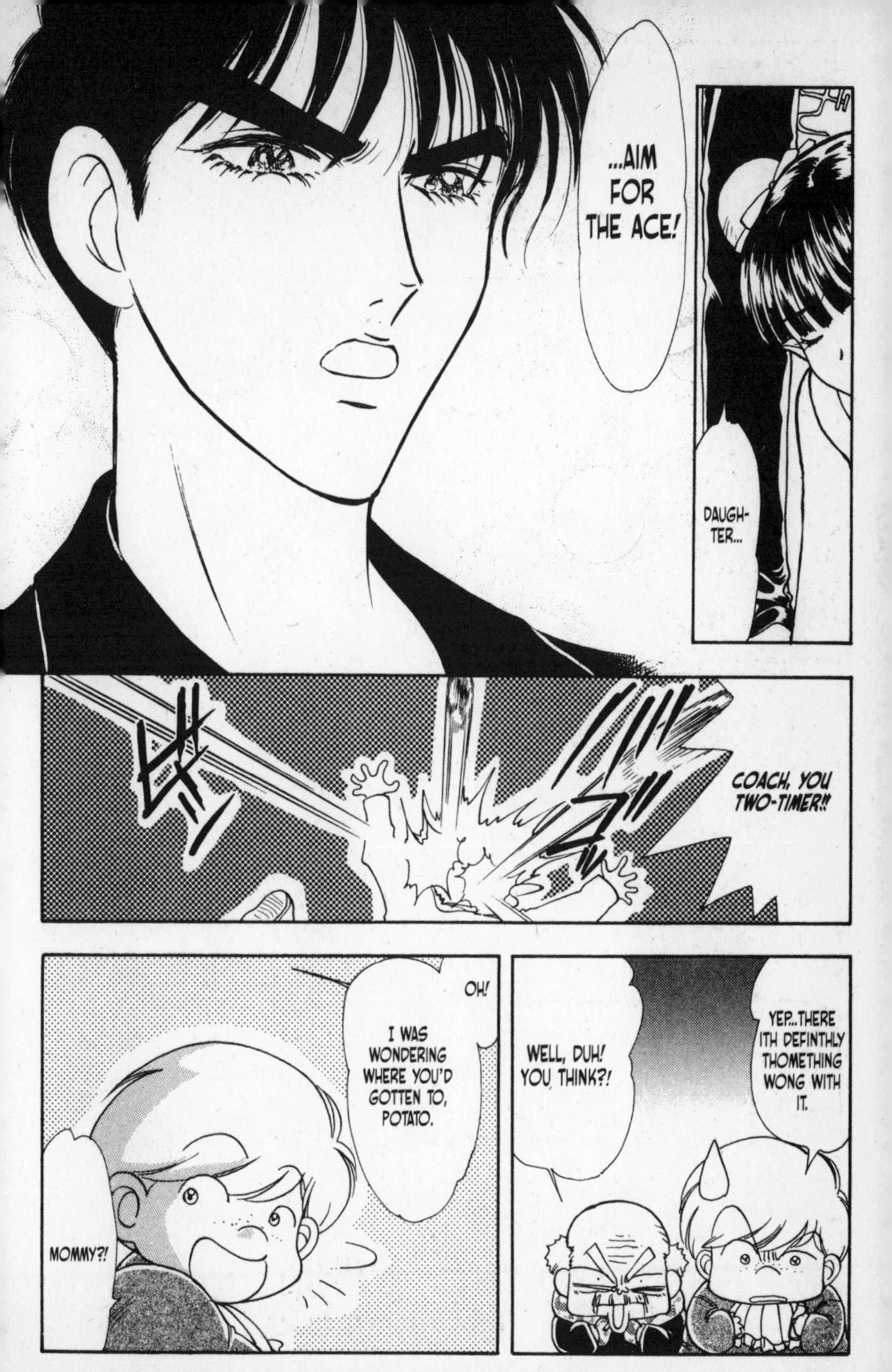
DAUGH-TER...
...AIM FOR THE ACE!
COACH, YOU TWO-TIMER!!
YEP...THERE ITH DEFINTHLY THOMETHING WONG WITH IT.
WELL, DUH! YOU THINK?!
OH!
I WAS WONDERING WHERE YOU'D GOTTEN TO, POTATO.
MOMMY?!

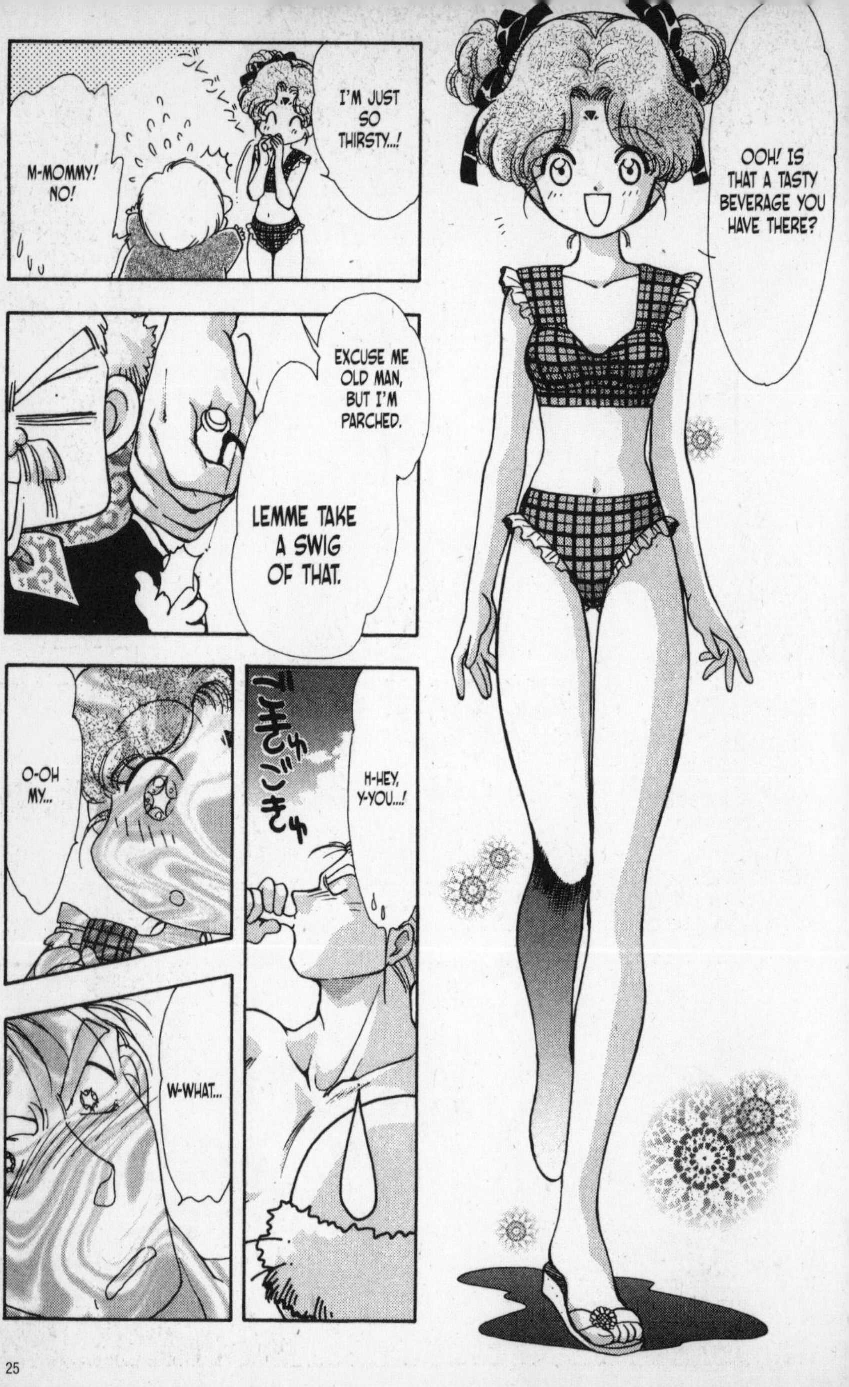
OOH! IS THAT A TASTY BEVERAGE YOU HAVE THERE?
I'M JUST SO THIRSTY...!
M-MOMMY! NO!
EXCUSE ME OLD MAN, BUT I'M PARCHED.
LEMME TAKE A SWIG OF THAT.
ごきゅごきゅ
H-HEY, Y-YOU...!
O-OH MY...
W-WHAT...

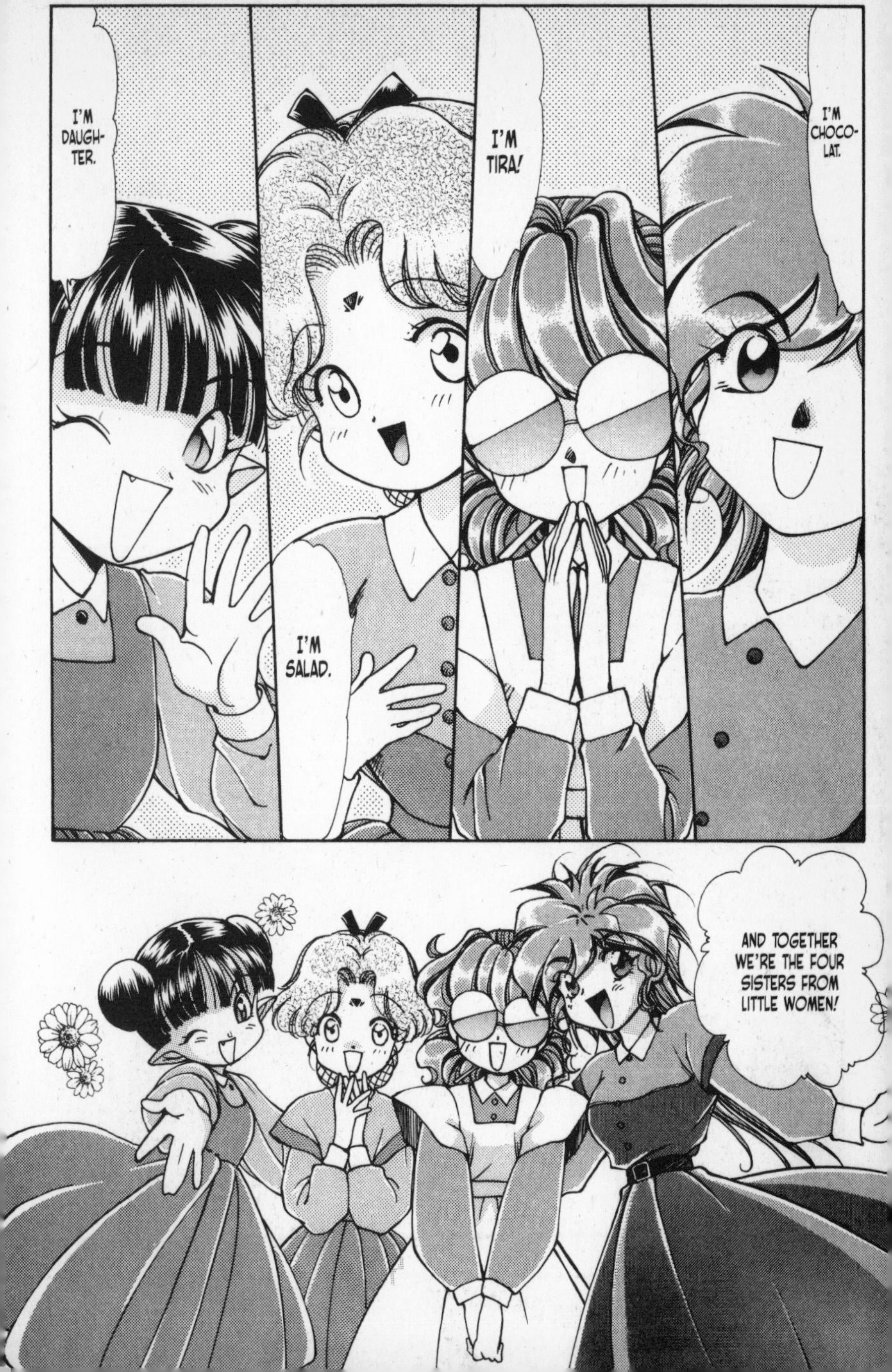
I'M CHOCO-LAT.
I'M TIRA!
I'M SALAD.
I'M DAUGH-TER.
AND TOGETHER WE'RE THE FOUR SISTERS FROM LITTLE WOMEN!

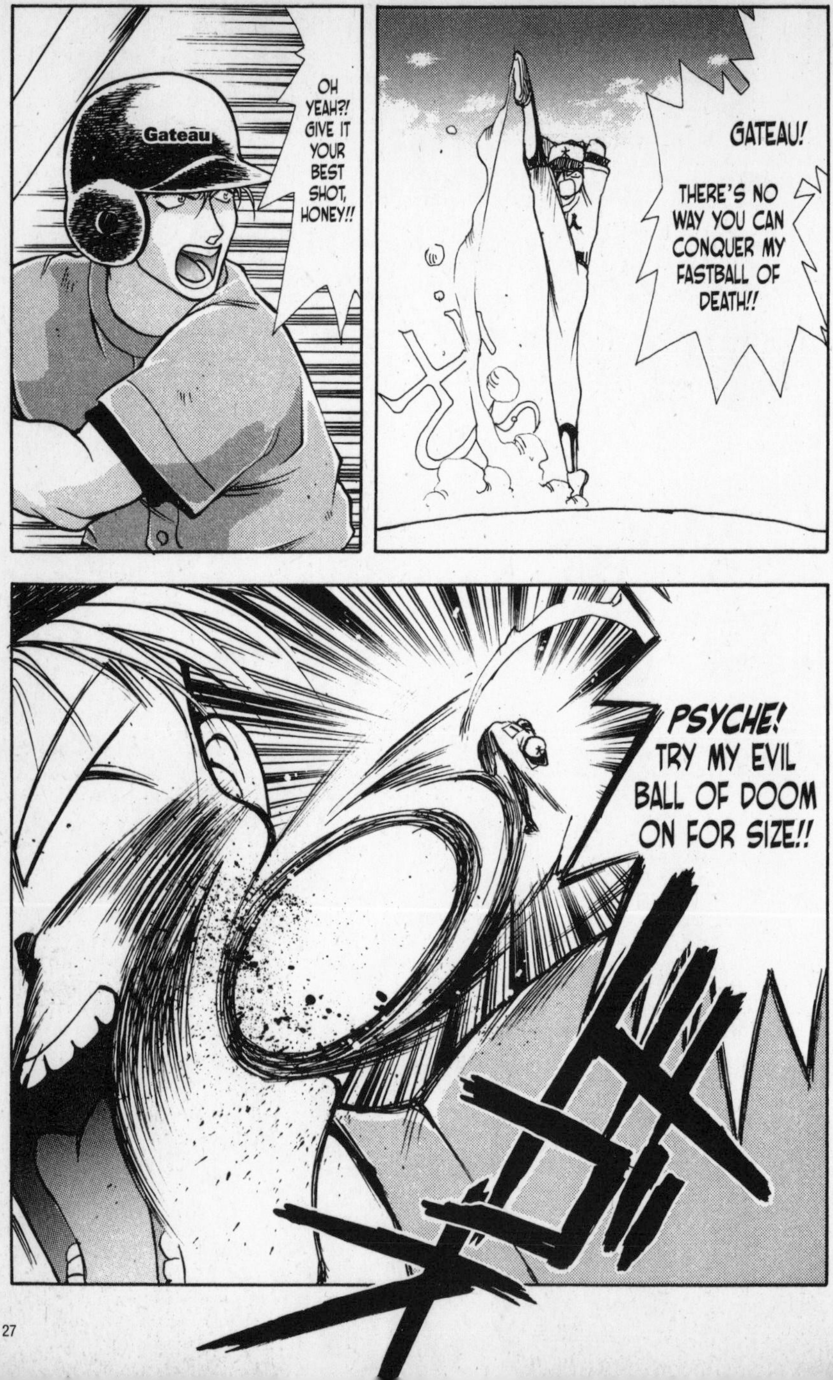
GATEAU!
THERE'S NO WAY YOU CAN CONQUER MY FASTBALL OF DEATH!!
OH YEAH?! GIVE IT YOUR BEST SHOT, HONEY!!
Gateau
PSYCHE! TRY MY EVIL BALL OF DOOM ON FOR SIZE!!

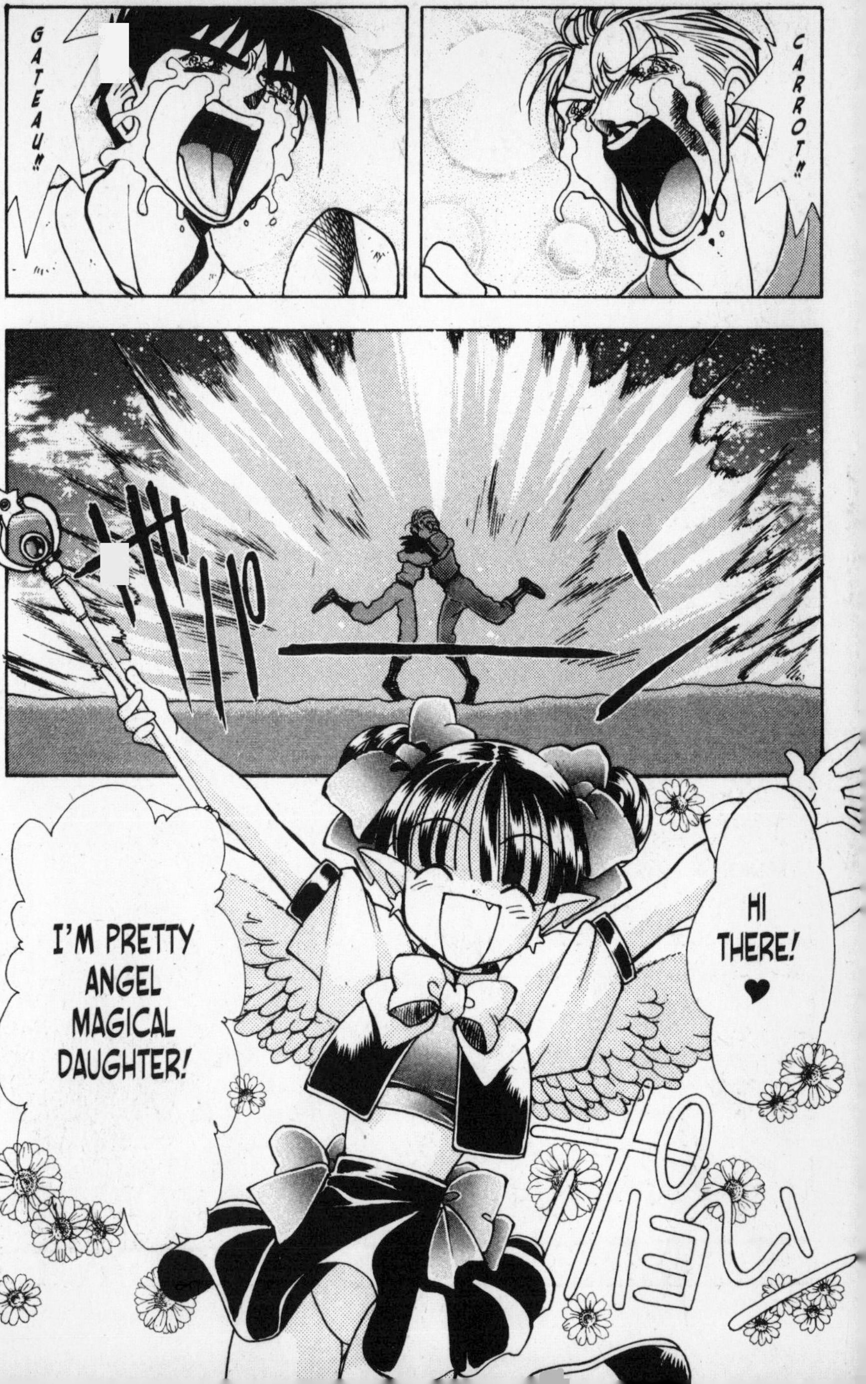
CARROT!!
GATEAU!!
HI THERE! ♥
I'M PRETTY ANGEL MAGICAL DAUGHTER!

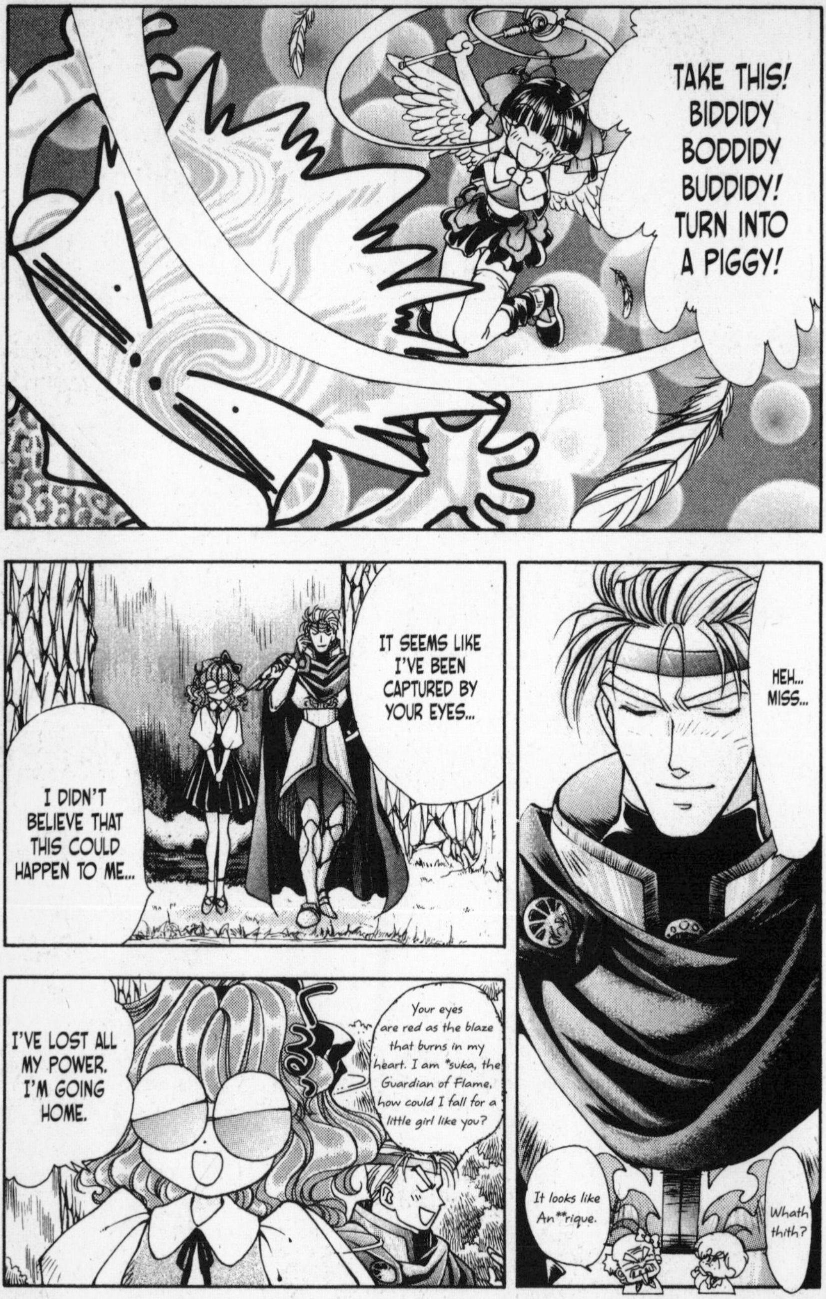
TAKE THIS! BIDDIDY BODDIDY BUDDIDY! TURN INTO A PIGGY!
HEH... MISS...
Whath thith?
It looks like An**rique.
IT SEEMS LIKE I'VE BEEN CAPTURED BY YOUR EYES...
I DIDN'T BELIEVE THAT THIS COULD HAPPEN TO ME...
Your eyes are red as the blaze that burns in my heart. I am *suka, the Guardian of Flame, how could I fall for a little girl like you?
I'VE LOST ALL MY POWER. I'M GOING HOME.

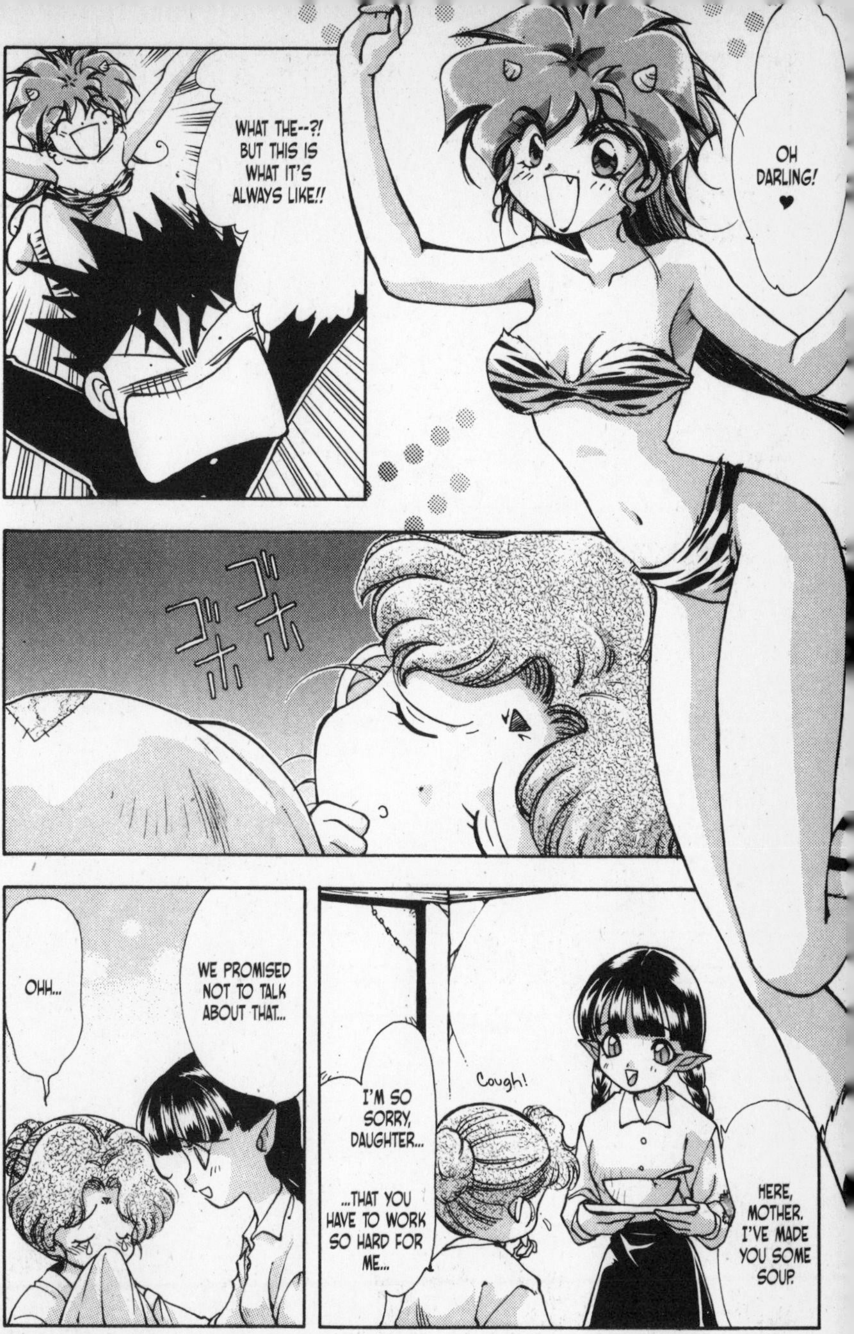
OH DARLING! ♥
WHAT THE--?! BUT THIS IS WHAT IT'S ALWAYS LIKE!!
ゴホゴホ
HERE, MOTHER. I'VE MADE YOU SOME SOUP.
Cough!
I'M SO SORRY, DAUGHTER...
...THAT YOU HAVE TO WORK SO HARD FOR ME...
WE PROMISED NOT TO TALK ABOUT THAT...
OHH...

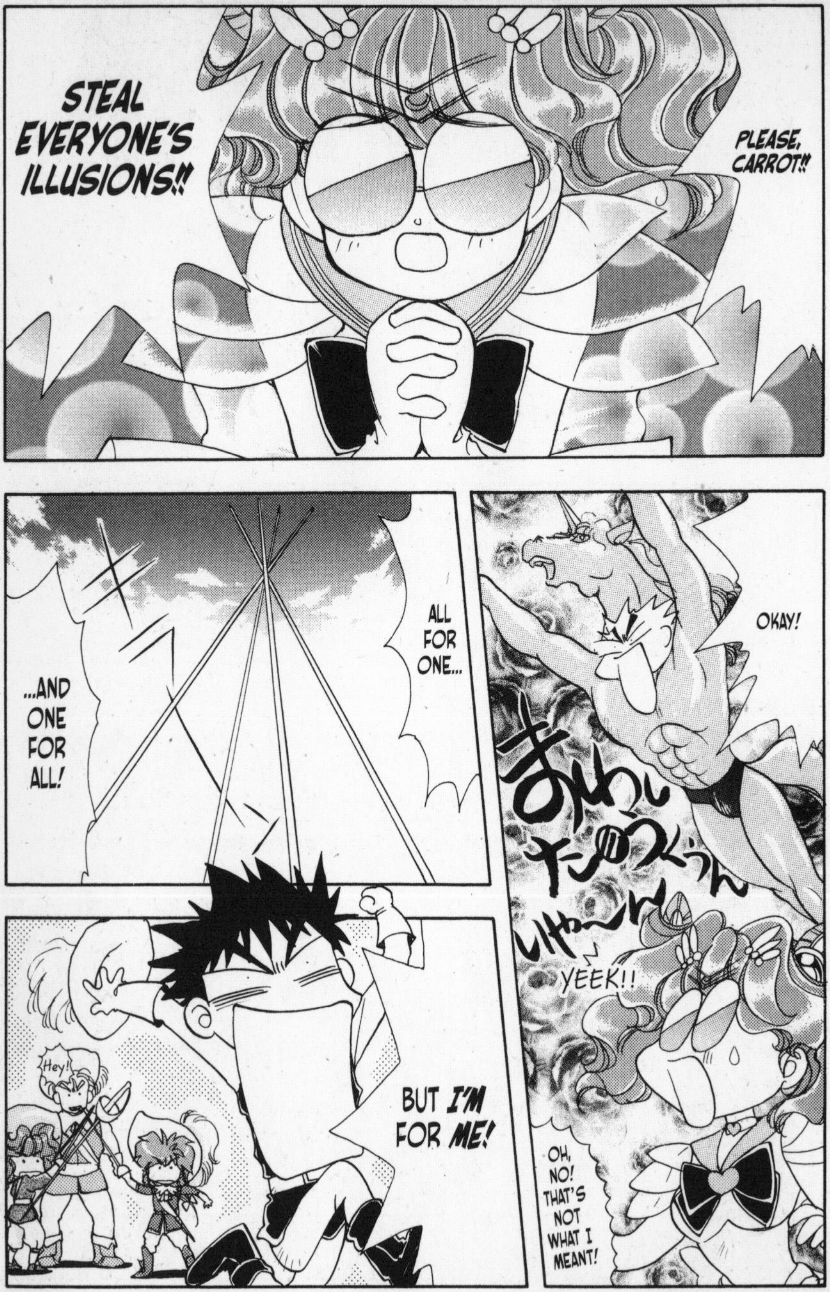
PLEASE, CARROT!!
STEAL EVERYONE'S ILLUSIONS!!
OKAY!
YEEK!!
OH, NO! THAT'S NOT WHAT I MEANT!
ALL FOR ONE...
...AND ONE FOR ALL!
BUT *I'M* FOR *ME!*
Hey!

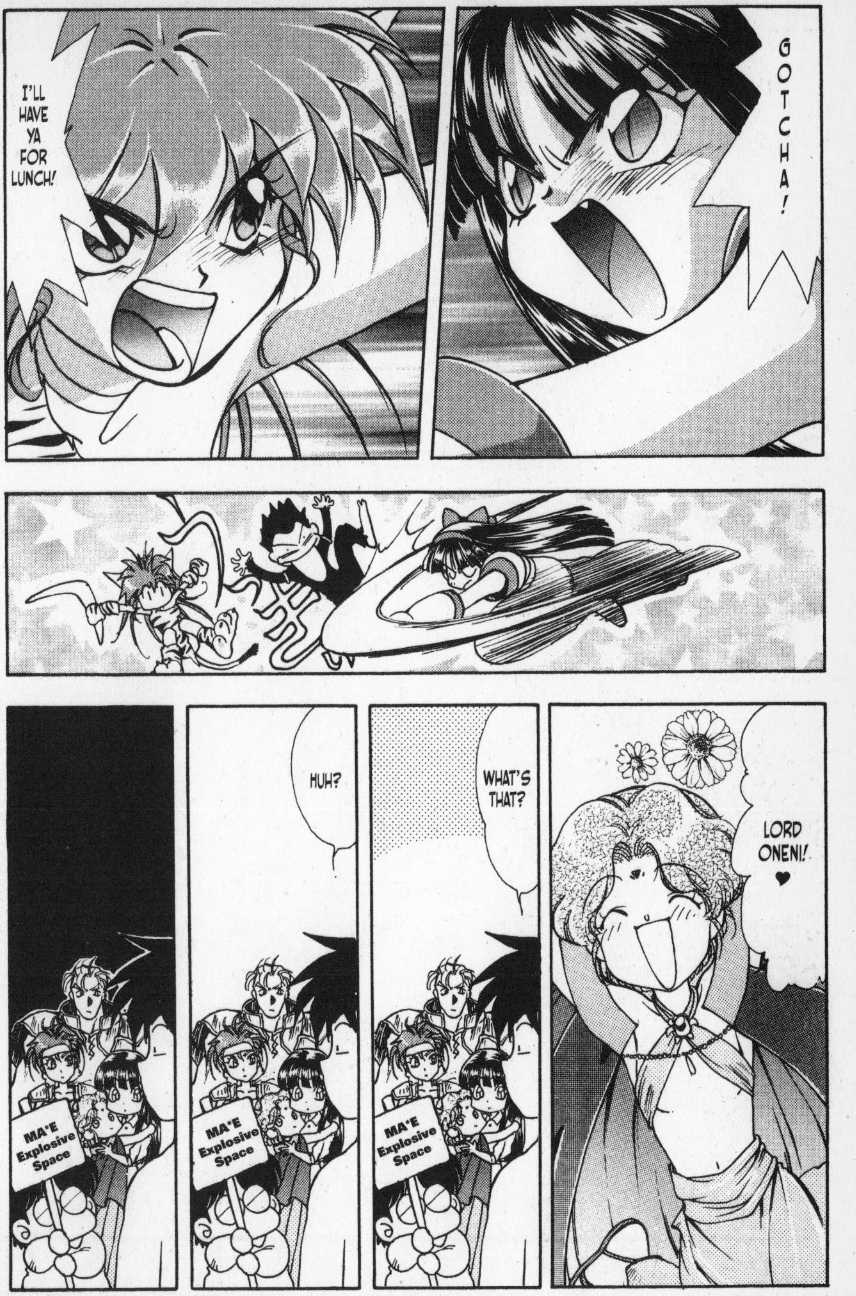
GOTCHA!
I'LL HAVE YA FOR LUNCH!
LORD ONENI! ♥
WHAT'S THAT?
MA'E Explosive Space
HUH?
MA'E Explosive Space
MA'E Explosive Space

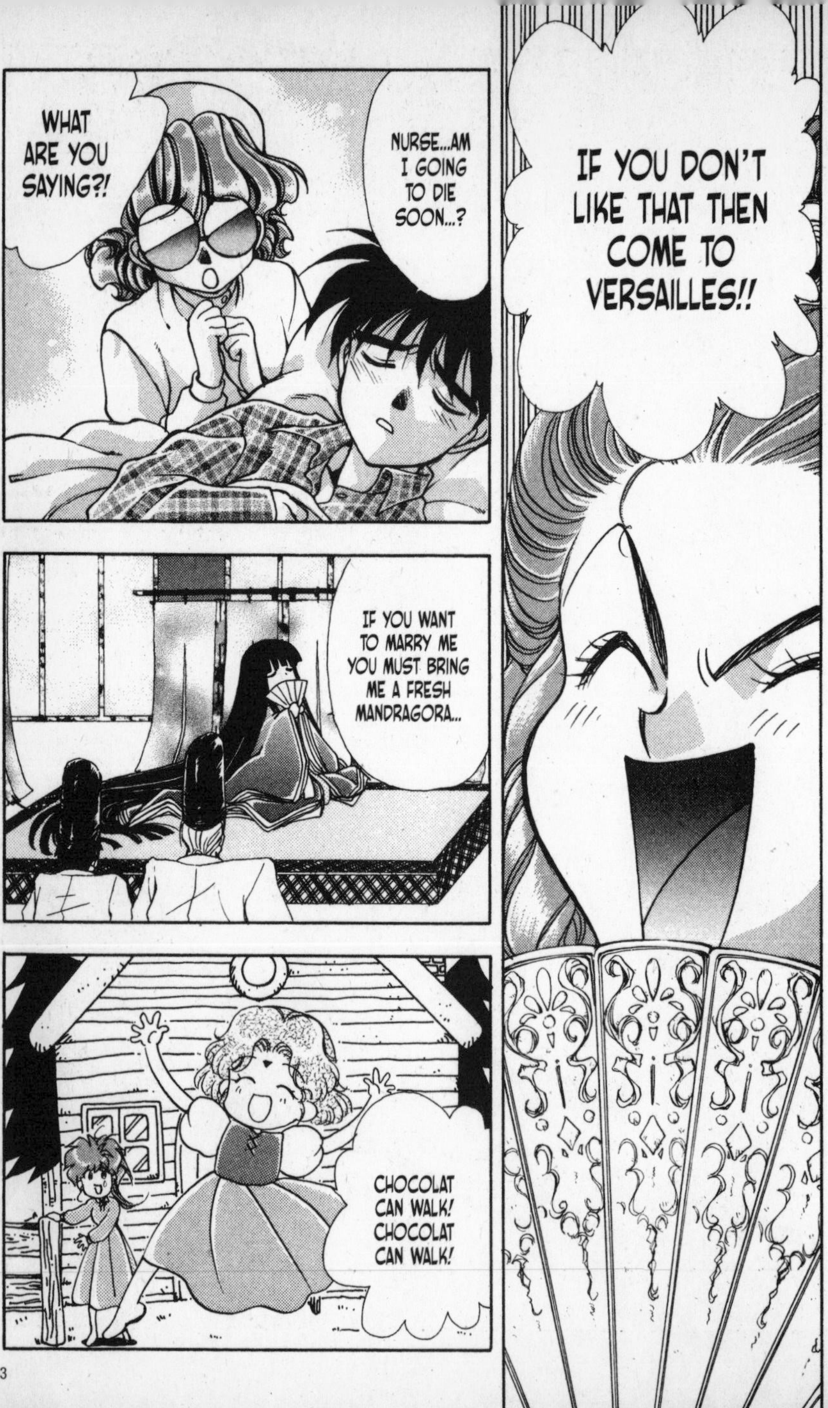
IF YOU DON'T LIKE THAT THEN COME TO VERSAILLES!!
NURSE...AM I GOING TO DIE SOON...?
WHAT ARE YOU SAYING?!
IF YOU WANT TO MARRY ME YOU MUST BRING ME A FRESH MANDRAGORA...
CHOCOLAT CAN WALK! CHOCOLAT CAN WALK!

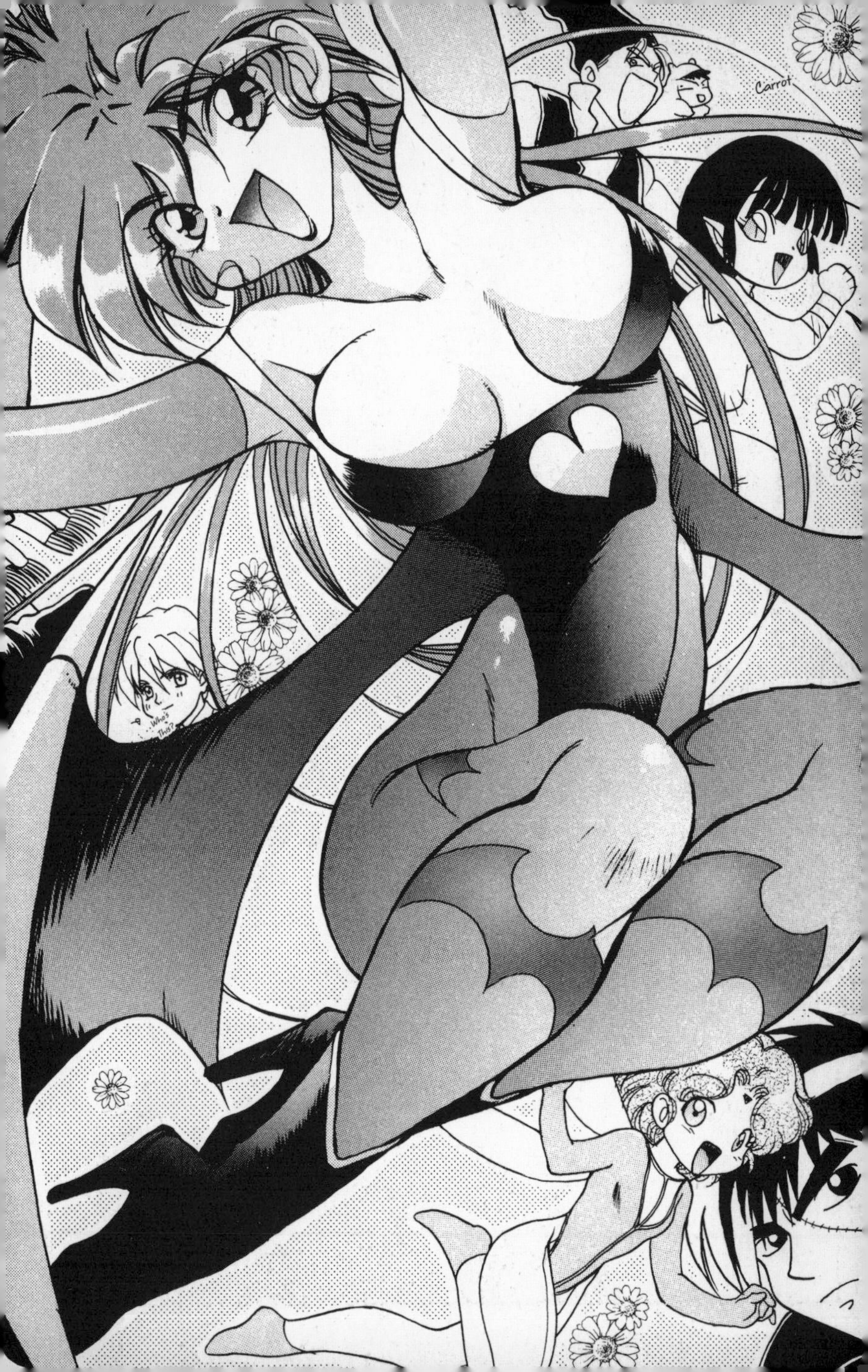
Carrot
Who's This?

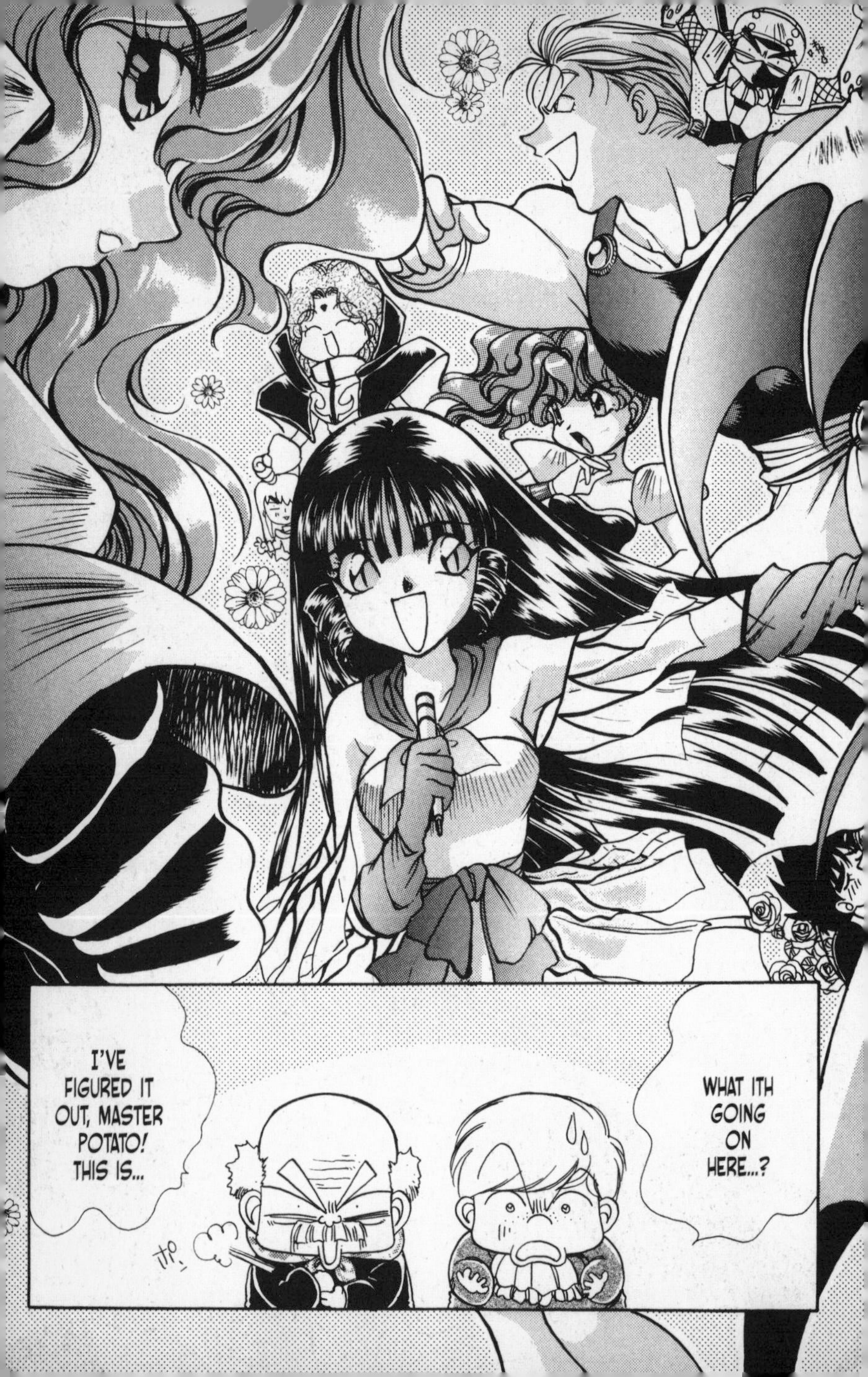
WHAT ITH GOING ON HERE...?
I'VE FIGURED IT OUT, MASTER POTATO! THIS IS...

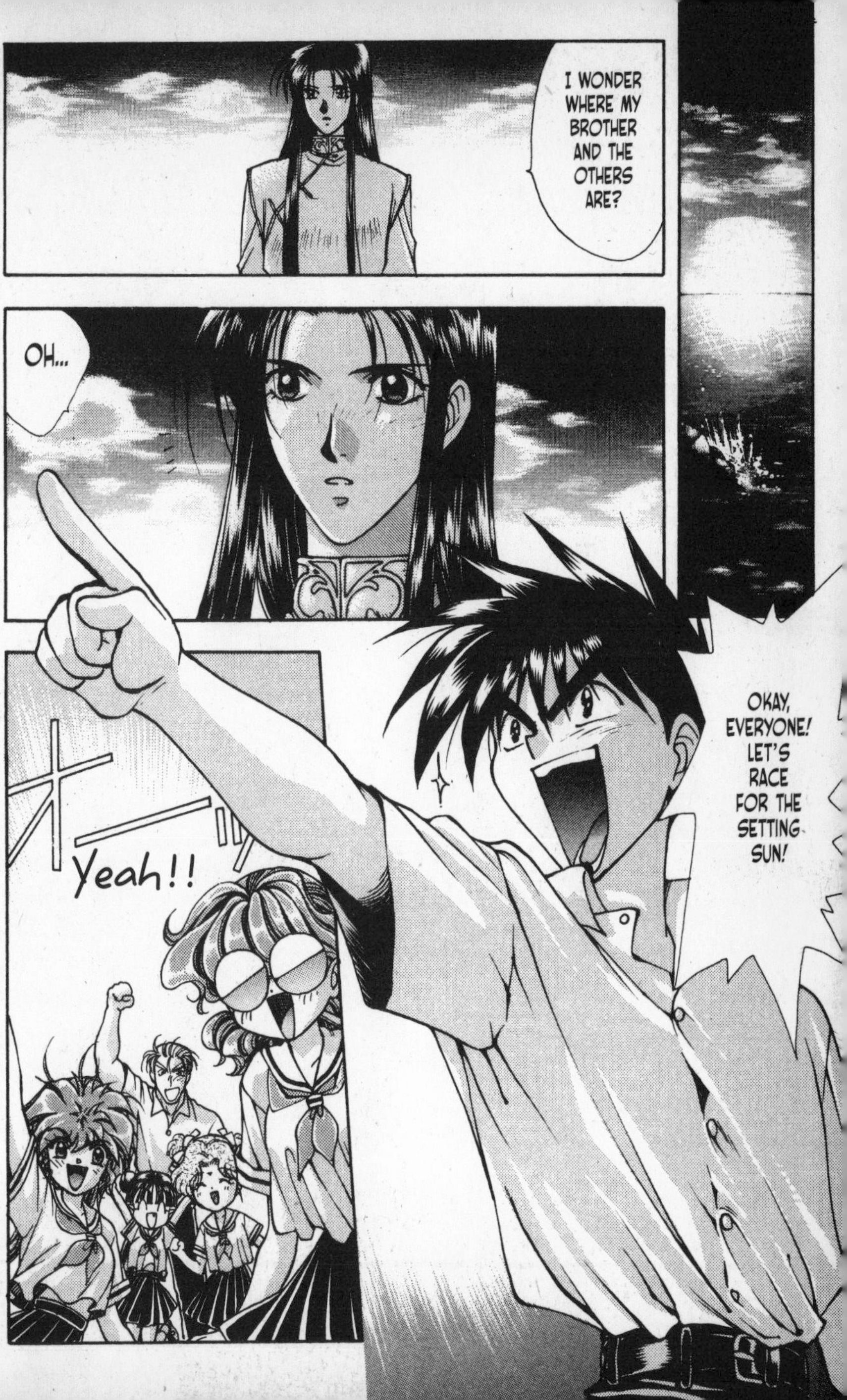
I WONDER WHERE MY BROTHER AND THE OTHERS ARE?
OH...
OKAY, EVERYONE! LET'S RACE FOR THE SETTING SUN!
Yeah!!

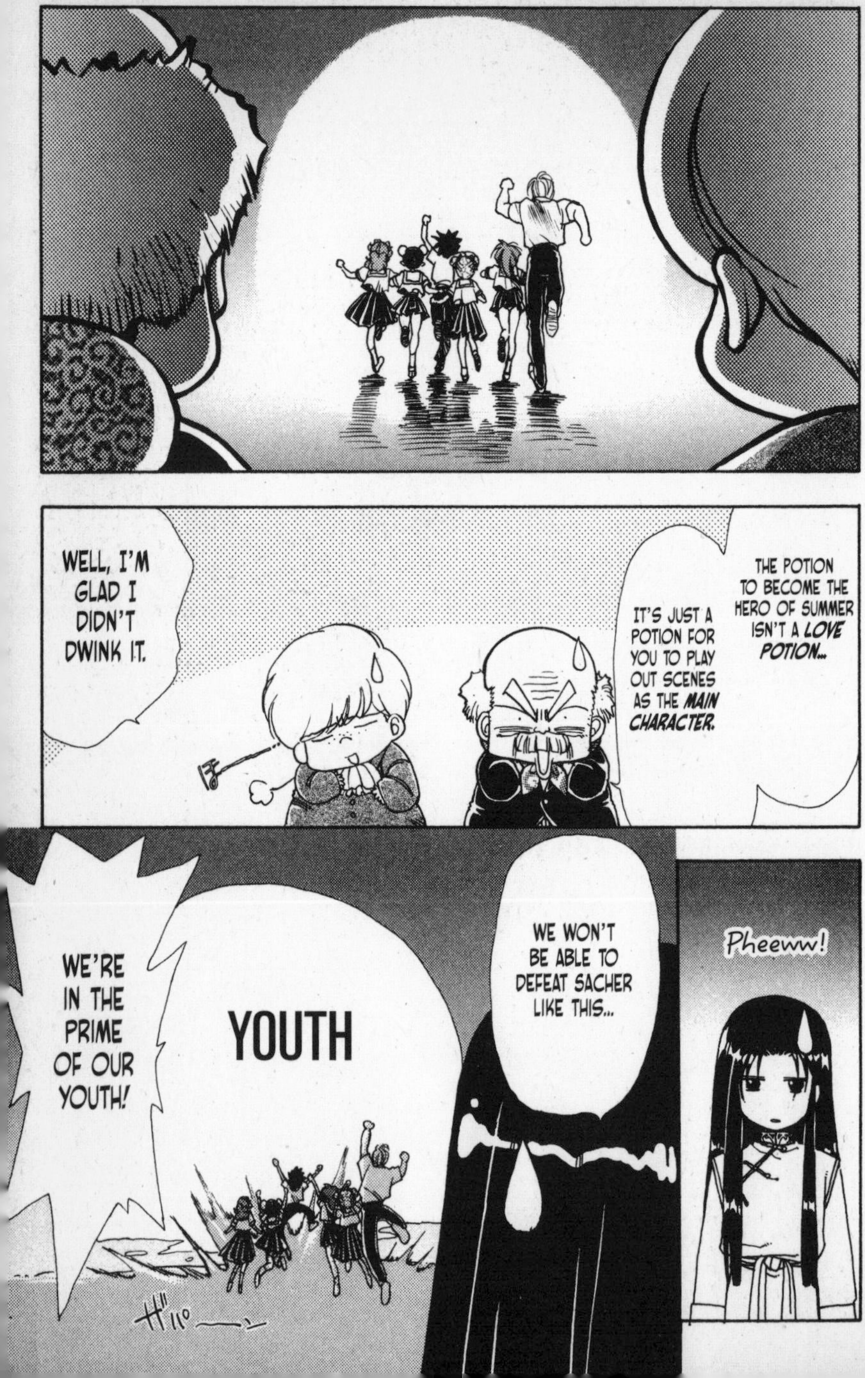
THE POTION TO BECOME THE HERO OF SUMMER ISN'T A *LOVE POTION*...
IT'S JUST A POTION FOR YOU TO PLAY OUT SCENES AS THE *MAIN CHARACTER*.
WELL, I'M GLAD I DIDN'T DWINK IT.
Pheeww!
WE WON'T BE ABLE TO DEFEAT SACHER LIKE THIS...
YOUTH
WE'RE IN THE PRIME OF OUR YOUTH!

37 THE LAST GUARDIAN SPIRIT?!

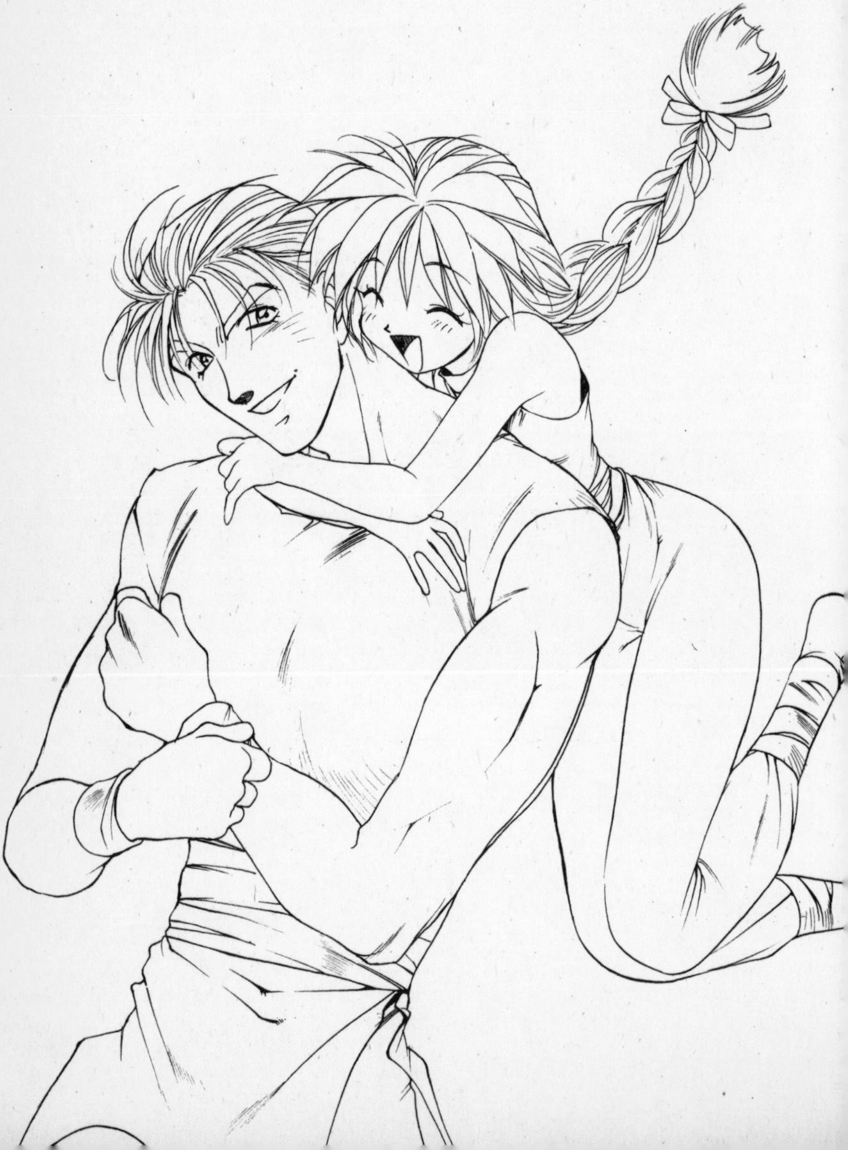

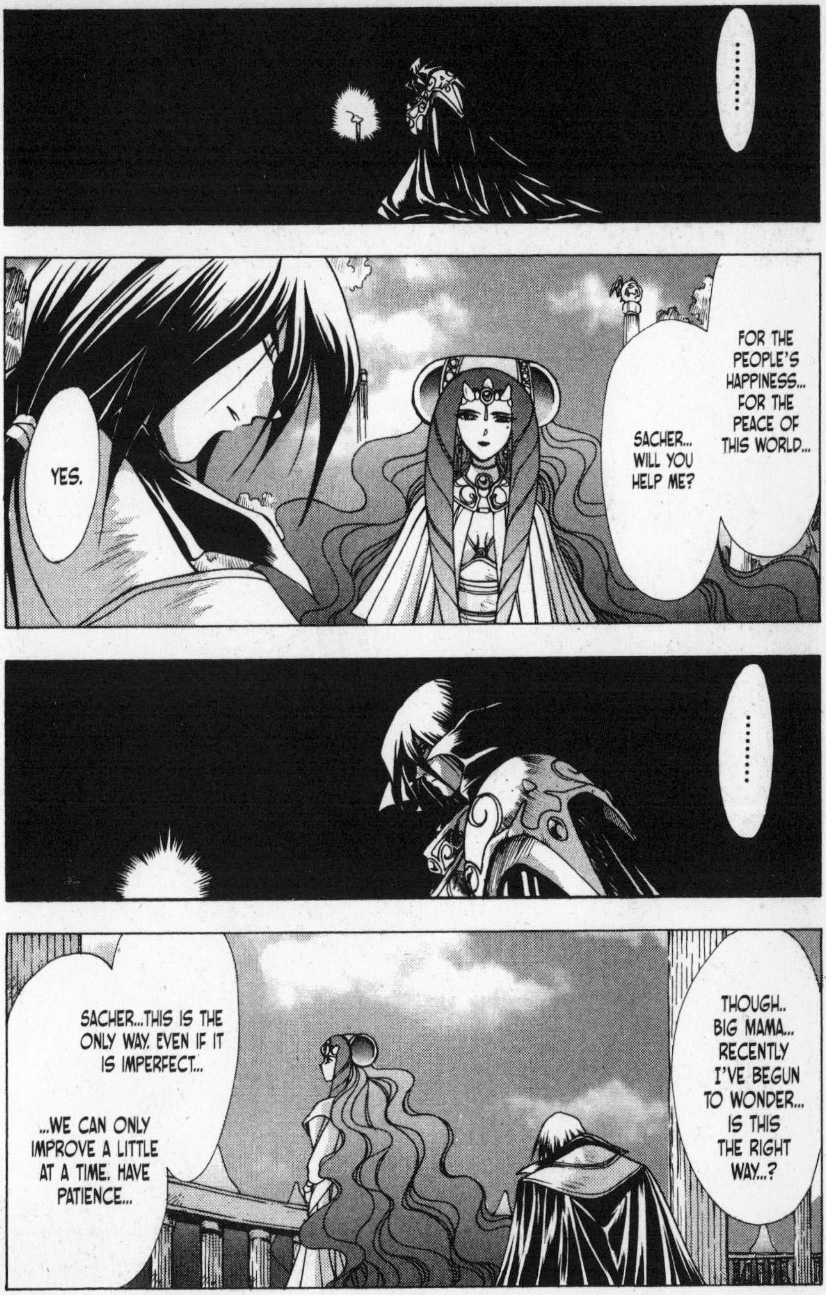
....
FOR THE PEOPLE'S HAPPINESS... FOR THE PEACE OF THIS WORLD...
SACHER... WILL YOU HELP ME?
YES.
....
THOUGH.. BIG MAMA... RECENTLY I'VE BEGUN TO WONDER... IS THIS THE RIGHT WAY...?
SACHER...THIS IS THE ONLY WAY. EVEN IF IT IS IMPERFECT...
...WE CAN ONLY IMPROVE A LITTLE AT A TIME. HAVE PATIENCE...

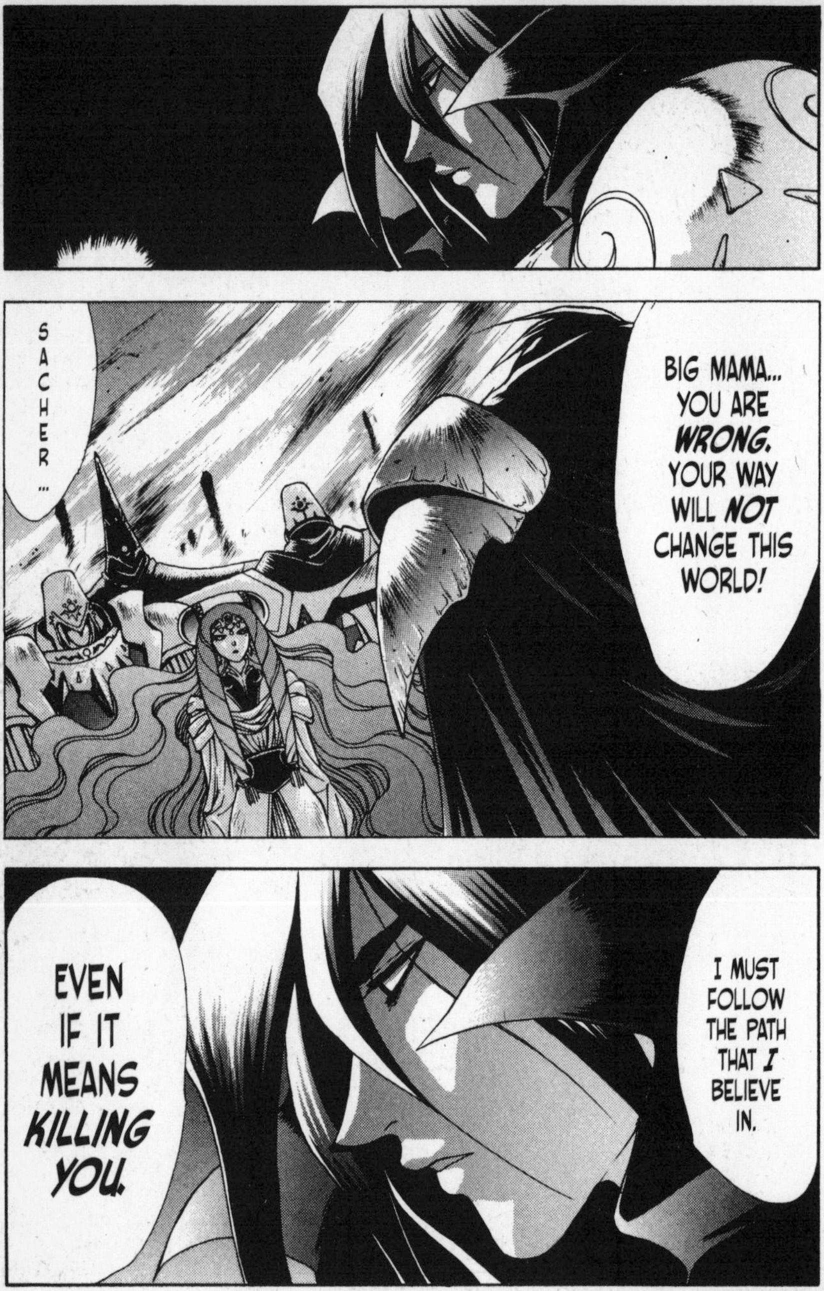
BIG MAMA... YOU ARE *WRONG.* YOUR WAY WILL *NOT* CHANGE THIS WORLD!
SACHER...
I MUST FOLLOW THE PATH THAT *I* BELIEVE IN.
EVEN IF IT MEANS *KILLING YOU.*

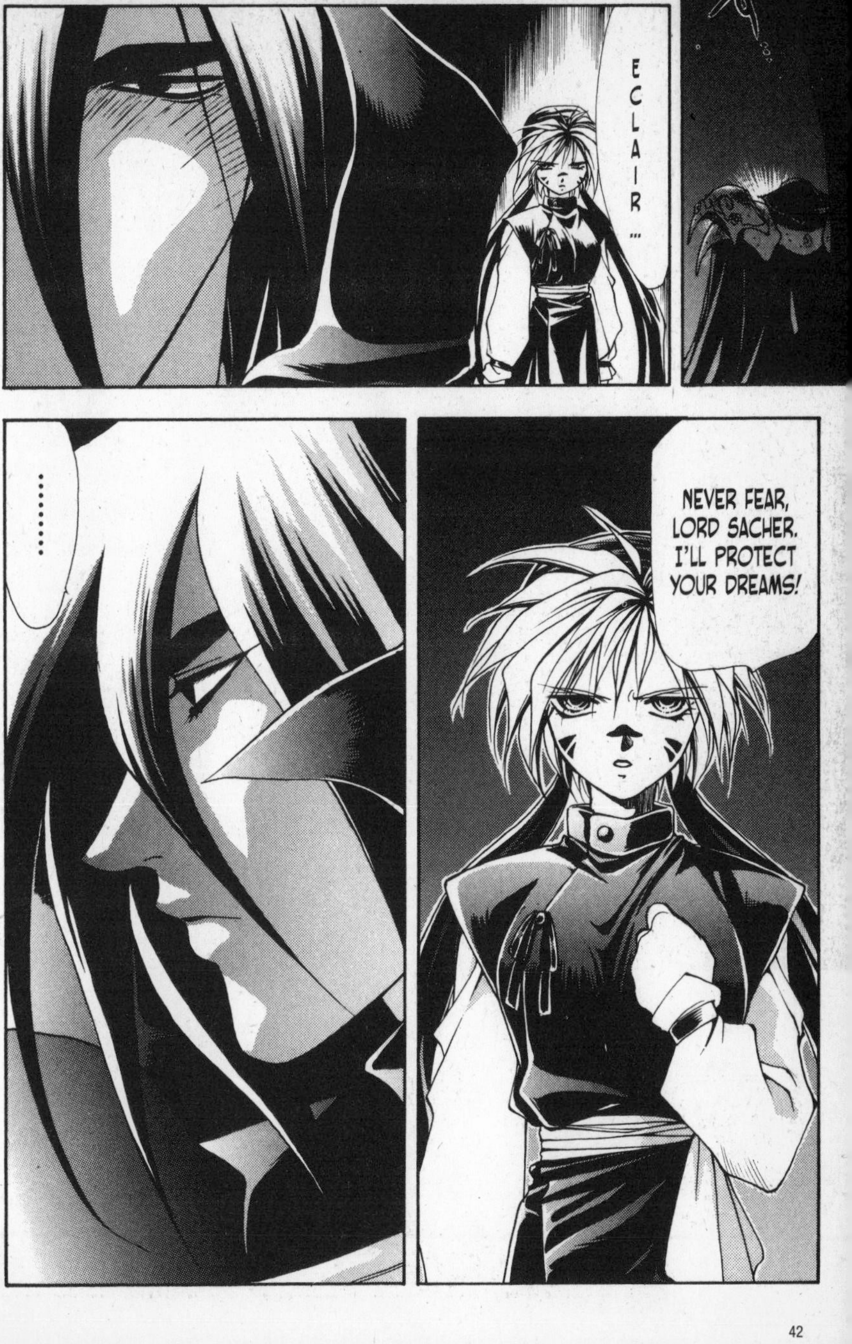
ECLAIR...
NEVER FEAR, LORD SACHER. I'LL PROTECT YOUR DREAMS!
....

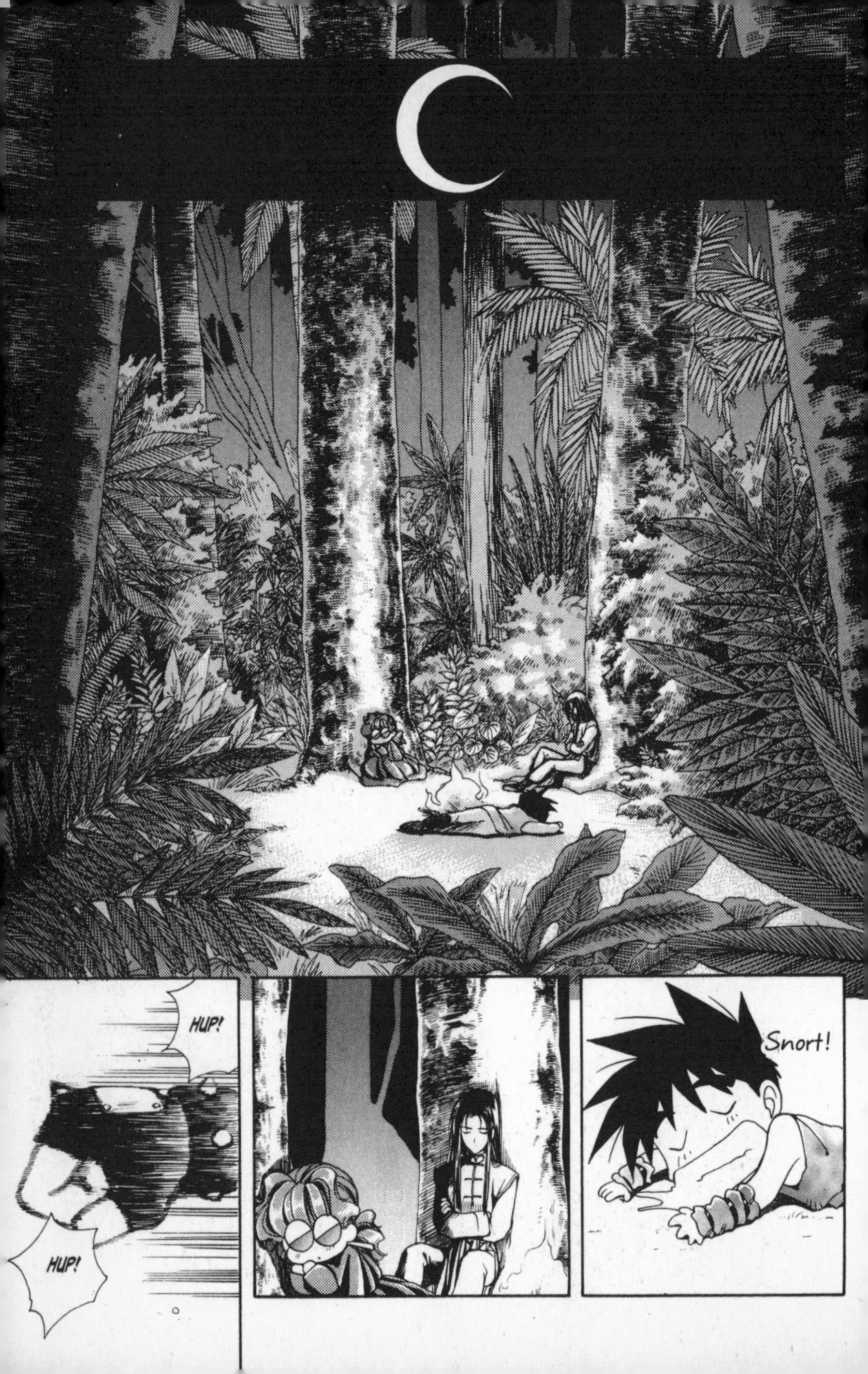
Snort!
HUP!
HUP!

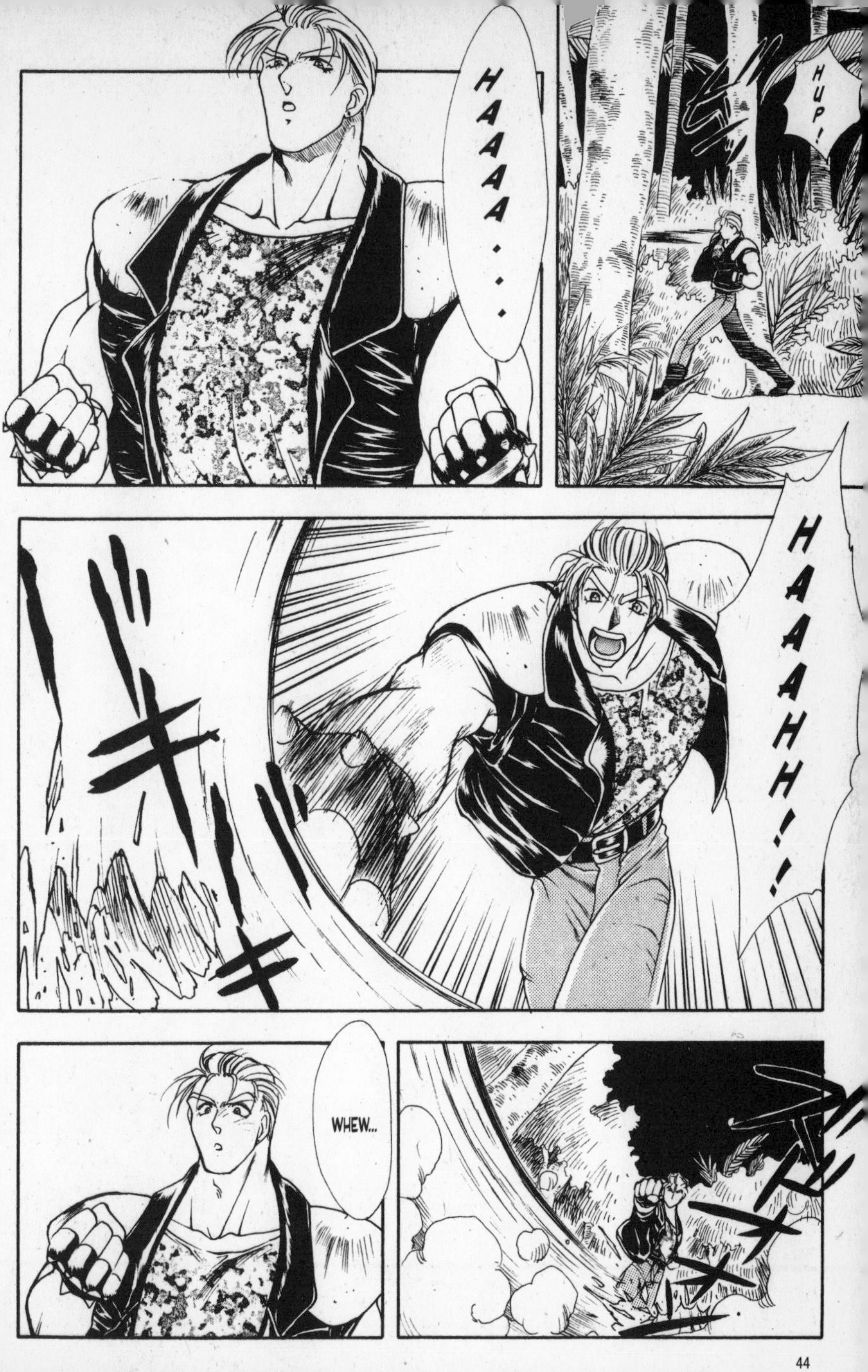
HUP!
HAAAA...
HAAAAHH!!!
WHEW...

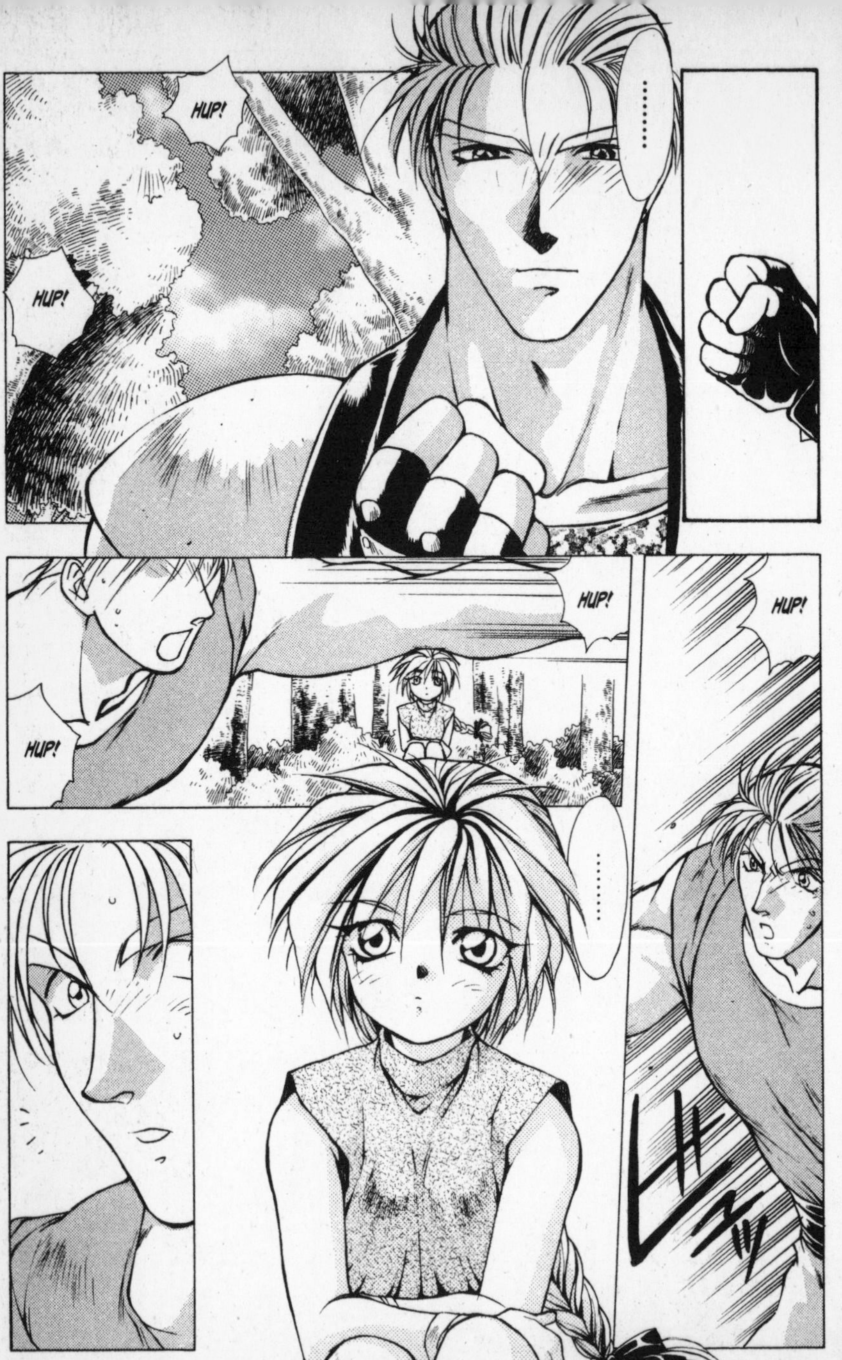
......
HUP!
HUP!
HUP!
HUP!
HUP!
......

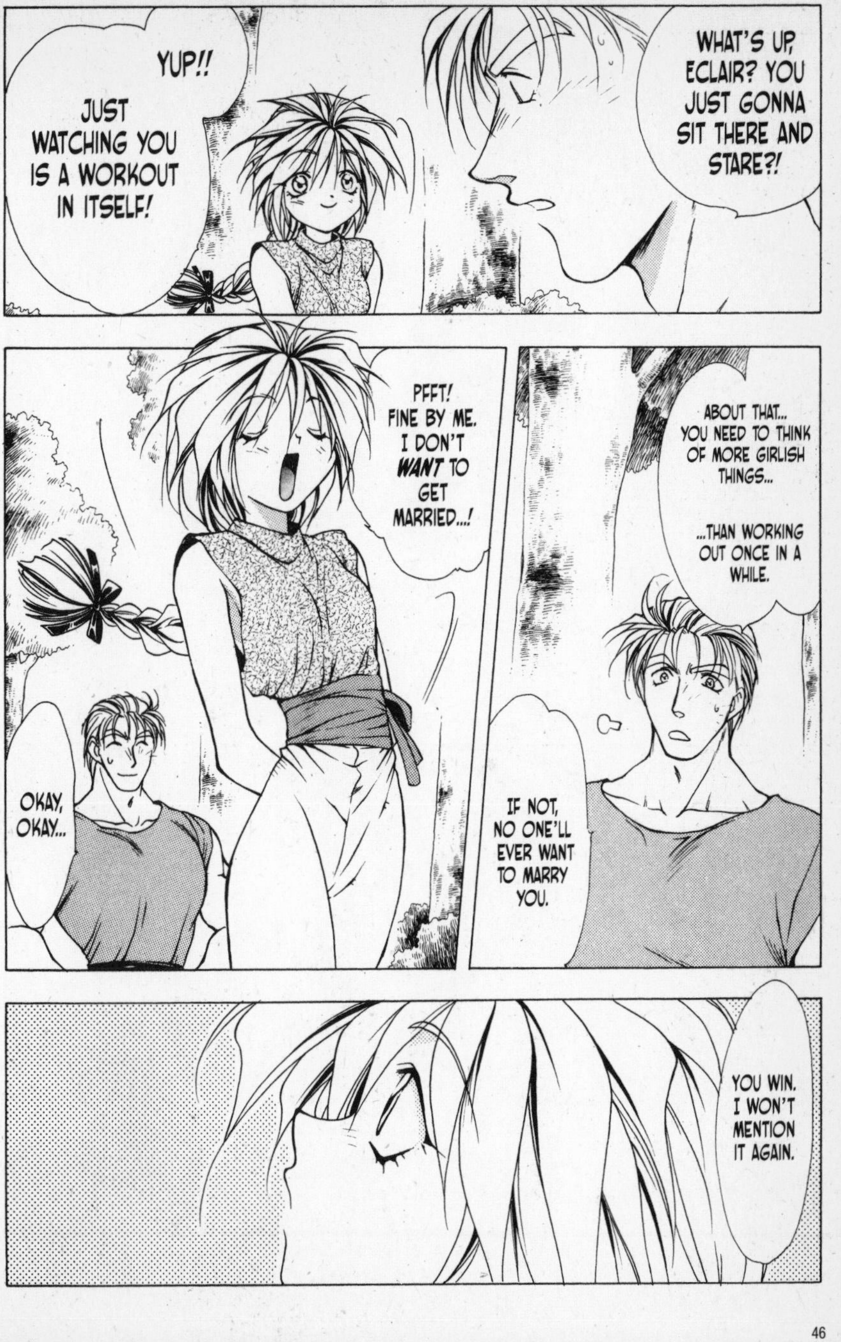
WHAT'S UP, ECLAIR? YOU JUST GONNA SIT THERE AND STARE?!
YUP!!
JUST WATCHING YOU IS A WORKOUT IN ITSELF!
ABOUT THAT... YOU NEED TO THINK OF MORE GIRLISH THINGS...
...THAN WORKING OUT ONCE IN A WHILE.
IF NOT, NO ONE'LL EVER WANT TO MARRY YOU.
PFFT! FINE BY ME. I DON'T *WANT* TO GET MARRIED...!
OKAY, OKAY...
YOU WIN. I WON'T MENTION IT AGAIN.

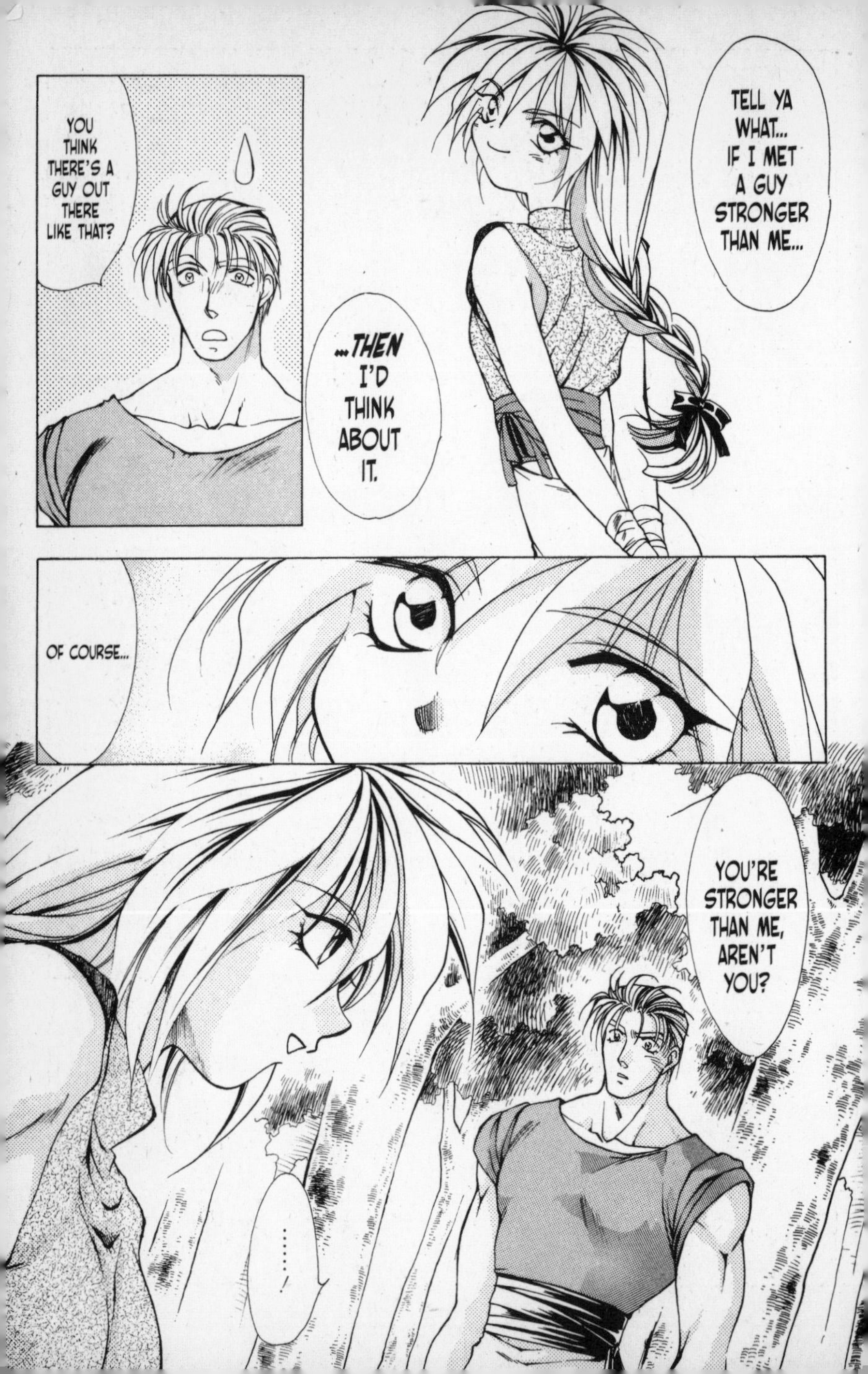
TELL YA WHAT... IF I MET A GUY STRONGER THAN ME...
...THEN I'D THINK ABOUT IT.
YOU THINK THERE'S A GUY OUT THERE LIKE THAT?
OF COURSE...
YOU'RE STRONGER THAN ME, AREN'T YOU?
......!

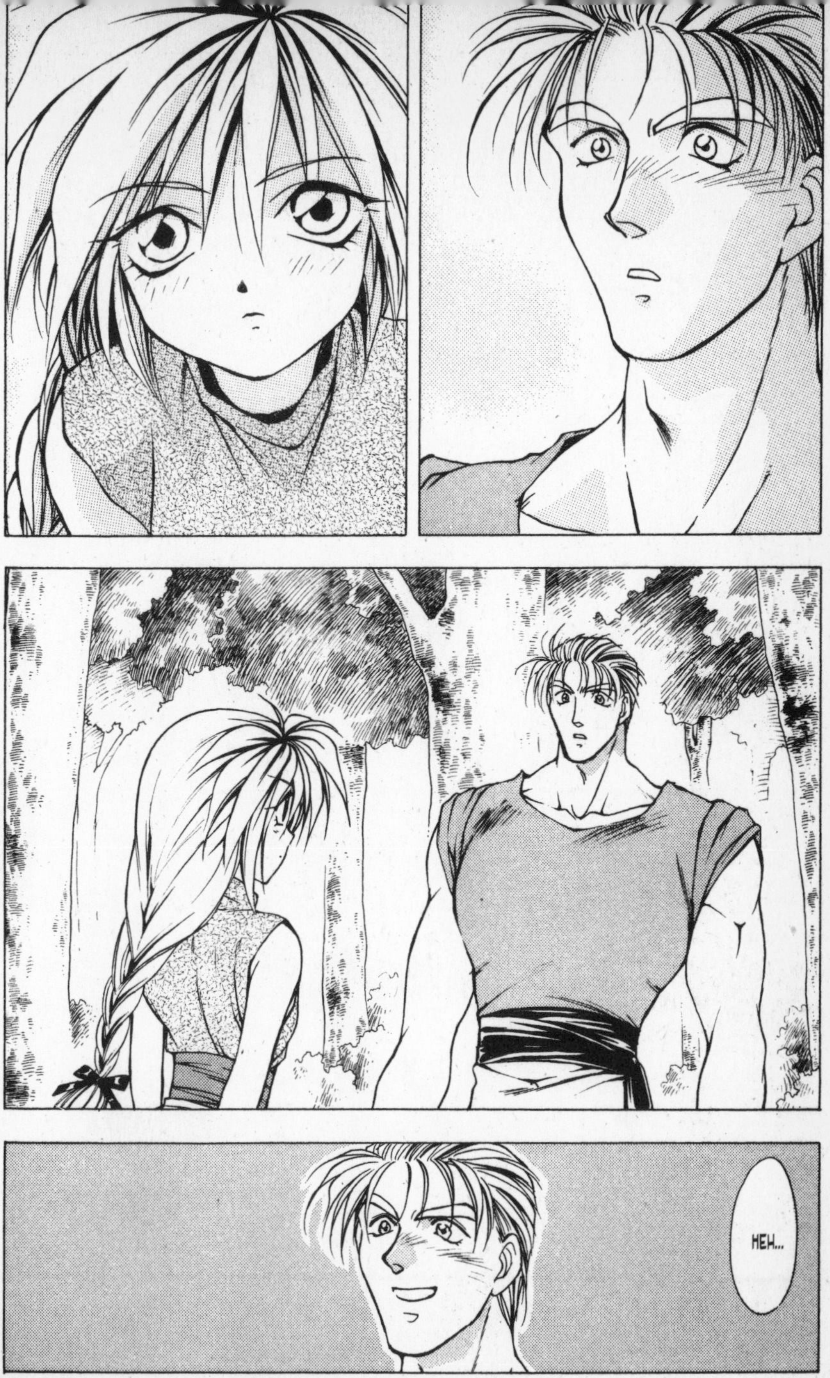
HEH...

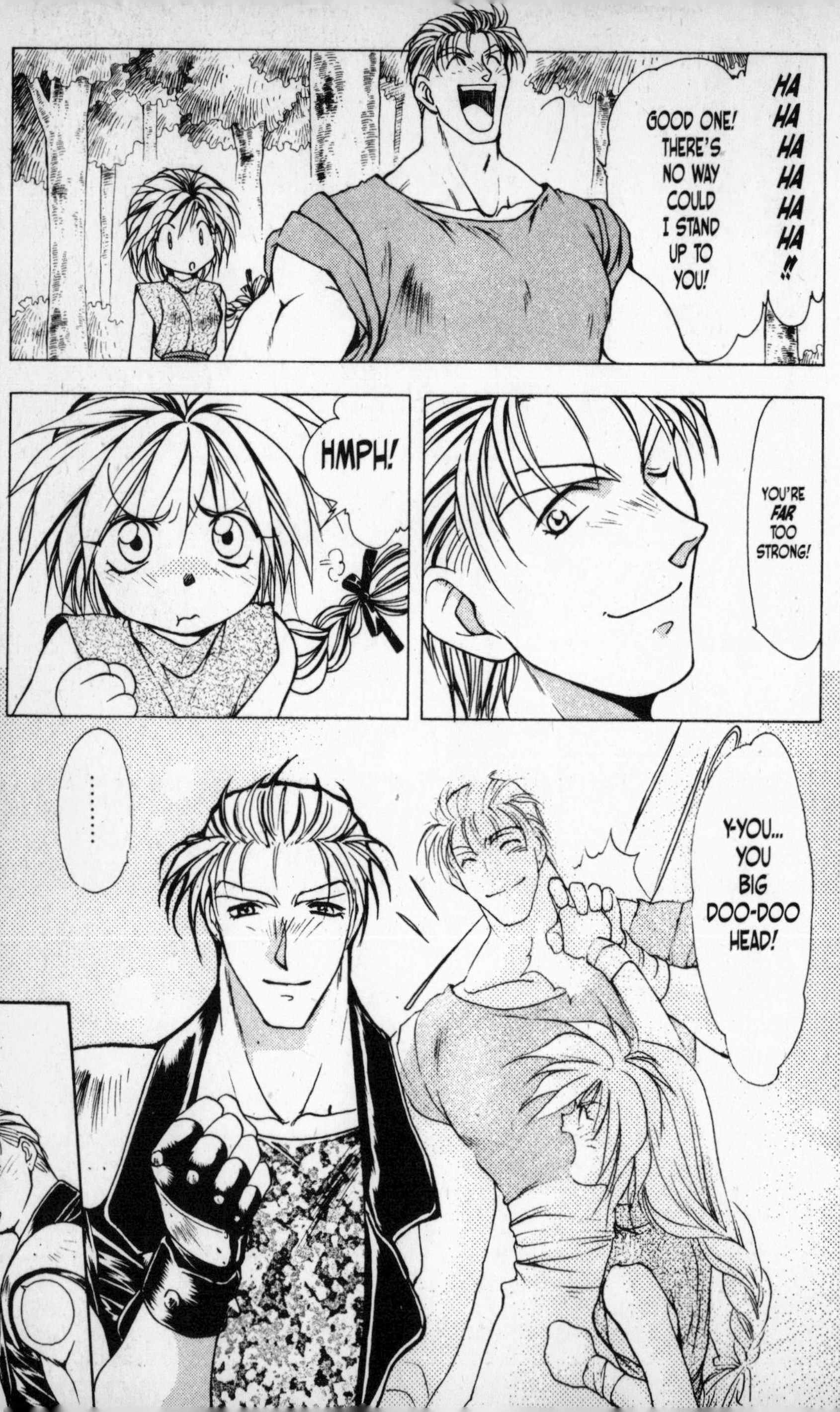
HA HA HA HA HA HA!!
GOOD ONE! THERE'S NO WAY COULD I STAND UP TO YOU!
YOU'RE FAR TOO STRONG!
HMPH!
Y-YOU... YOU BIG DOO-DOO HEAD!
......

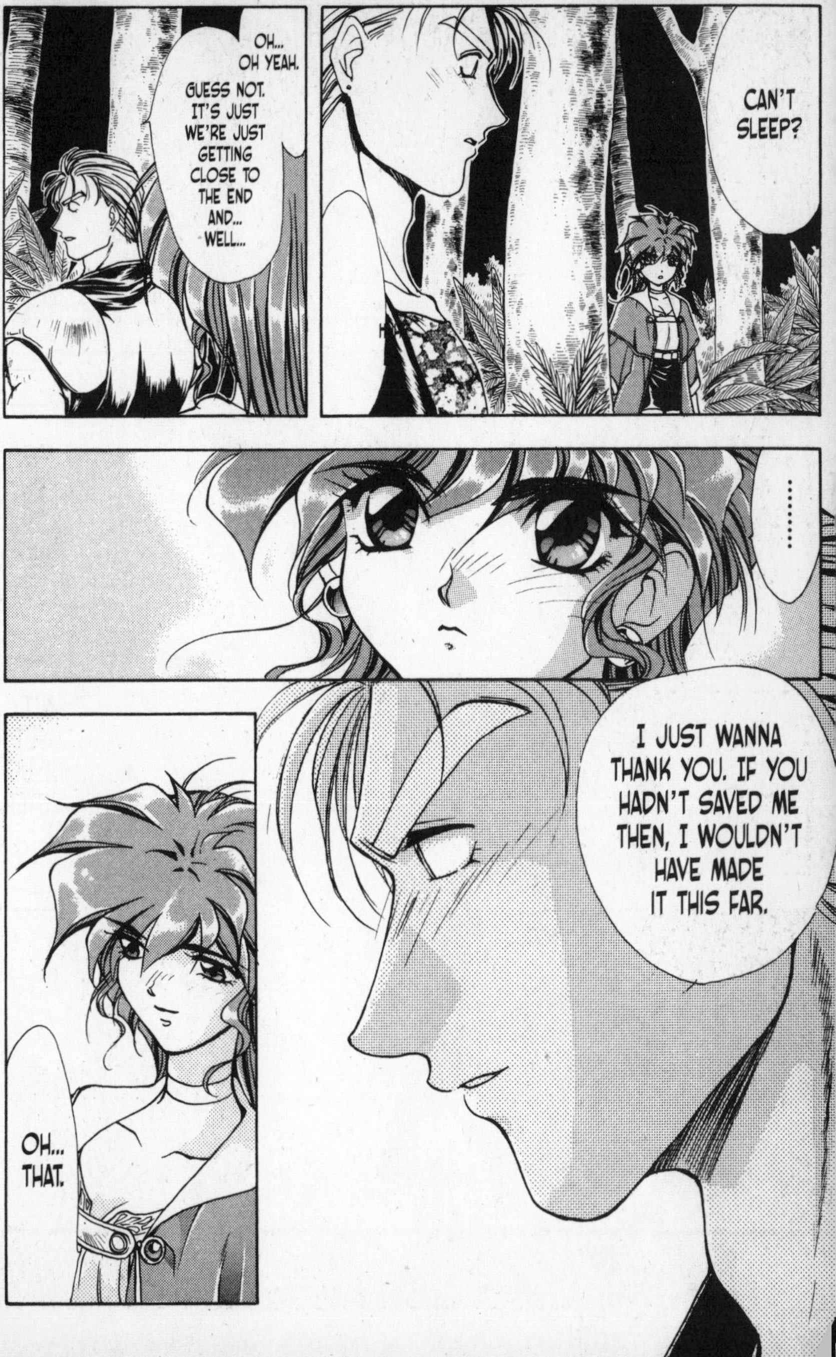
CAN'T SLEEP?
OH... OH YEAH. GUESS NOT. IT'S JUST WE'RE JUST GETTING CLOSE TO THE END AND... WELL...
....
I JUST WANNA THANK YOU. IF YOU HADN'T SAVED ME THEN, I WOULDN'T HAVE MADE IT THIS FAR.
OH... THAT.

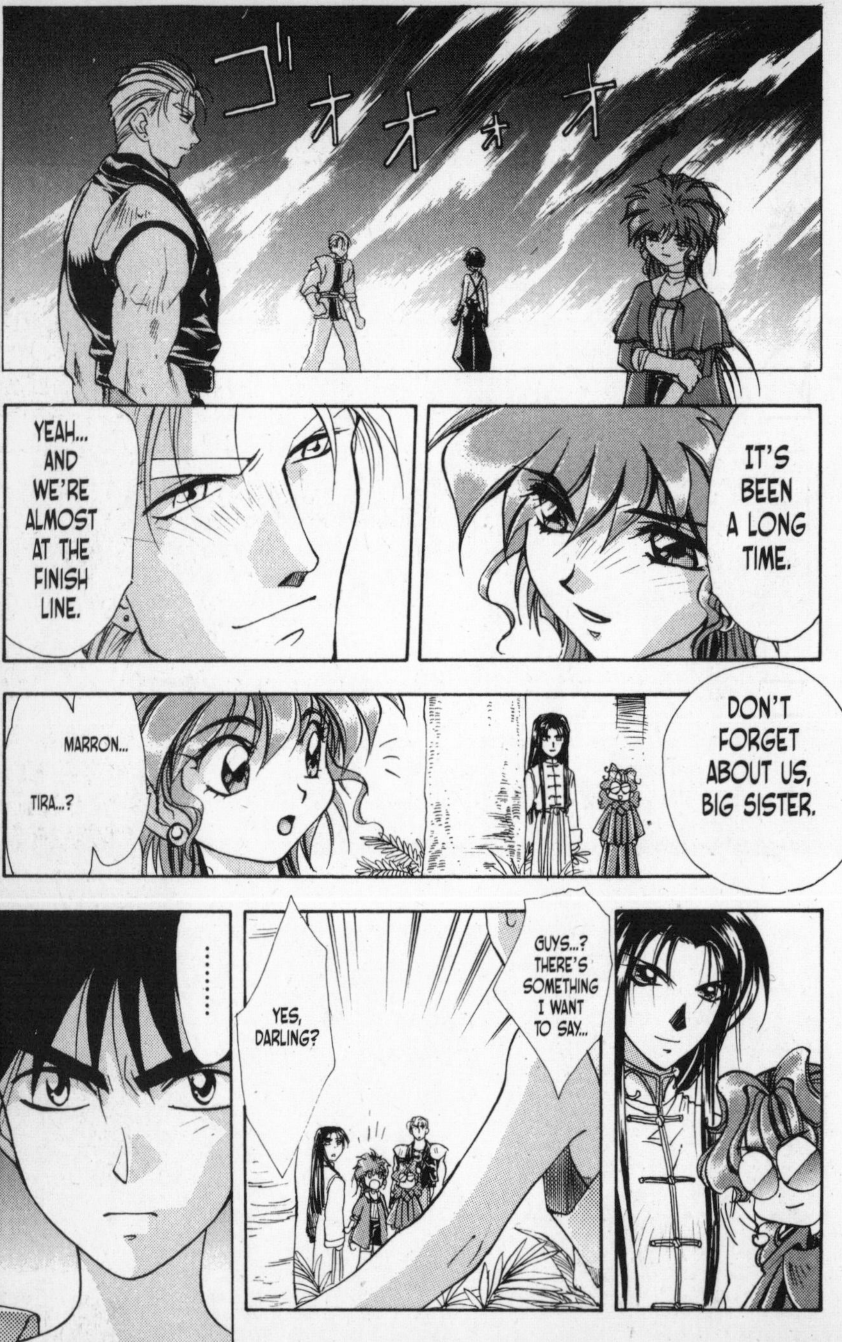
ゴオオォオ
IT'S BEEN A LONG TIME.
YEAH... AND WE'RE ALMOST AT THE FINISH LINE.
DON'T FORGET ABOUT US, BIG SISTER.
MARRON...
TIRA...?
GUYS...? THERE'S SOMETHING I WANT TO SAY...
YES, DARLING?
......

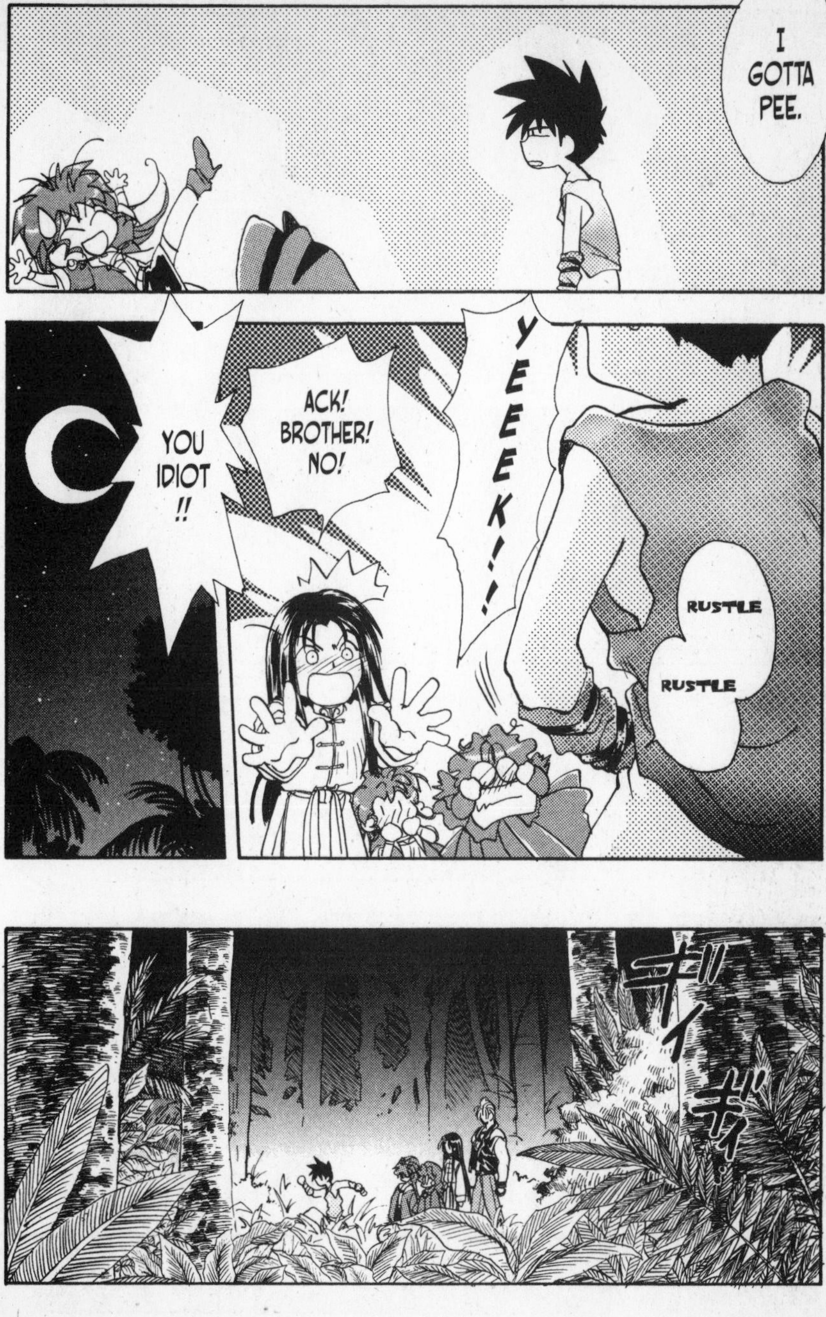
I GOTTA PEE.
YEEEK!!!
ACK! BROTHER! NO!
RUSTLE
RUSTLE
YOU IDIOT!!

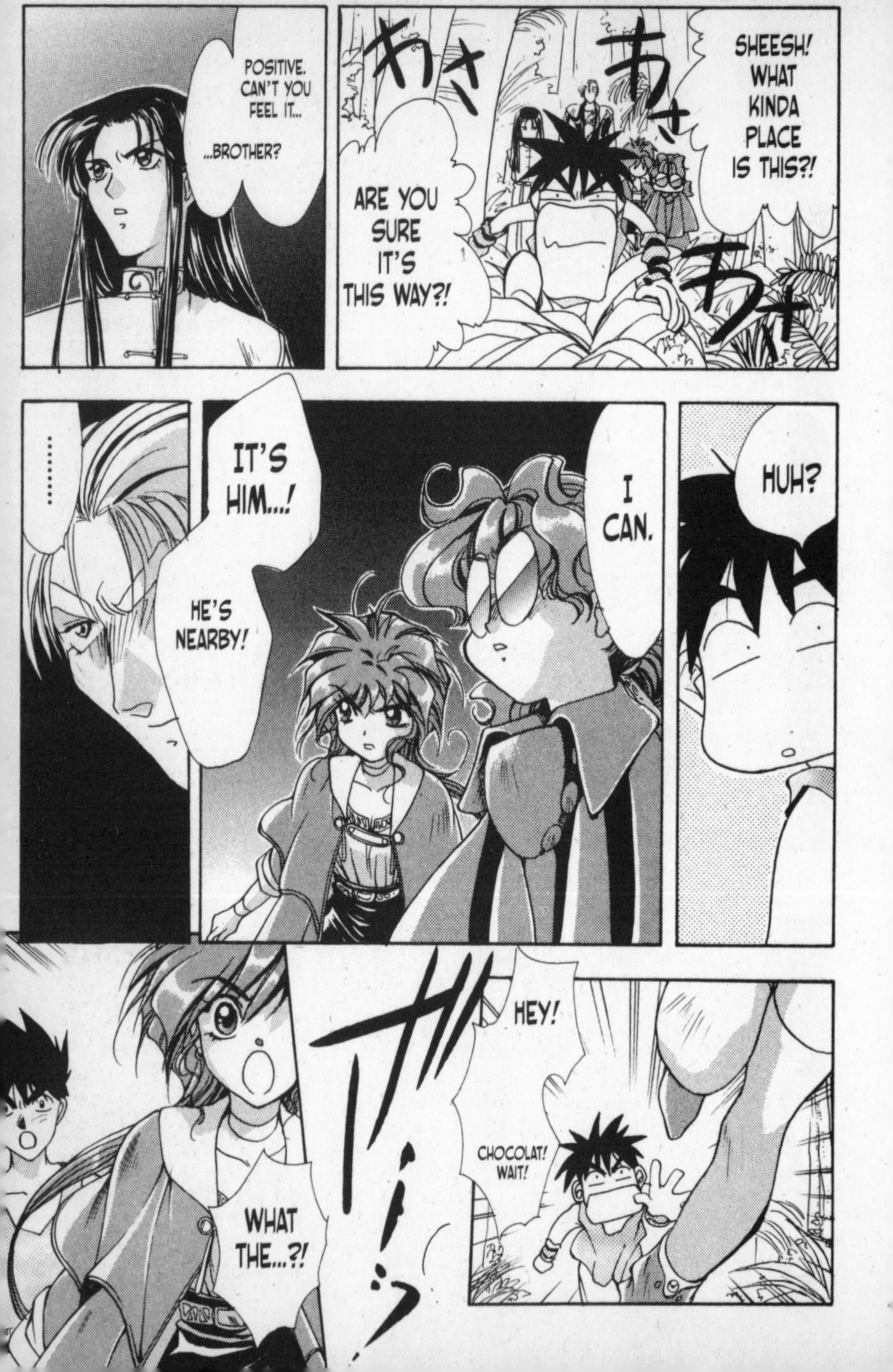
SHEESH! WHAT KINDA PLACE IS THIS?!
ARE YOU SURE IT'S THIS WAY?!
POSITIVE. CAN'T YOU FEEL IT...
...BROTHER?
HUH?
I CAN.
IT'S HIM...!
HE'S NEARBY!
....
HEY!
CHOCOLAT! WAIT!
WHAT THE...?!

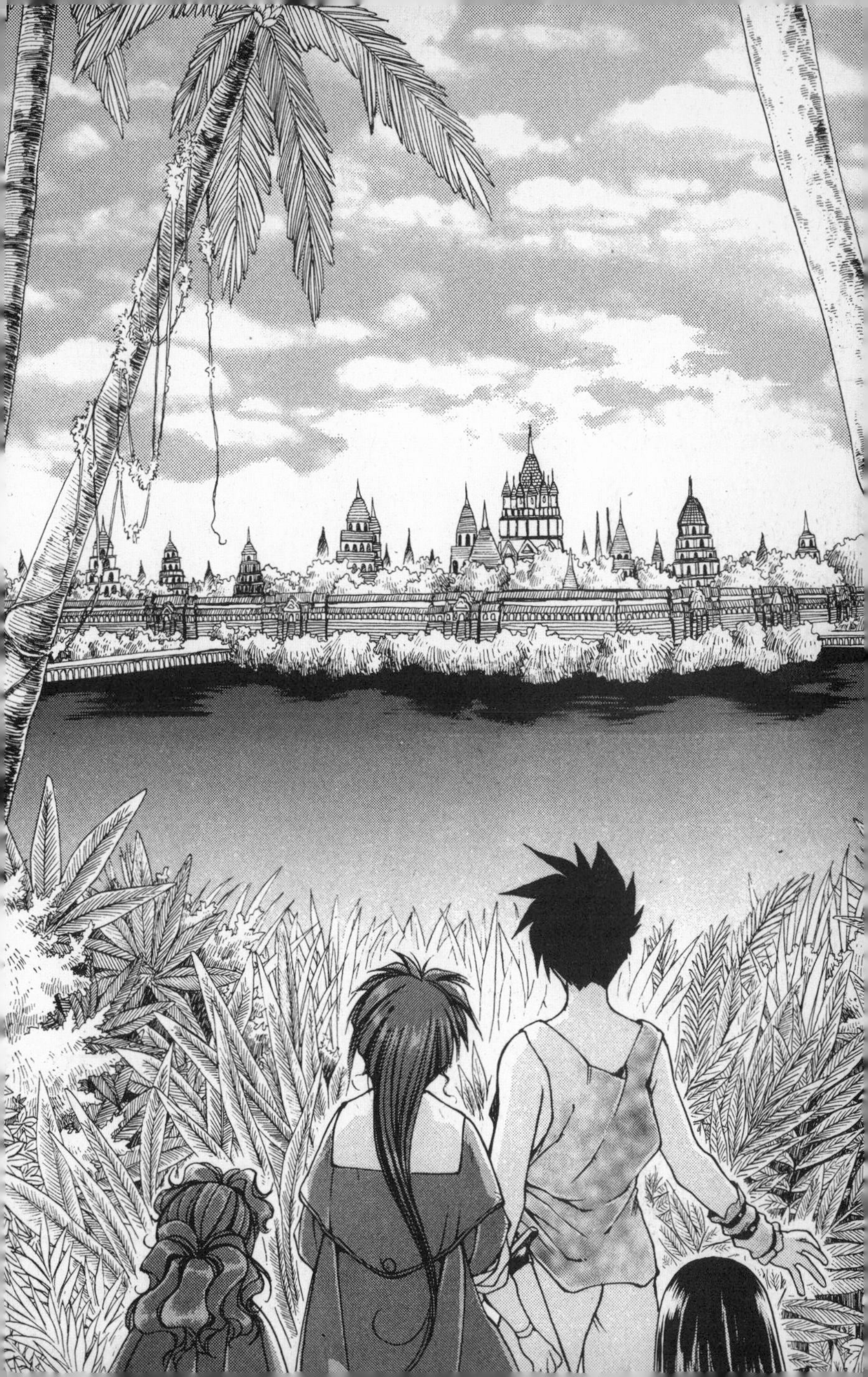

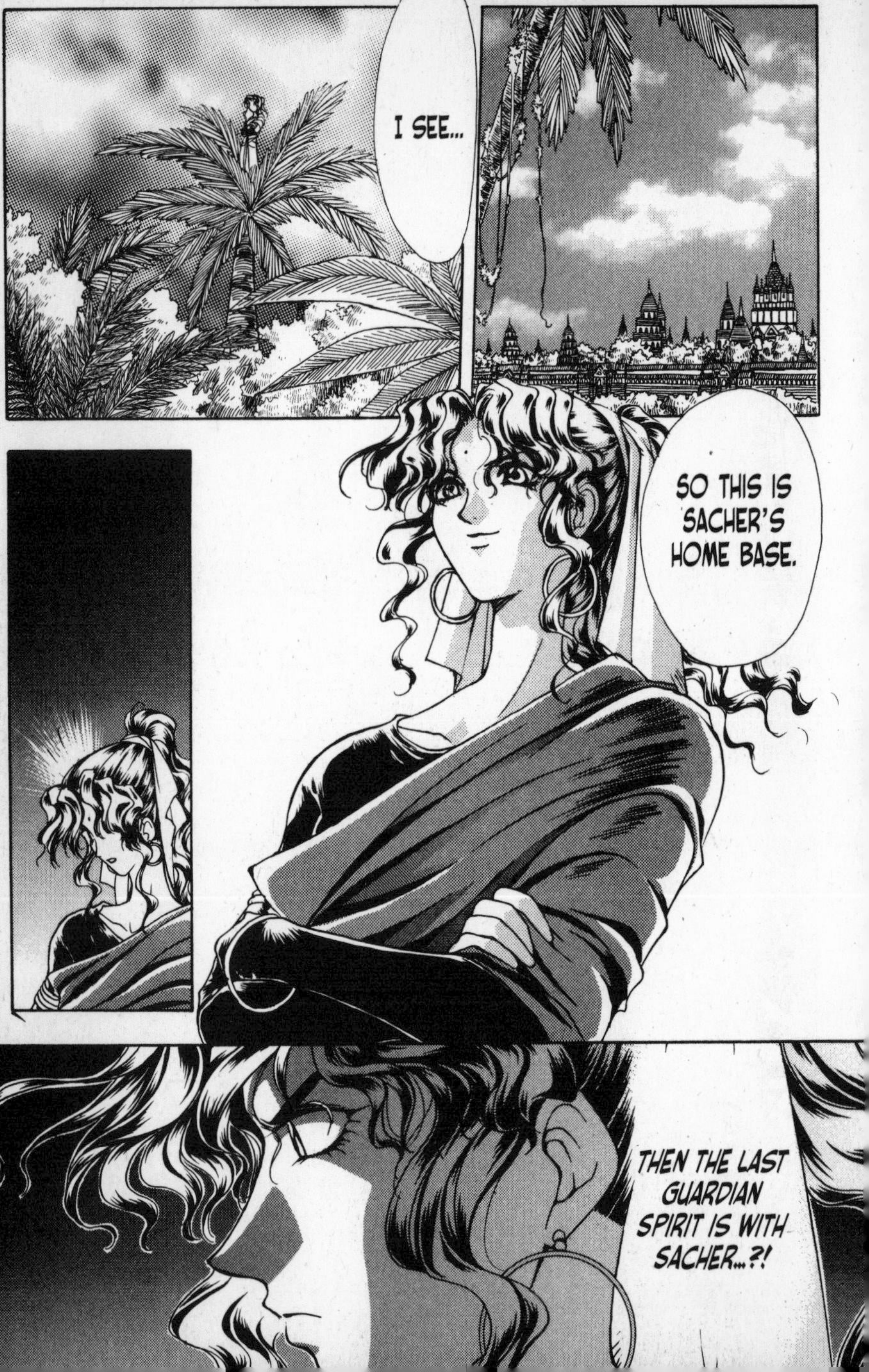
I SEE...
SO THIS IS SACHER'S HOME BASE.
THEN THE LAST GUARDIAN SPIRIT IS WITH SACHER...?!

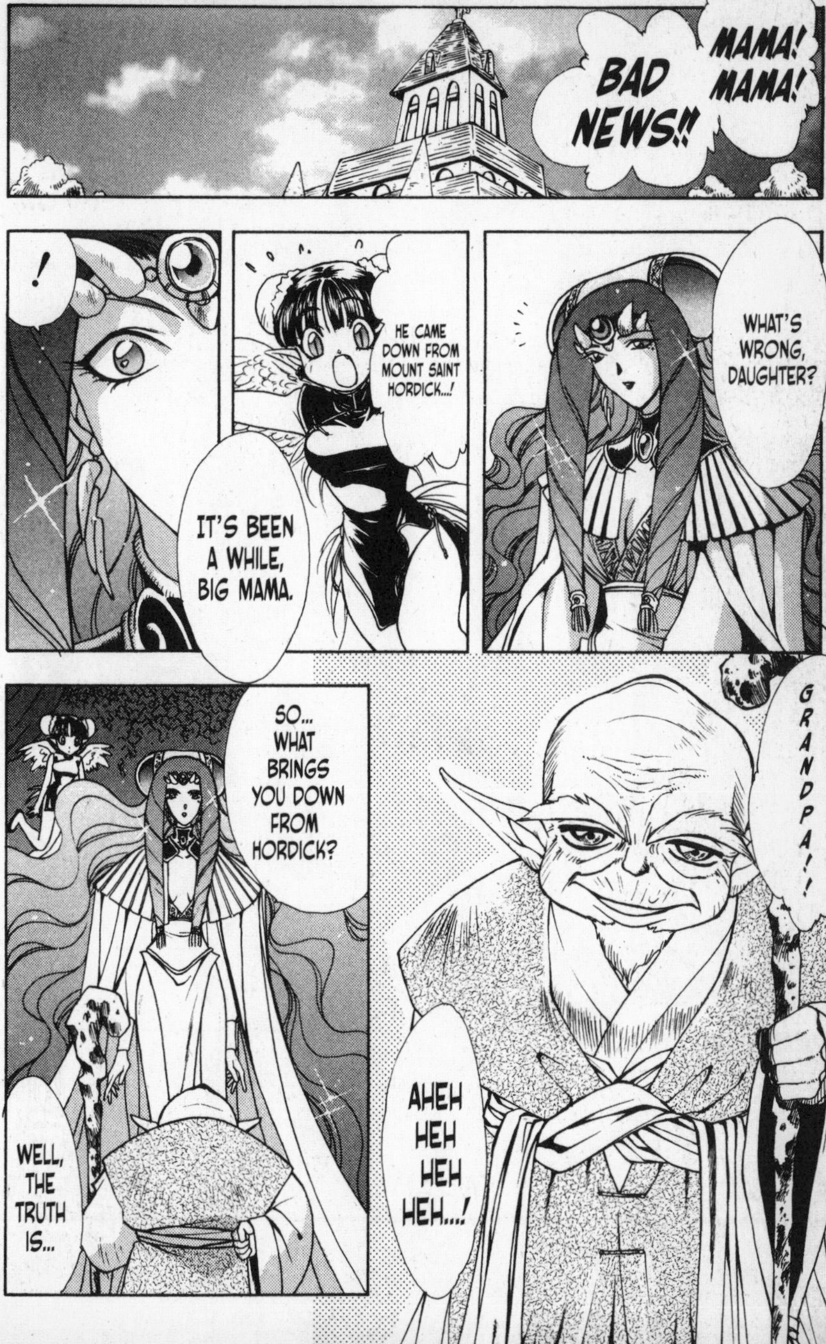
MAMA! MAMA!
BAD NEWS!!
WHAT'S WRONG, DAUGHTER?
HE CAME DOWN FROM MOUNT SAINT HORDICK...!
IT'S BEEN A WHILE, BIG MAMA.
!
GRANDPA!!
AHEH HEH HEH HEH...!
SO... WHAT BRINGS YOU DOWN FROM HORDICK?
WELL, THE TRUTH IS...

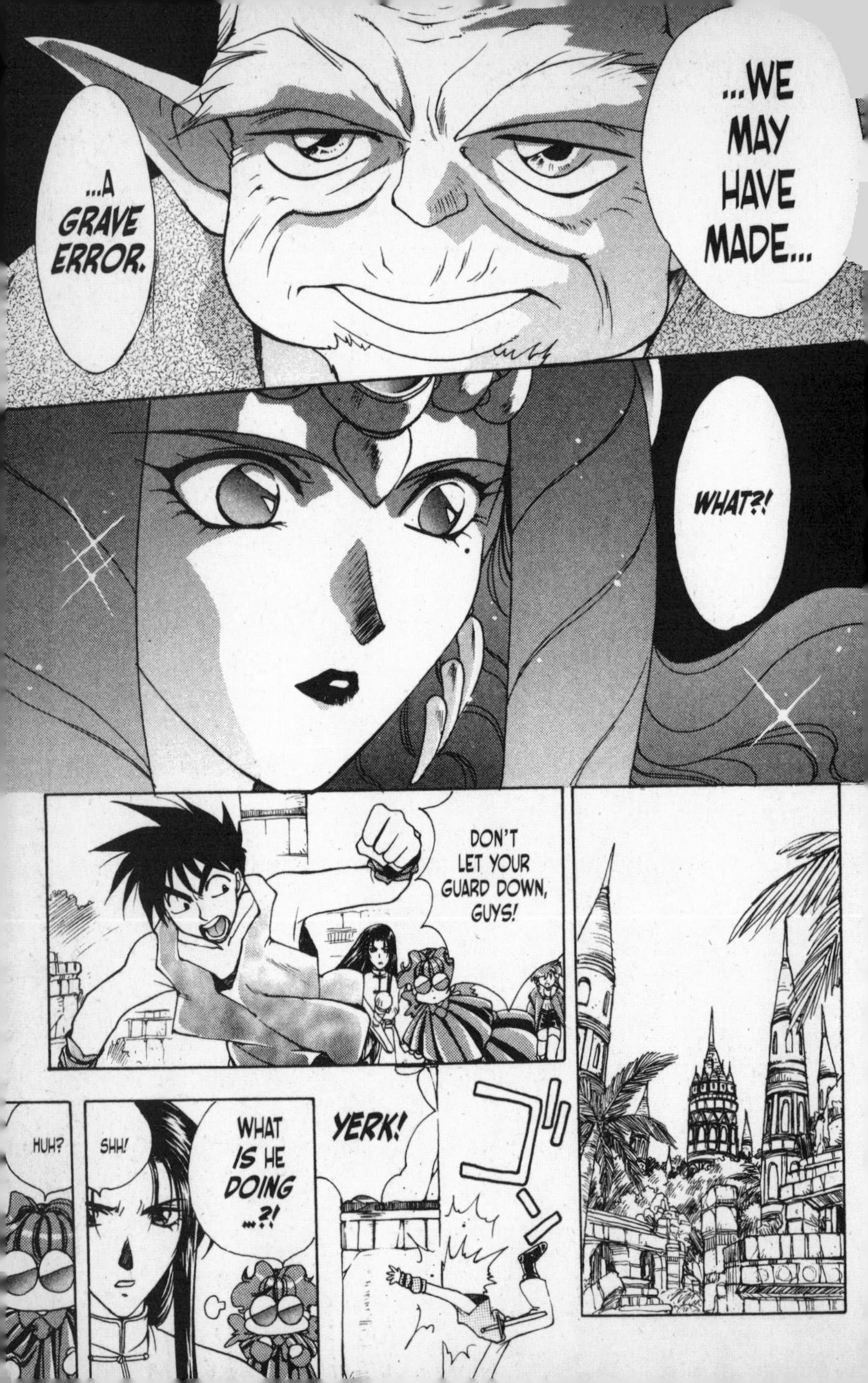
...WE MAY HAVE MADE...
...A GRAVE ERROR.
WHAT?!
DON'T LET YOUR GUARD DOWN, GUYS!
YERK!
WHAT IS HE DOING ...?!
SHH!
HUH?

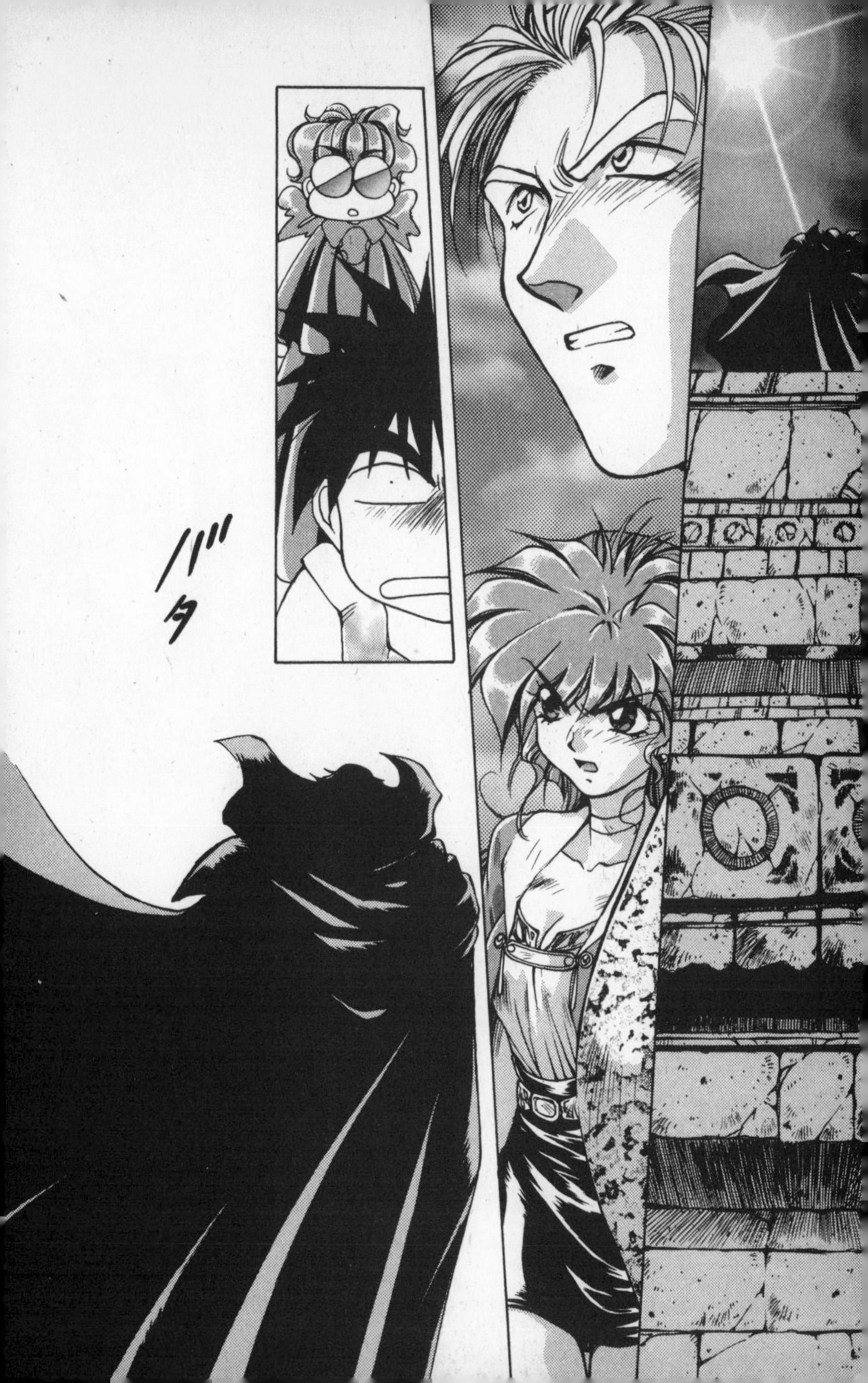
バタ

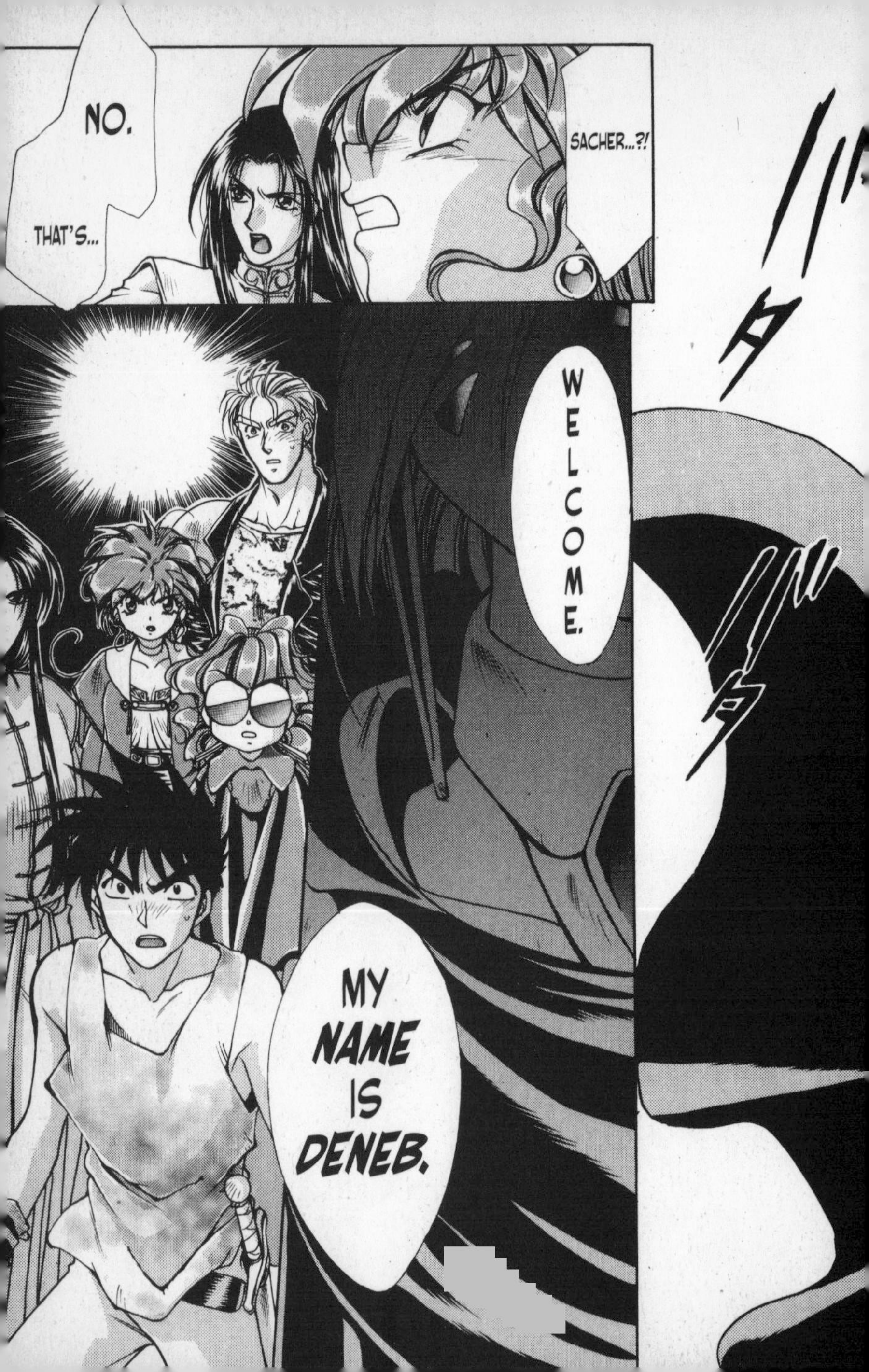
SACHER...?!
NO.
THAT'S...
WELCOME.
MY NAME IS DENEB.

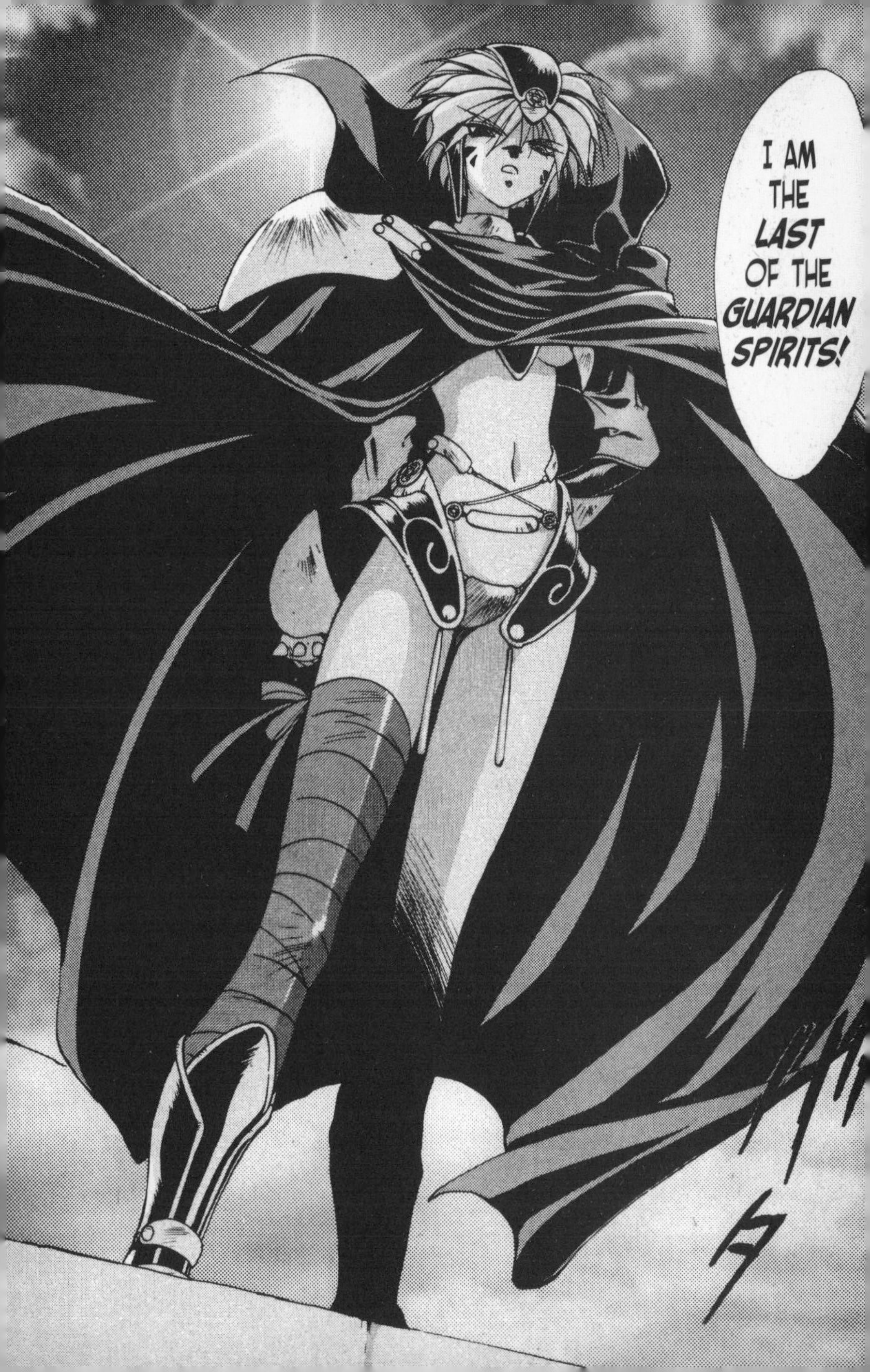
I AM THE LAST OF THE GUARDIAN SPIRITS!

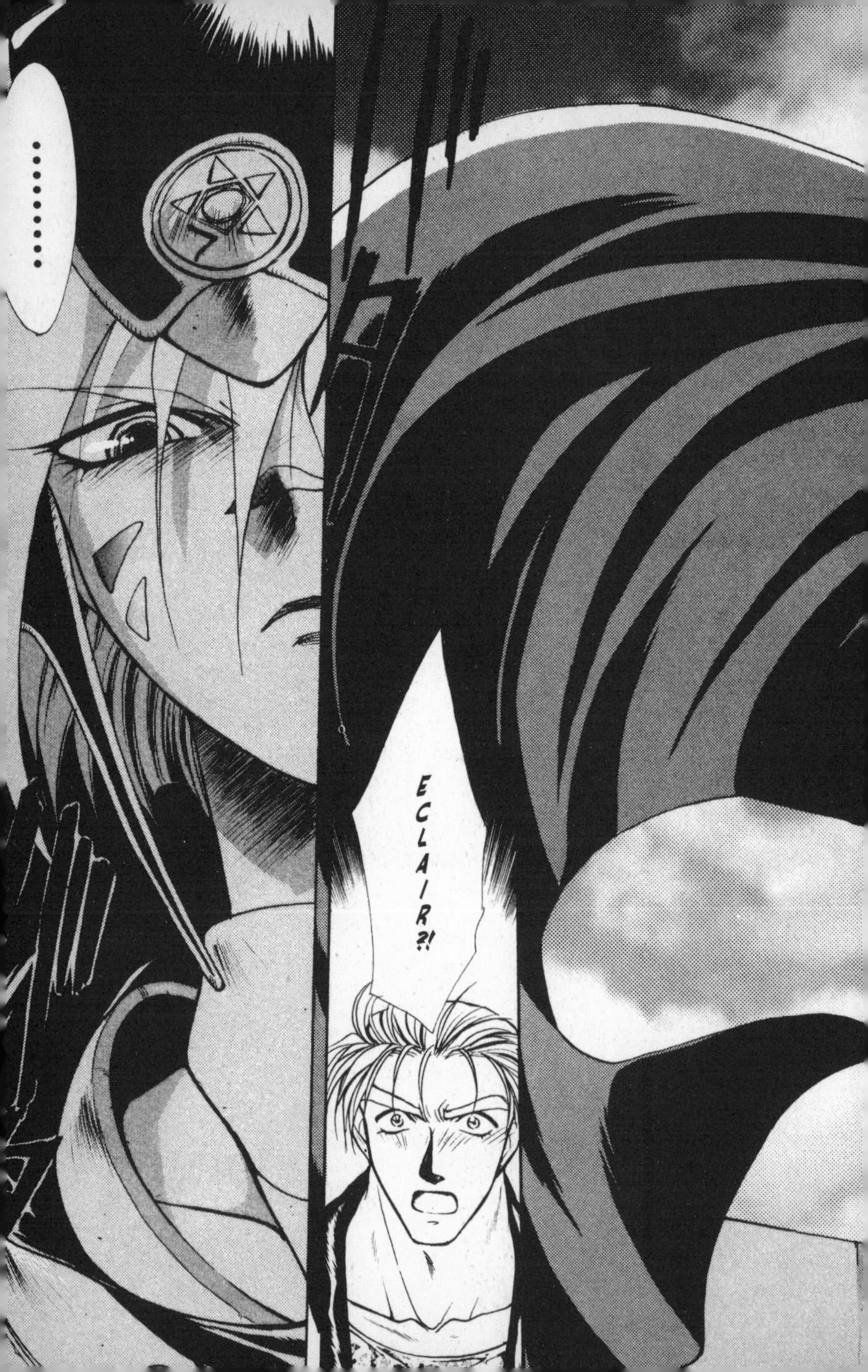
ECLAIR?!
......

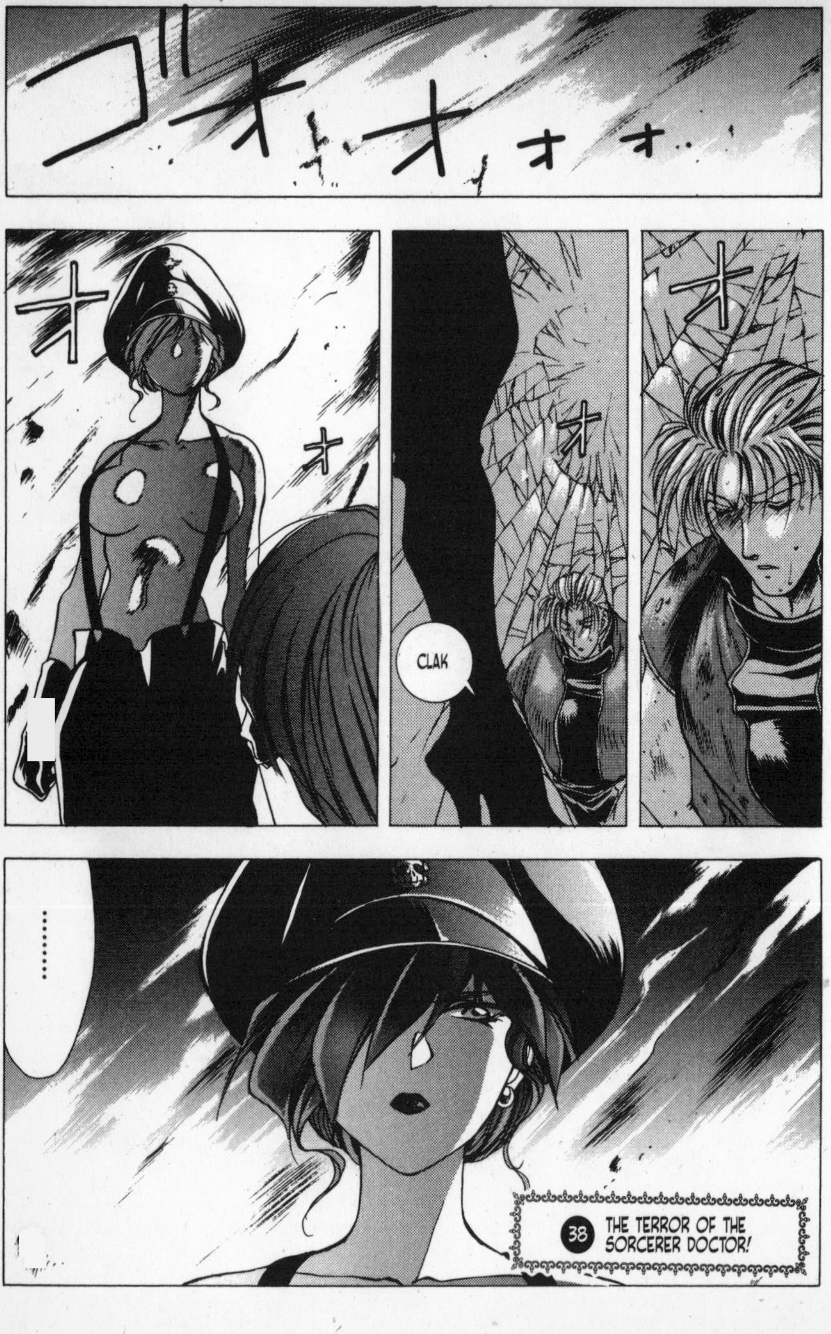
ゴオォオォォォ…
オ
オ
CLAK
オ
オ
......
38 THE TERROR OF THE SORCERER DOCTOR!

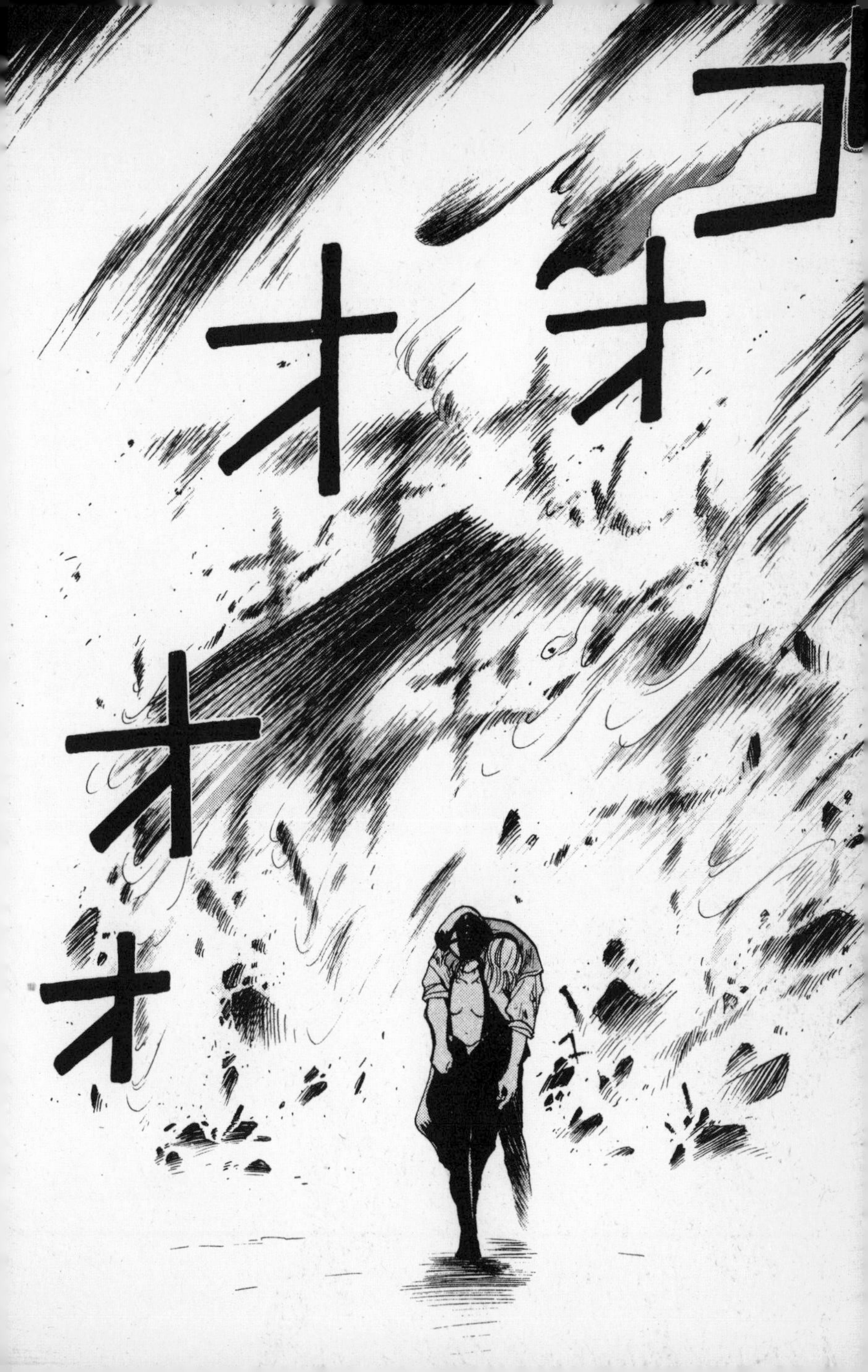
ゴオオオオ

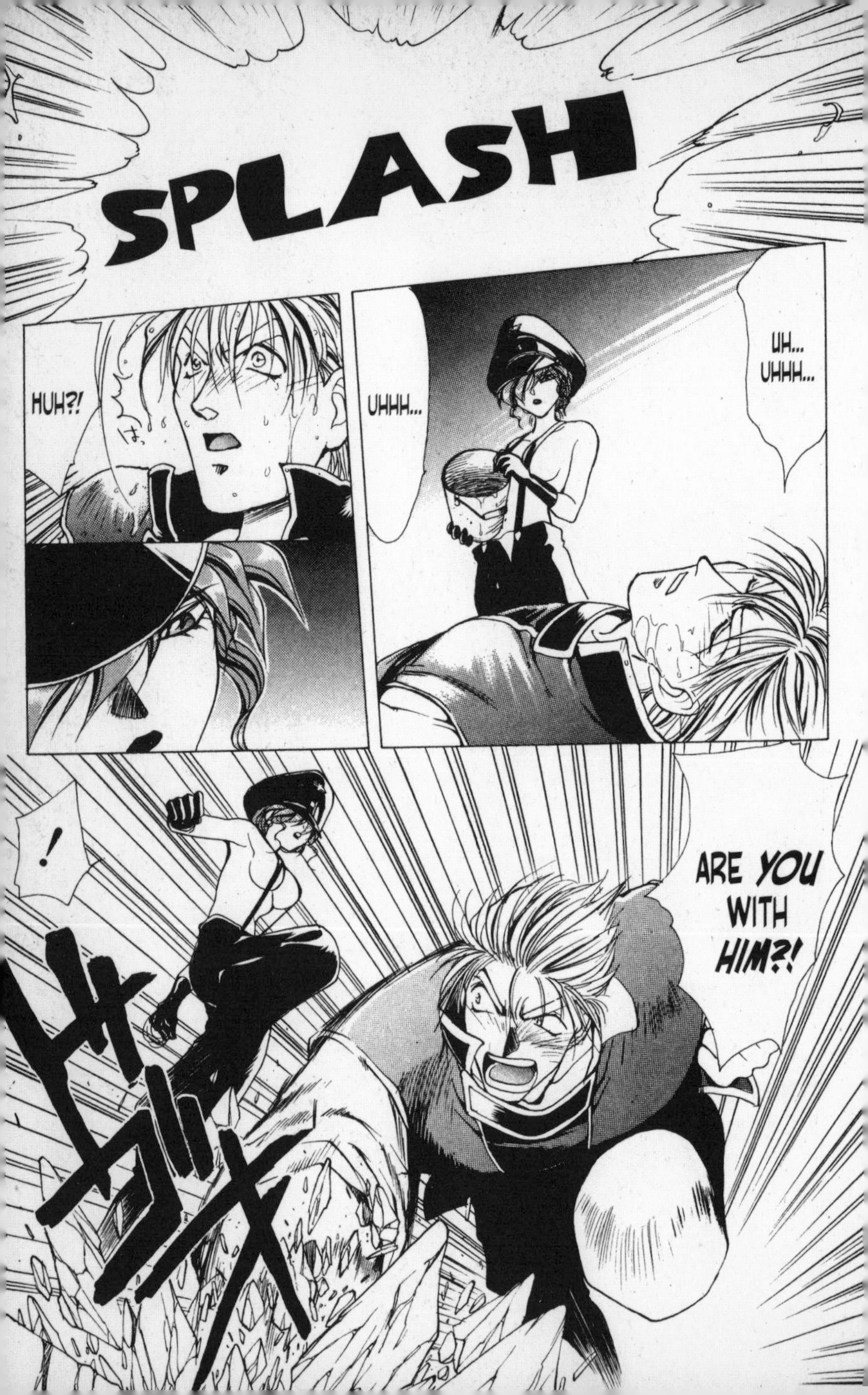
SPLASH
UH... UHHH...
UHHH...
HUH?!
はっ
ARE YOU WITH HIM?!
!

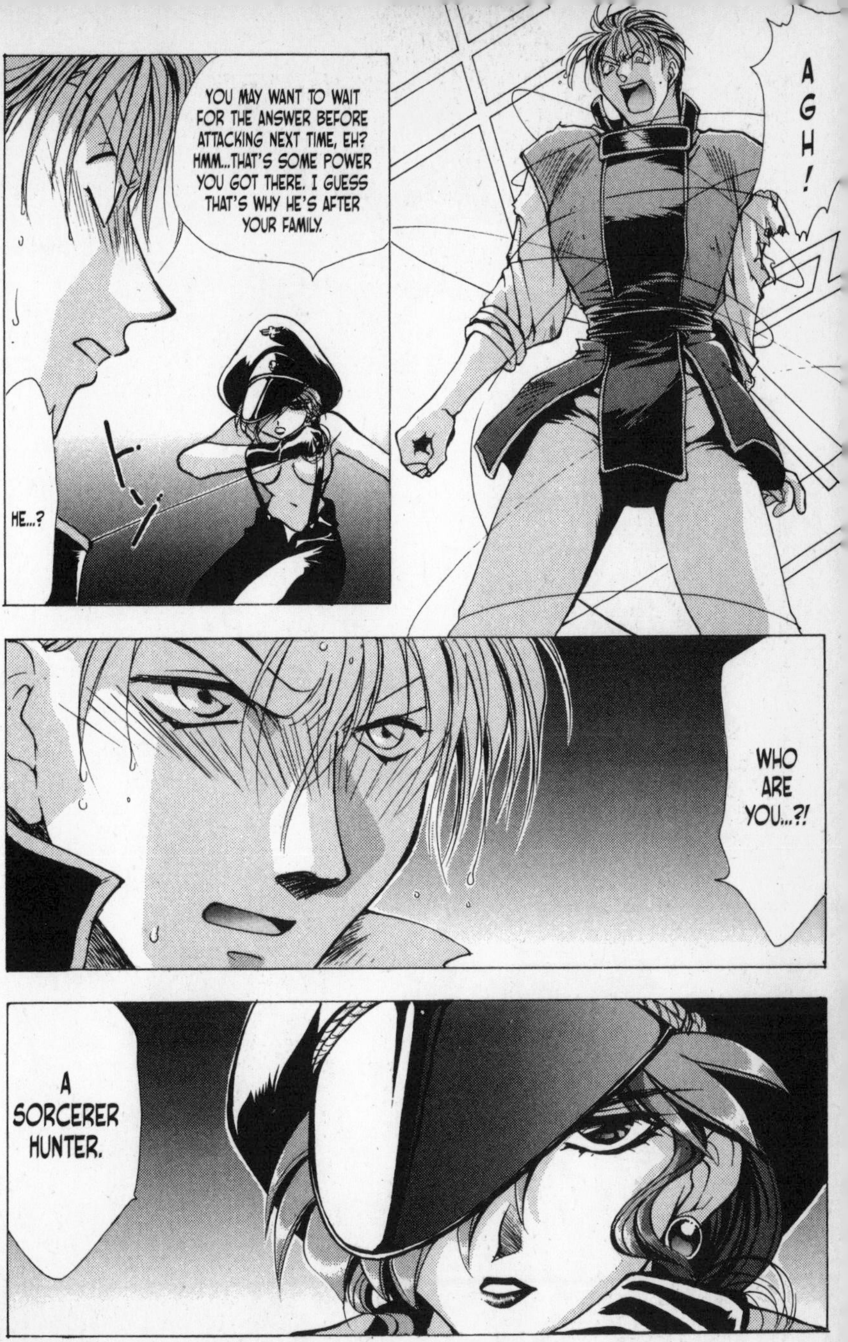
AGH!
YOU MAY WANT TO WAIT FOR THE ANSWER BEFORE ATTACKING NEXT TIME, EH? HMM...THAT'S SOME POWER YOU GOT THERE. I GUESS THAT'S WHY HE'S AFTER YOUR FAMILY.
HE...?
WHO ARE YOU...?!
A SORCERER HUNTER.

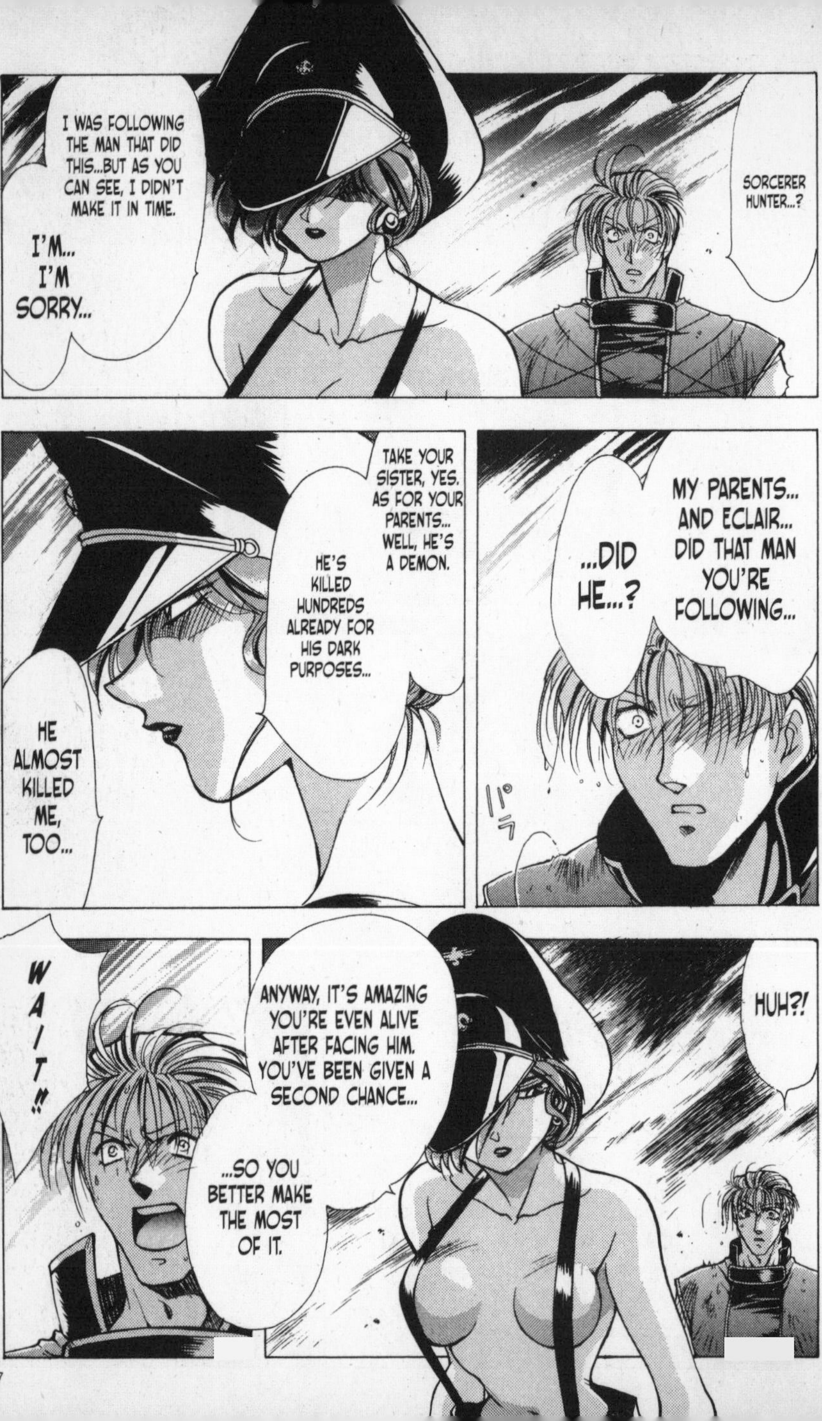
SORCERER HUNTER...?
I WAS FOLLOWING THE MAN THAT DID THIS...BUT AS YOU CAN SEE, I DIDN'T MAKE IT IN TIME.
I'M... I'M SORRY...
MY PARENTS... AND ECLAIR... DID THAT MAN YOU'RE FOLLOWING...
...DID HE...?
パラ
TAKE YOUR SISTER, YES. AS FOR YOUR PARENTS... WELL, HE'S A DEMON.
HE'S KILLED HUNDREDS ALREADY FOR HIS DARK PURPOSES...
HE ALMOST KILLED ME, TOO...
HUH?!
ANYWAY, IT'S AMAZING YOU'RE EVEN ALIVE AFTER FACING HIM. YOU'VE BEEN GIVEN A SECOND CHANCE...
...SO YOU BETTER MAKE THE MOST OF IT.
WAIT!!

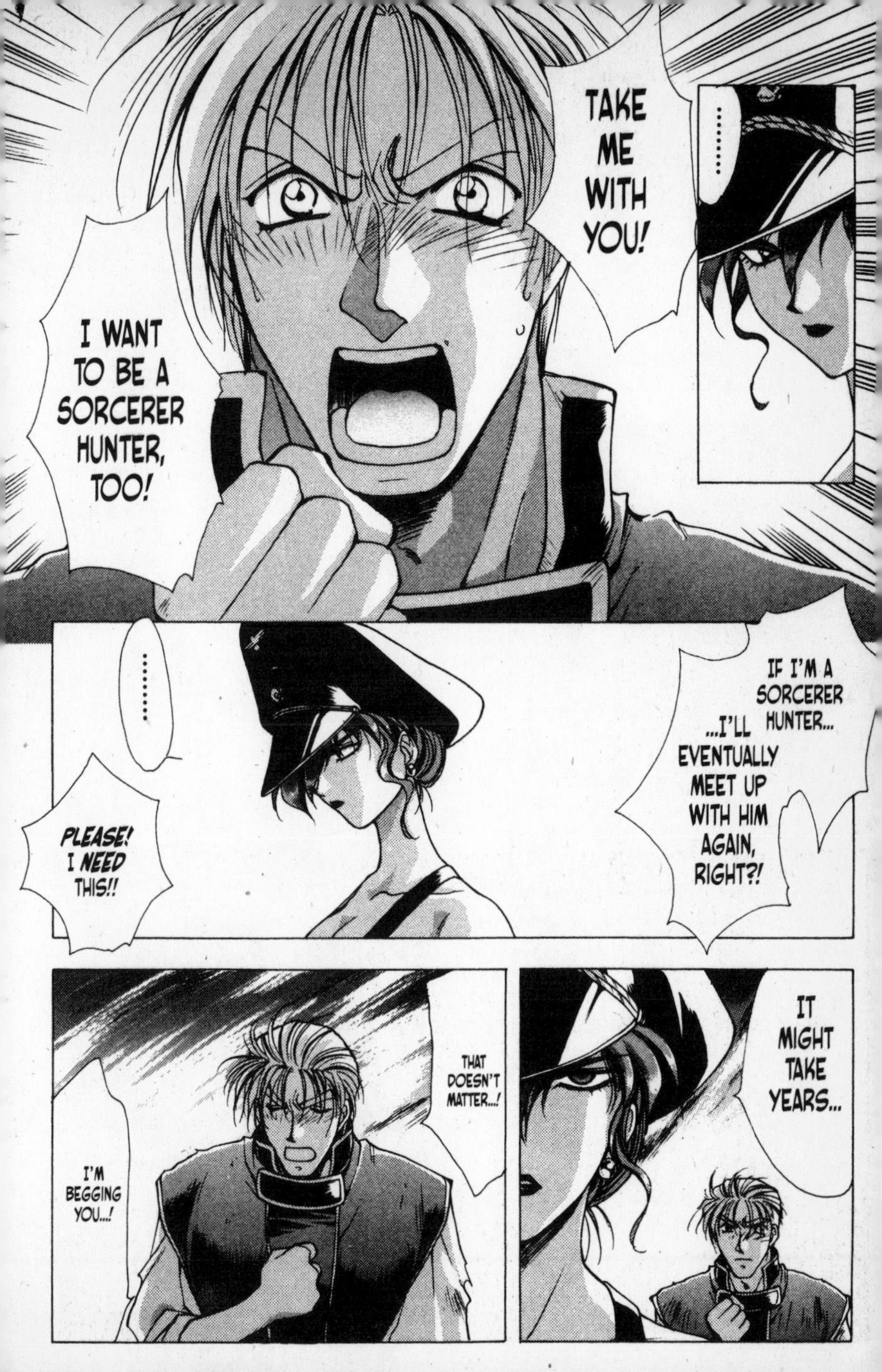
......
TAKE ME WITH YOU!
I WANT TO BE A SORCERER HUNTER, TOO!
IF I'M A SORCERER HUNTER...
...I'LL EVENTUALLY MEET UP WITH HIM AGAIN, RIGHT?!
......
PLEASE! I NEED THIS!!
IT MIGHT TAKE YEARS...
THAT DOESN'T MATTER...!
I'M BEGGING YOU...!

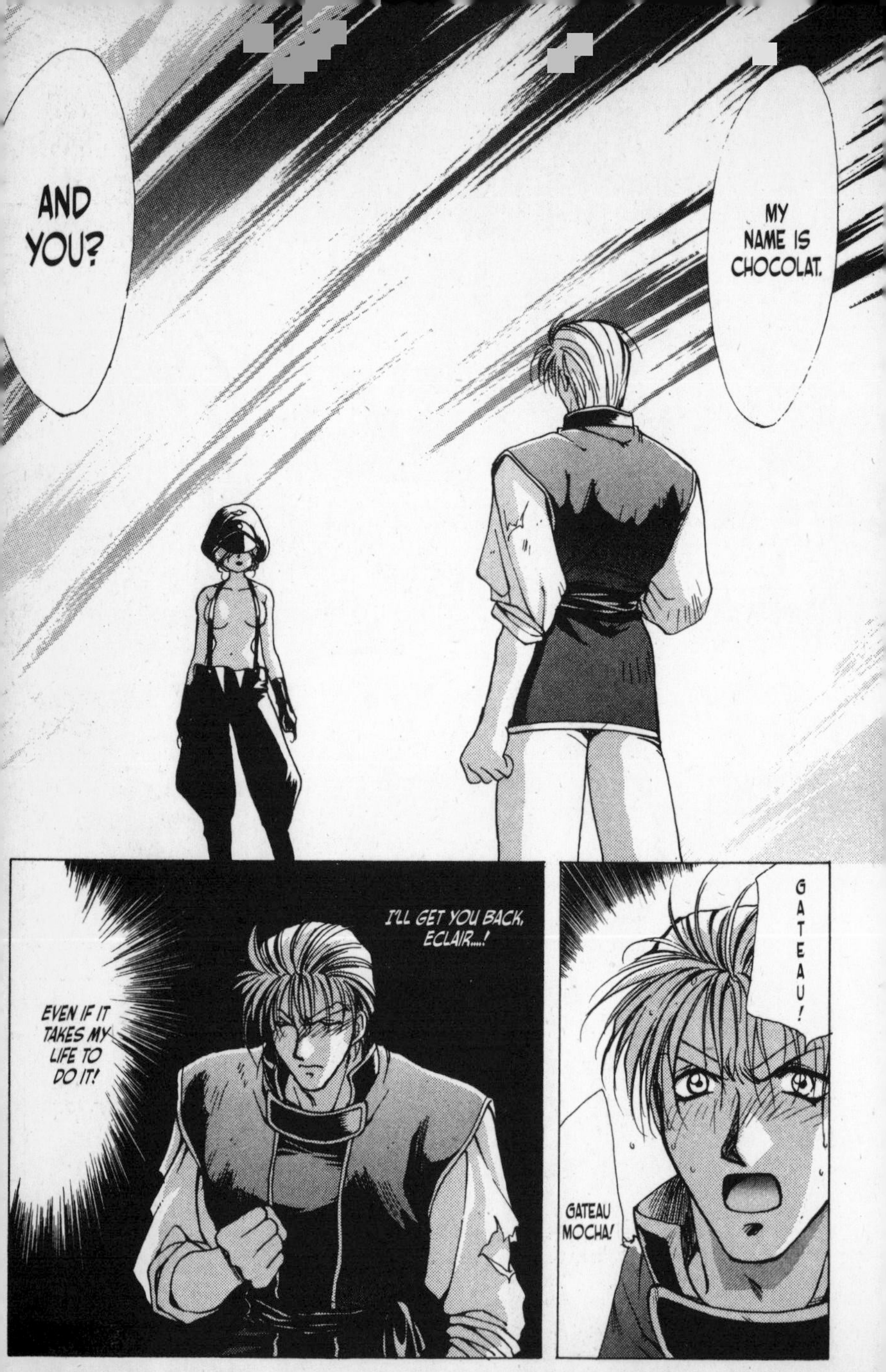
MY NAME IS CHOCOLAT.
AND YOU?
GATEAU!
GATEAU MOCHA!
I'LL GET YOU BACK, ECLAIR....!
EVEN IF IT TAKES MY LIFE TO DO IT!

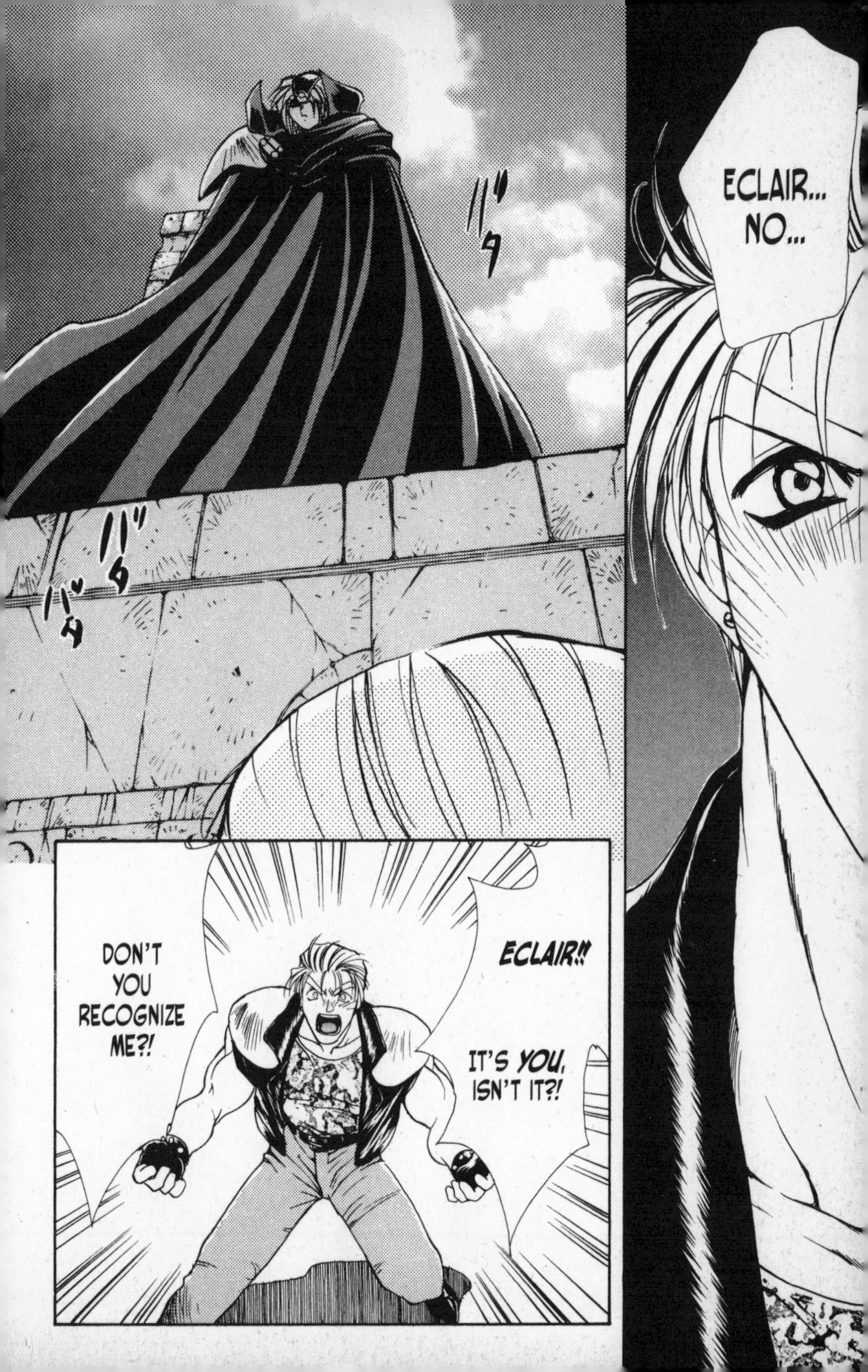
ECLAIR... NO...
ECLAIR!!
IT'S *YOU*, ISN'T IT?!
DON'T YOU RECOGNIZE ME?!

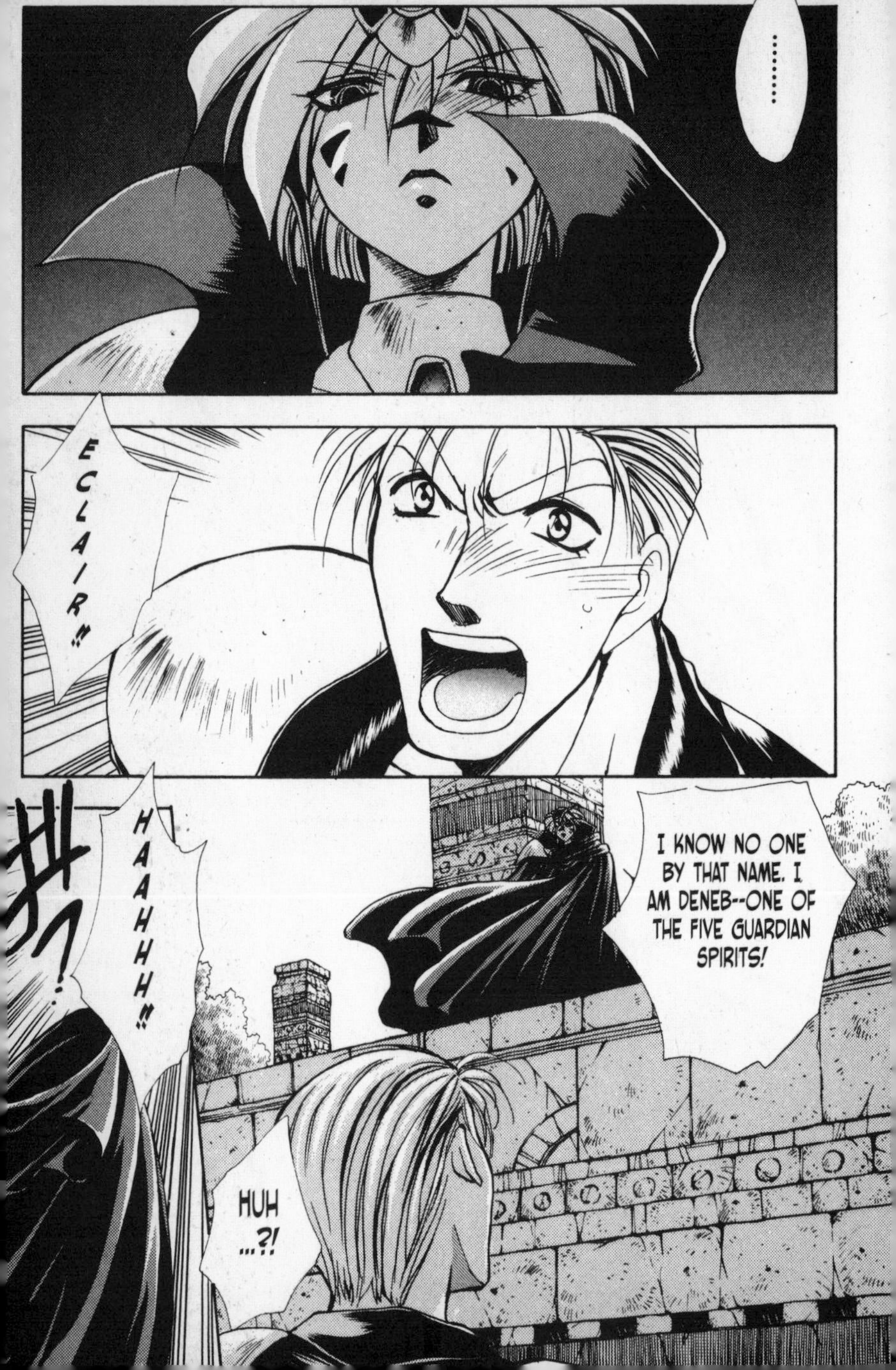
......
ECLAIR!!
I KNOW NO ONE BY THAT NAME. I AM DENEB--ONE OF THE FIVE GUARDIAN SPIRITS!
HAAHHH!!
HUH ...?!

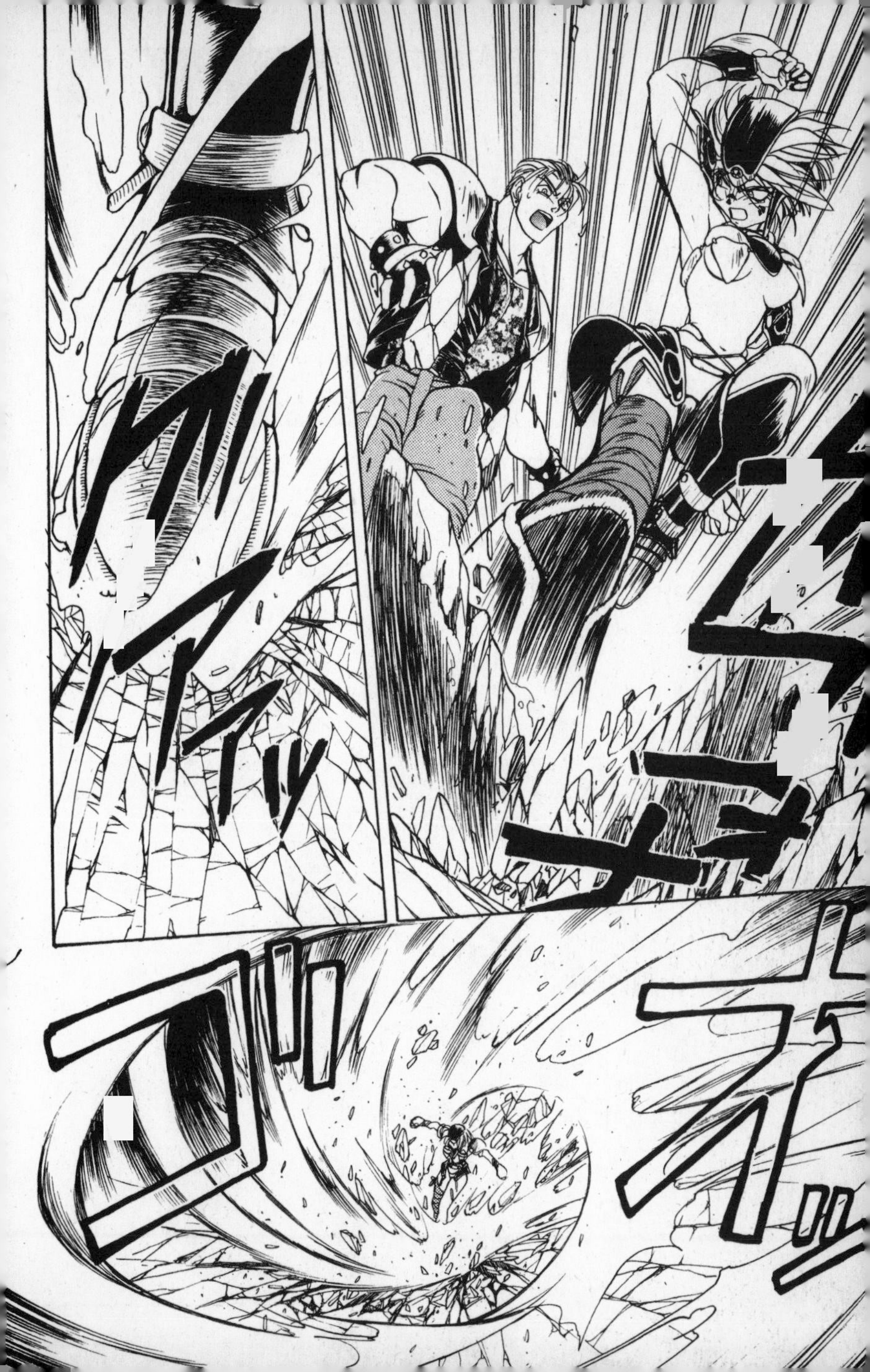

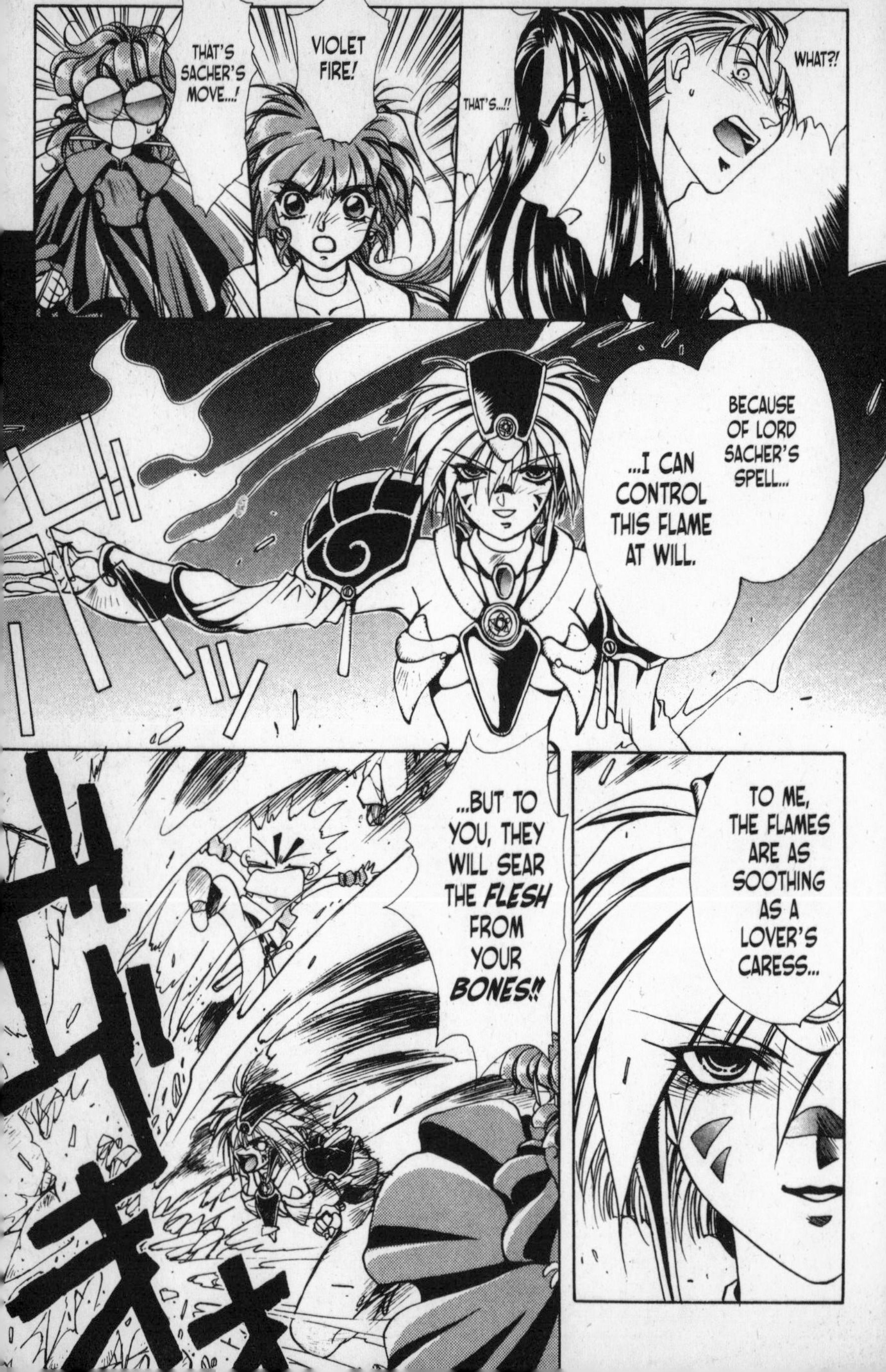
WHAT?!
THAT'S...!!
VIOLET FIRE!
THAT'S SACHER'S MOVE...!
BECAUSE OF LORD SACHER'S SPELL...
...I CAN CONTROL THIS FLAME AT WILL.
TO ME, THE FLAMES ARE AS SOOTHING AS A LOVER'S CARESS...
...BUT TO YOU, THEY WILL SEAR THE *FLESH* FROM YOUR *BONES!!*

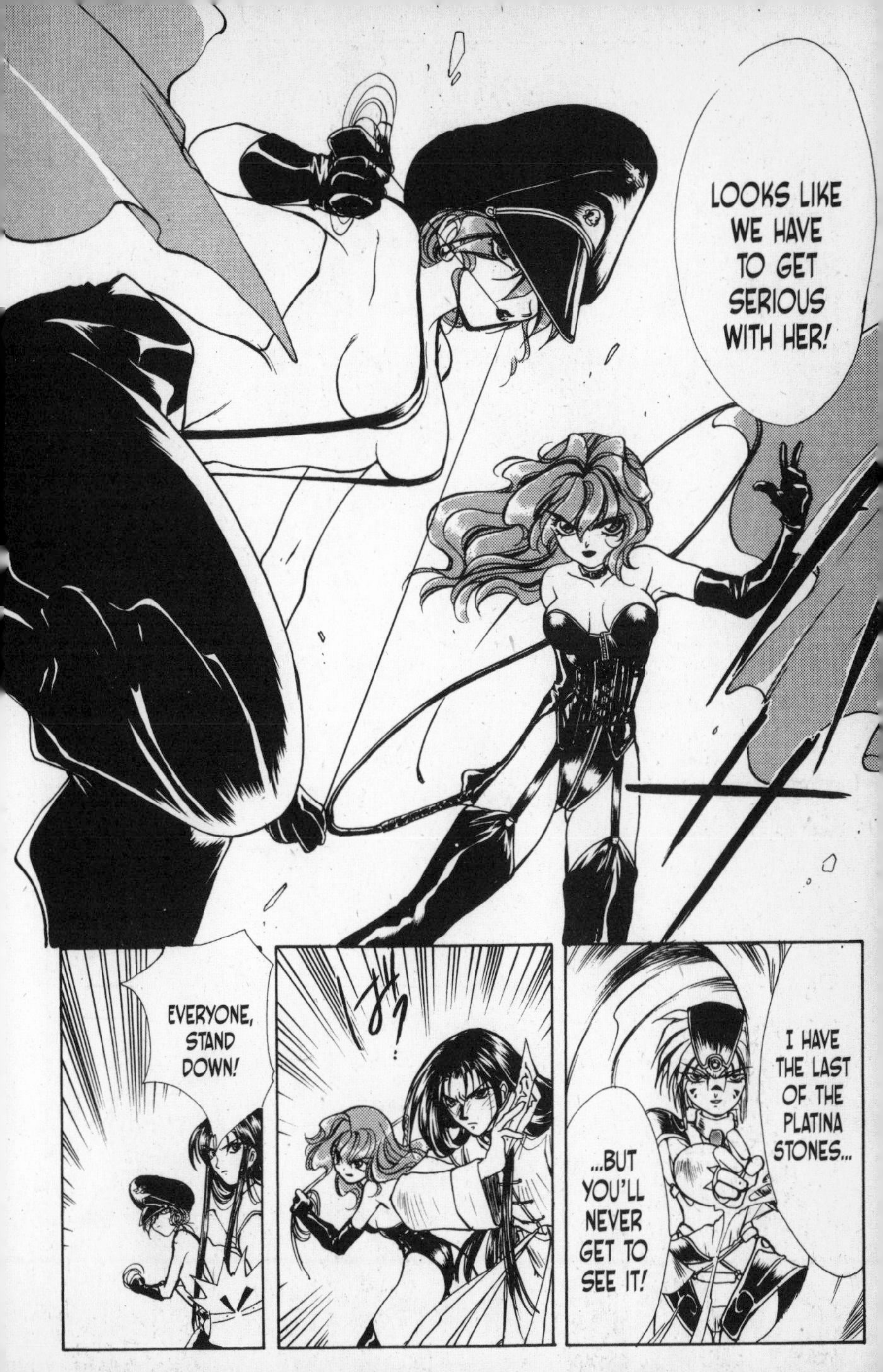
LOOKS LIKE WE HAVE TO GET SERIOUS WITH HER!
I HAVE THE LAST OF THE PLATINA STONES...
...BUT YOU'LL NEVER GET TO SEE IT!
EVERYONE, STAND DOWN!

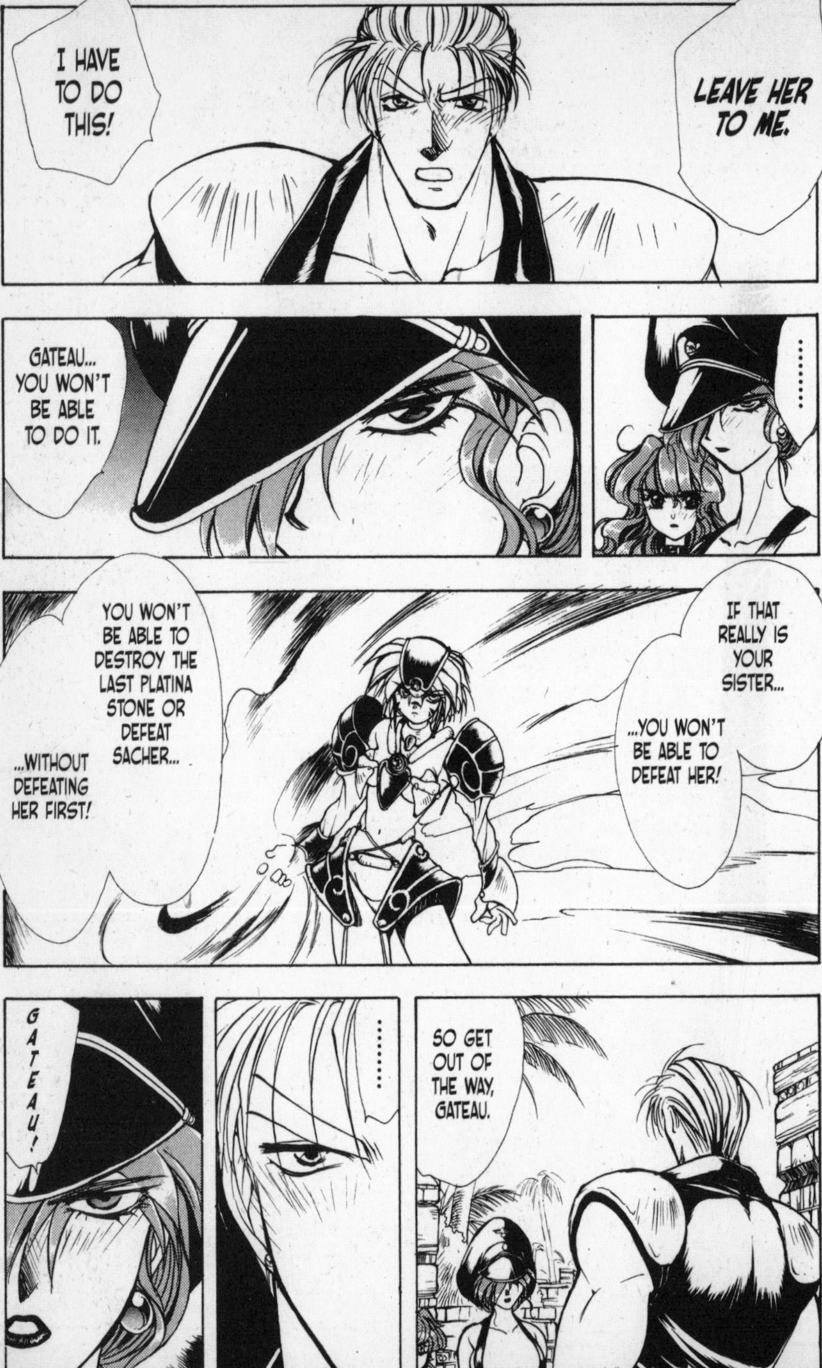
LEAVE HER TO ME.
I HAVE TO DO THIS!
......
GATEAU... YOU WON'T BE ABLE TO DO IT.
IF THAT REALLY IS YOUR SISTER...
...YOU WON'T BE ABLE TO DEFEAT HER!
YOU WON'T BE ABLE TO DESTROY THE LAST PLATINA STONE OR DEFEAT SACHER...
...WITHOUT DEFEATING HER FIRST!
SO GET OUT OF THE WAY, GATEAU.
....
GATEAU!

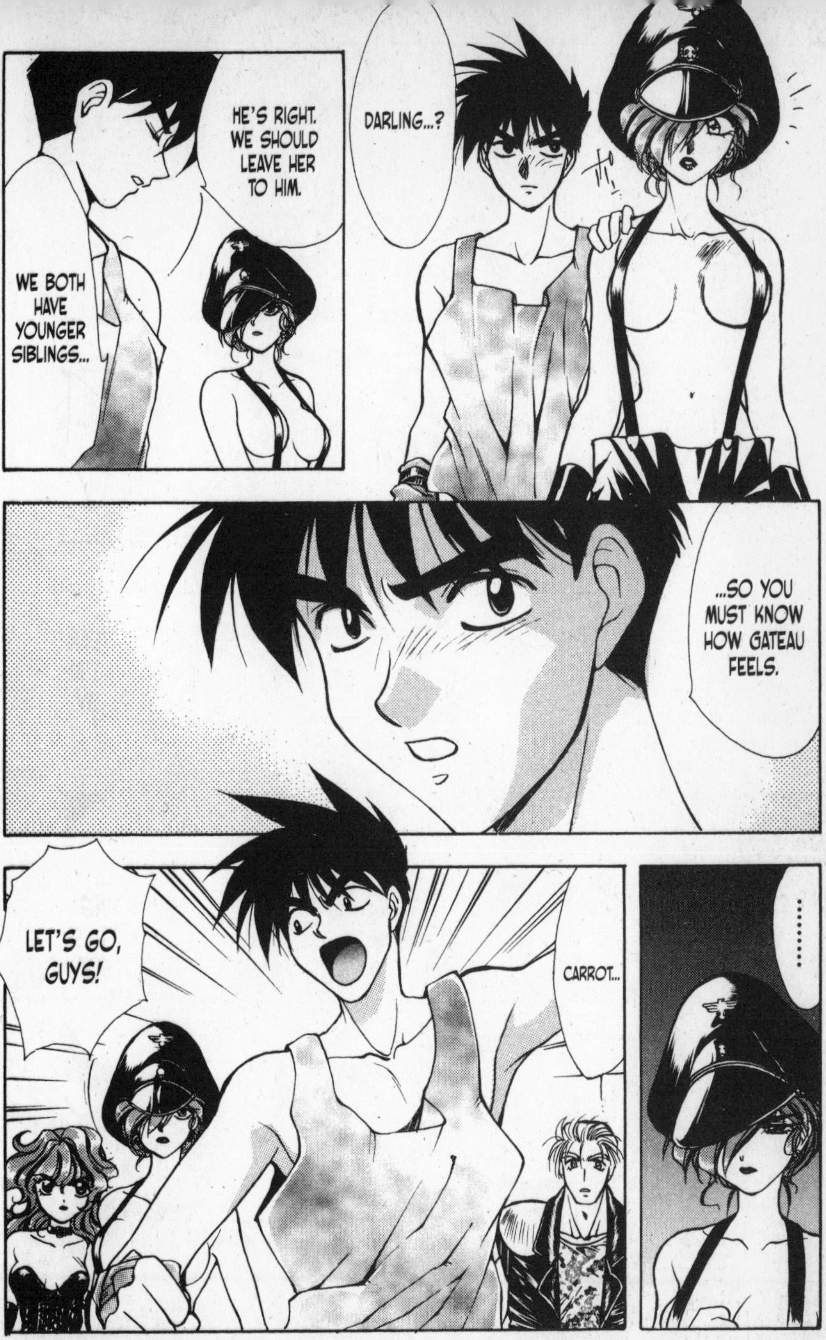
DARLING...?
HE'S RIGHT. WE SHOULD LEAVE HER TO HIM.
WE BOTH HAVE YOUNGER SIBLINGS...
...SO YOU MUST KNOW HOW GATEAU FEELS.
......
CARROT...
LET'S GO, GUYS!

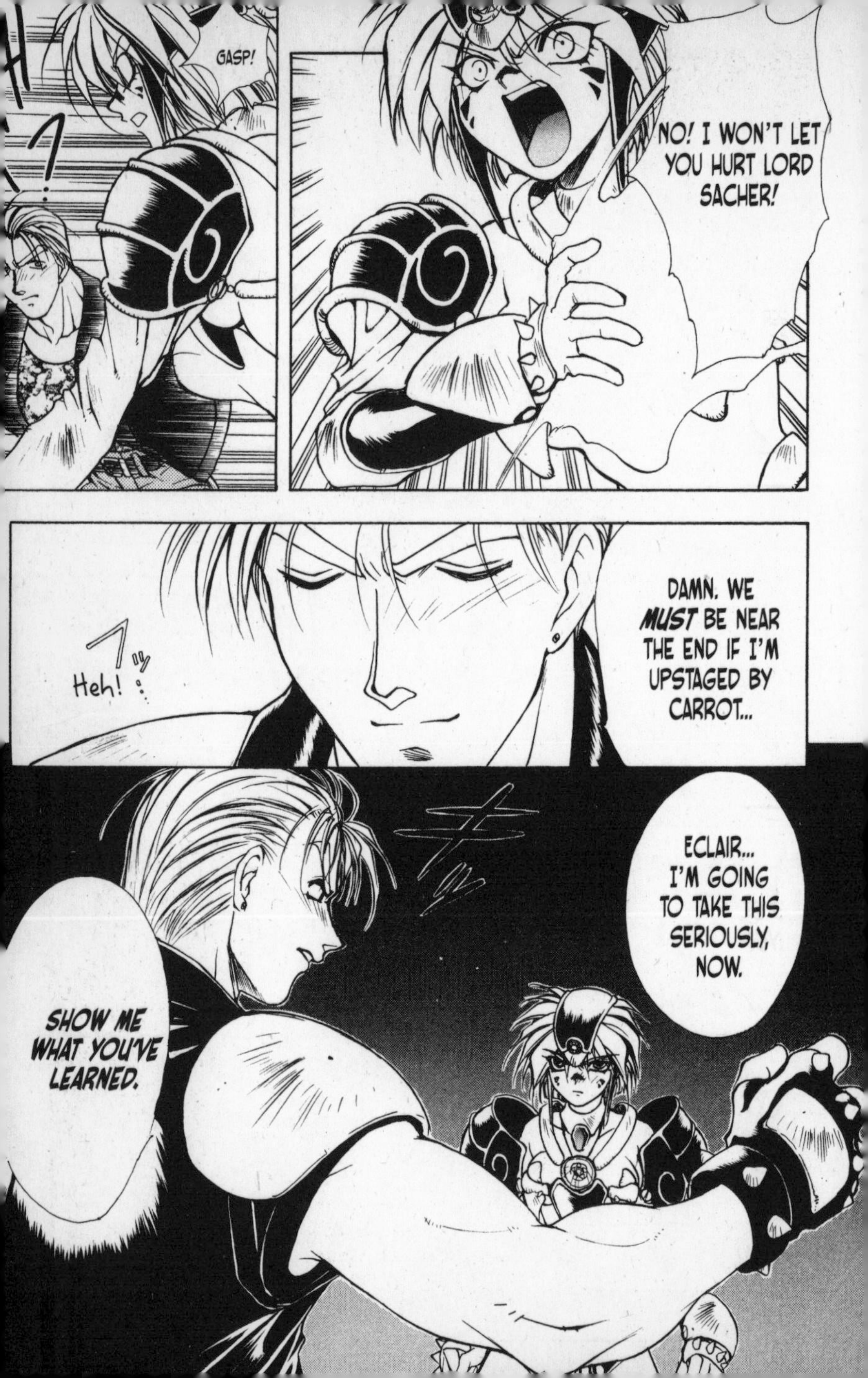
NO! I WON'T LET YOU HURT LORD SACHER!
GASP!
DAMN. WE *MUST* BE NEAR THE END IF I'M UPSTAGED BY CARROT...
Heh!
ECLAIR... I'M GOING TO TAKE THIS SERIOUSLY, NOW.
SHOW ME WHAT YOU'VE LEARNED.

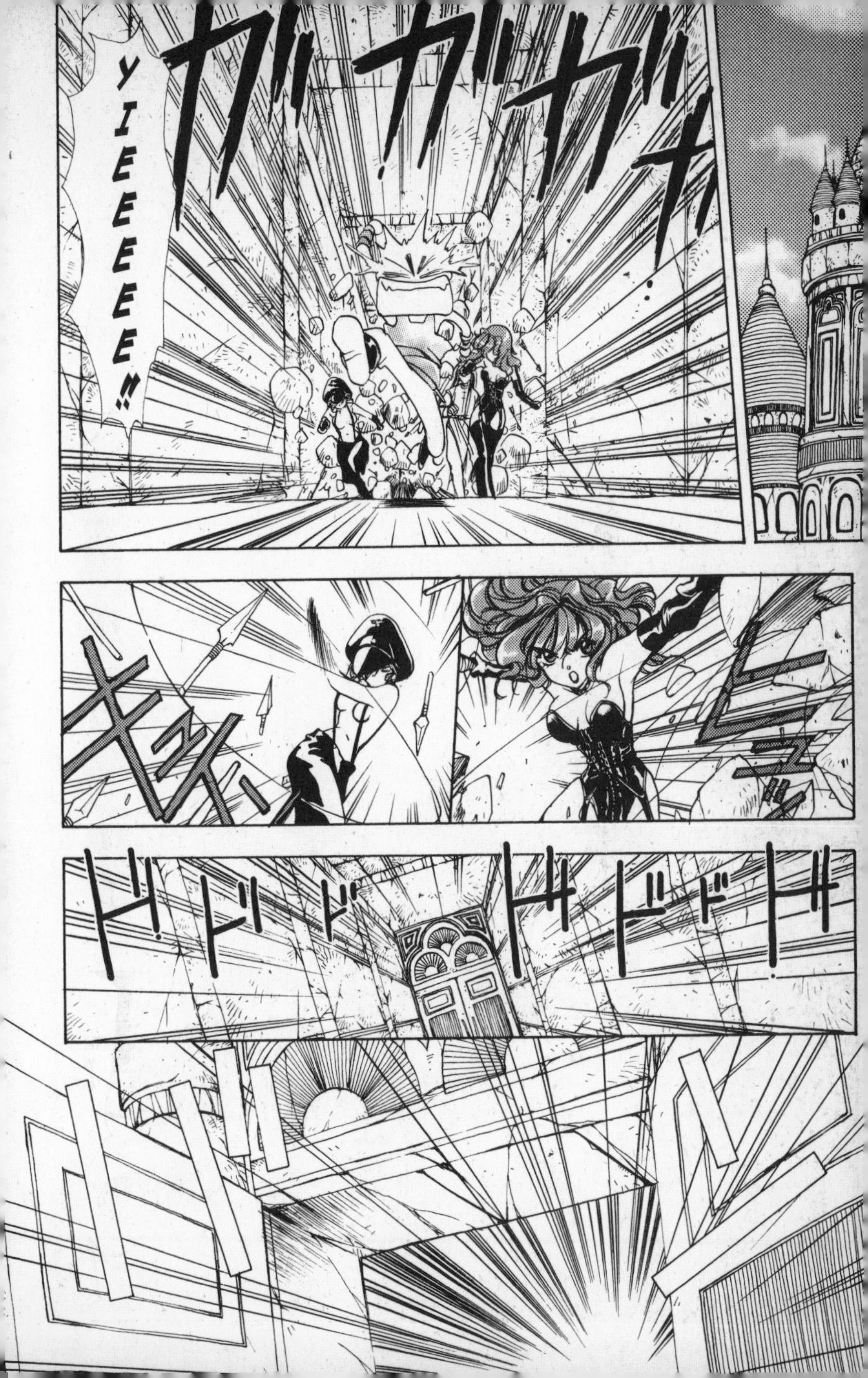
YIEEEEE!!

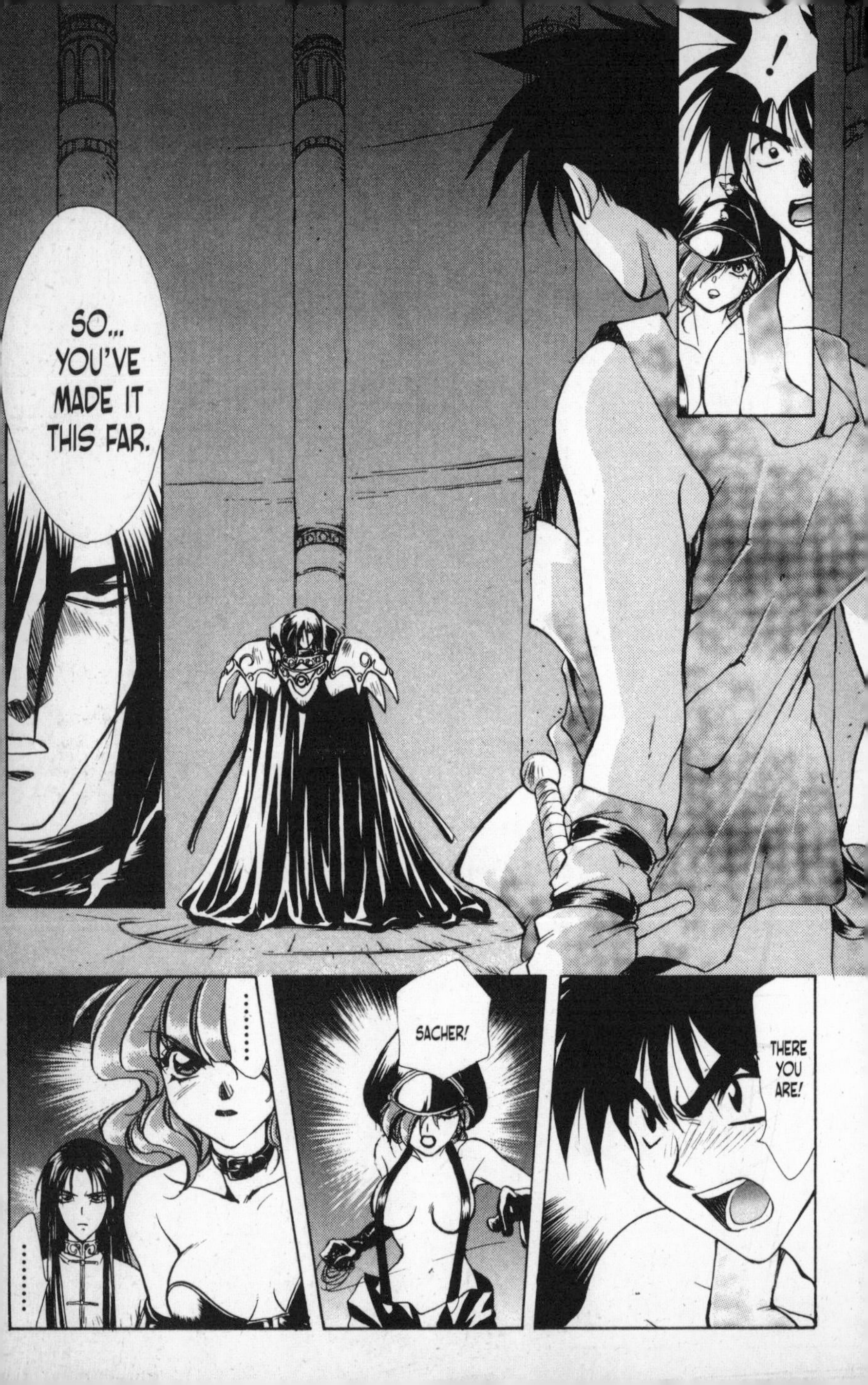
!
SO... YOU'VE MADE IT THIS FAR.
THERE YOU ARE!
SACHER!
......
......

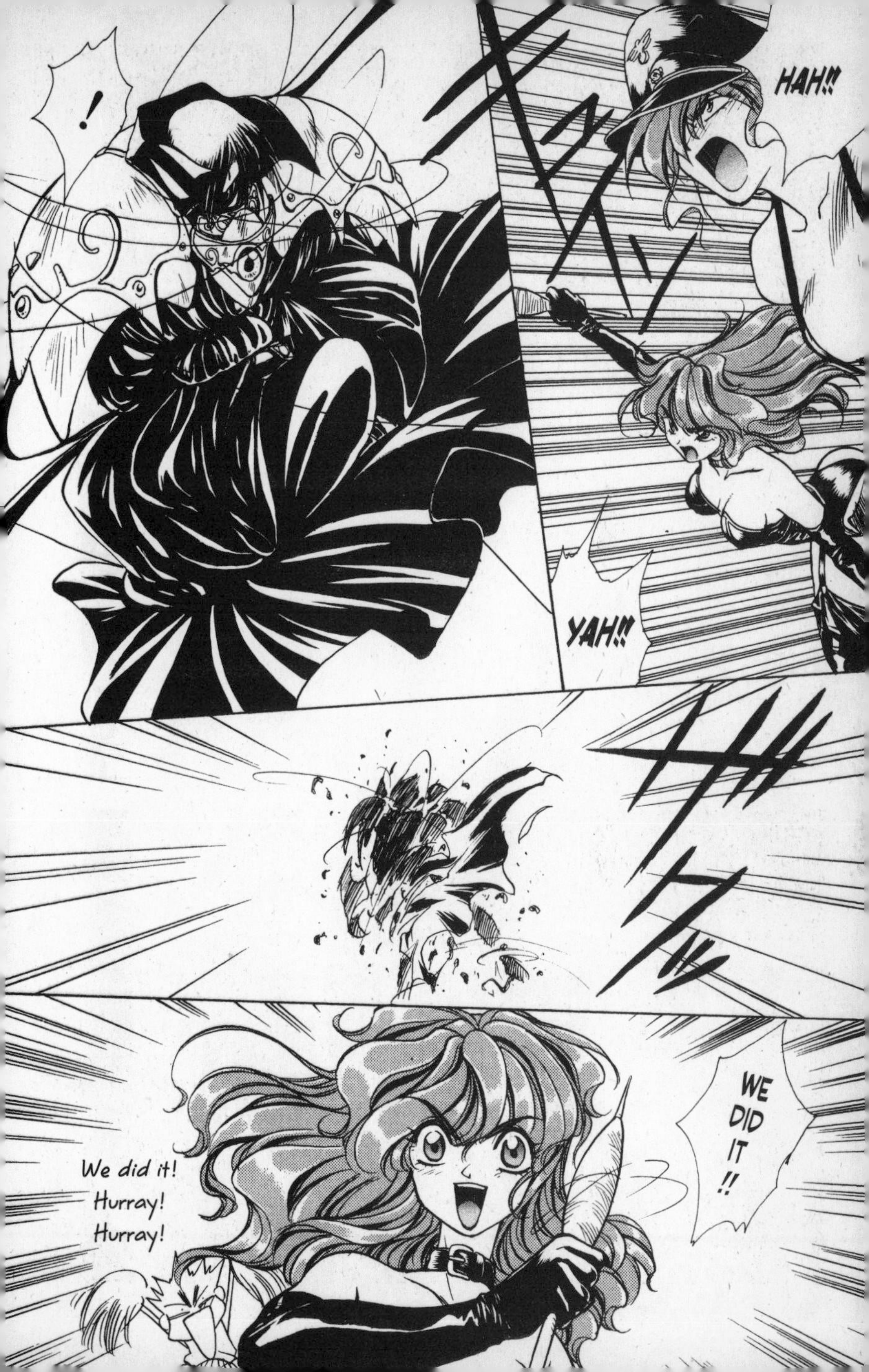
HAH!!
YAH!!
!
WE DID IT!!
We did it! Hurray! Hurray!

NO...IT CAN'T BE THIS EASY...

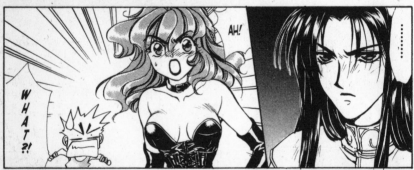

AH!

WHAT?!

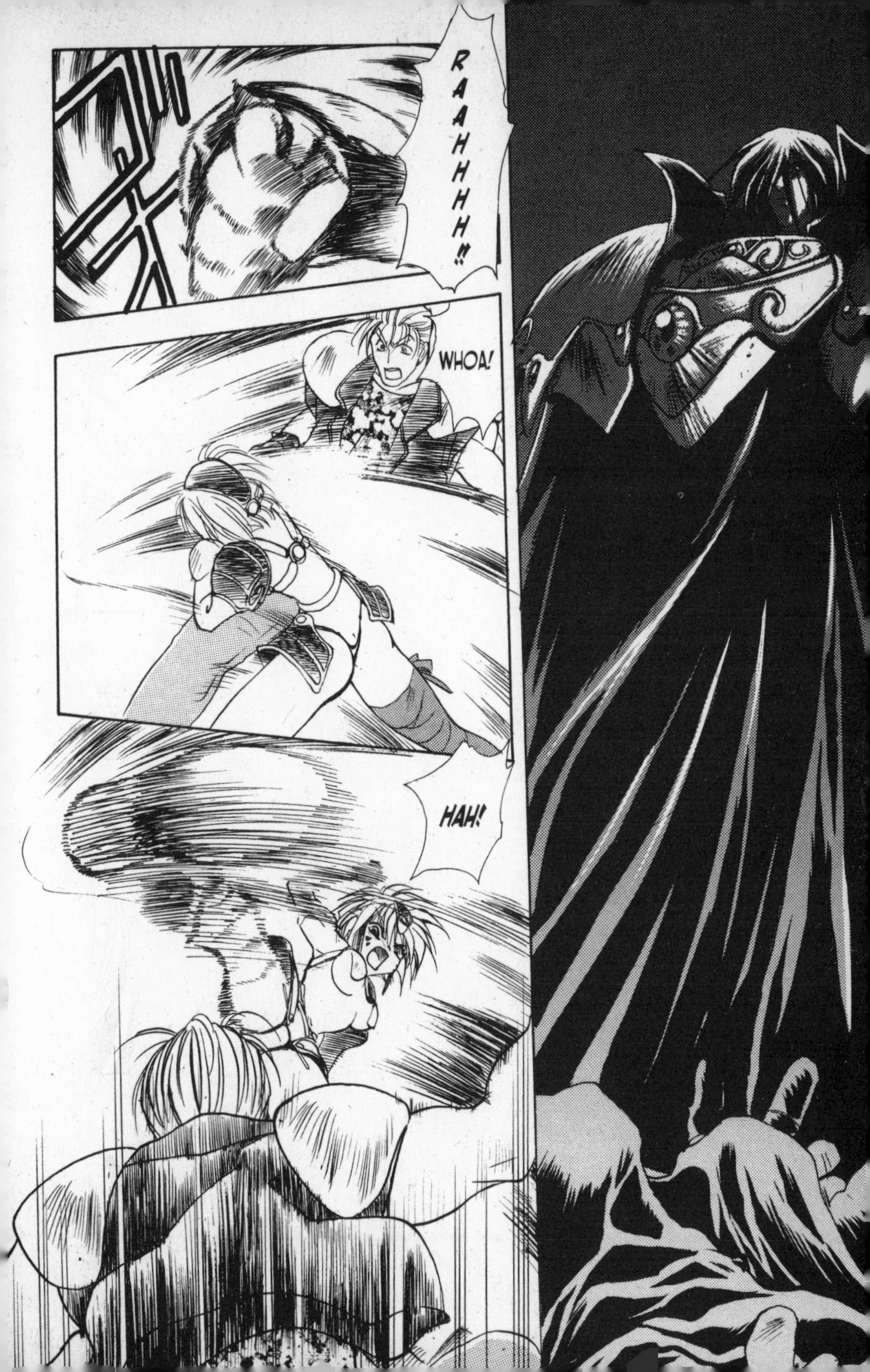
RAAHHHHH!!
WHOA!
HAH!

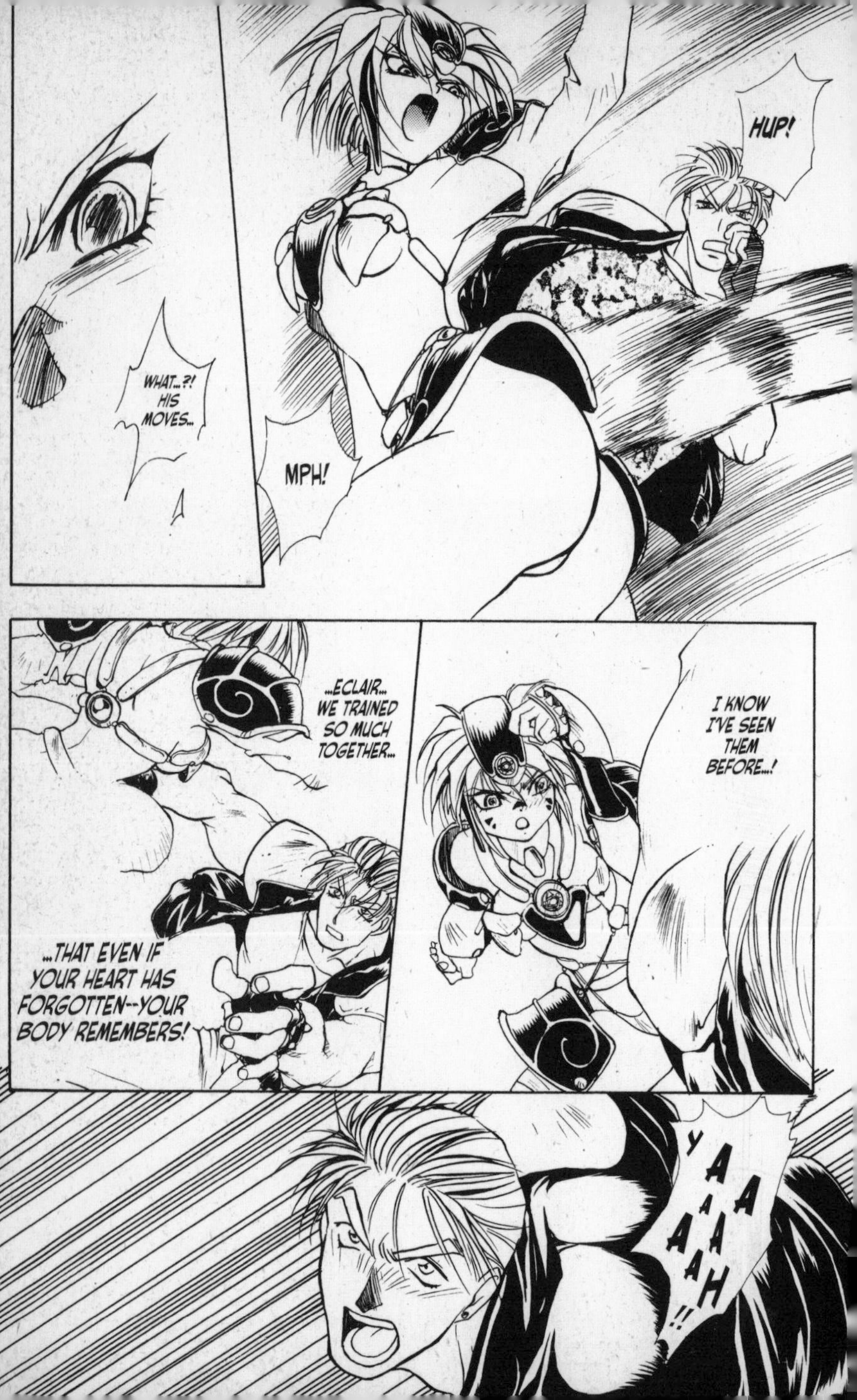
HUP!
MPH!
WHAT...?! HIS MOVES...
I KNOW I'VE SEEN THEM BEFORE...!
...ECLAIR... WE TRAINED SO MUCH TOGETHER...
...THAT EVEN IF YOUR HEART HAS FORGOTTEN--YOUR BODY REMEMBERS!
YAAAAAAAH!!

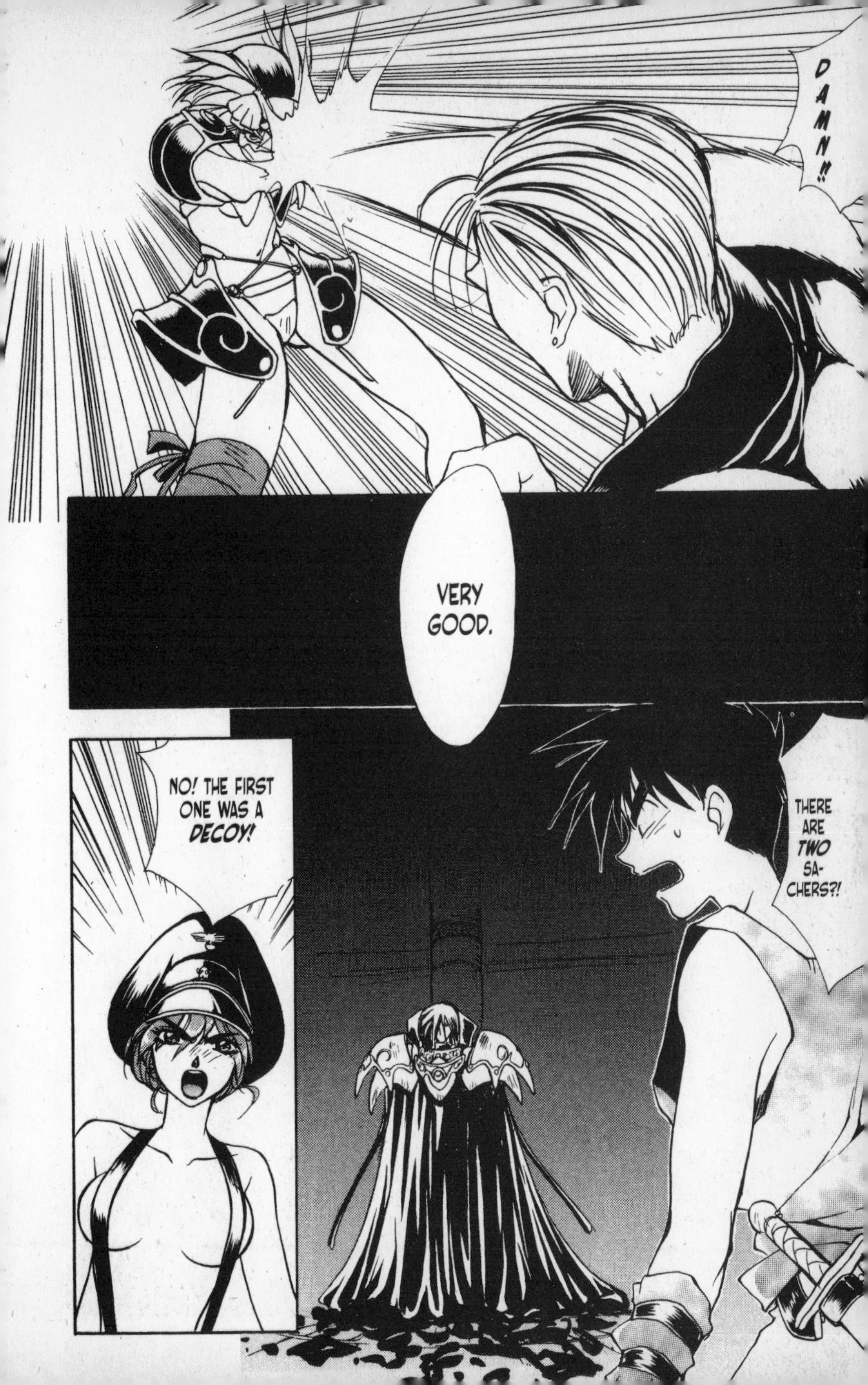
DAMN!!
VERY GOOD.
THERE ARE TWO SA-CHERS?!
NO! THE FIRST ONE WAS A DECOY!

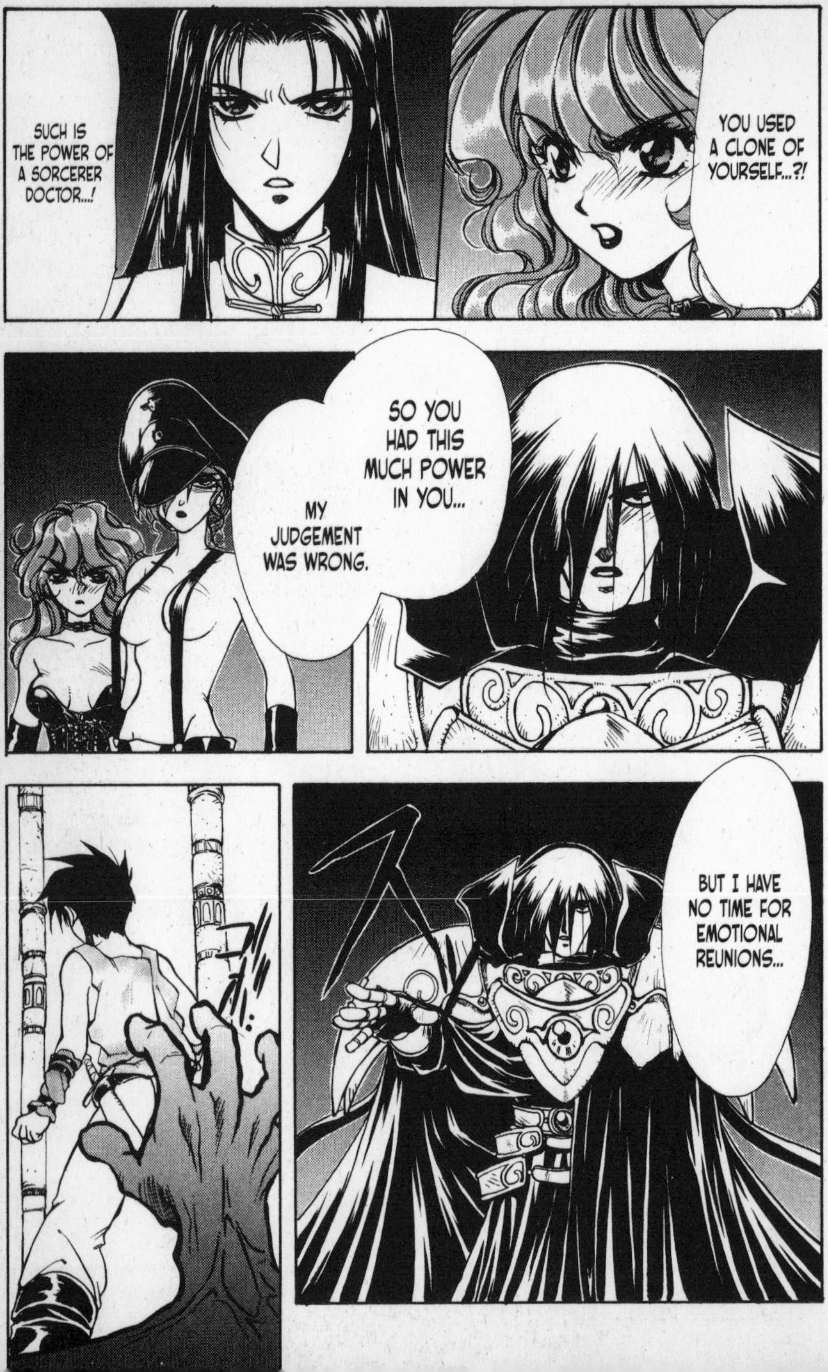
YOU USED A CLONE OF YOURSELF...?!
SUCH IS THE POWER OF A SORCERER DOCTOR...!
SO YOU HAD THIS MUCH POWER IN YOU... MY JUDGEMENT WAS WRONG.
BUT I HAVE NO TIME FOR EMOTIONAL REUNIONS...

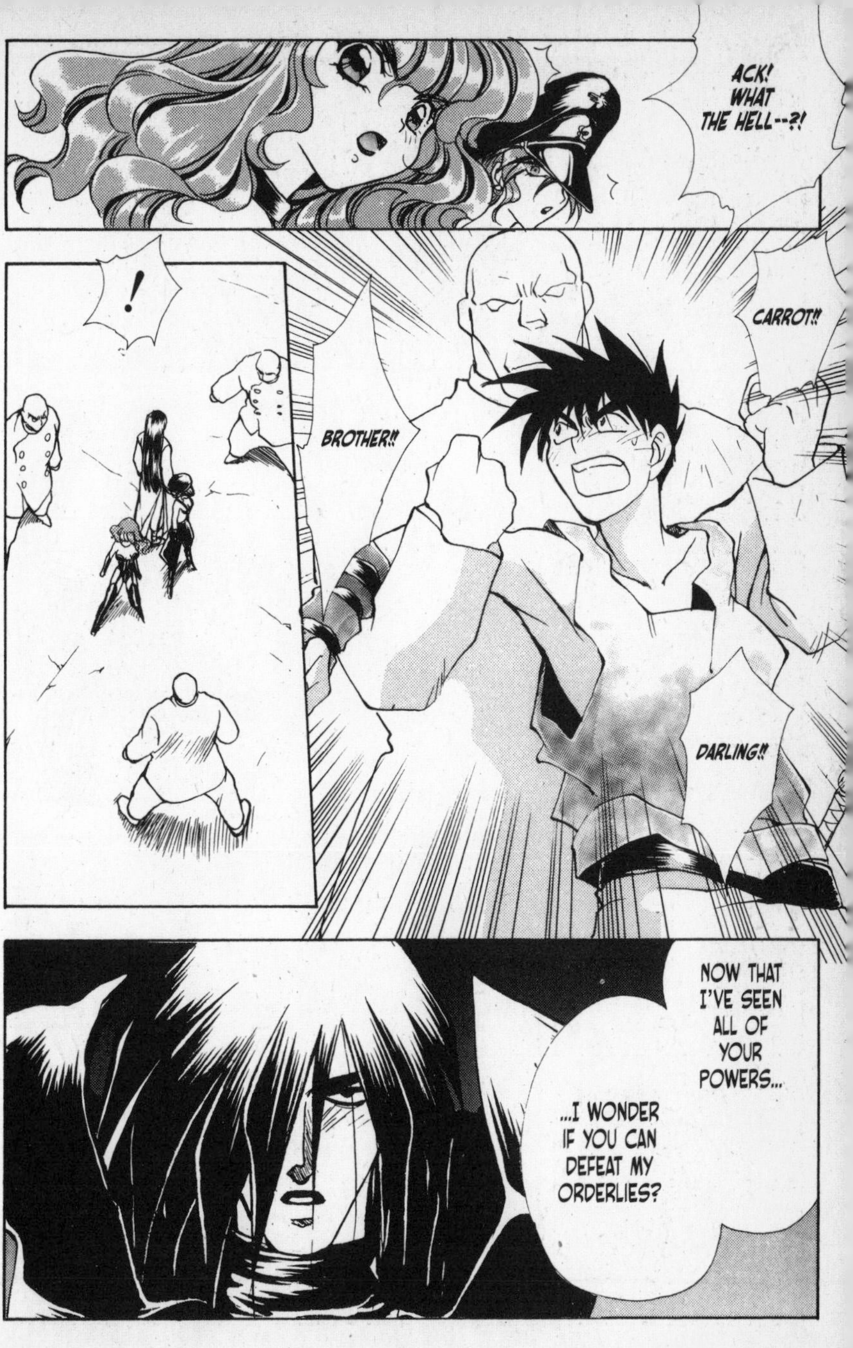
ACK! WHAT THE HELL--?!
CARROT!!
BROTHER!!
DARLING!!
!
NOW THAT I'VE SEEN ALL OF YOUR POWERS...
...I WONDER IF YOU CAN DEFEAT MY ORDERLIES?

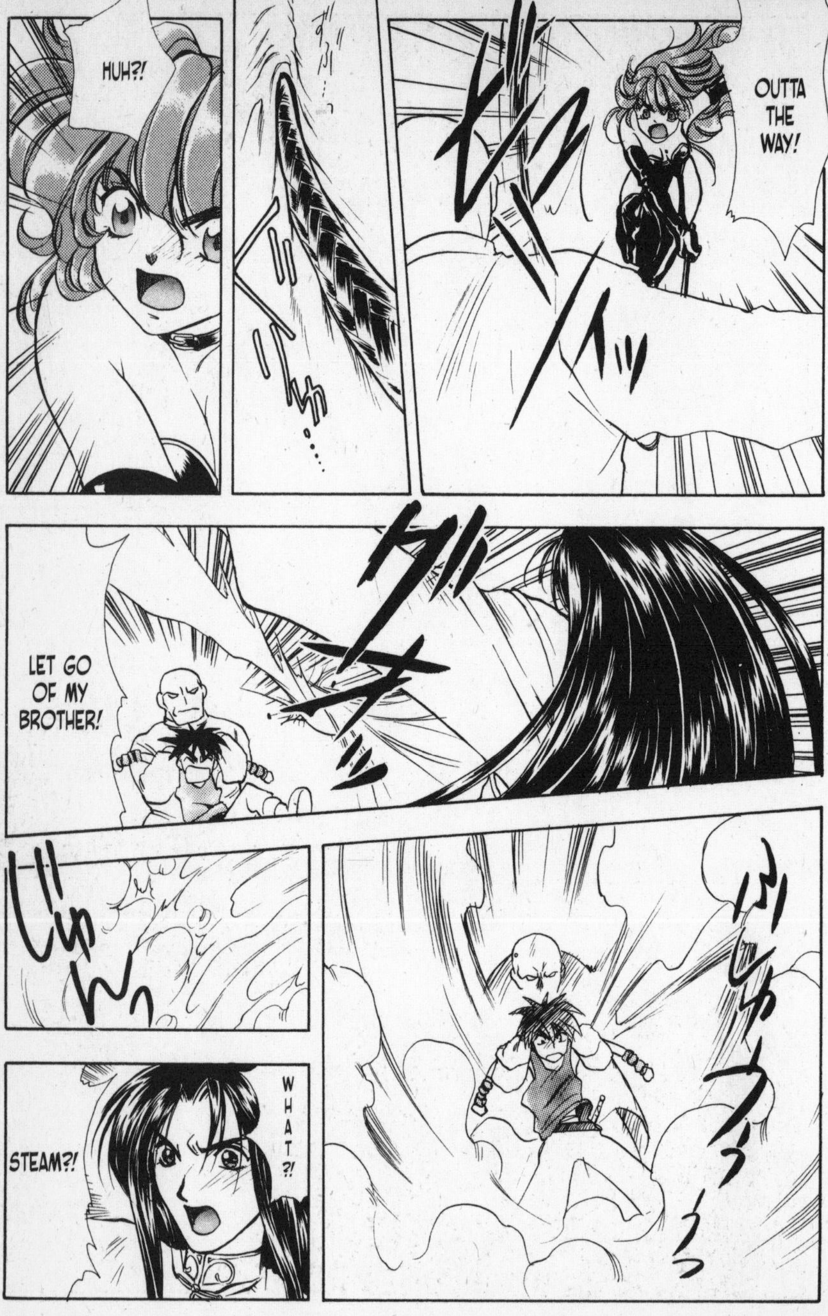
OUTTA THE WAY!
HUH?!
LET GO OF MY BROTHER!
WHAT?!
STEAM?!

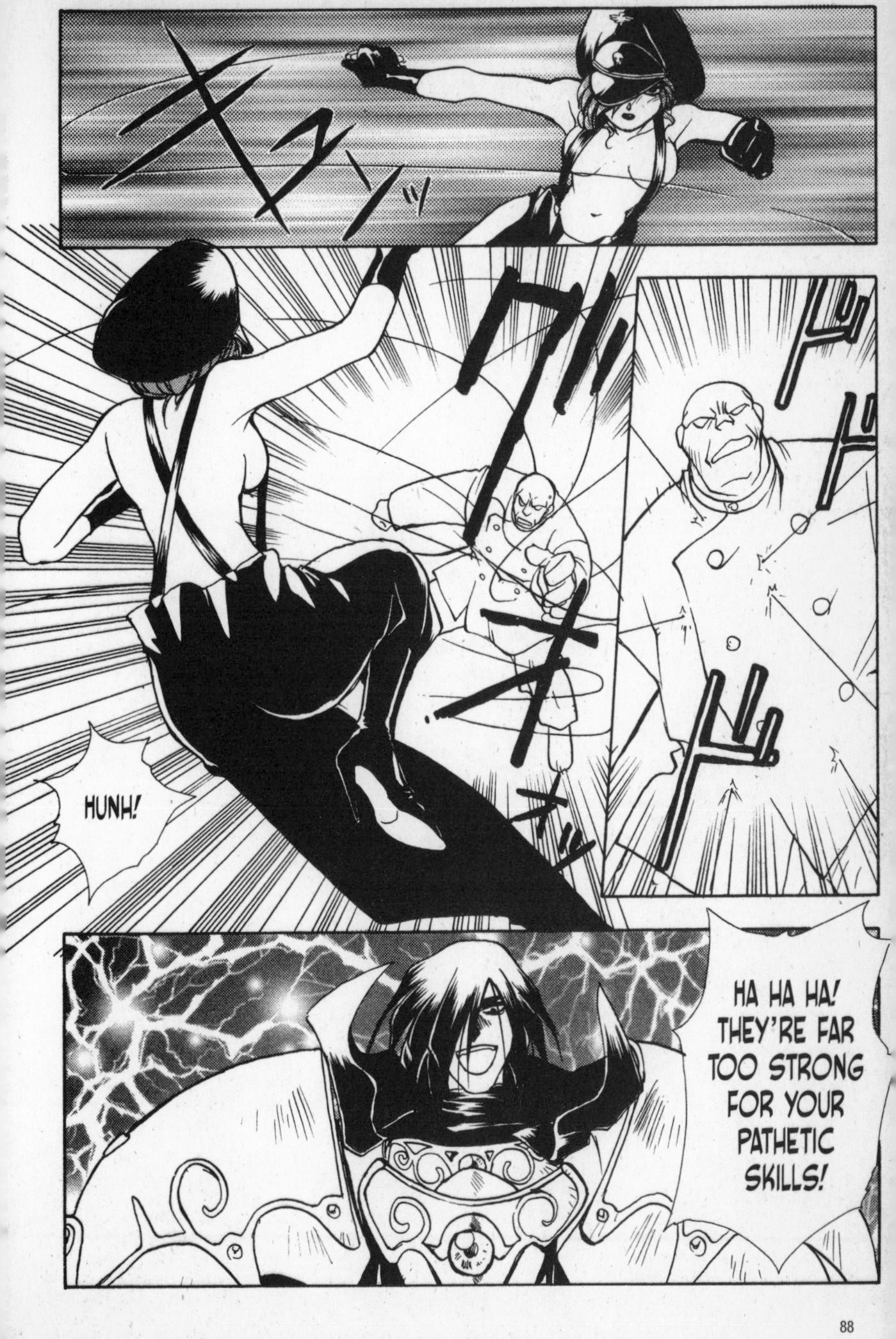
HUNH!
HA HA HA! THEY'RE FAR TOO STRONG FOR YOUR PATHETIC SKILLS!

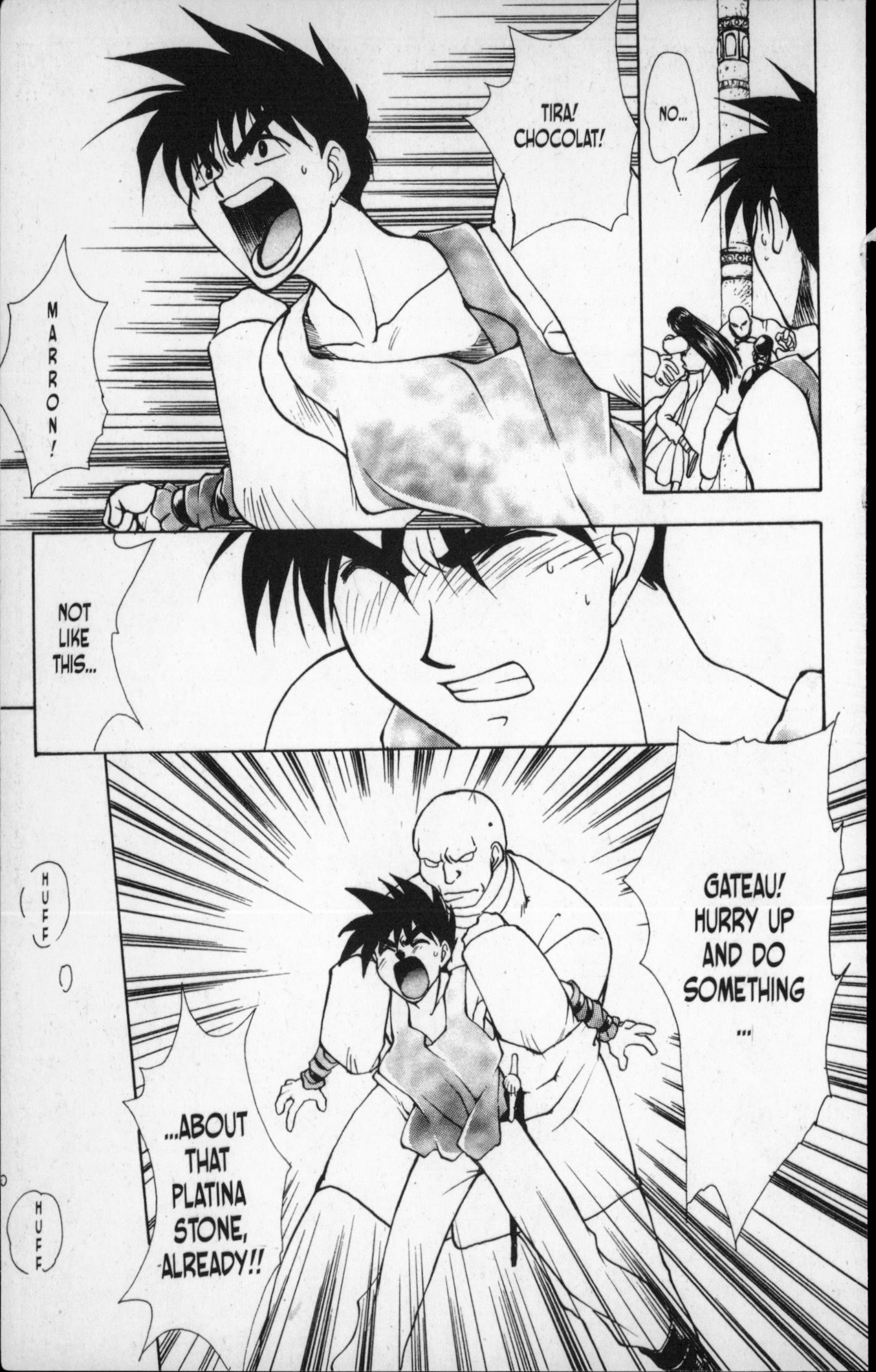
NO...
TIRA! CHOCOLAT!
MARRON!
NOT LIKE THIS...
HUFF
GATEAU! HURRY UP AND DO SOMETHING ...
...ABOUT THAT PLATINA STONE, ALREADY!!
HUFF

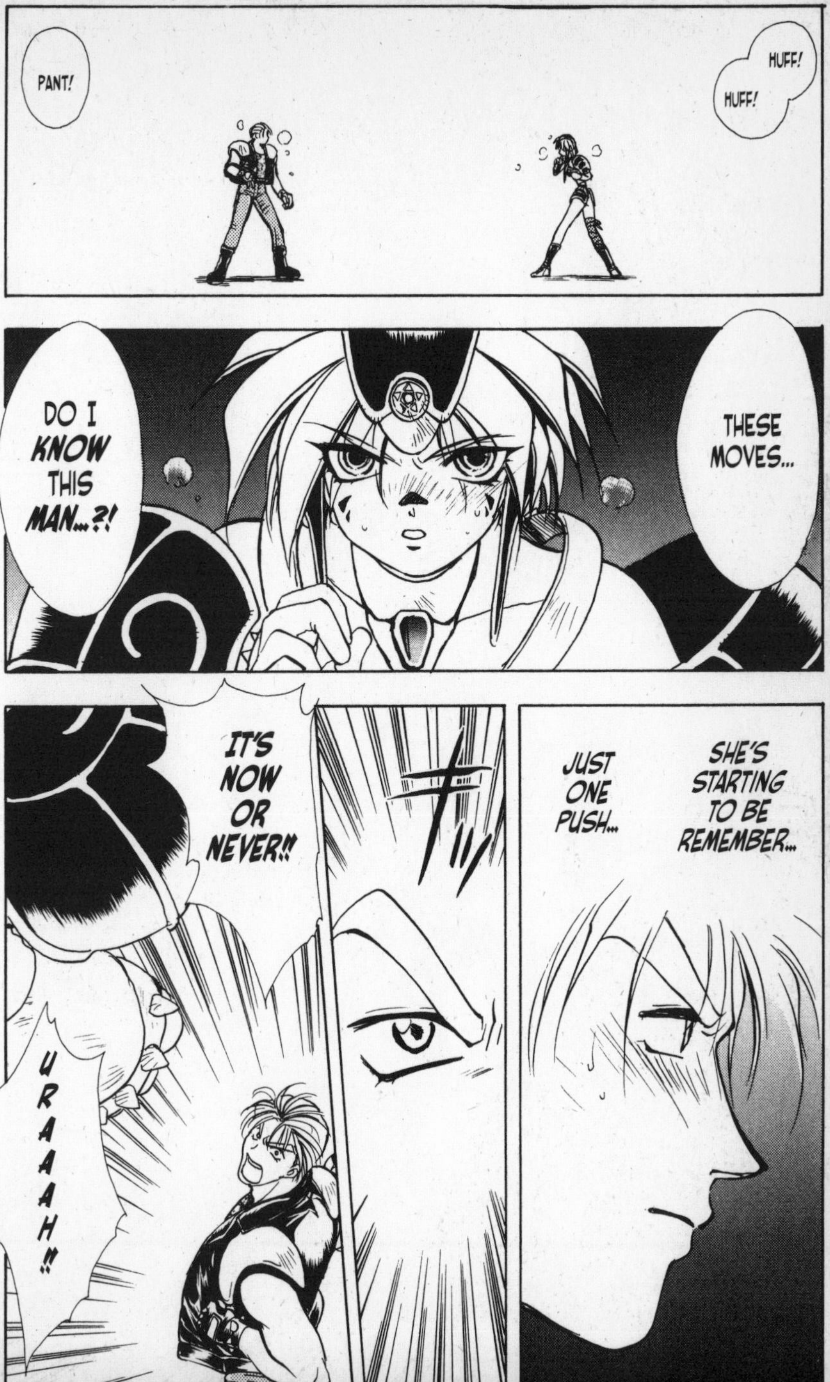
HUFF! HUFF!
PANT!
THESE MOVES...
DO I KNOW THIS MAN...?!
SHE'S STARTING TO BE REMEMBER...
JUST ONE PUSH...
IT'S NOW OR NEVER!!
URAAAAH!!

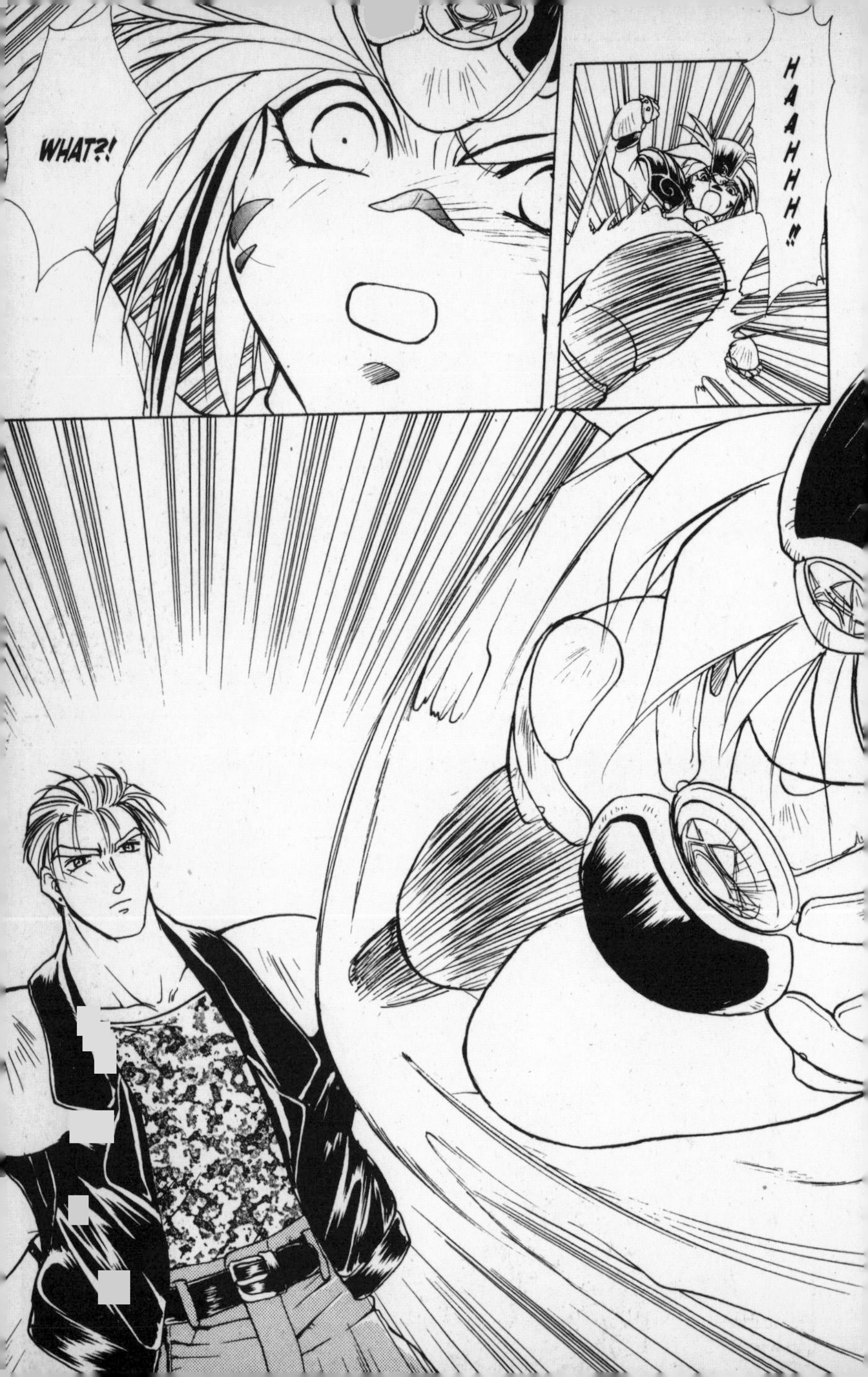
HAAAHHH!!
WHAT?!

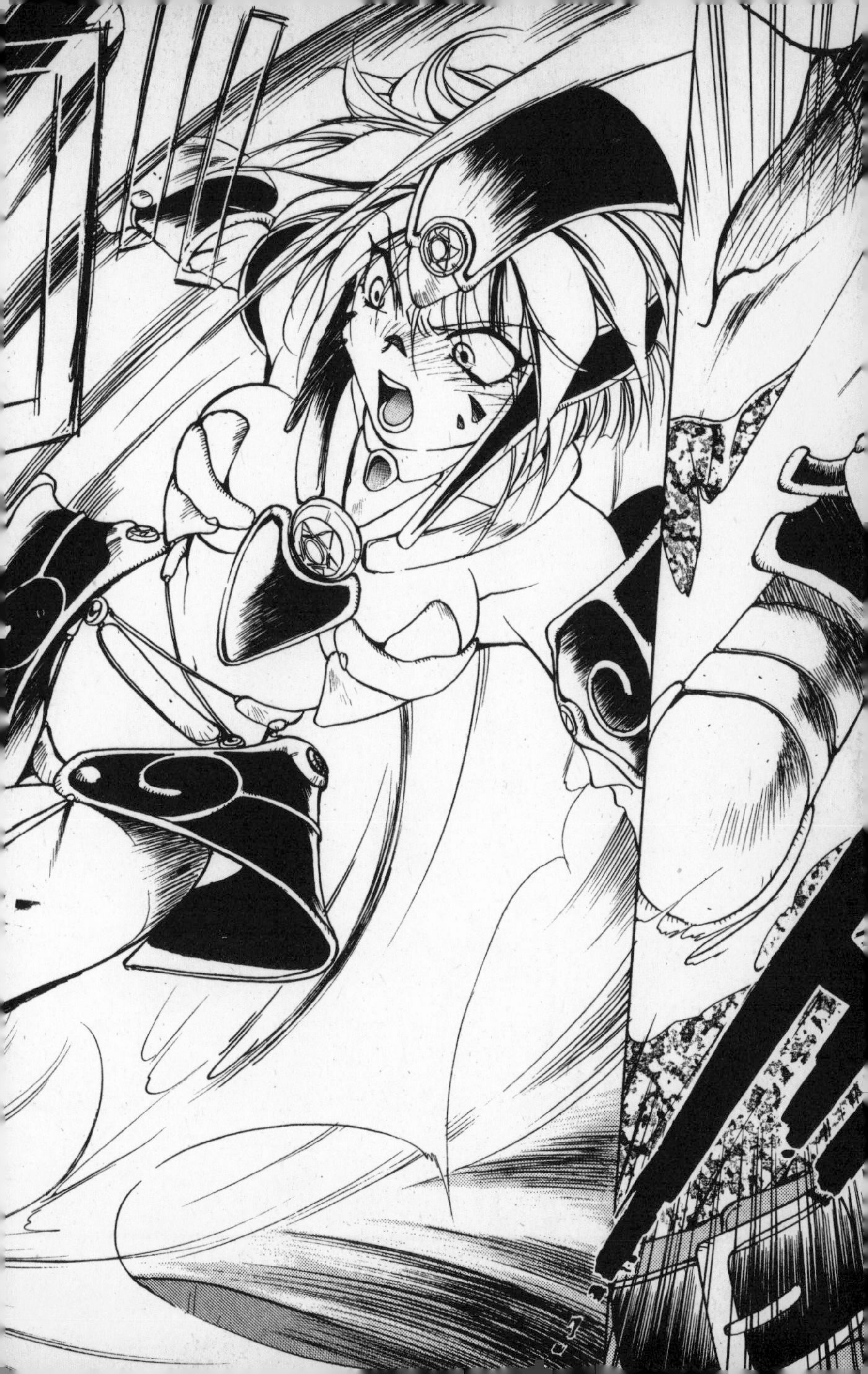

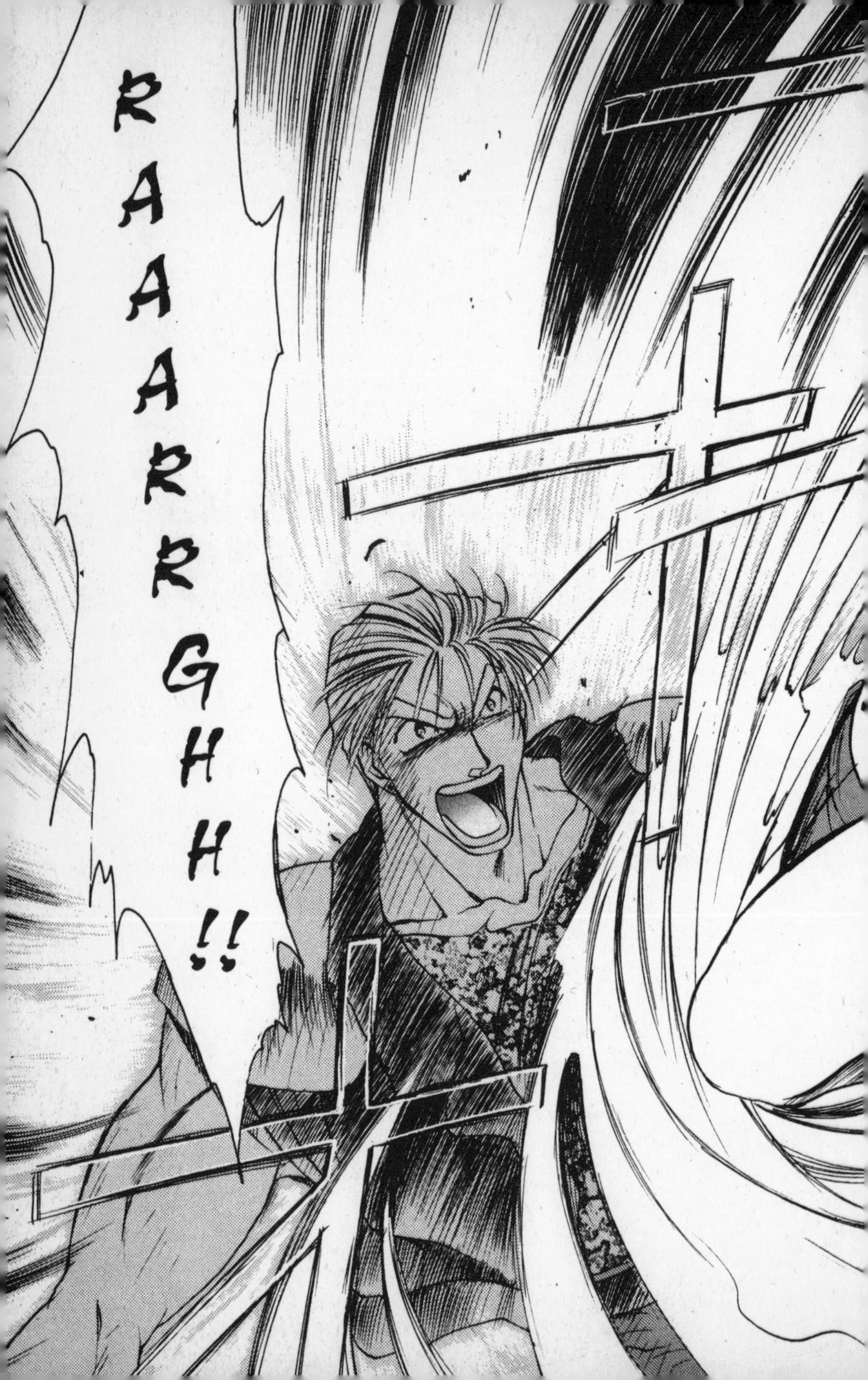
RAAARRGHH!!

SORCERER HUNTERS ™

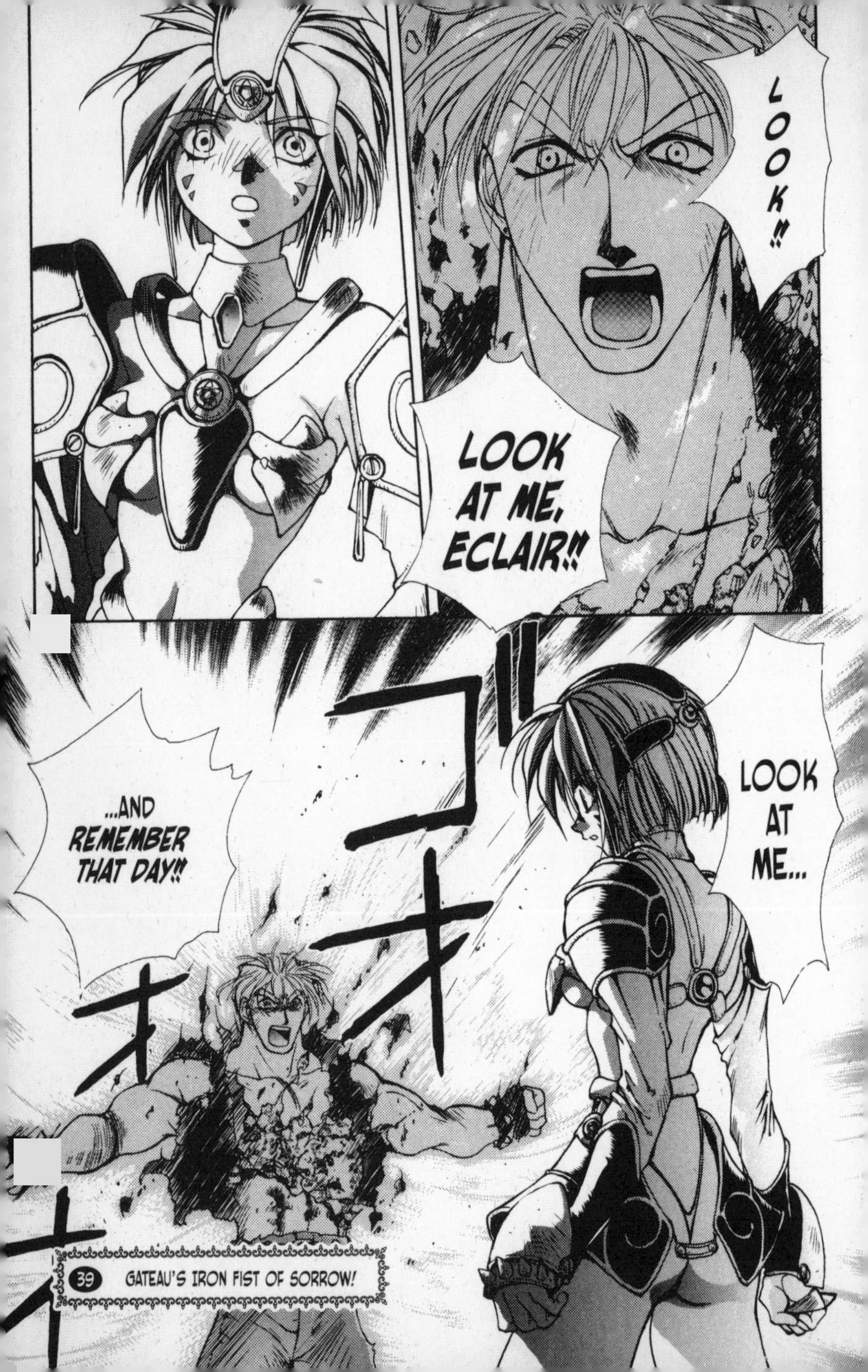
LOOK!!
LOOK AT ME, ECLAIR!!
LOOK AT ME...
...AND REMEMBER THAT DAY!!
ゴオオ
39 GATEAU'S IRON FIST OF SORROW!

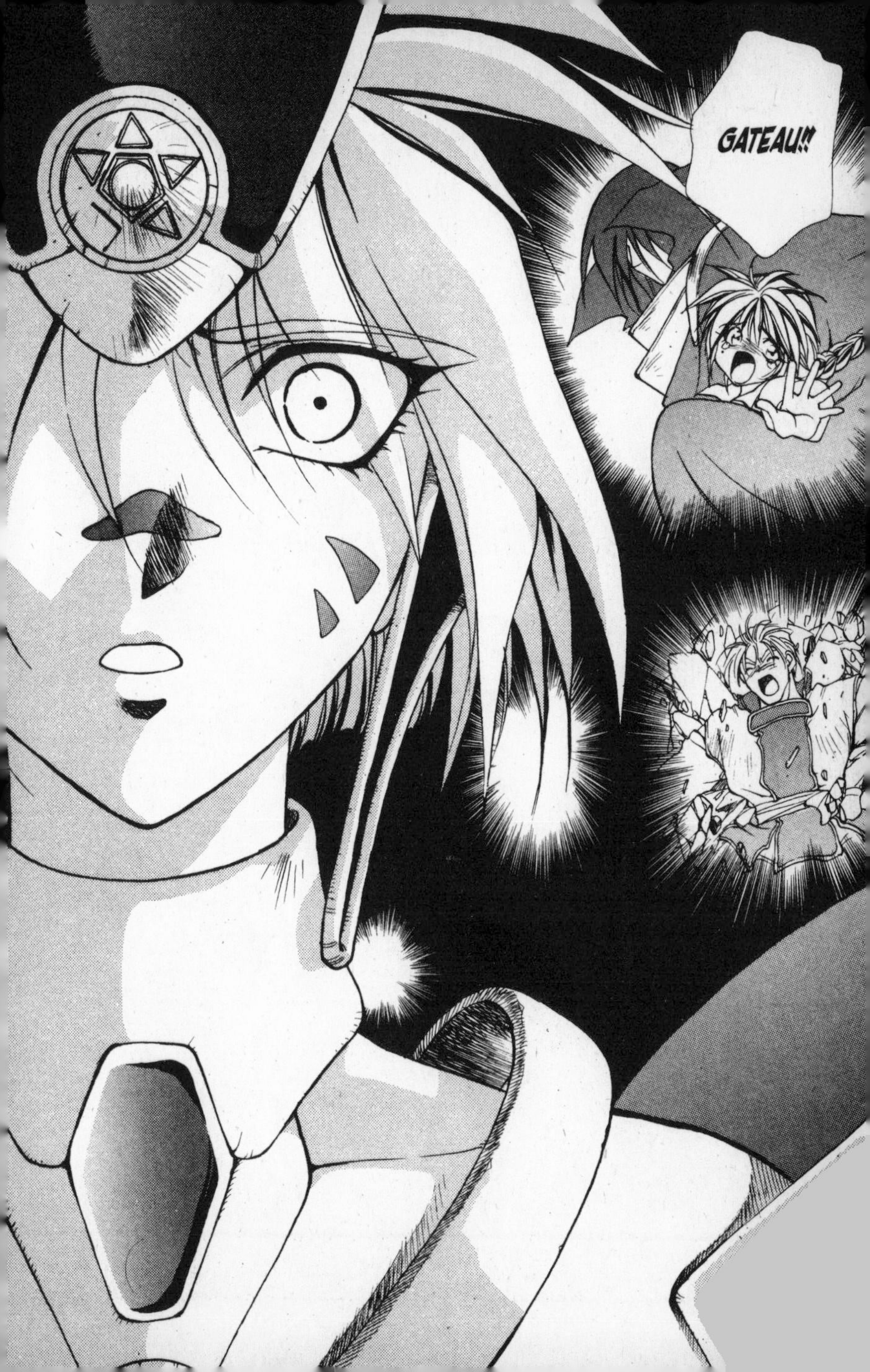
GATEAU!!

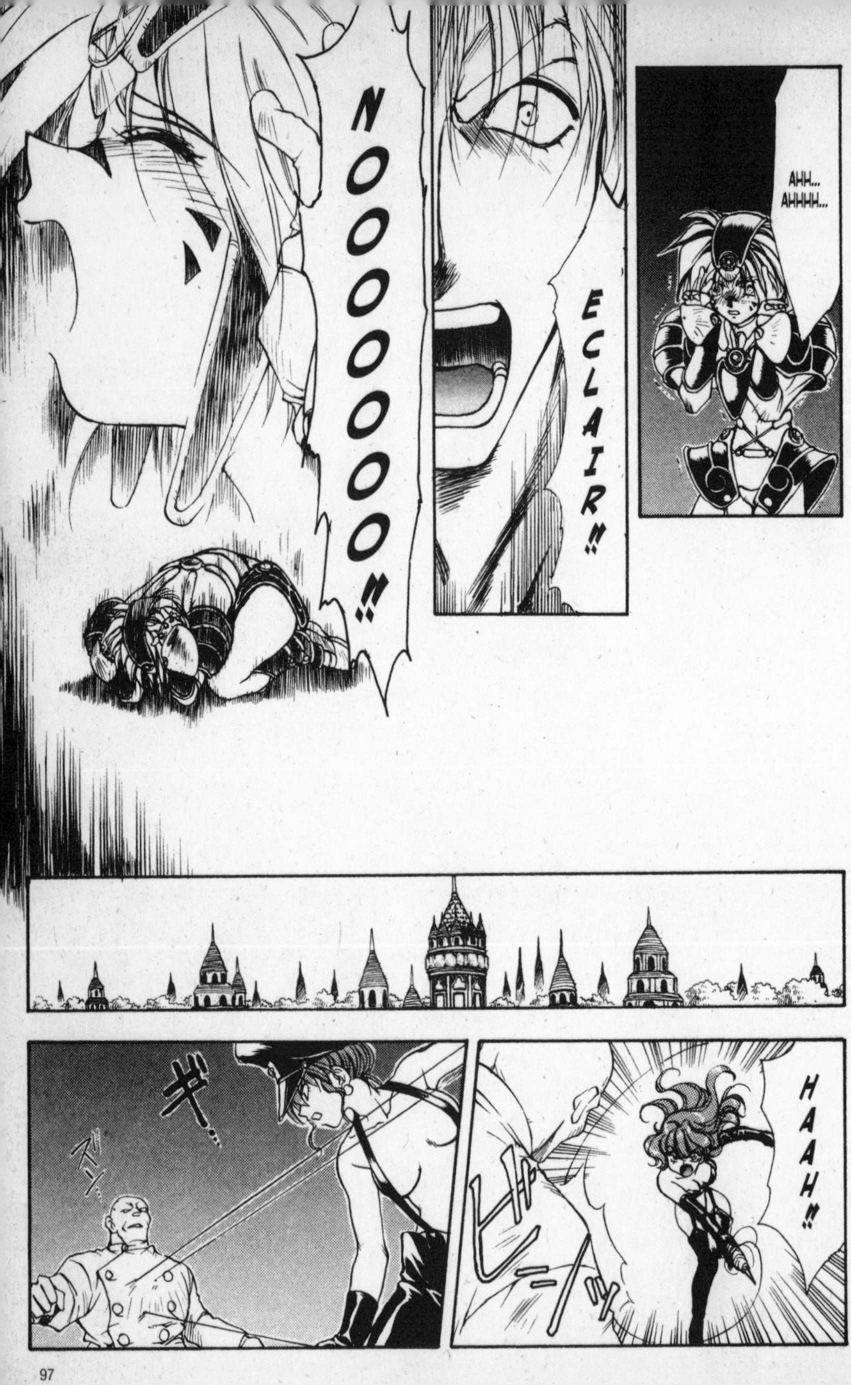
AHH... AHHHH...
ECLAIR!!
NOOOOOOO!!
HAAH!!

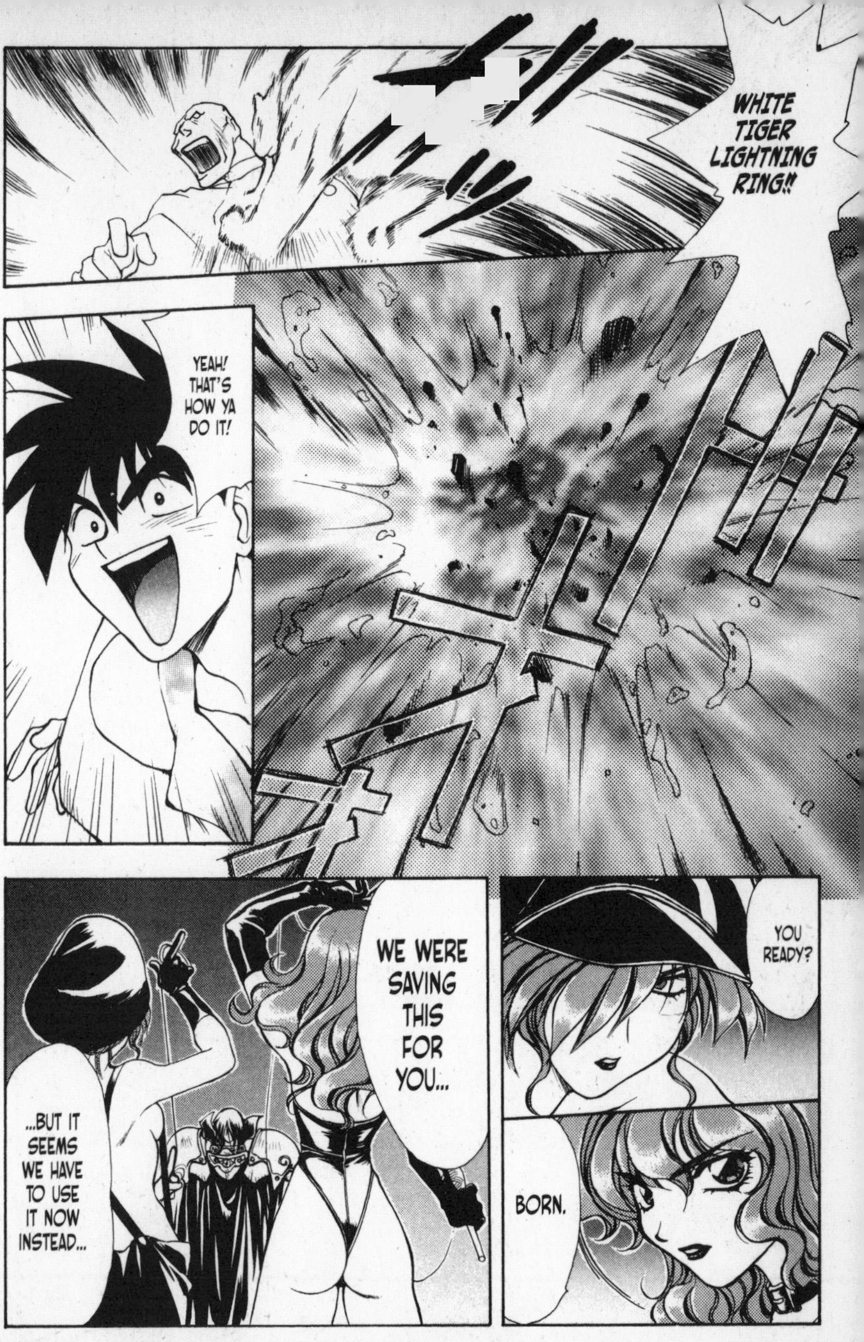
WHITE TIGER LIGHTNING RING!!
YEAH! THAT'S HOW YA DO IT!
YOU READY?
BORN.
WE WERE SAVING THIS FOR YOU...
...BUT IT SEEMS WE HAVE TO USE IT NOW INSTEAD...

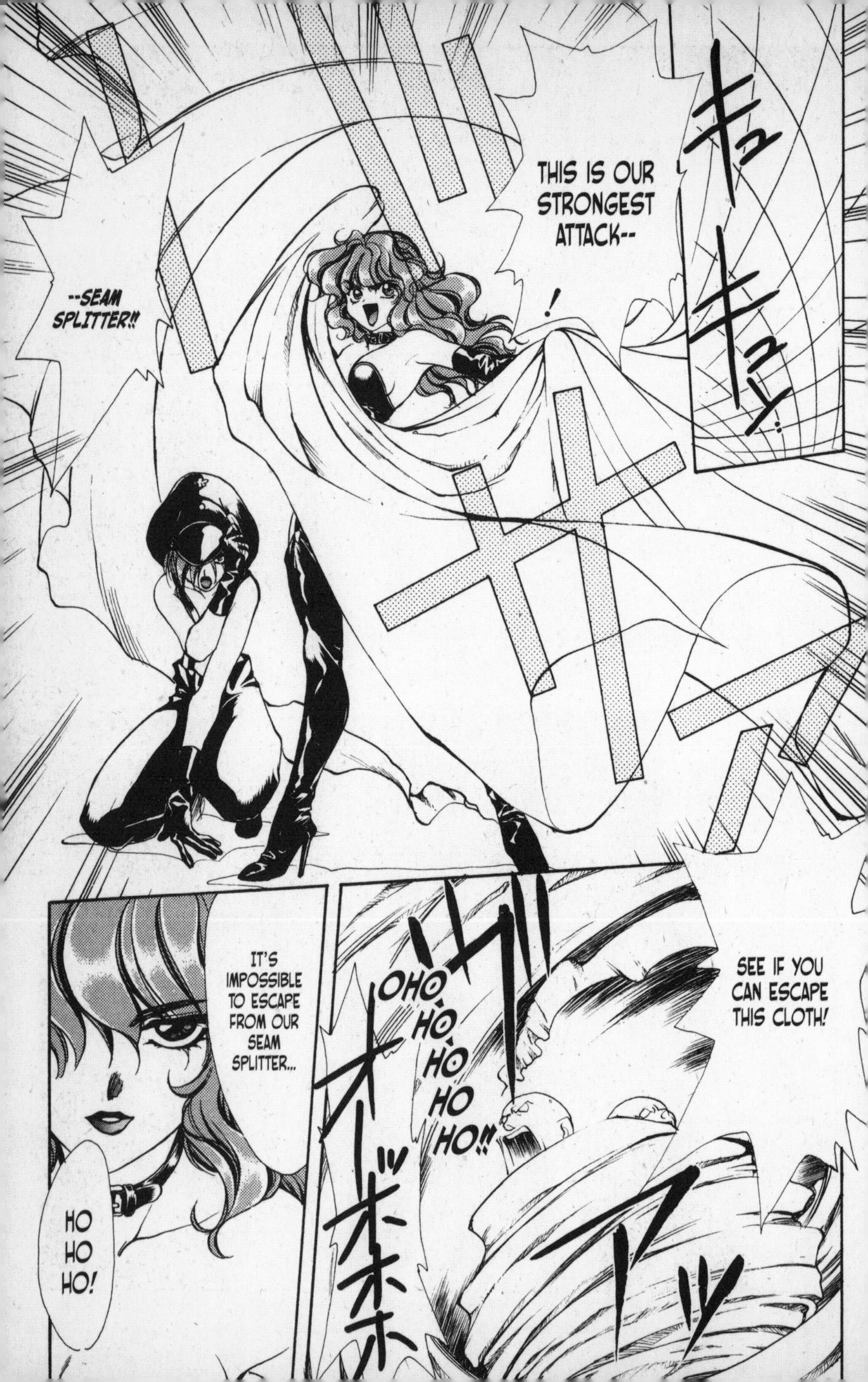
THIS IS OUR STRONGEST ATTACK--
--SEAM SPLITTER!!
SEE IF YOU CAN ESCAPE THIS CLOTH!
OHO HO HO HO HO!!
IT'S IMPOSSIBLE TO ESCAPE FROM OUR SEAM SPLITTER...
HO HO HO!

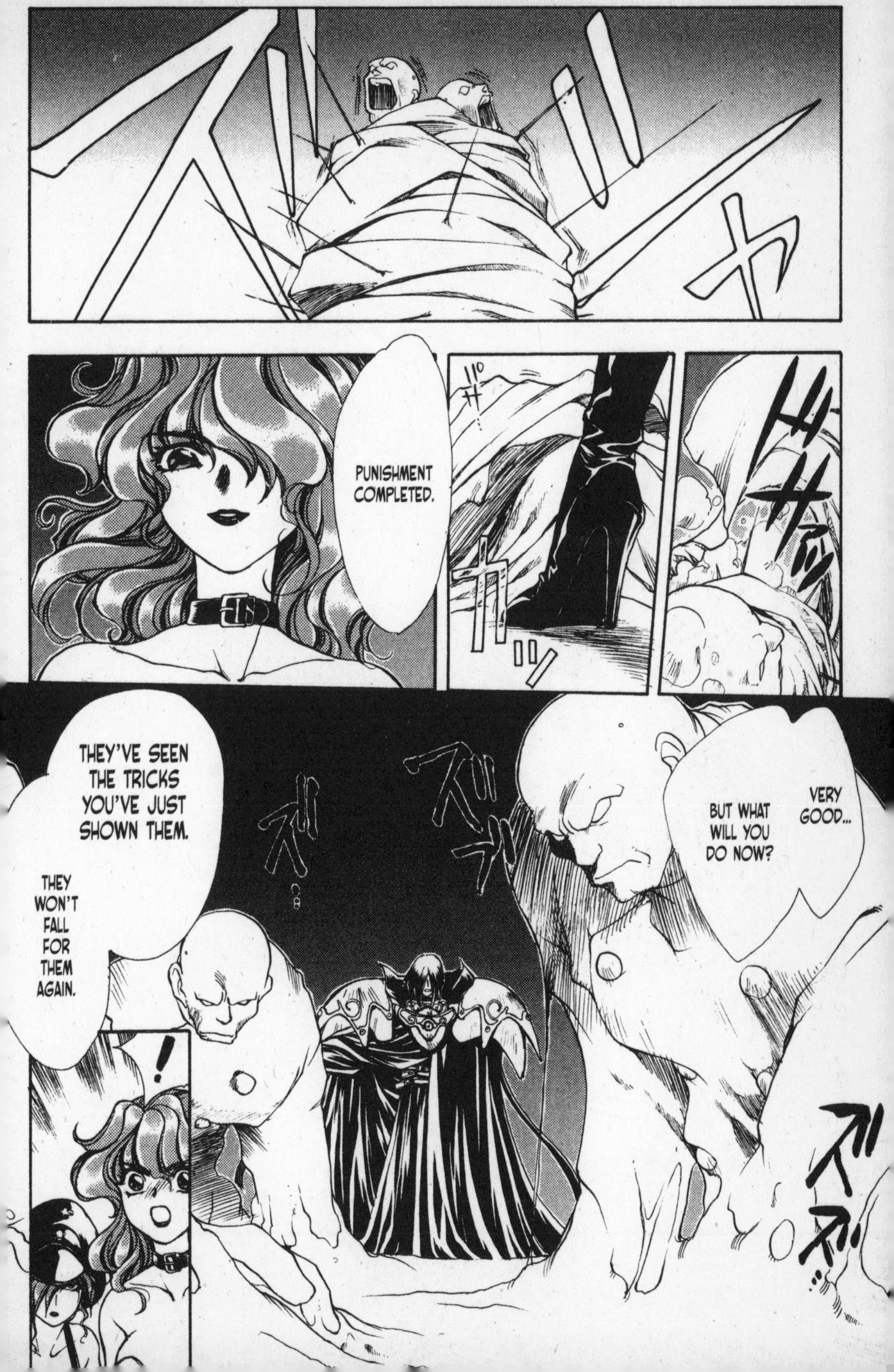
PUNISHMENT COMPLETED.
VERY GOOD...
BUT WHAT WILL YOU DO NOW?
THEY'VE SEEN THE TRICKS YOU'VE JUST SHOWN THEM.
THEY WON'T FALL FOR THEM AGAIN.
!

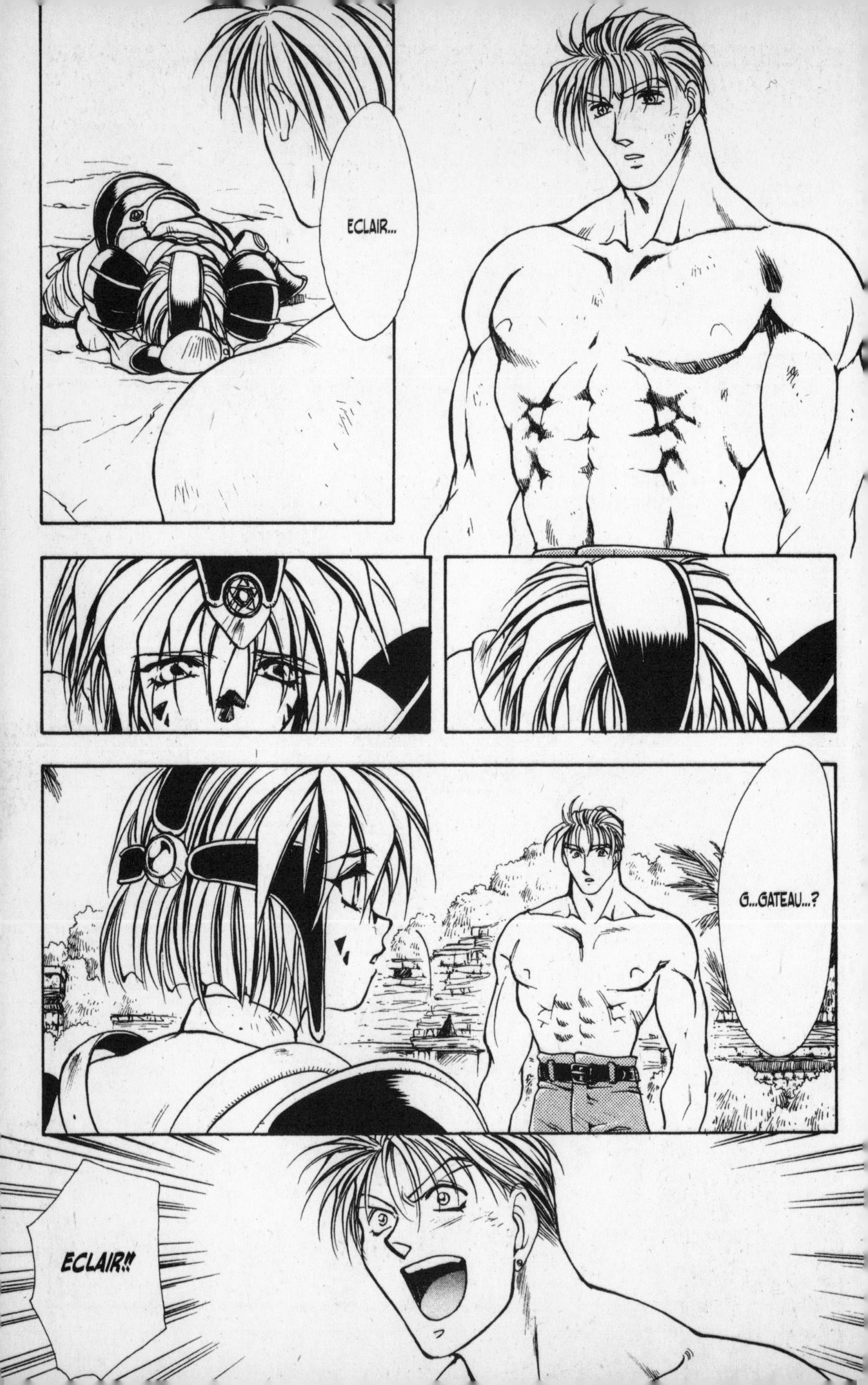
ECLAIR...
G...GATEAU...?
ECLAIR!!

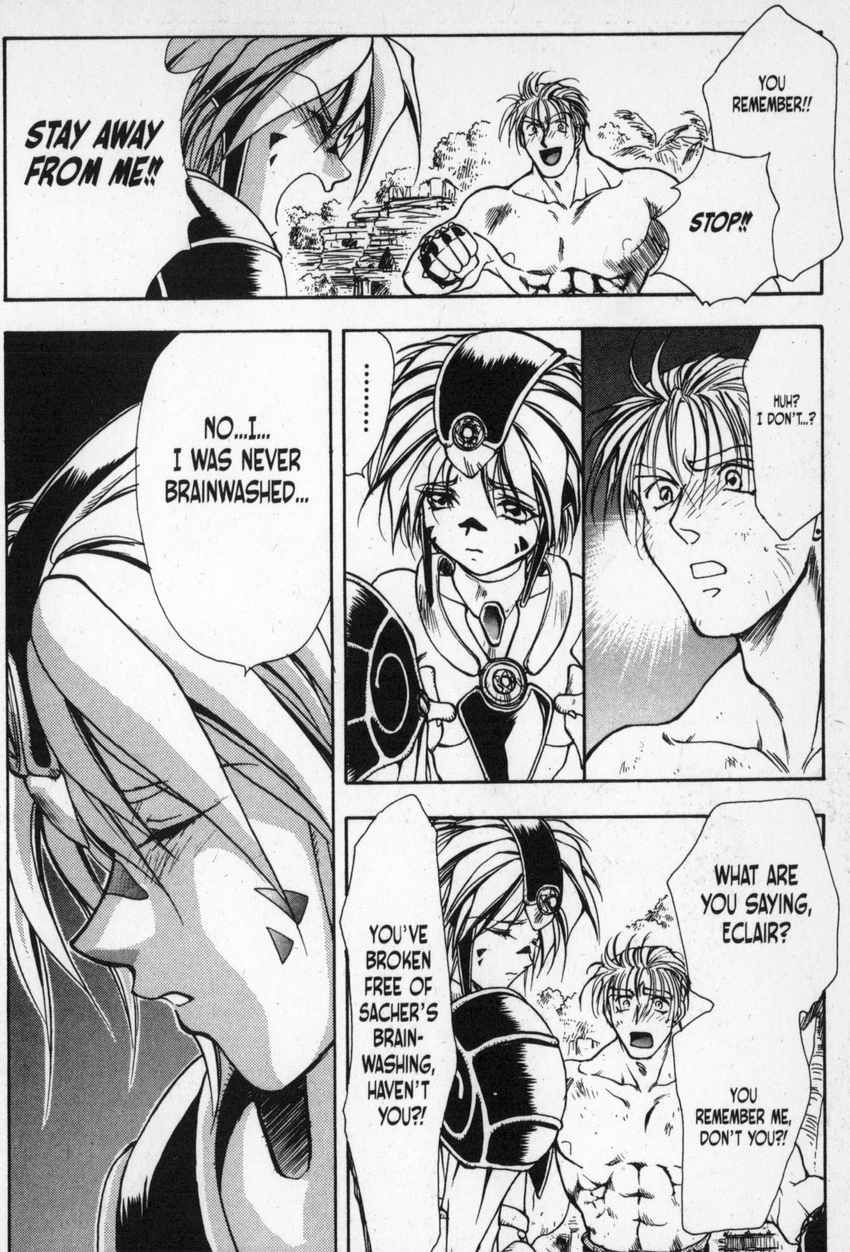
YOU REMEMBER!!
STOP!!
STAY AWAY FROM ME!!
HUH? I DON'T...?
......
WHAT ARE YOU SAYING, ECLAIR?
YOU REMEMBER ME, DON'T YOU?!
YOU'VE BROKEN FREE OF SACHER'S BRAIN-WASHING, HAVEN'T YOU?!
NO...I... I WAS NEVER BRAINWASHED...

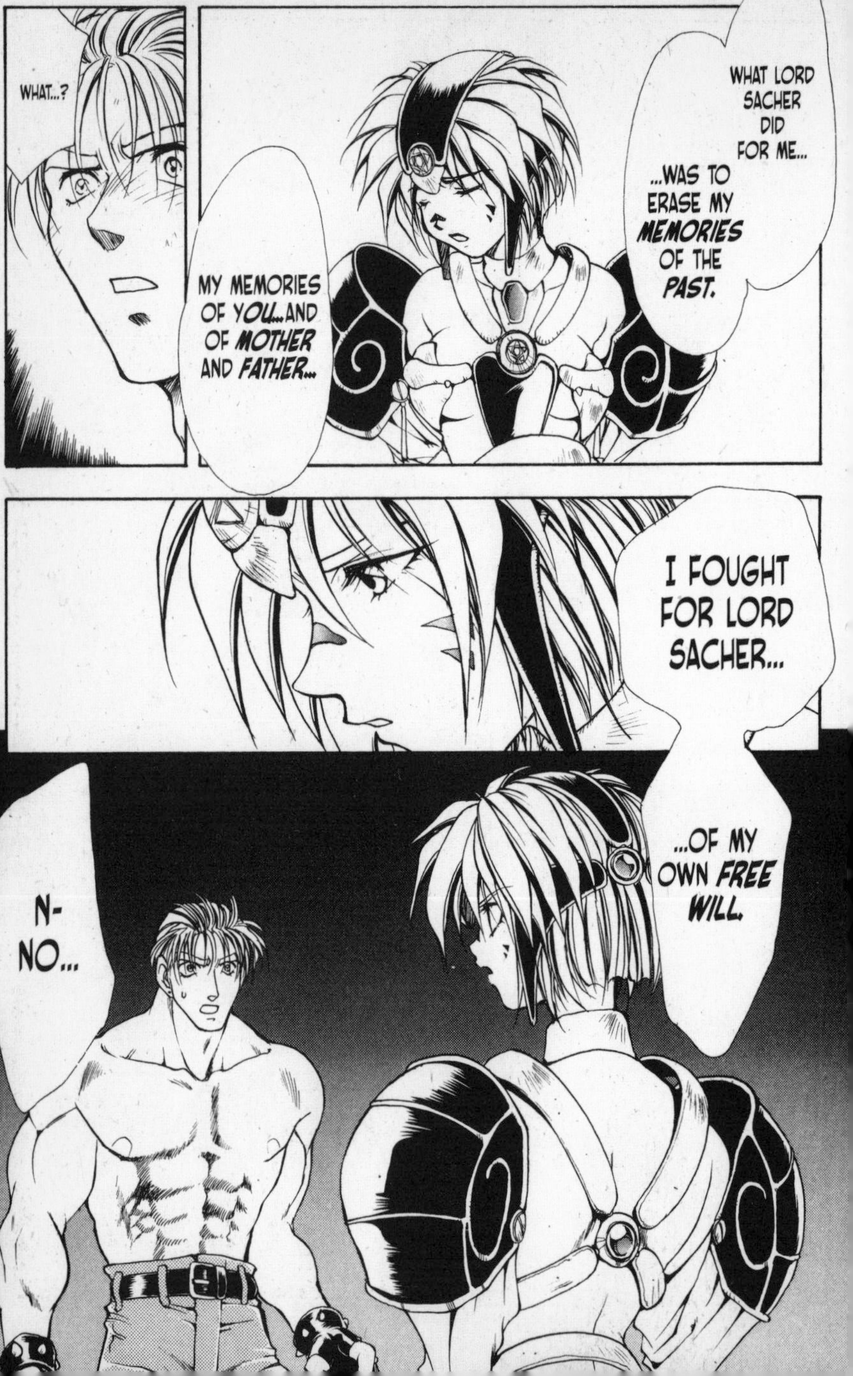
WHAT LORD SACHER DID FOR ME...
...WAS TO ERASE MY MEMORIES OF THE PAST.
MY MEMORIES OF YOU...AND OF MOTHER AND FATHER...
WHAT...?
I FOUGHT FOR LORD SACHER...
...OF MY OWN FREE WILL.
N-NO...

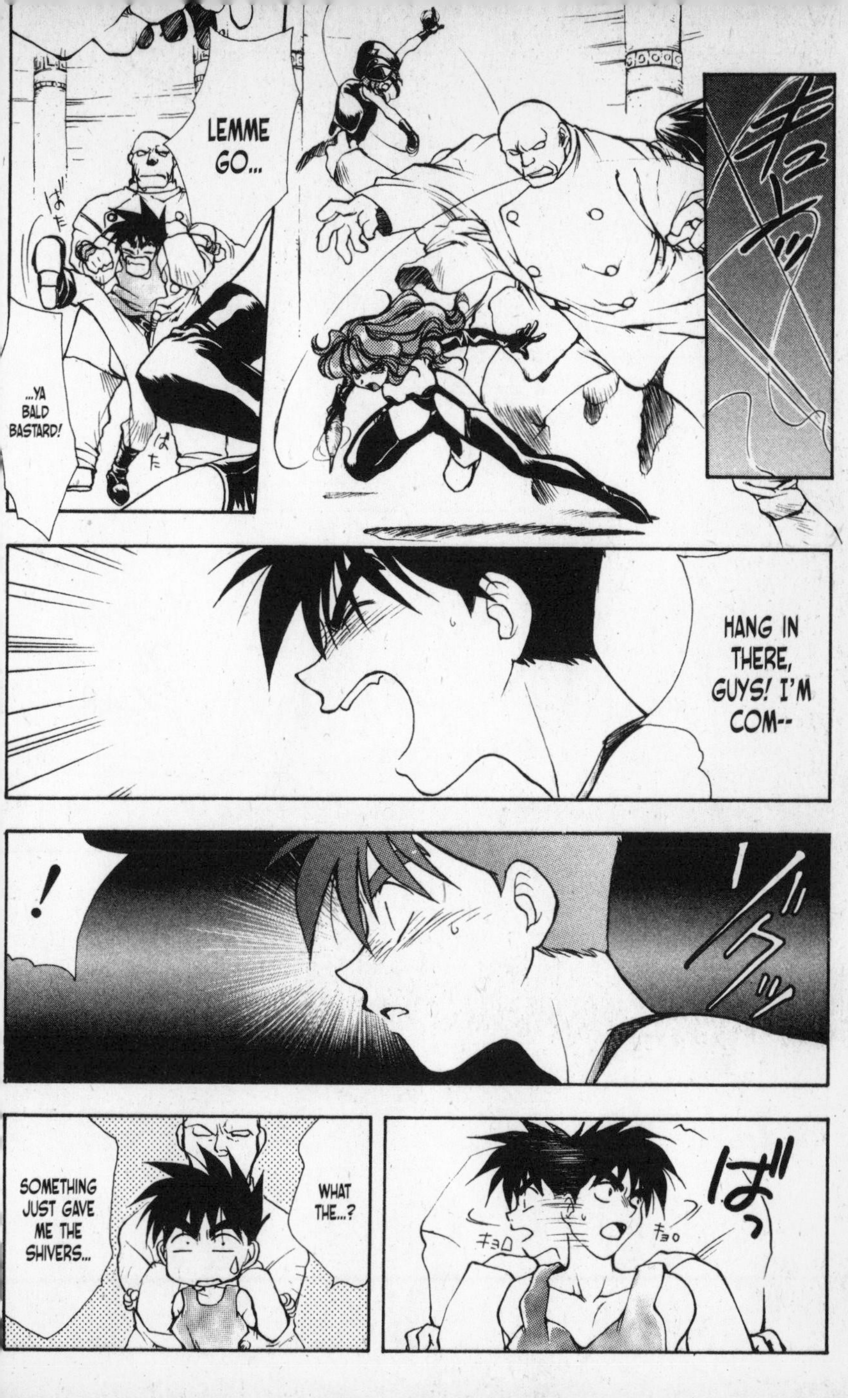
LEMME GO...
ばた
...YA BALD BASTARD!
ばた
HANG IN THERE, GUYS! I'M COM--
ゾクッ
!
ばっ
キョロ
キョロ
WHAT THE...?
SOMETHING JUST GAVE ME THE SHIVERS...

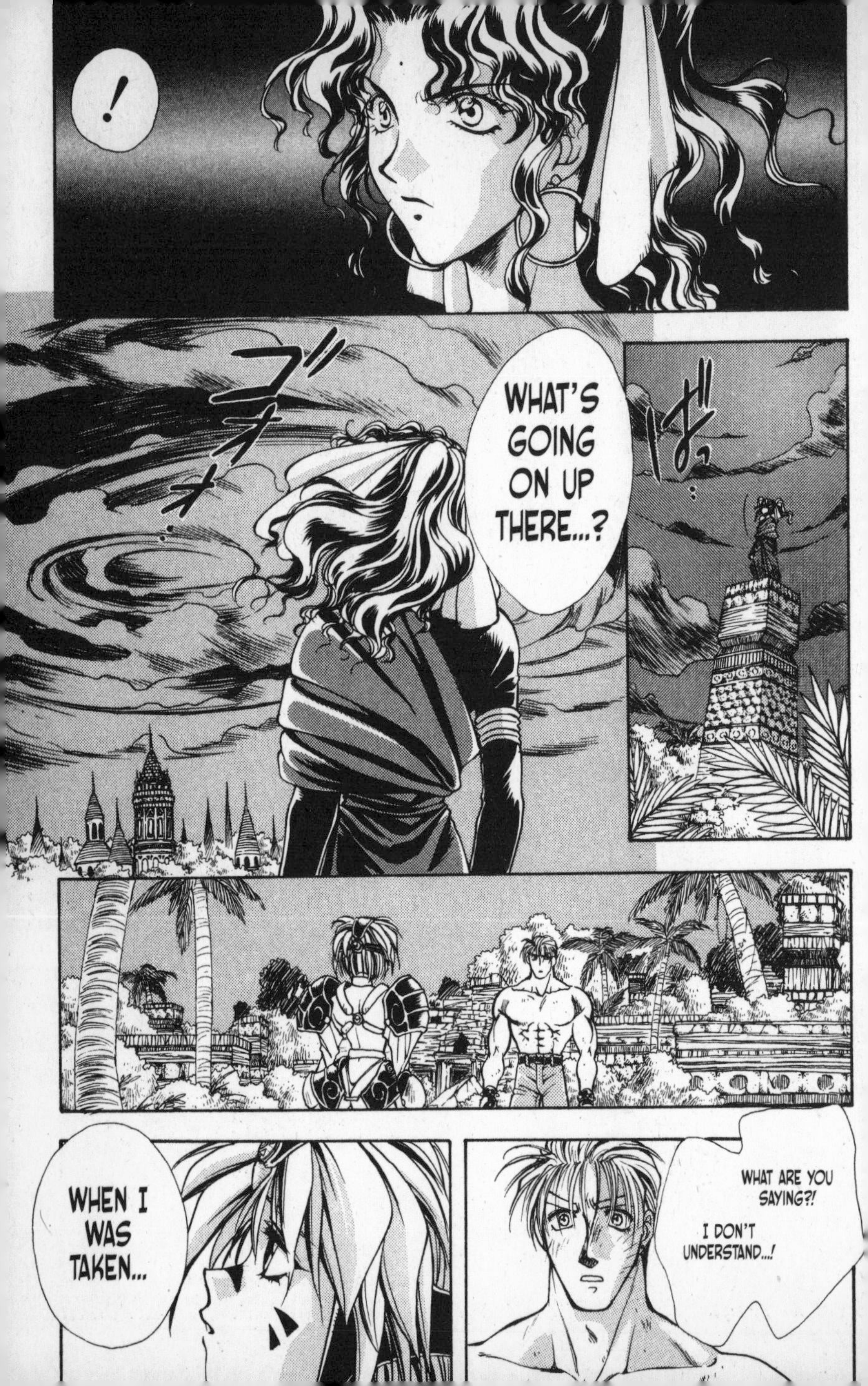
!
WHAT'S GOING ON UP THERE...?
WHAT ARE YOU SAYING?!
I DON'T UNDERSTAND...!
WHEN I WAS TAKEN...

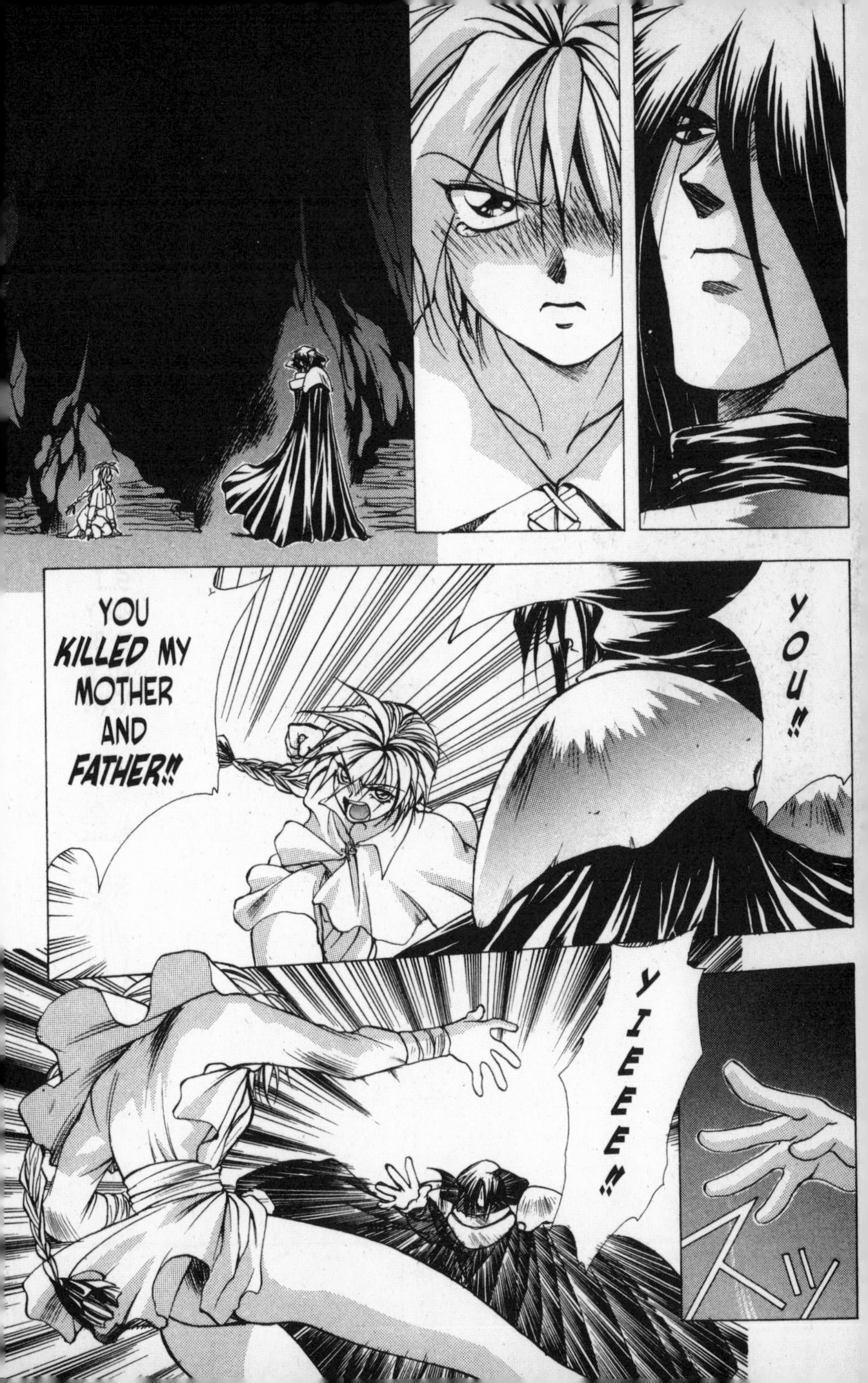
YOU!!
YOU KILLED MY MOTHER AND FATHER!!
ズッ
YIEEEE!!

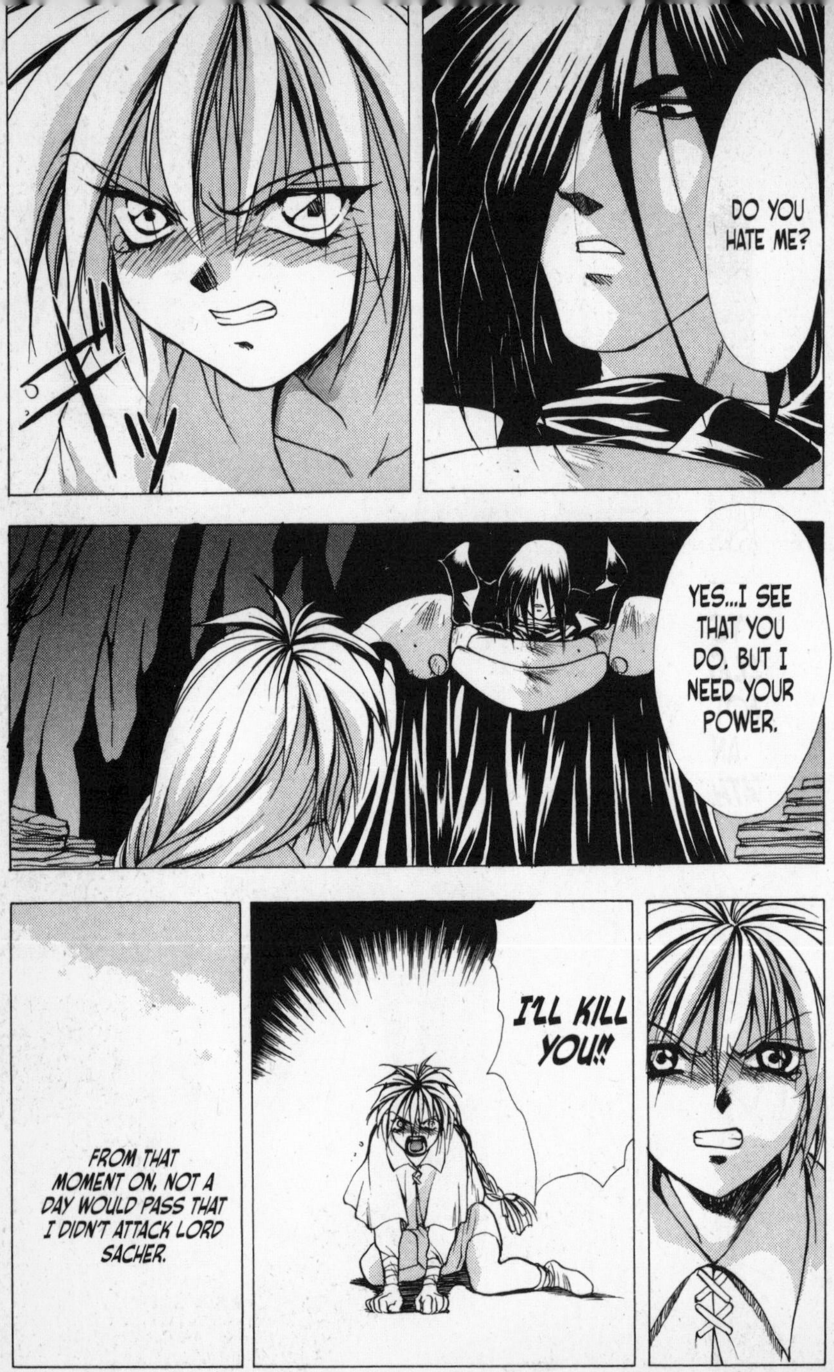
DO YOU HATE ME?
YES...I SEE THAT YOU DO. BUT I NEED YOUR POWER.
I'LL KILL YOU!!
FROM THAT MOMENT ON, NOT A DAY WOULD PASS THAT I DIDN'T ATTACK LORD SACHER.

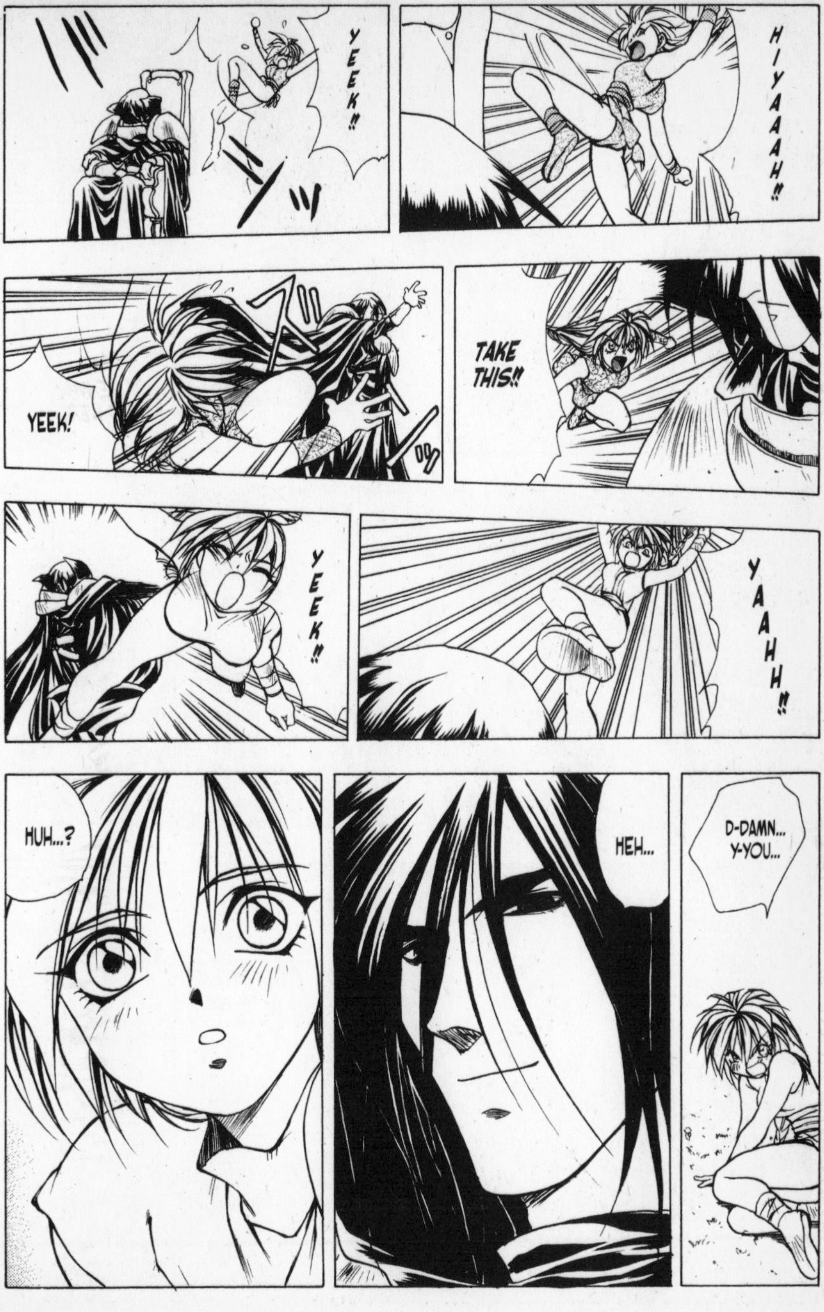
HIYAAAAH!!
YEEK!!
TAKE THIS!!
YEEK!
YAAHH!!
YEEK!!
D-DAMN... Y-YOU...
HEH...
HUH...?

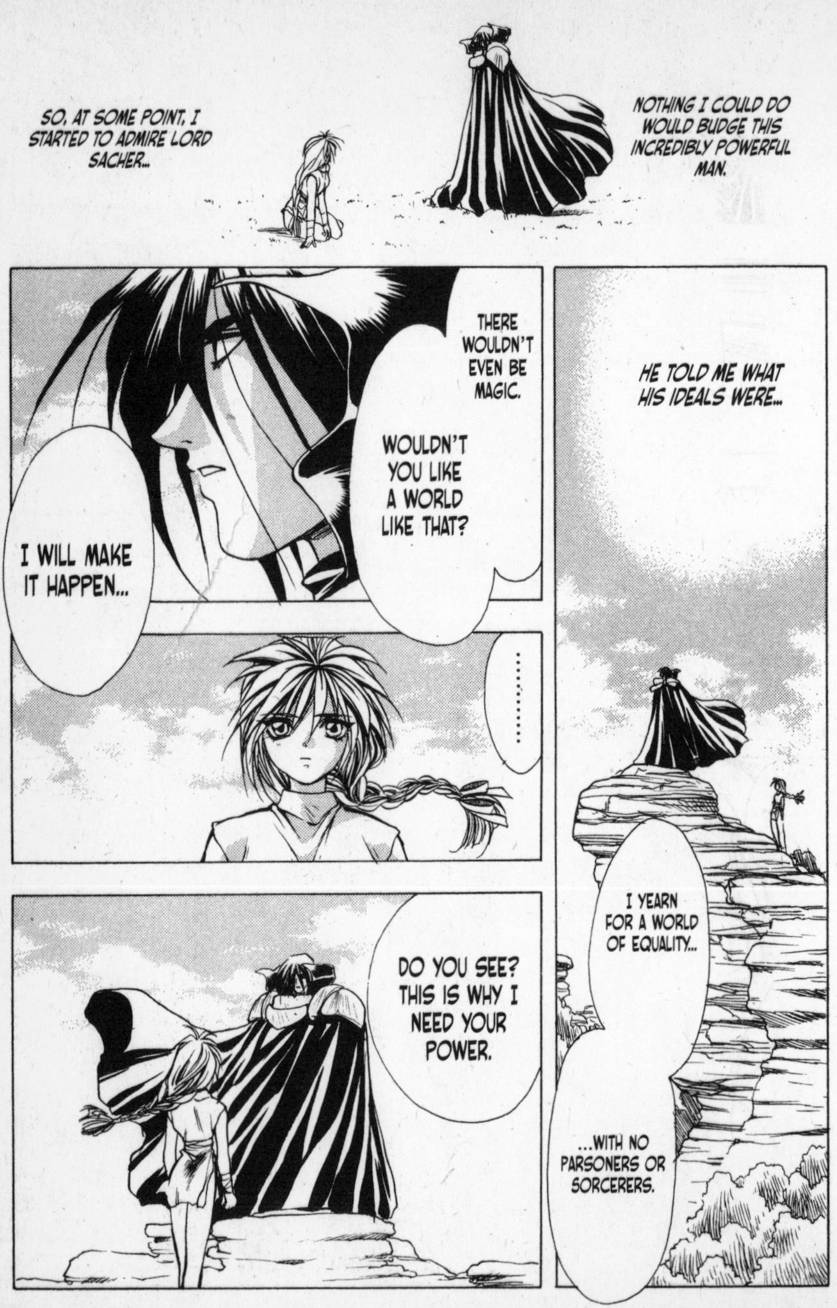
NOTHING I COULD DO WOULD BUDGE THIS INCREDIBLY POWERFUL MAN.
SO, AT SOME POINT, I STARTED TO ADMIRE LORD SACHER...
HE TOLD ME WHAT HIS IDEALS WERE...
I YEARN FOR A WORLD OF EQUALITY...
...WITH NO PARSONERS OR SORCERERS.
THERE WOULDN'T EVEN BE MAGIC.
WOULDN'T YOU LIKE A WORLD LIKE THAT?
I WILL MAKE IT HAPPEN...
....
DO YOU SEE? THIS IS WHY I NEED YOUR POWER.

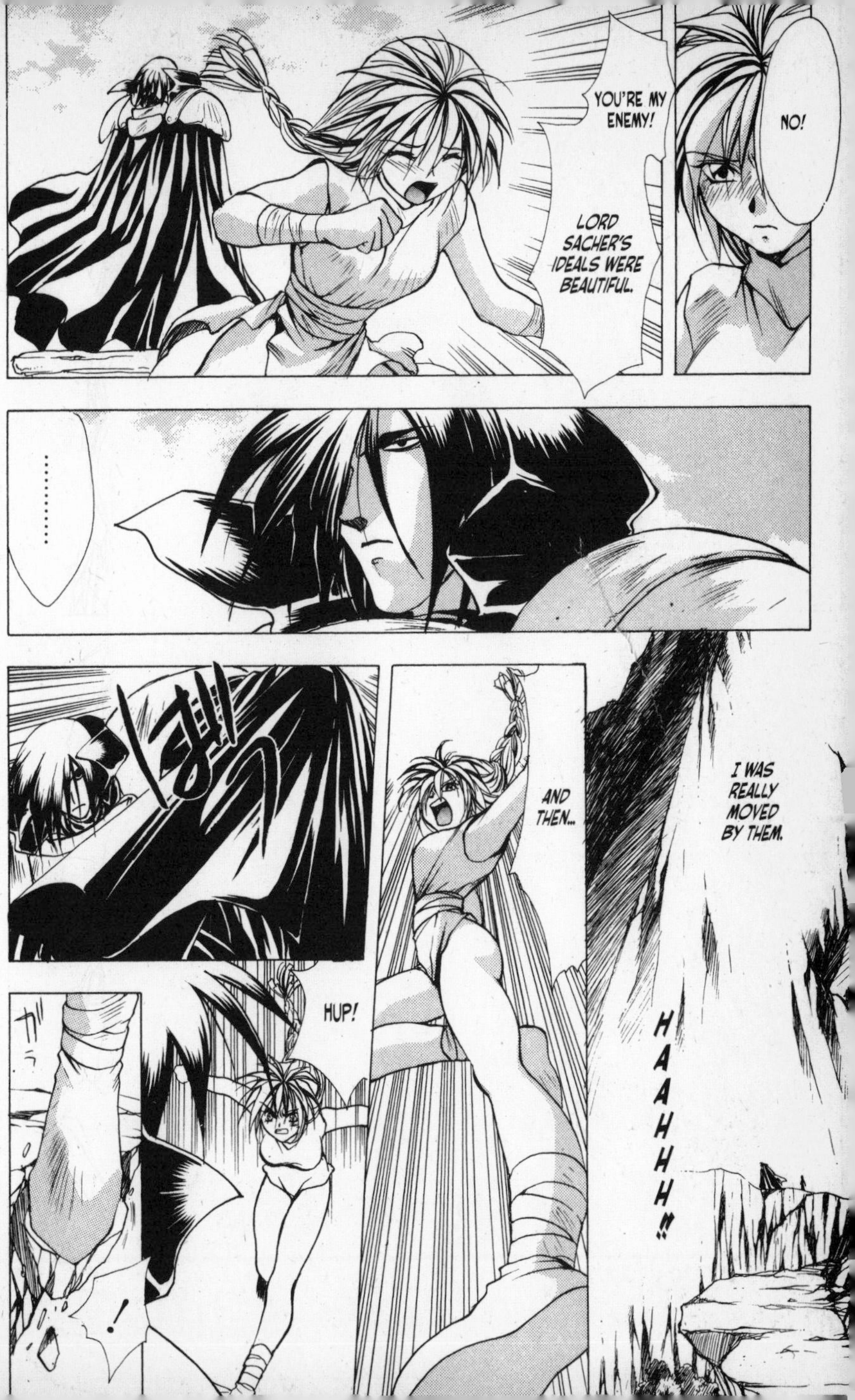
NO!
YOU'RE MY ENEMY!
LORD SACHER'S IDEALS WERE BEAUTIFUL.
......
I WAS REALLY MOVED BY THEM.
AND THEN...
HAAAHHH!!
HUP!
!

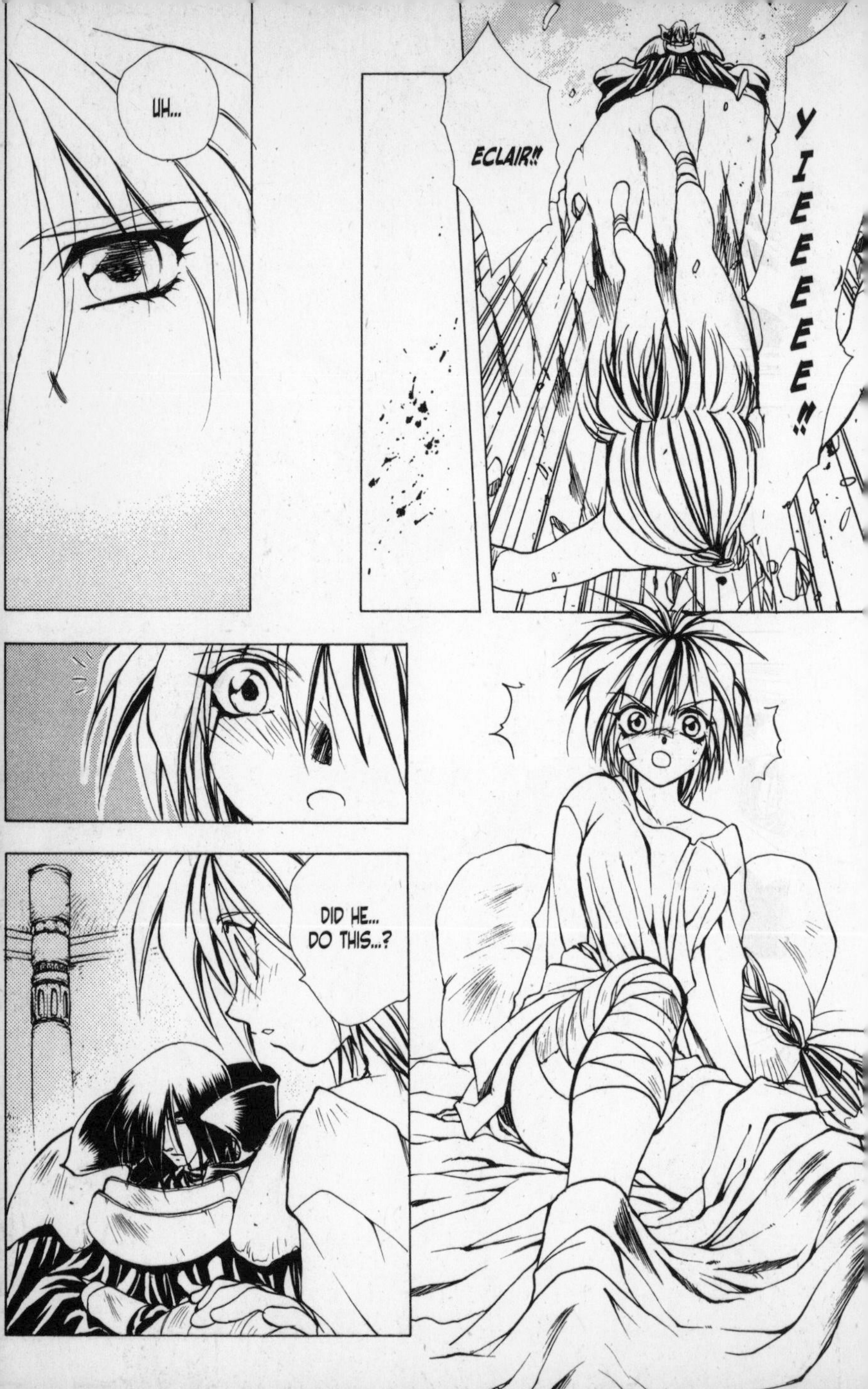
YIEEEEE!!
ECLAIR!!
UH...
DID HE... DO THIS...?

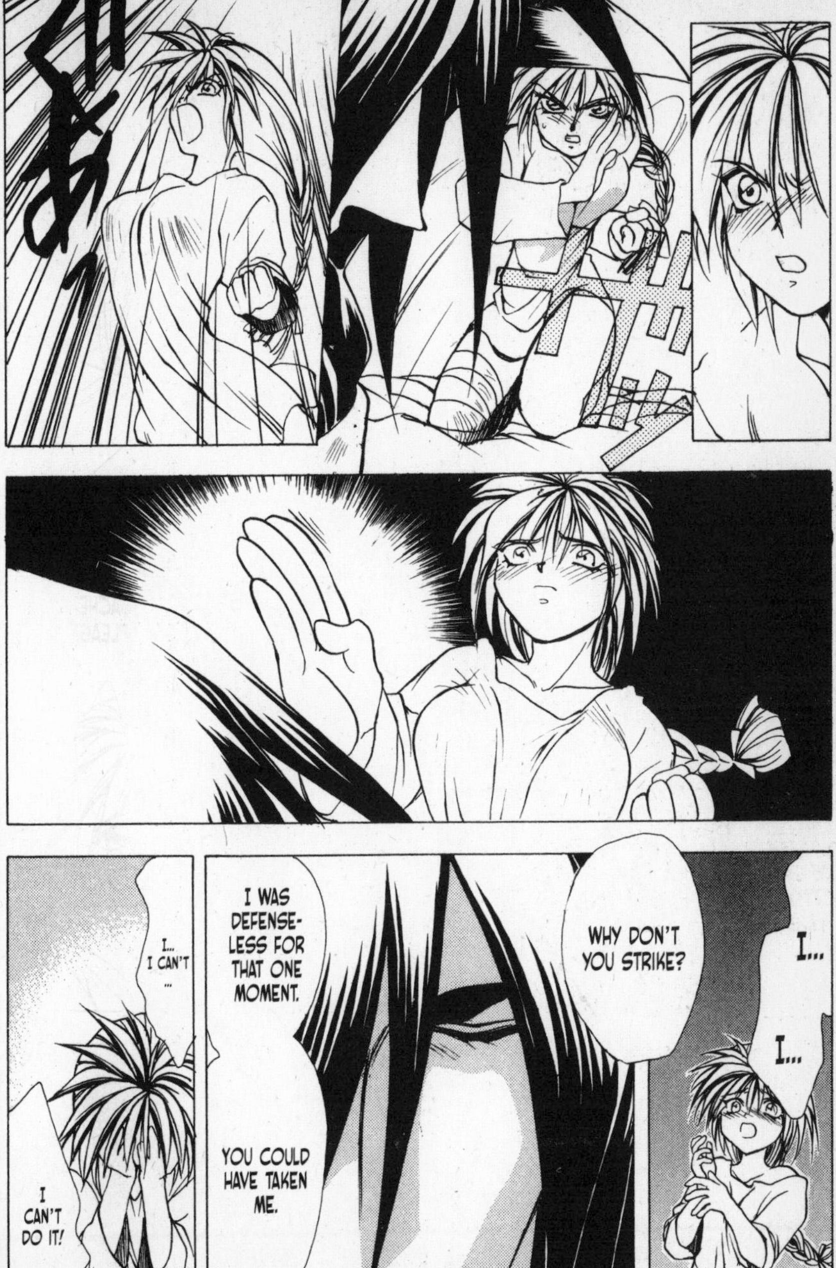
I...
I...
WHY DON'T YOU STRIKE?
I WAS DEFENSE-LESS FOR THAT ONE MOMENT.
YOU COULD HAVE TAKEN ME.
I... I CAN'T ...
I CAN'T DO IT!

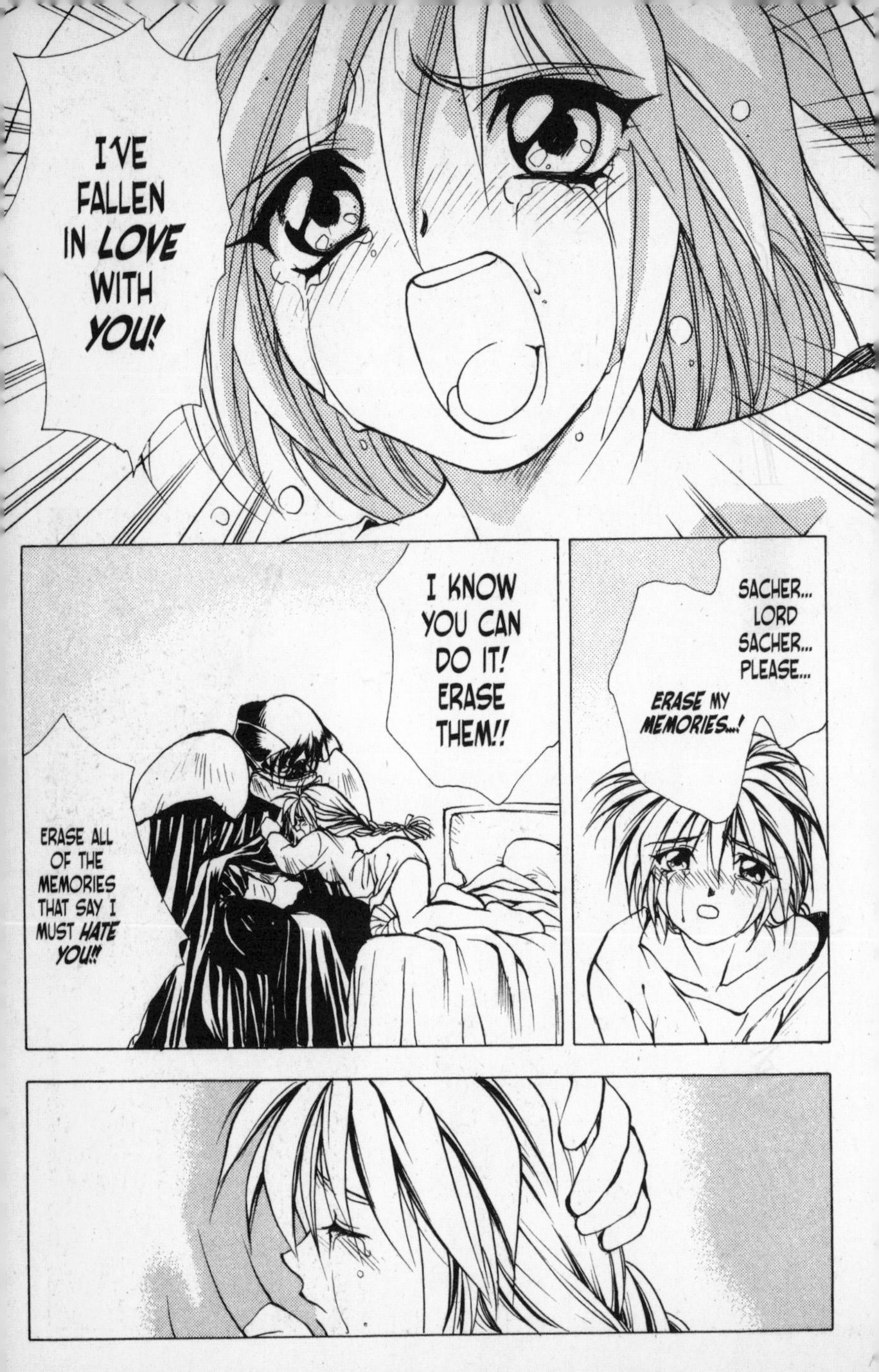
I'VE FALLEN IN LOVE WITH YOU!
SACHER... LORD SACHER... PLEASE...
ERASE MY MEMORIES...!
I KNOW YOU CAN DO IT! ERASE THEM!!
ERASE ALL OF THE MEMORIES THAT SAY I MUST HATE YOU!!

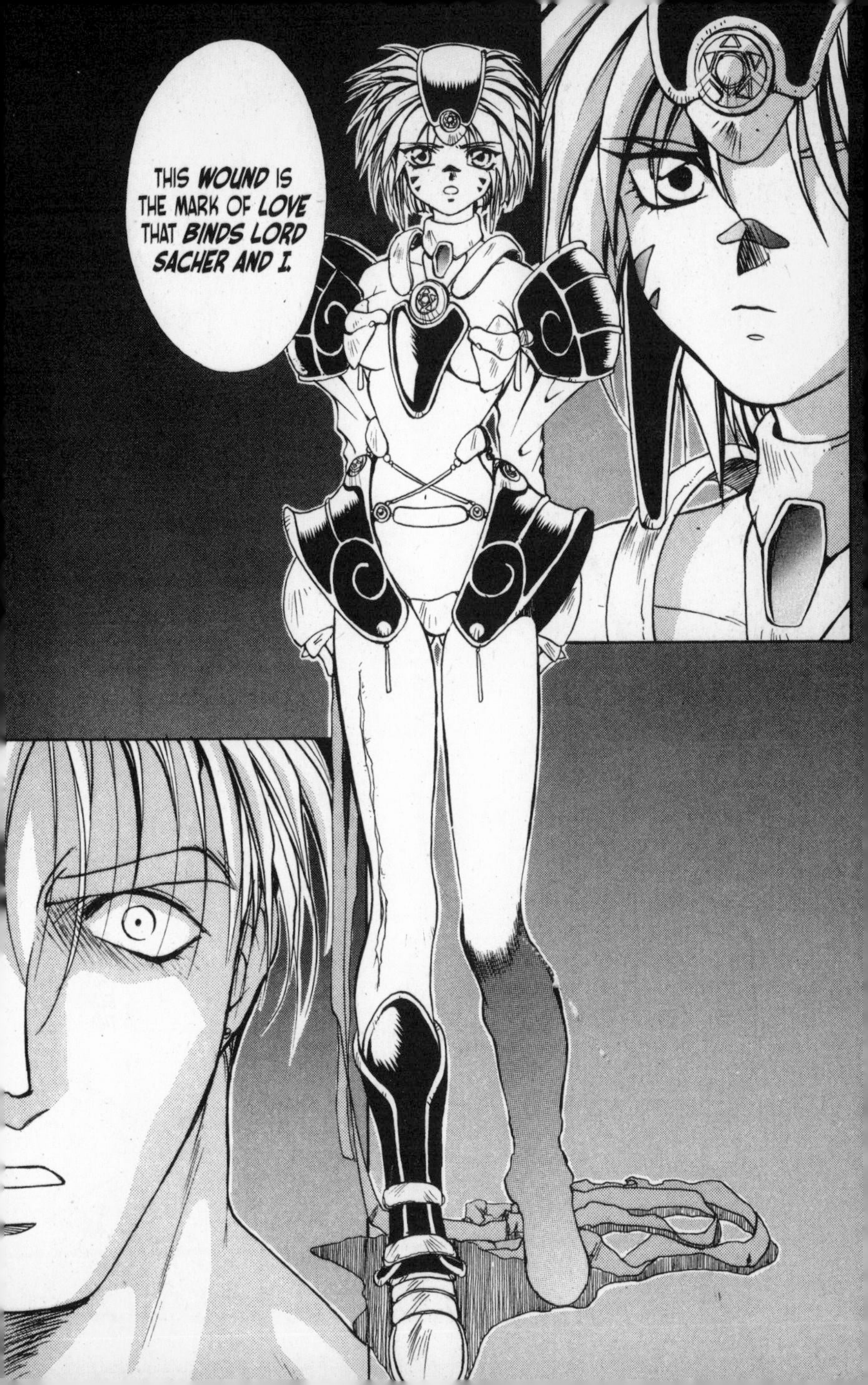
THIS WOUND IS THE MARK OF LOVE THAT BINDS LORD SACHER AND I.

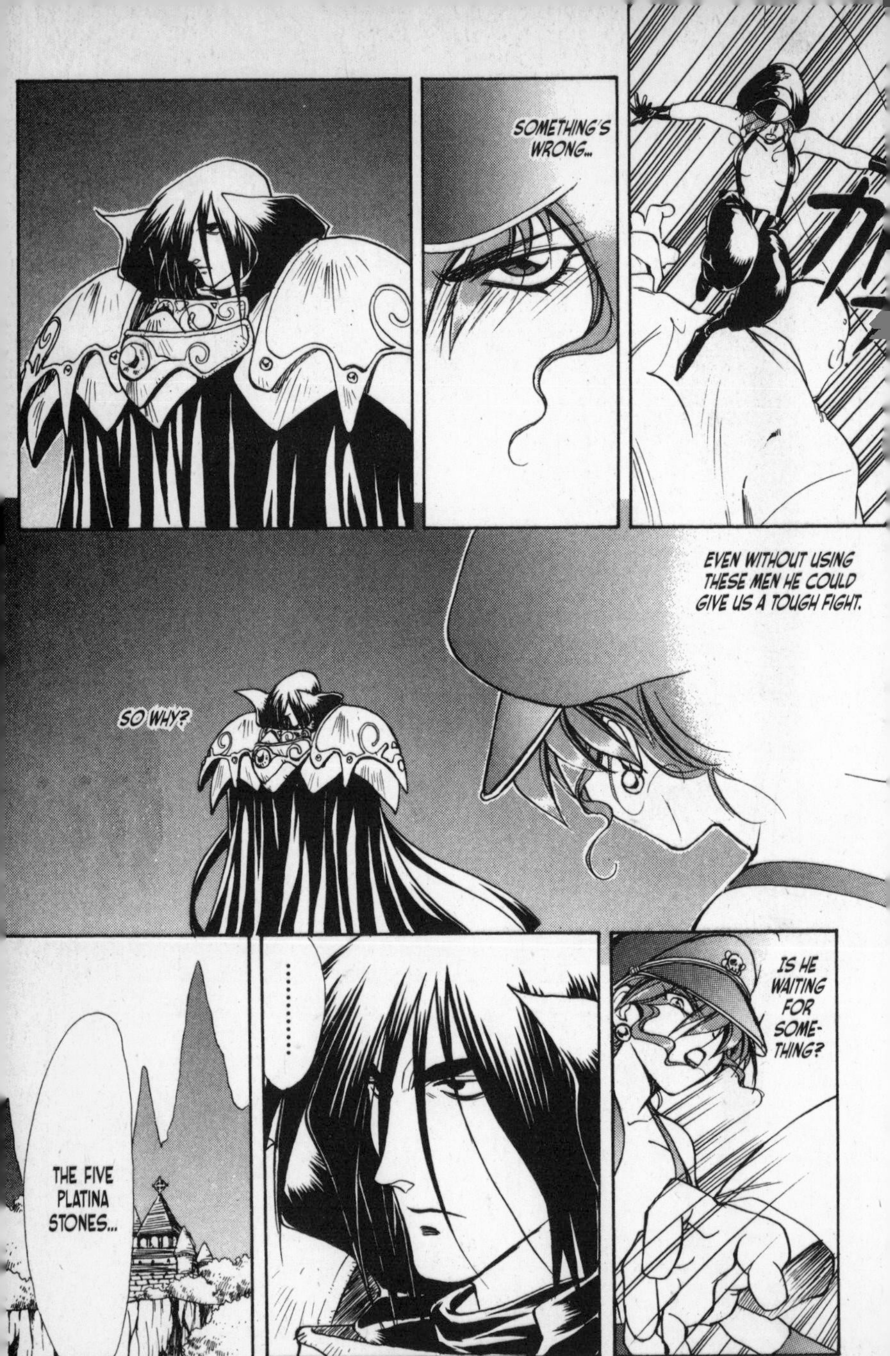
SOMETHING'S WRONG...
EVEN WITHOUT USING THESE MEN HE COULD GIVE US A TOUGH FIGHT.
SO WHY?
IS HE WAITING FOR SOME-THING?
......
THE FIVE PLATINA STONES...

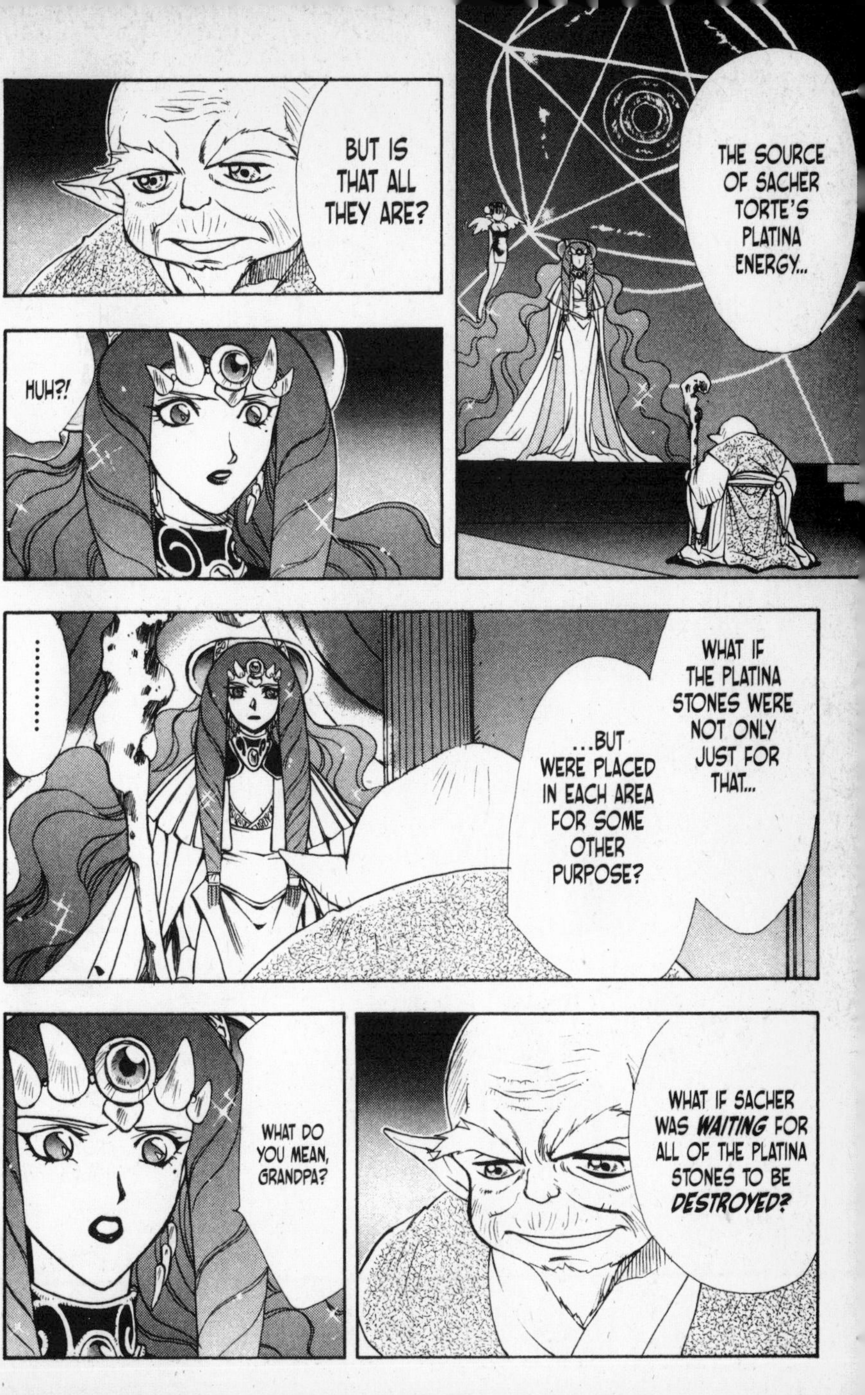
THE SOURCE OF SACHER TORTE'S PLATINA ENERGY...
BUT IS THAT ALL THEY ARE?
HUH?!
WHAT IF THE PLATINA STONES WERE NOT ONLY JUST FOR THAT...
...BUT WERE PLACED IN EACH AREA FOR SOME OTHER PURPOSE?
......
WHAT IF SACHER WAS *WAITING* FOR ALL OF THE PLATINA STONES TO BE ***DESTROYED?***
WHAT DO YOU MEAN, GRANDPA?

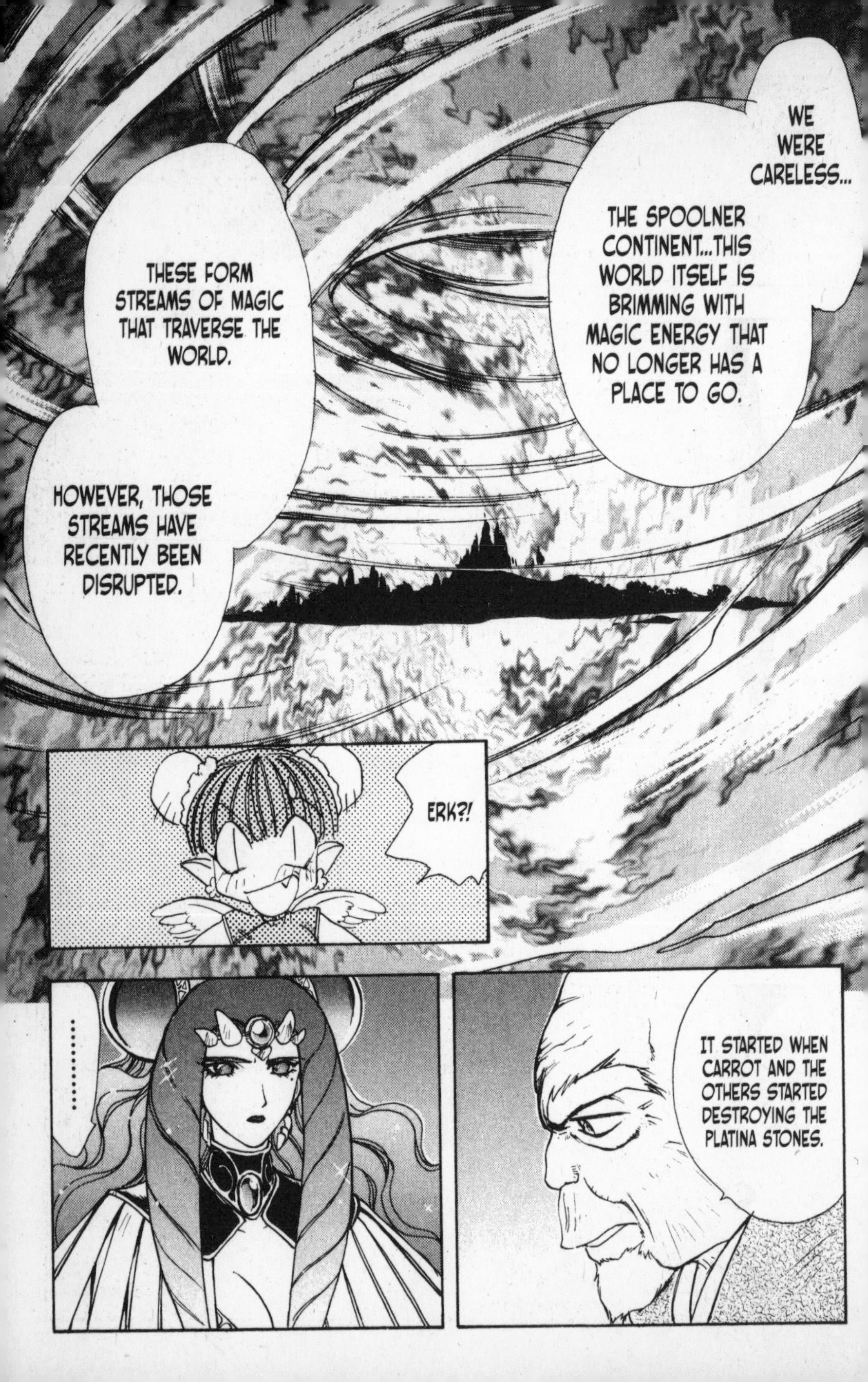
WE WERE CARELESS...
THE SPOOLNER CONTINENT...THIS WORLD ITSELF IS BRIMMING WITH MAGIC ENERGY THAT NO LONGER HAS A PLACE TO GO.
THESE FORM STREAMS OF MAGIC THAT TRAVERSE THE WORLD.
HOWEVER, THOSE STREAMS HAVE RECENTLY BEEN DISRUPTED.
ERK?!
IT STARTED WHEN CARROT AND THE OTHERS STARTED DESTROYING THE PLATINA STONES.
....

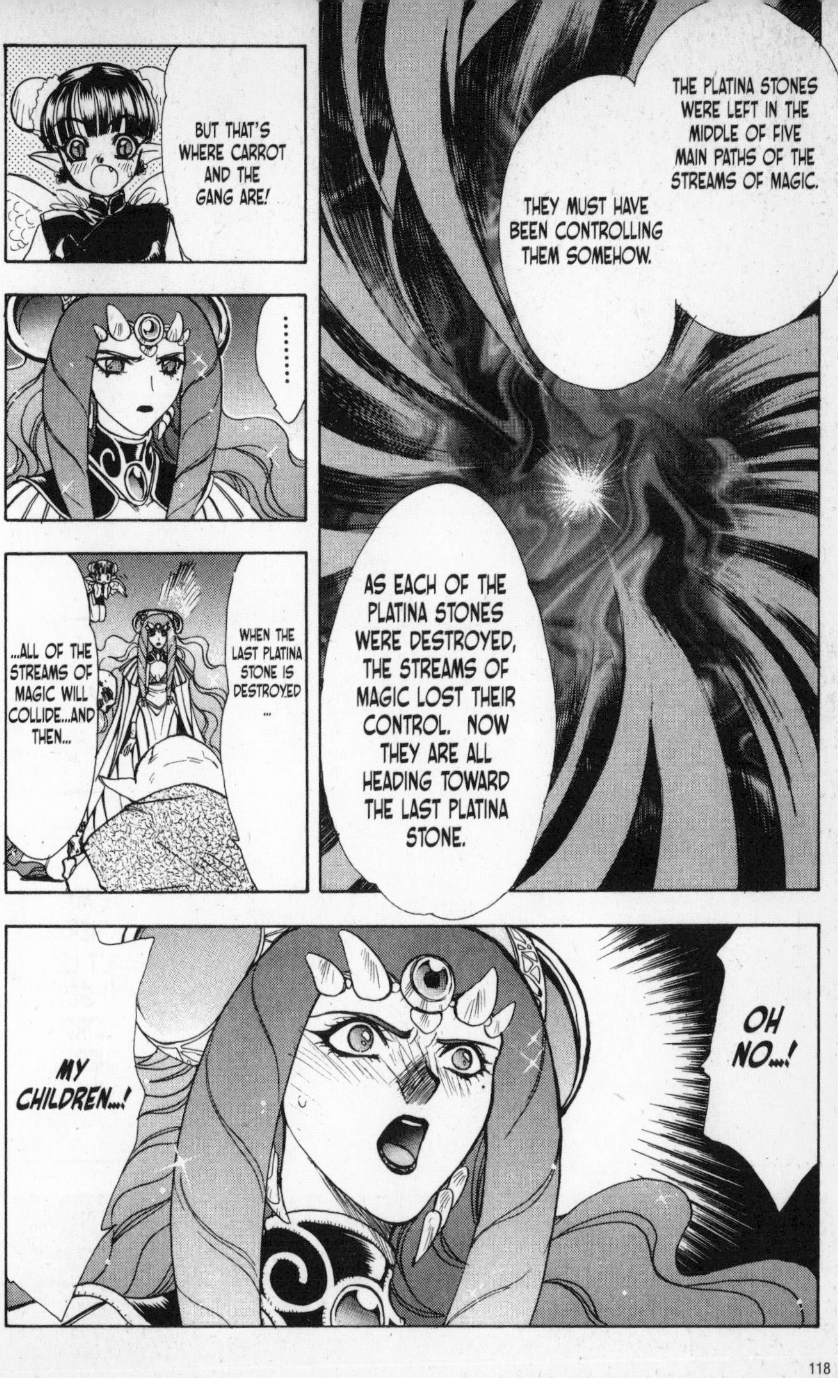
THE PLATINA STONES WERE LEFT IN THE MIDDLE OF FIVE MAIN PATHS OF THE STREAMS OF MAGIC.
THEY MUST HAVE BEEN CONTROLLING THEM SOMEHOW.
AS EACH OF THE PLATINA STONES WERE DESTROYED, THE STREAMS OF MAGIC LOST THEIR CONTROL. NOW THEY ARE ALL HEADING TOWARD THE LAST PLATINA STONE.
BUT THAT'S WHERE CARROT AND THE GANG ARE!
....
WHEN THE LAST PLATINA STONE IS DESTROYED ...
...ALL OF THE STREAMS OF MAGIC WILL COLLIDE...AND THEN...
OH NO...!
MY CHILDREN...!

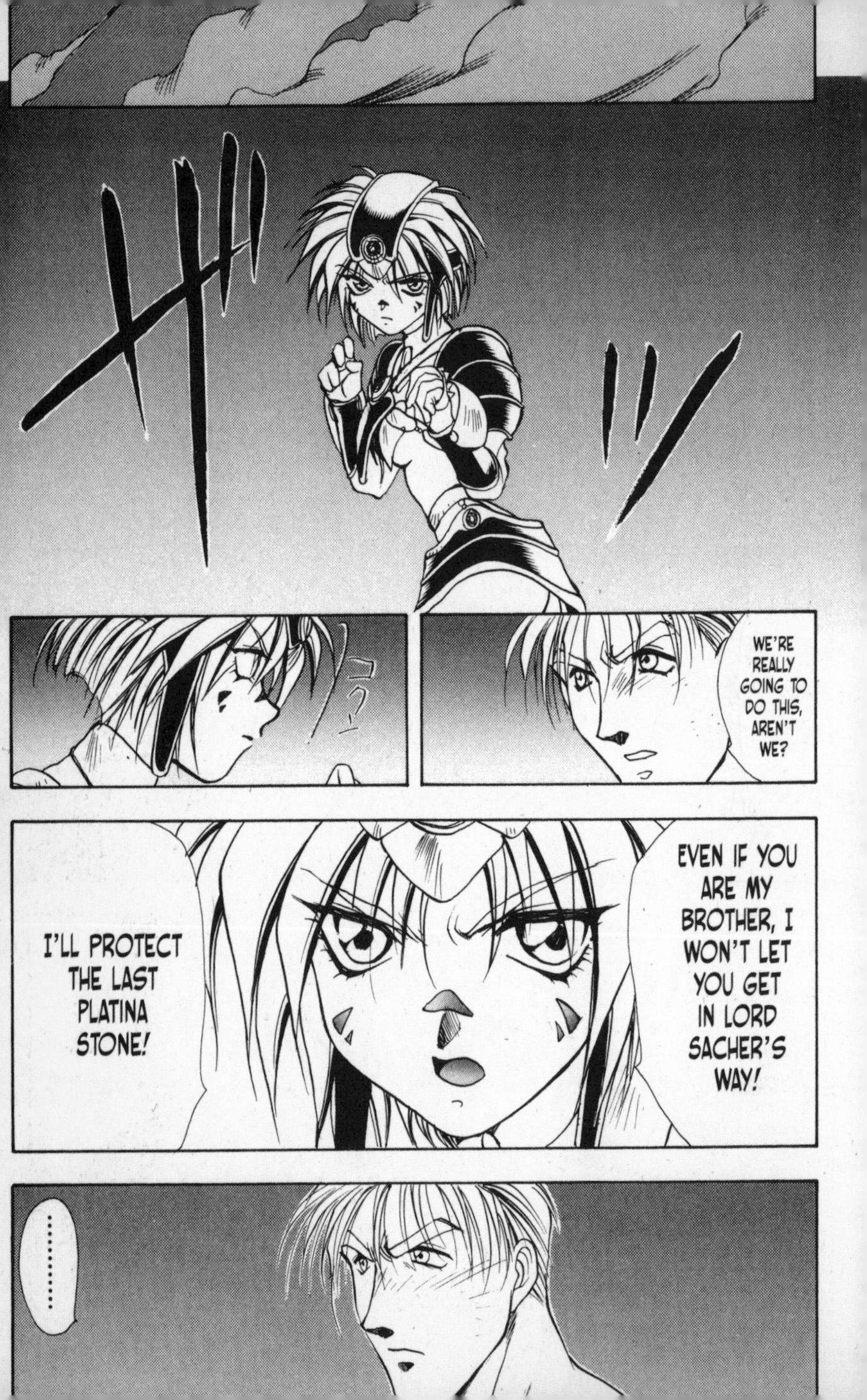
WE'RE REALLY GOING TO DO THIS, AREN'T WE?
EVEN IF YOU ARE MY BROTHER, I WON'T LET YOU GET IN LORD SACHER'S WAY!
I'LL PROTECT THE LAST PLATINA STONE!
....

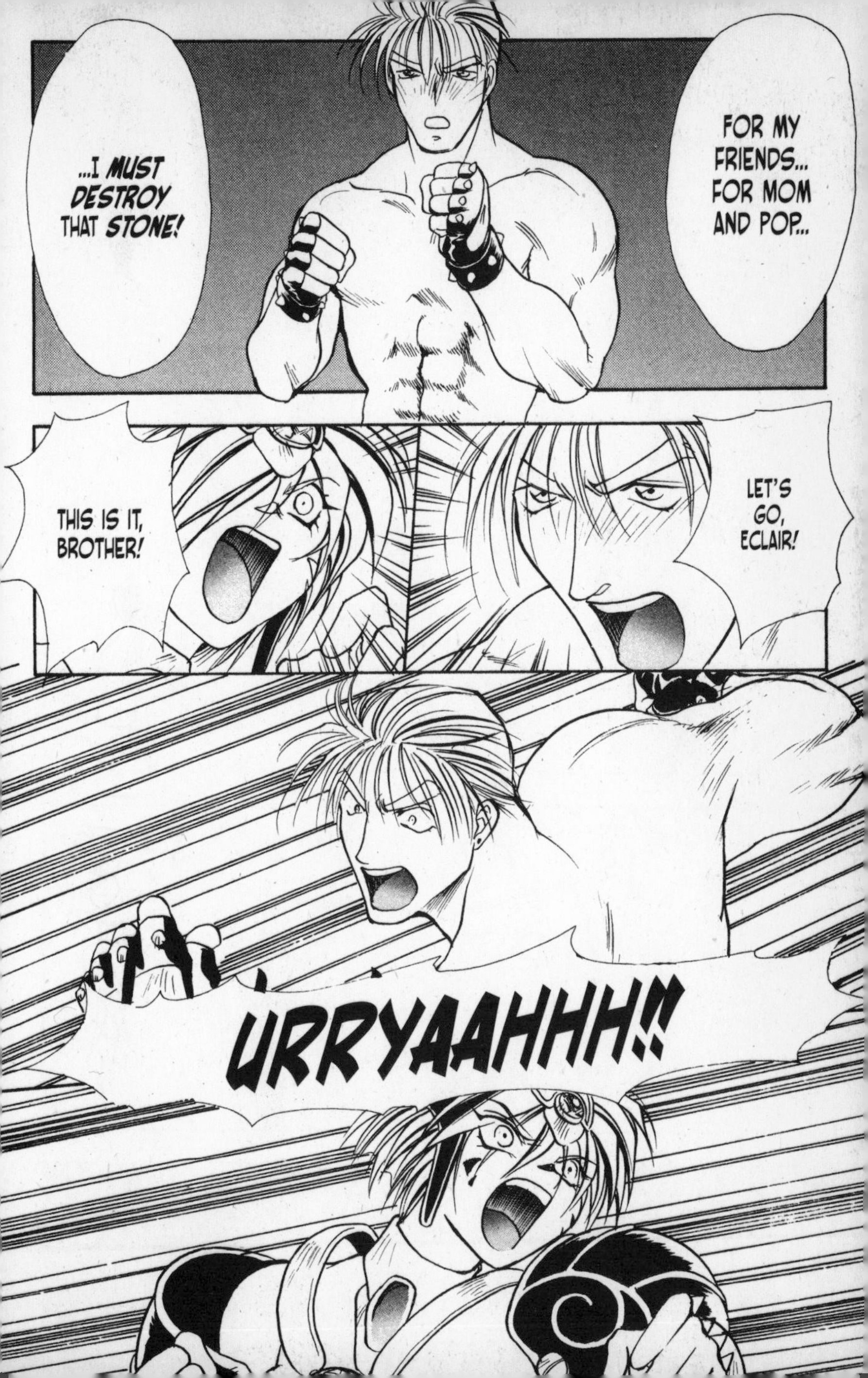
FOR MY FRIENDS... FOR MOM AND POP...
...I MUST DESTROY THAT STONE!
LET'S GO, ECLAIR!
THIS IS IT, BROTHER!
URRYAAHHH!!

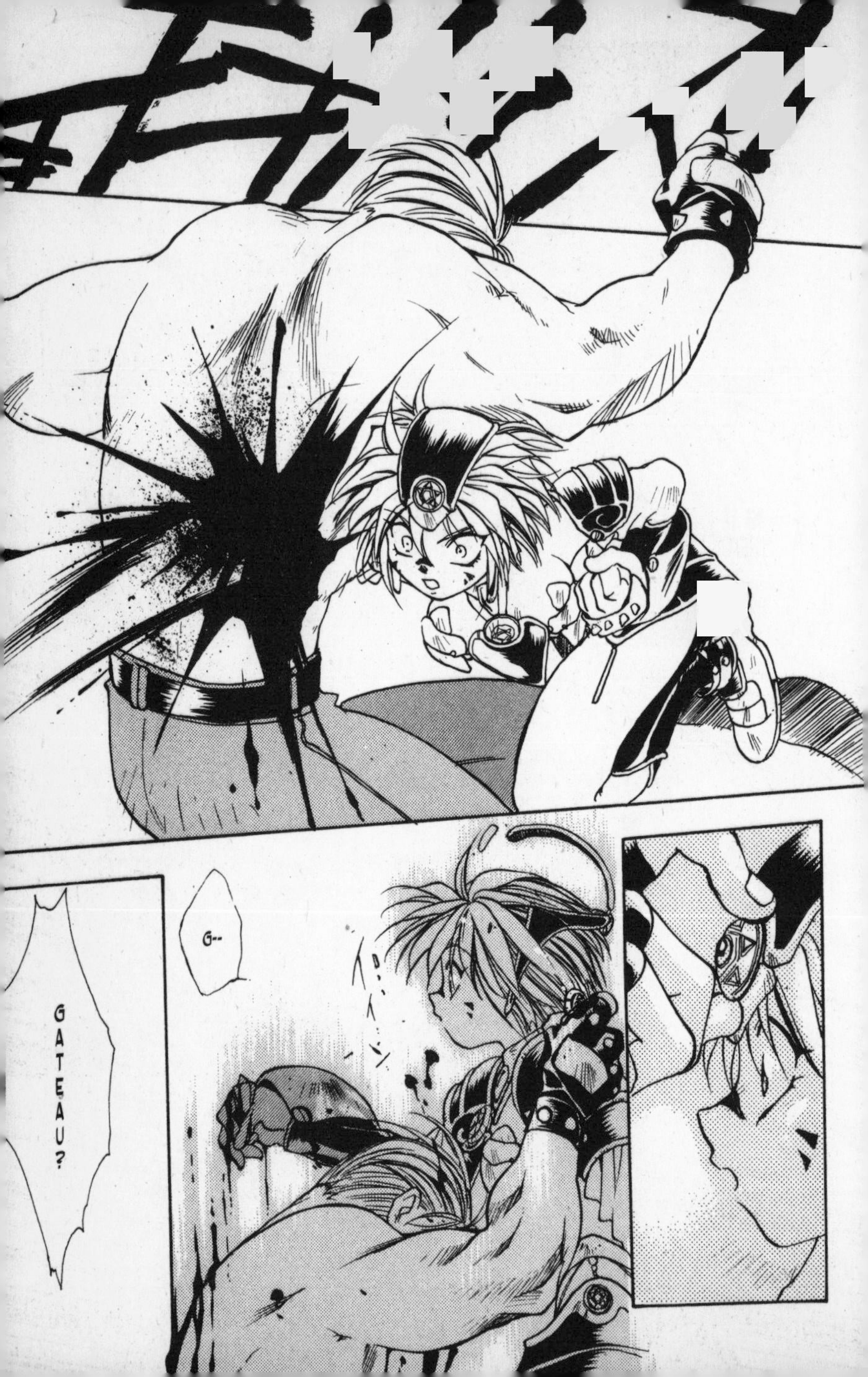
G--
GATEAU?

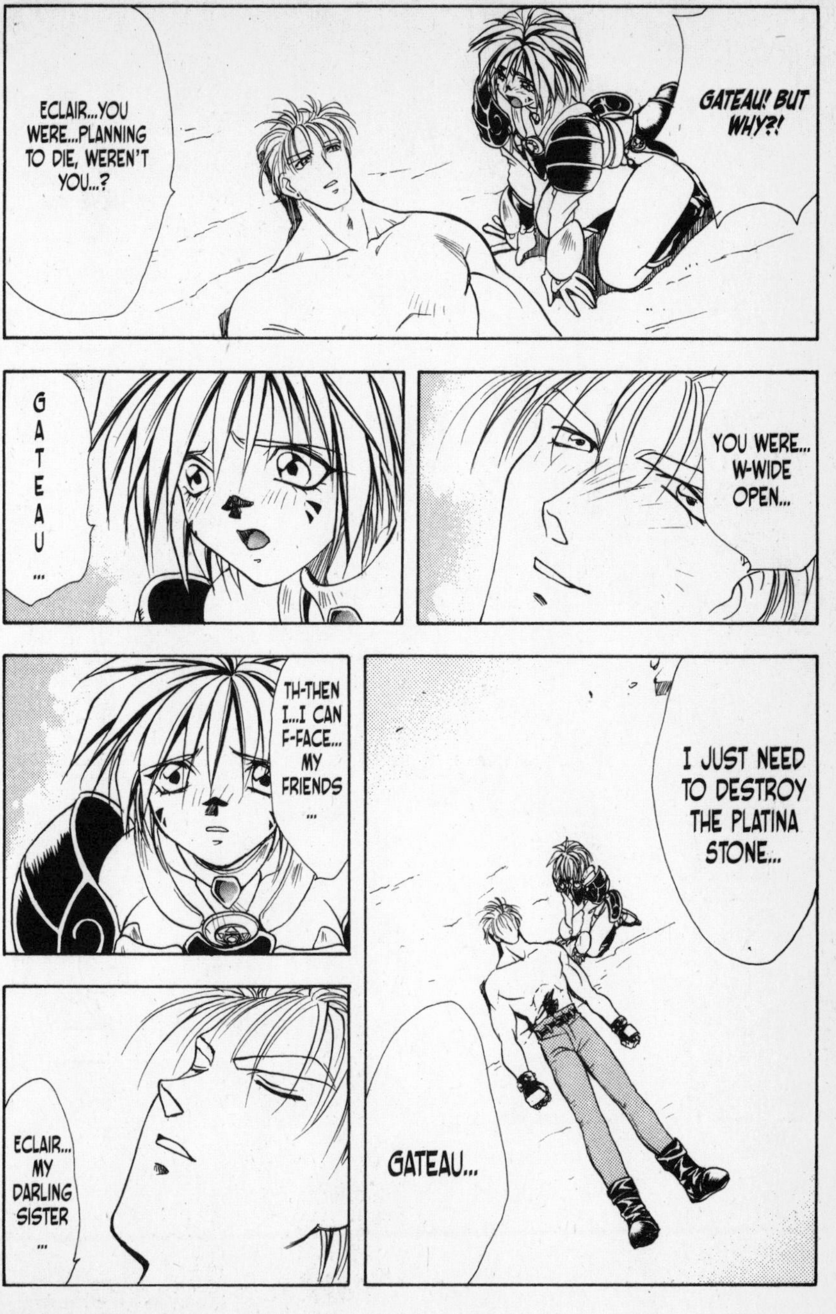
GATEAU! BUT WHY?!
ECLAIR...YOU WERE...PLANNING TO DIE, WEREN'T YOU...?
YOU WERE... W-WIDE OPEN...
GATEAU...
I JUST NEED TO DESTROY THE PLATINA STONE...
GATEAU...
TH-THEN I...I CAN F-FACE... MY FRIENDS...
ECLAIR... MY DARLING SISTER...

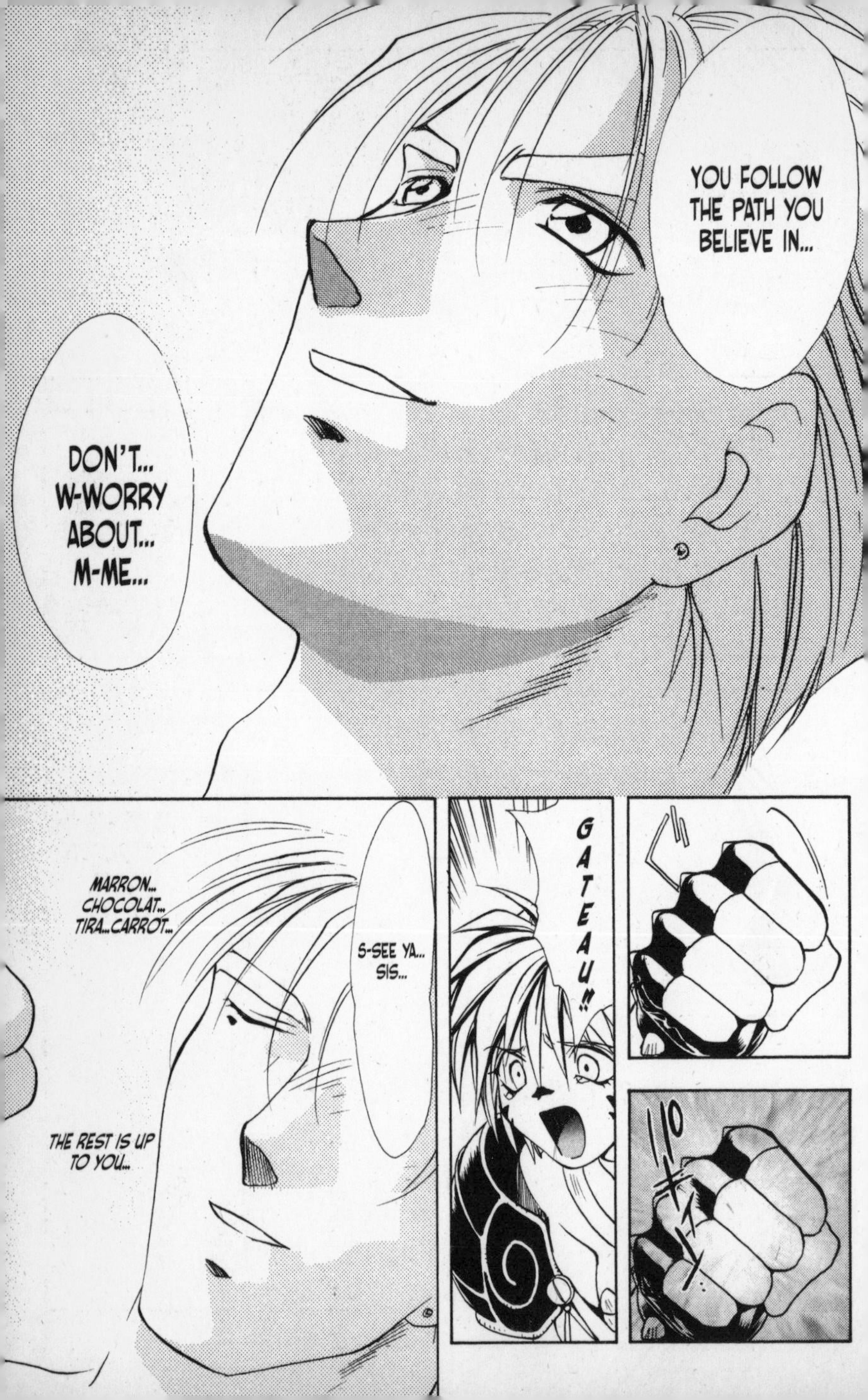
YOU FOLLOW THE PATH YOU BELIEVE IN...
DON'T... W-WORRY ABOUT... M-ME...
GATEAU!!
S-SEE YA... SIS...
MARRON... CHOCOLAT... TIRA...CARROT...
THE REST IS UP TO YOU...

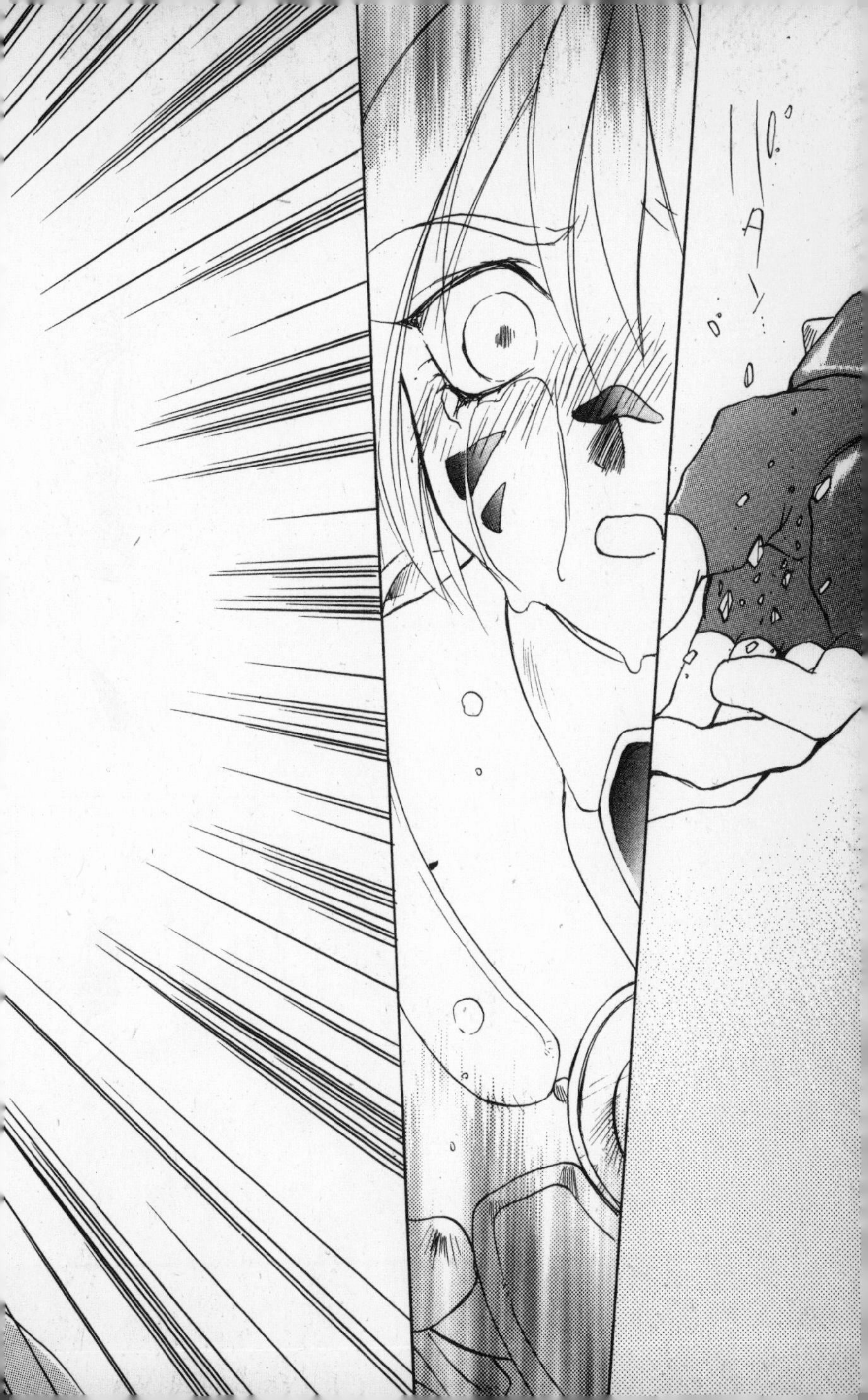
A...

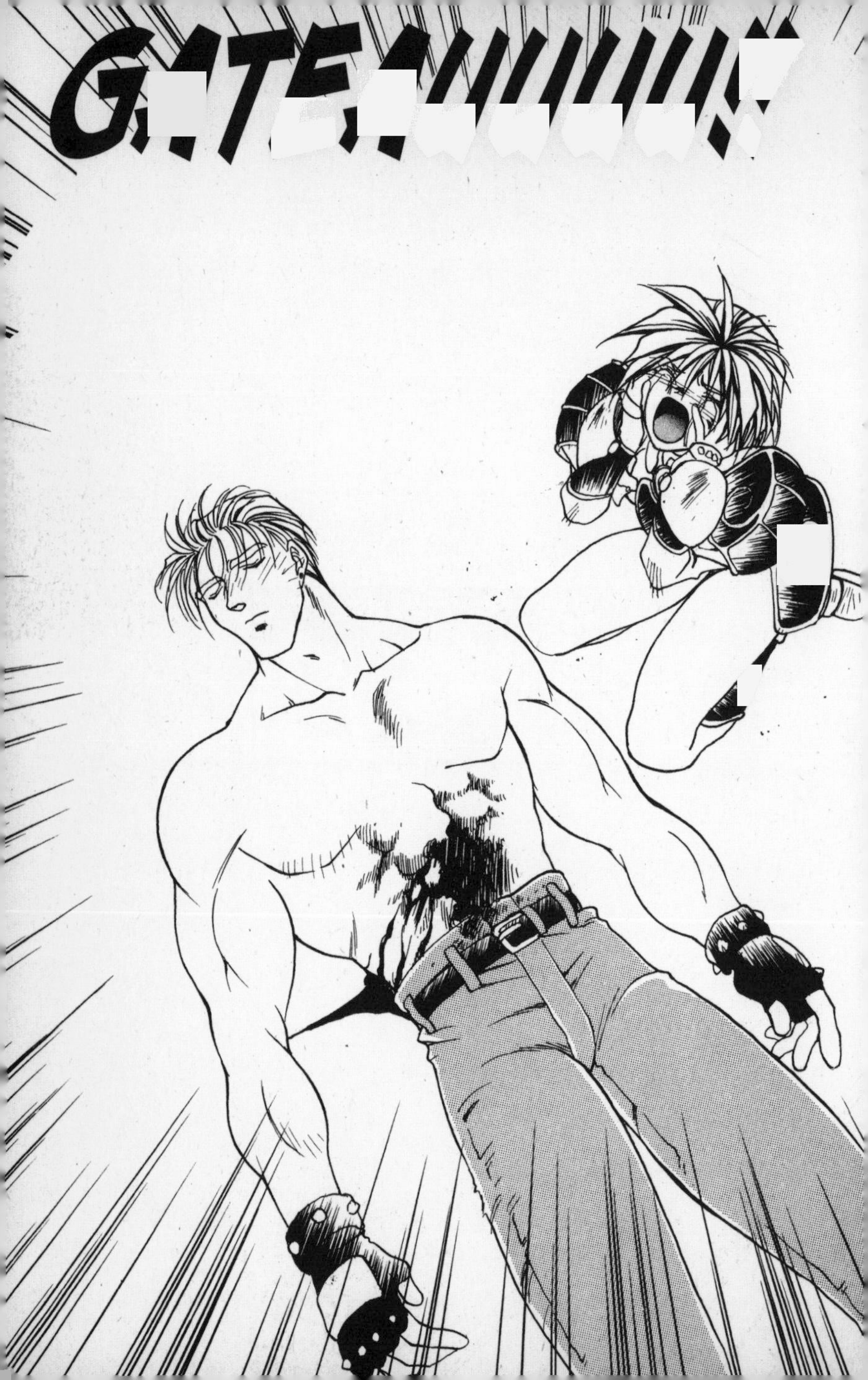
GATEAUUUUUU!

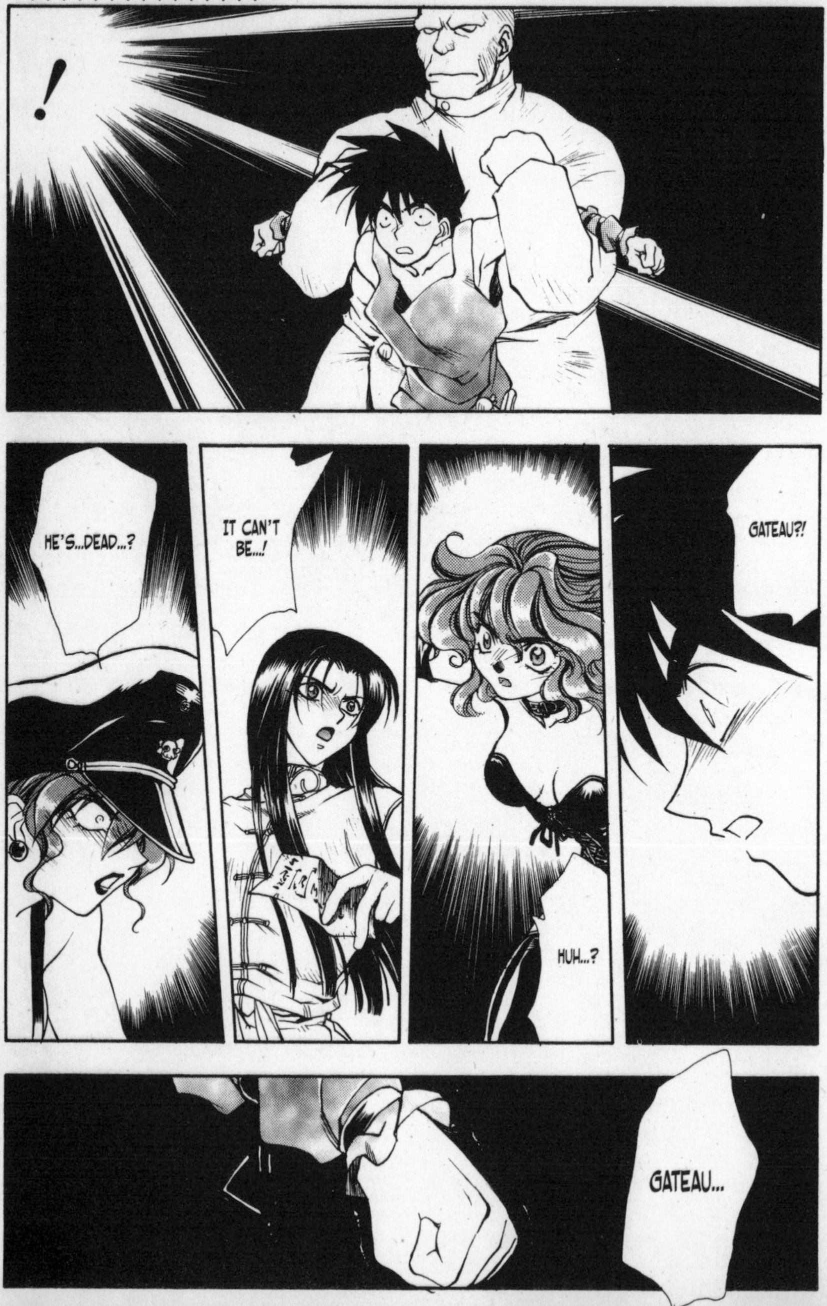
!
GATEAU?!
HUH...?
IT CAN'T BE...!
HE'S...DEAD...?
GATEAU...

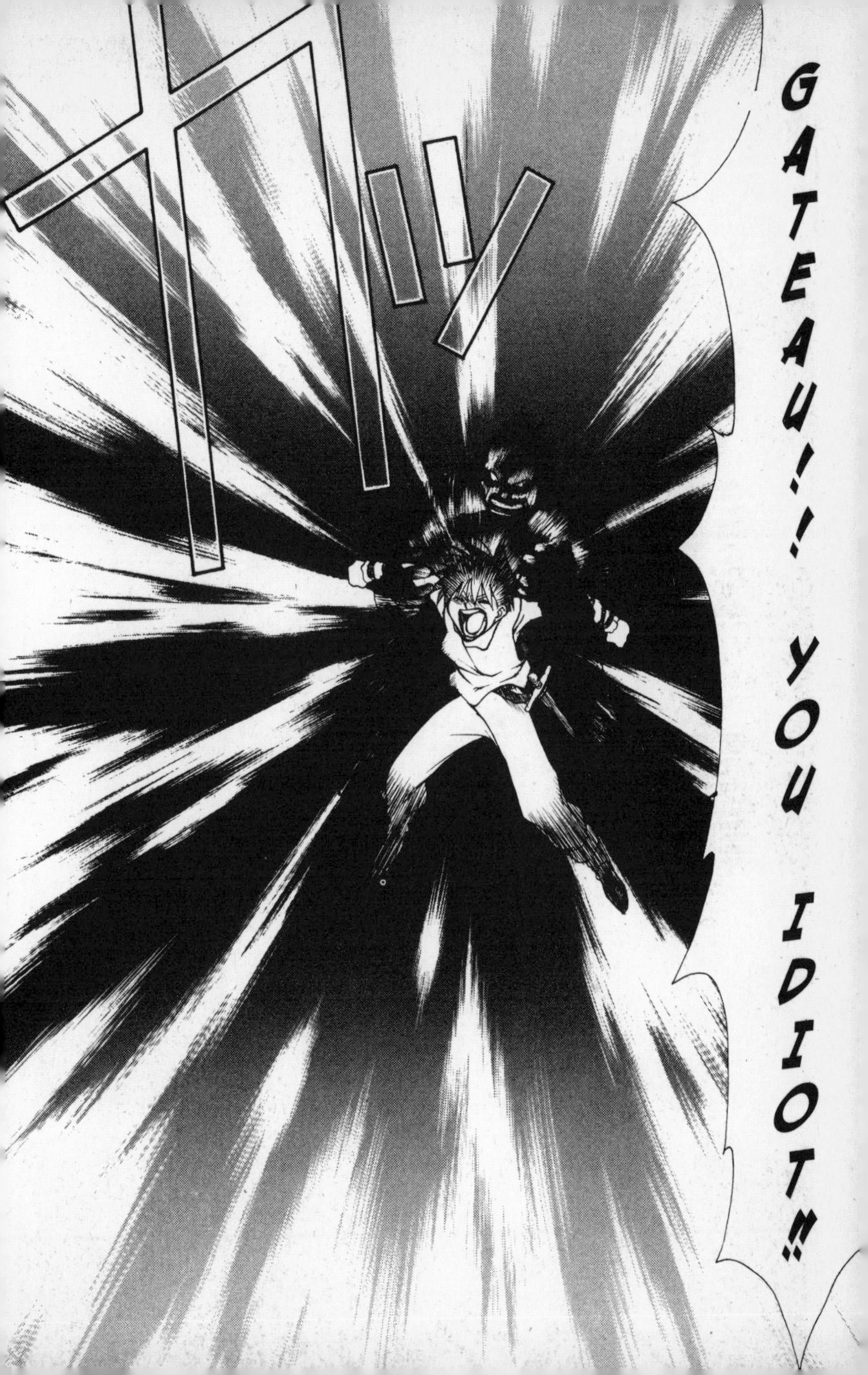
GATEAU!!! YOU IDIOT!!

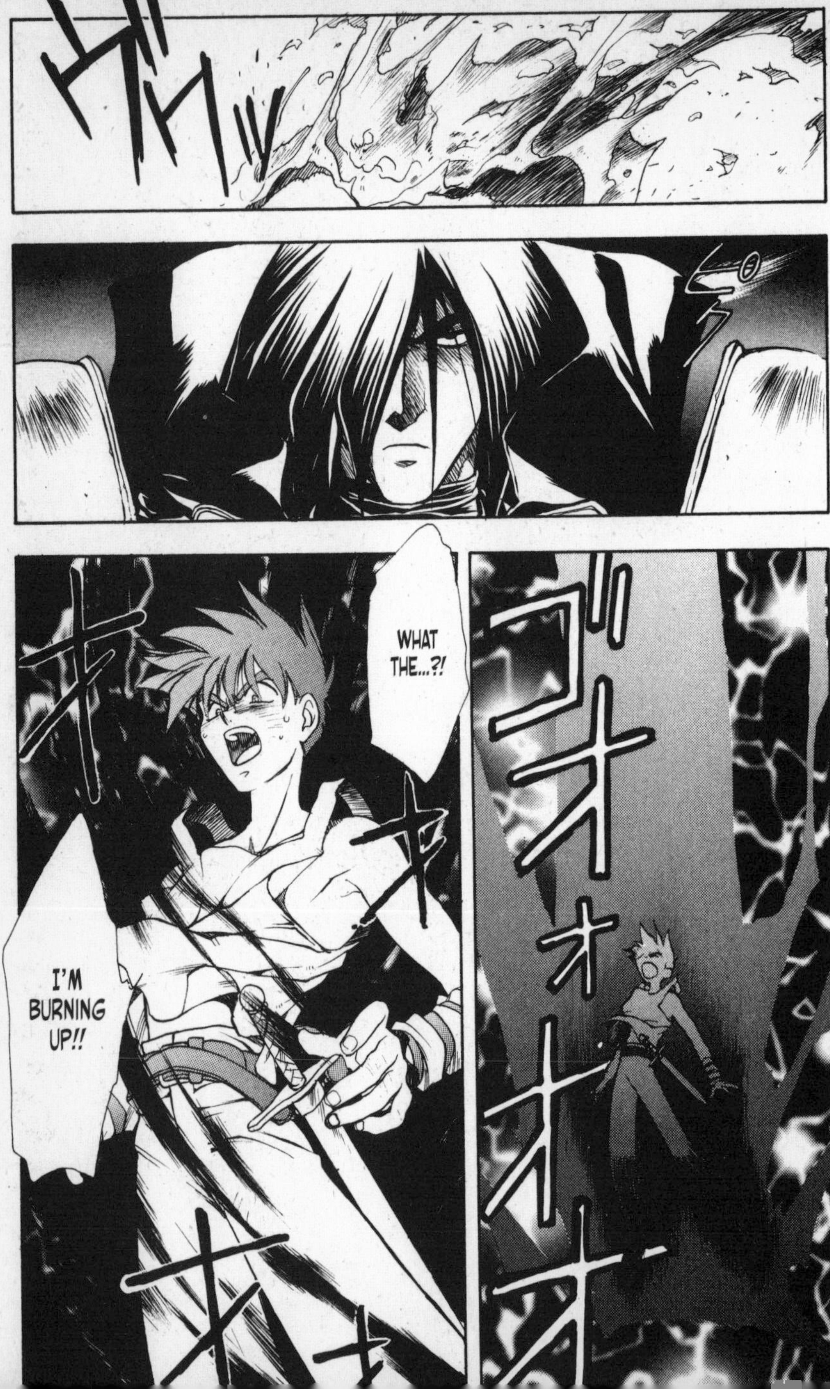
WHAT THE...?!
I'M BURNING UP!!

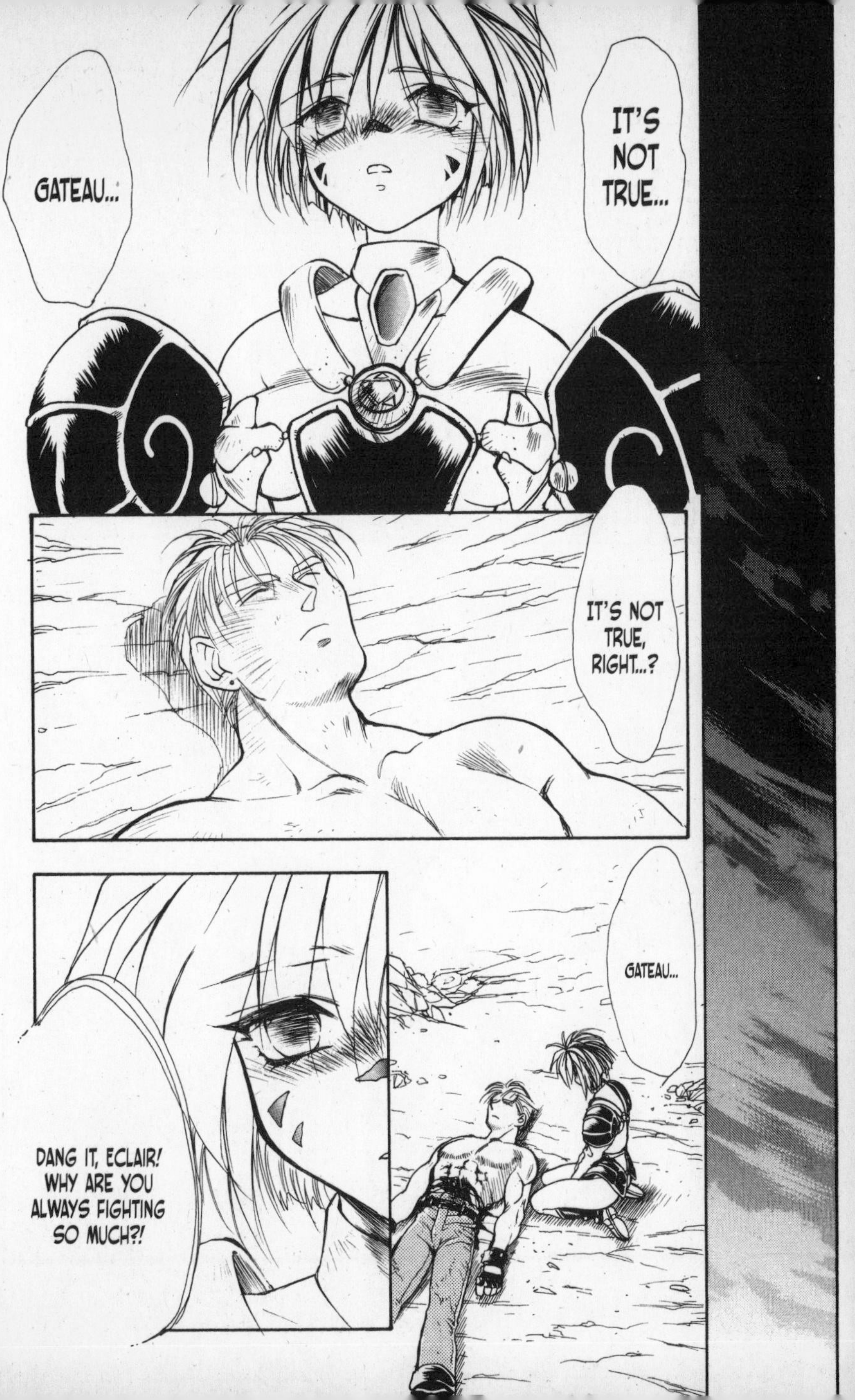
IT'S NOT TRUE...
GATEAU...
IT'S NOT TRUE, RIGHT...?
GATEAU...
DANG IT, ECLAIR! WHY ARE YOU ALWAYS FIGHTING SO MUCH?!

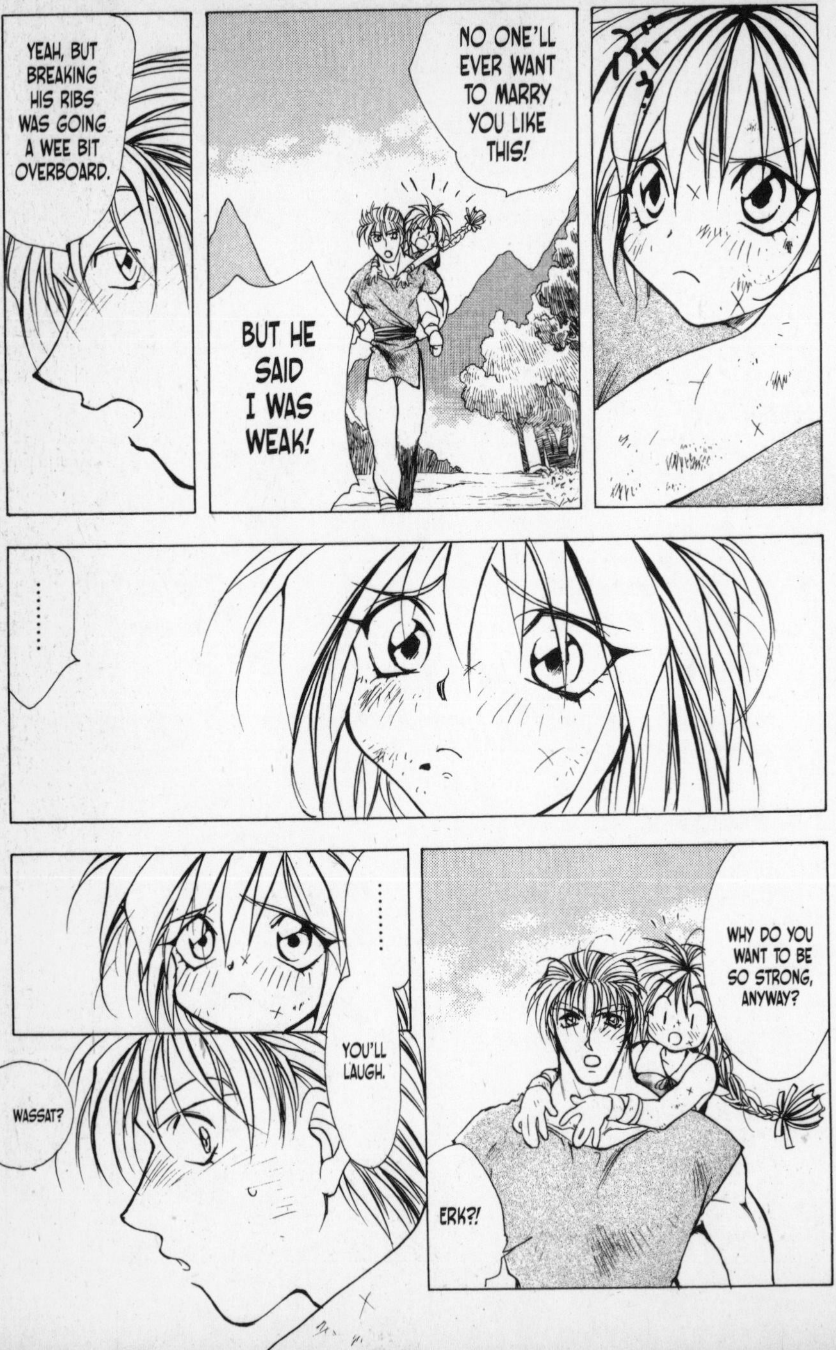
NO ONE'LL EVER WANT TO MARRY YOU LIKE THIS!
BUT HE SAID I WAS WEAK!
YEAH, BUT BREAKING HIS RIBS WAS GOING A WEE BIT OVERBOARD.
......
WHY DO YOU WANT TO BE SO STRONG, ANYWAY?
ERK?!
......
YOU'LL LAUGH.
WASSAT?

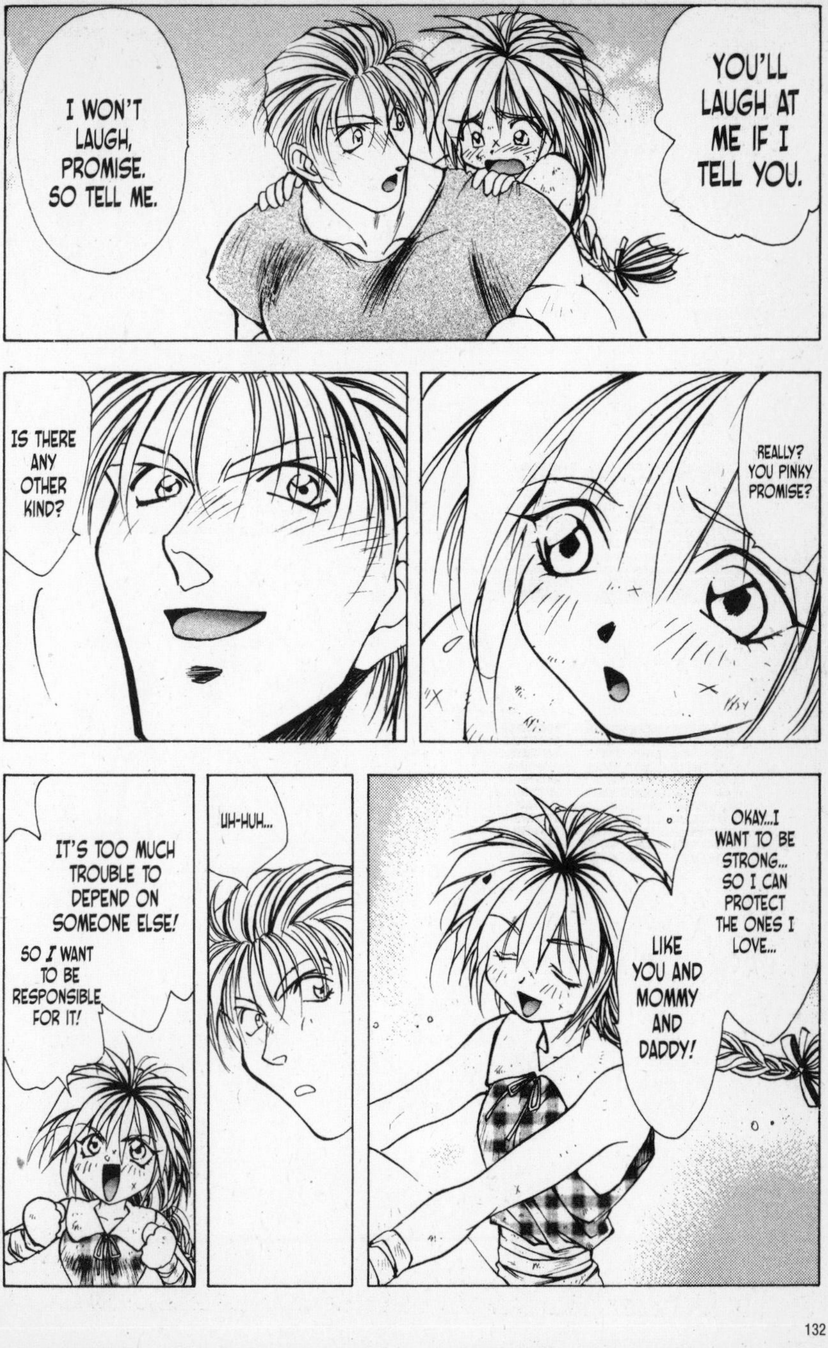
YOU'LL LAUGH AT ME IF I TELL YOU.
I WON'T LAUGH, PROMISE. SO TELL ME.
REALLY? YOU PINKY PROMISE?
IS THERE ANY OTHER KIND?
OKAY...I WANT TO BE STRONG... SO I CAN PROTECT THE ONES I LOVE...
LIKE YOU AND MOMMY AND DADDY!
UH-HUH...
IT'S TOO MUCH TROUBLE TO DEPEND ON SOMEONE ELSE!
SO *I* WANT TO BE RESPONSIBLE FOR IT!

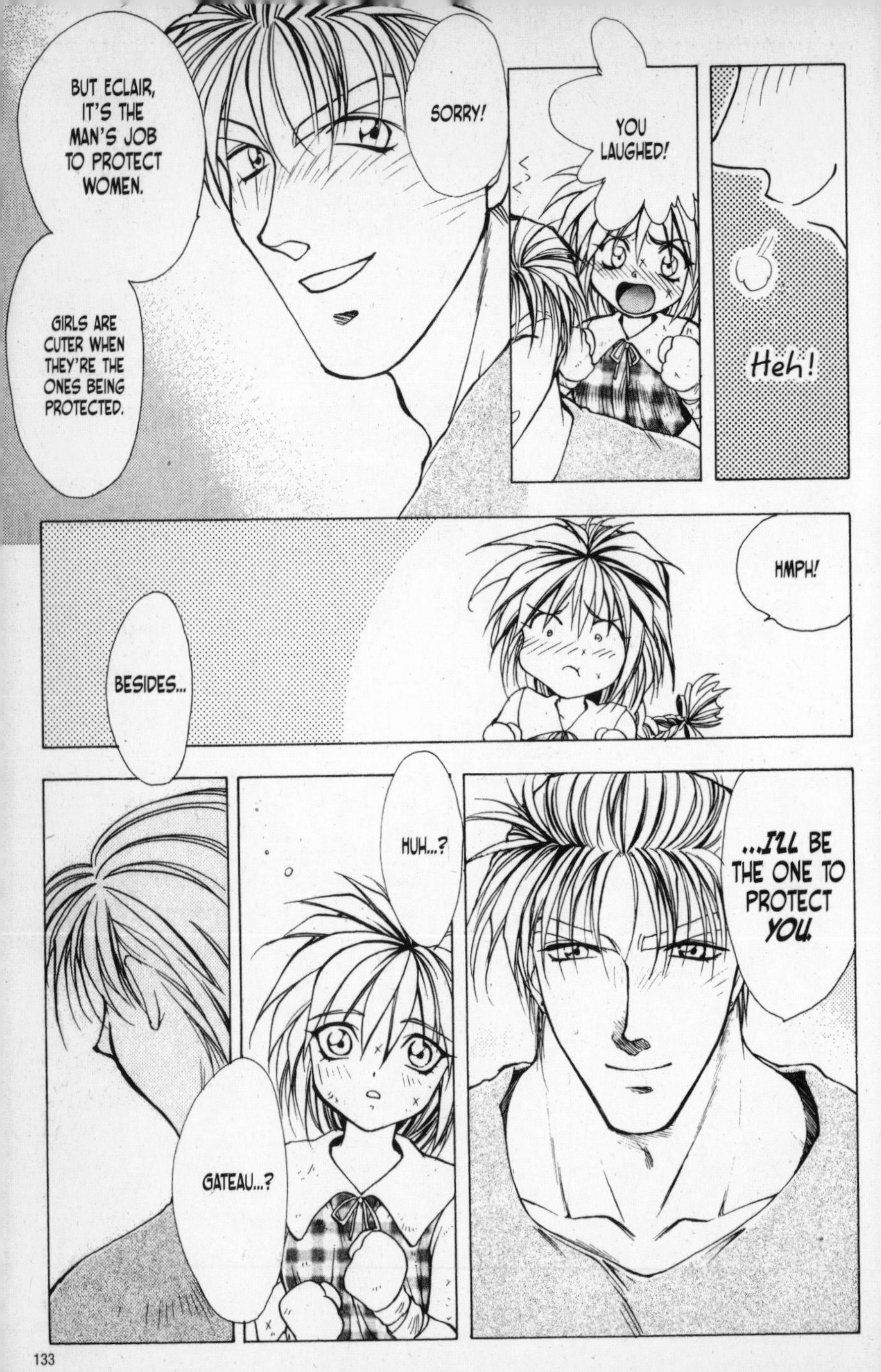
Heh!
YOU LAUGHED!
SORRY!
BUT ECLAIR, IT'S THE MAN'S JOB TO PROTECT WOMEN.
GIRLS ARE CUTER WHEN THEY'RE THE ONES BEING PROTECTED.
HMPH!
BESIDES...
...I'LL BE THE ONE TO PROTECT YOU.
HUH...?
GATEAU...?

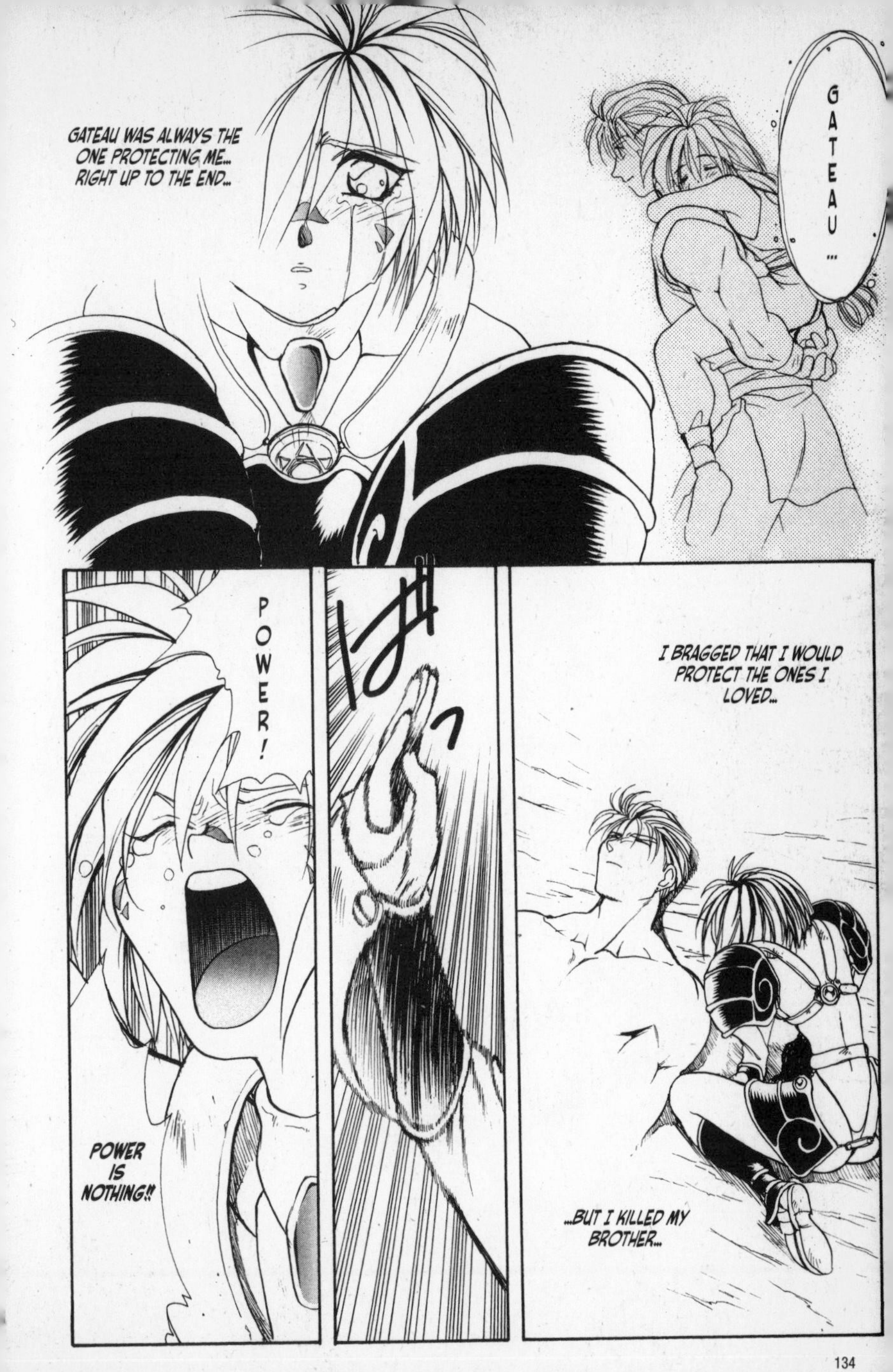
GATEAU...
GATEAU WAS ALWAYS THE ONE PROTECTING ME... RIGHT UP TO THE END...
I BRAGGED THAT I WOULD PROTECT THE ONES I LOVED...
...BUT I KILLED MY BROTHER...
POWER!
POWER IS NOTHING!!

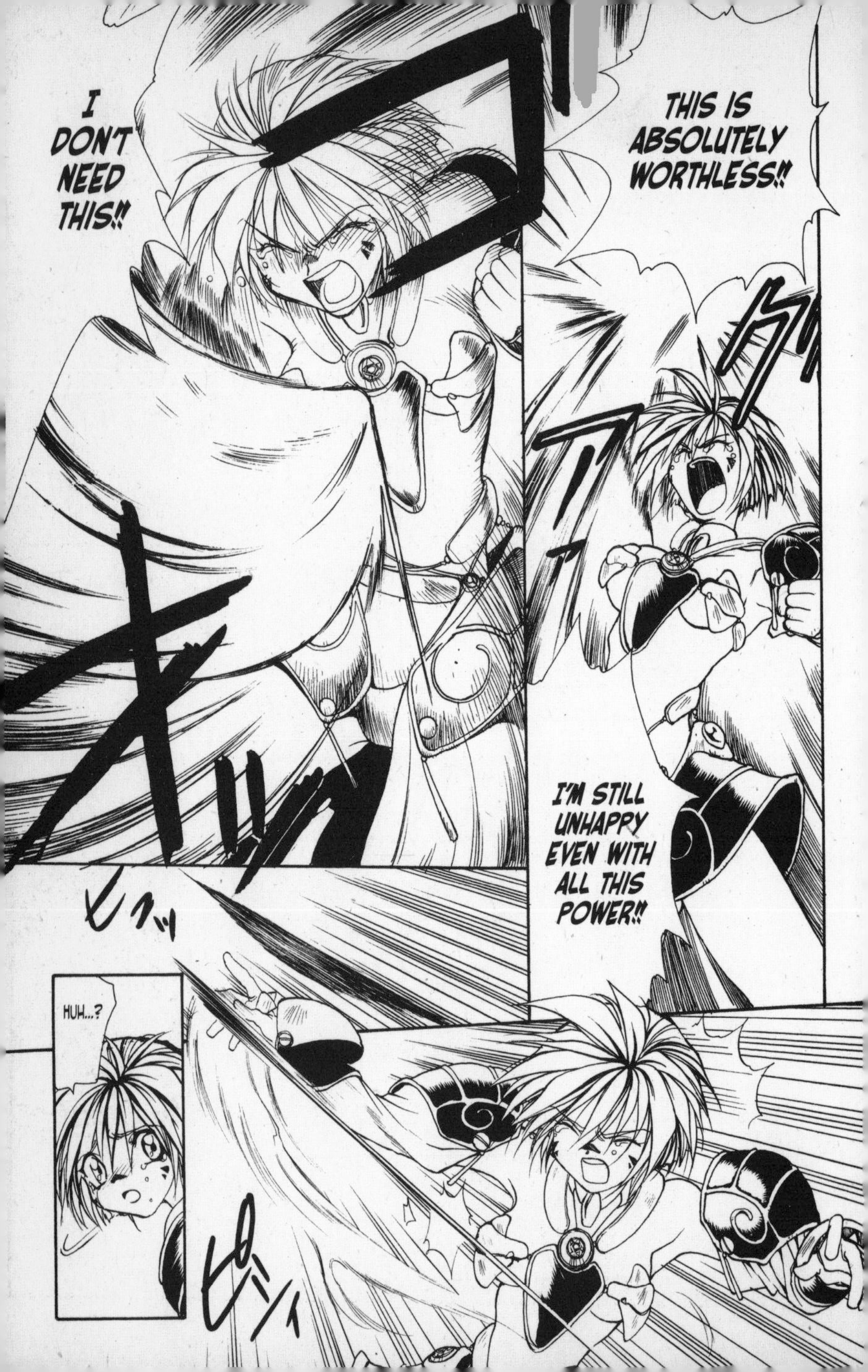
THIS IS ABSOLUTELY WORTHLESS!!
I'M STILL UNHAPPY EVEN WITH ALL THIS POWER!!
I DON'T NEED THIS!!
HUH...?

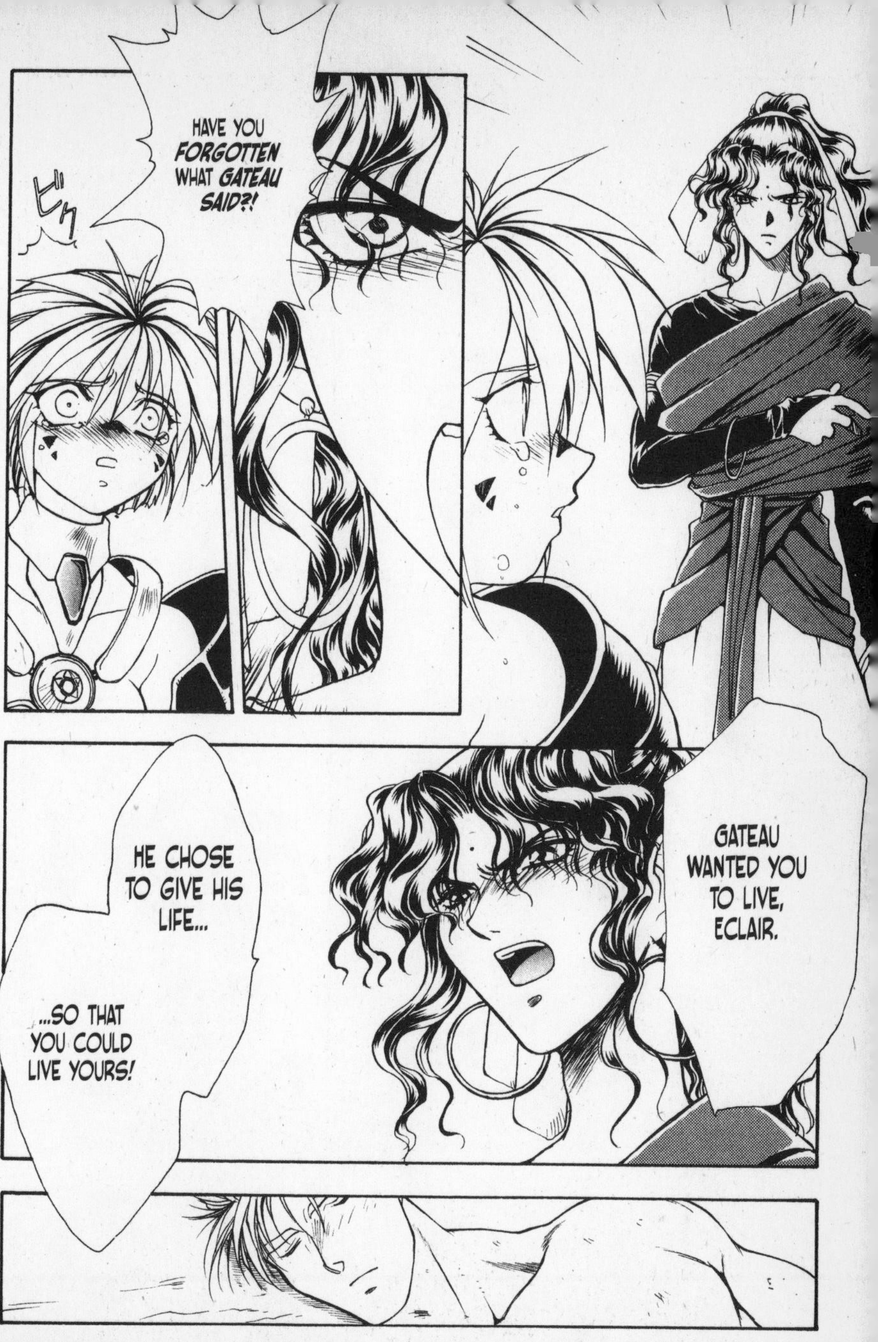
HAVE YOU FORGOTTEN WHAT GATEAU SAID?!
ビク
GATEAU WANTED YOU TO LIVE, ECLAIR.
HE CHOSE TO GIVE HIS LIFE...
...SO THAT YOU COULD LIVE YOURS!

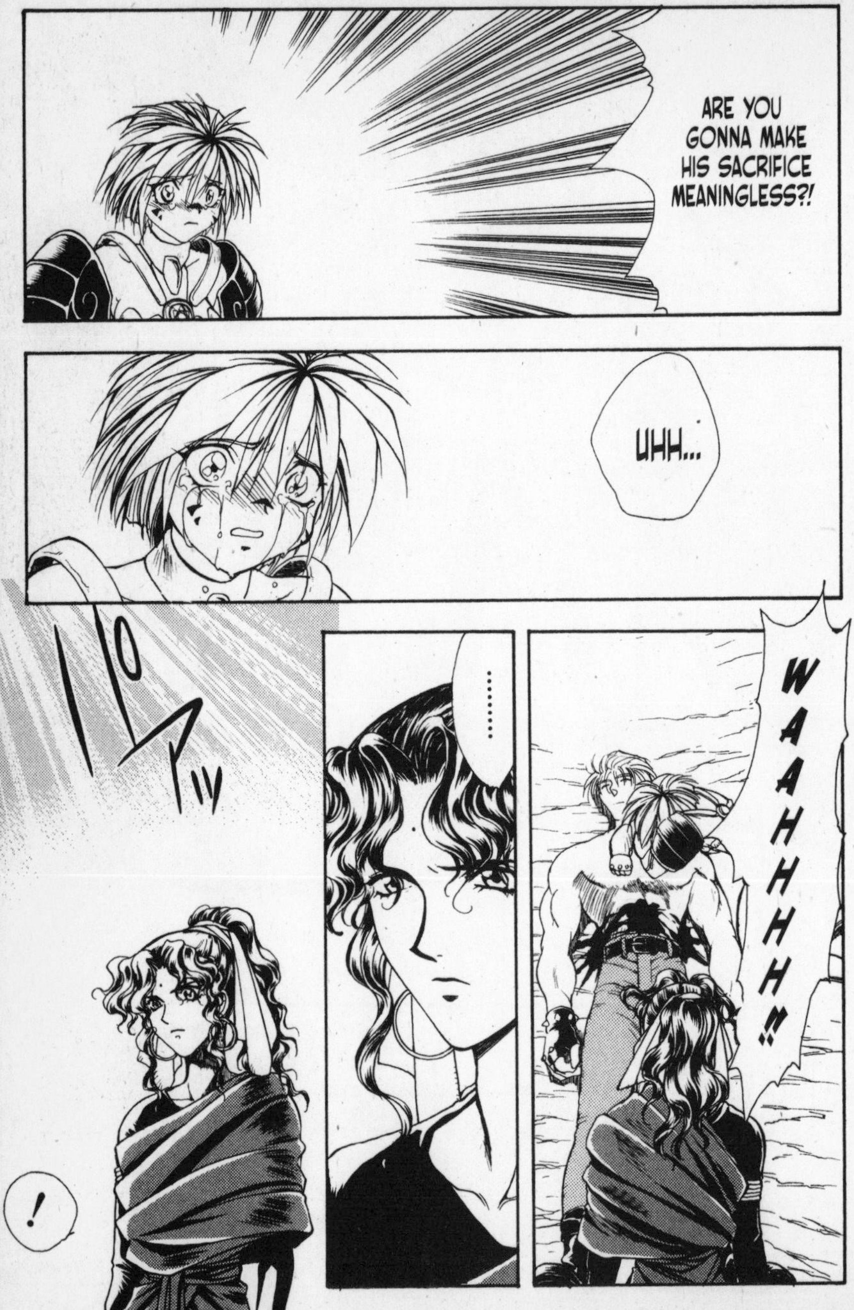
ARE YOU GONNA MAKE HIS SACRIFICE MEANINGLESS?!
UHH...
WAAHHHH!!
......
!

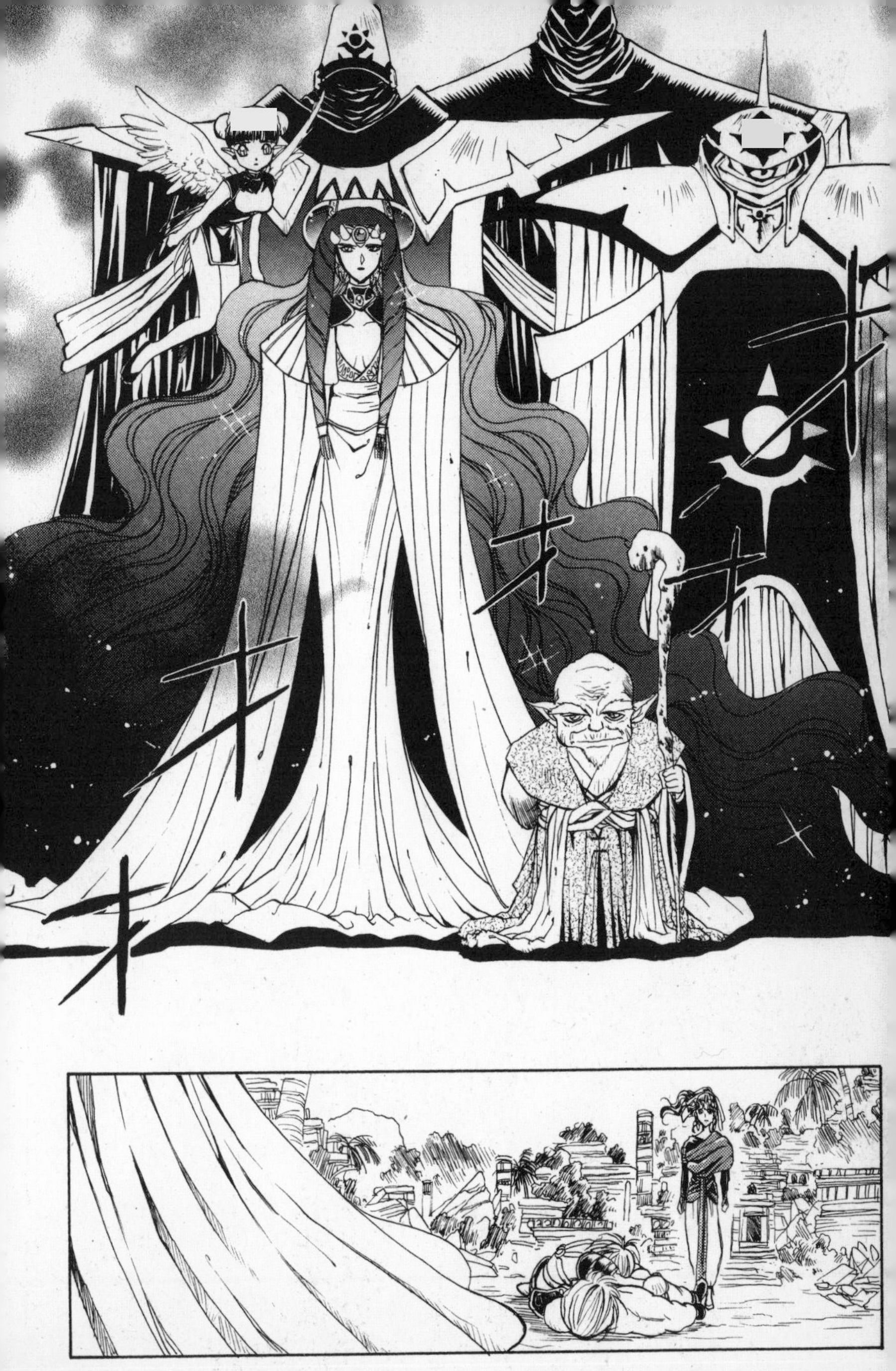
キ
キ
キ
キ
キ

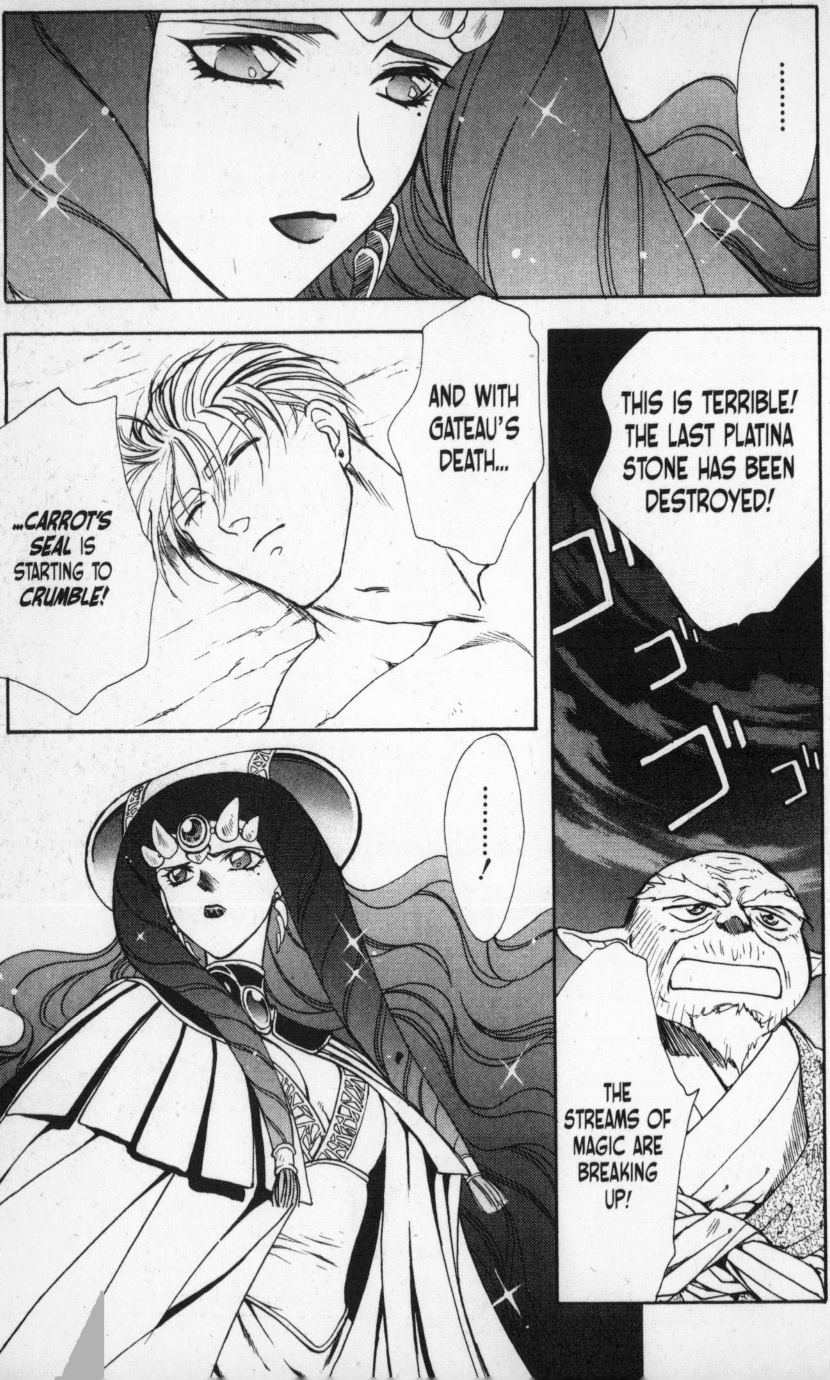
......
THIS IS TERRIBLE! THE LAST PLATINA STONE HAS BEEN DESTROYED!
ゴゴゴゴゴ
THE STREAMS OF MAGIC ARE BREAKING UP!
AND WITH GATEAU'S DEATH...
...CARROT'S SEAL IS STARTING TO CRUMBLE!
......!

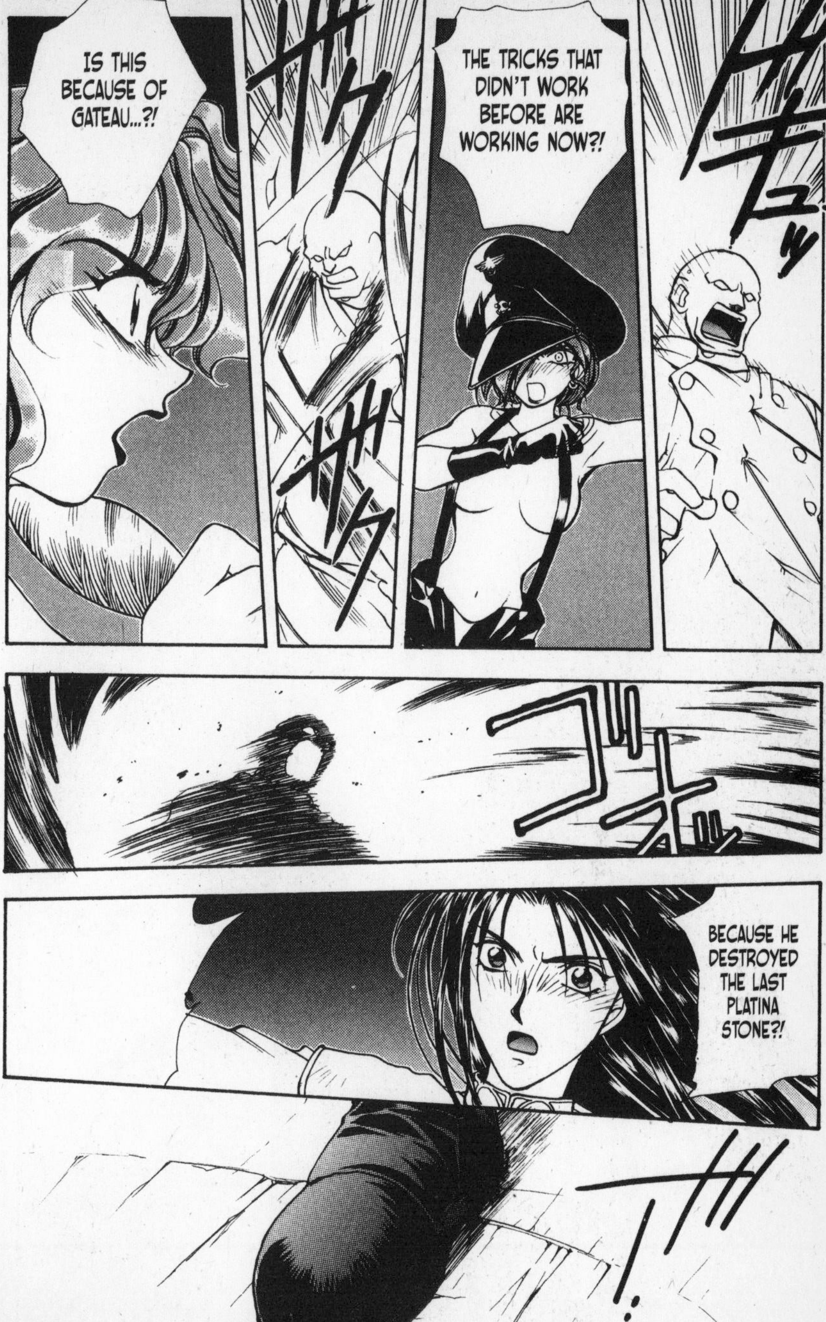
THE TRICKS THAT DIDN'T WORK BEFORE ARE WORKING NOW?!
IS THIS BECAUSE OF GATEAU...?!
BECAUSE HE DESTROYED THE LAST PLATINA STONE?!

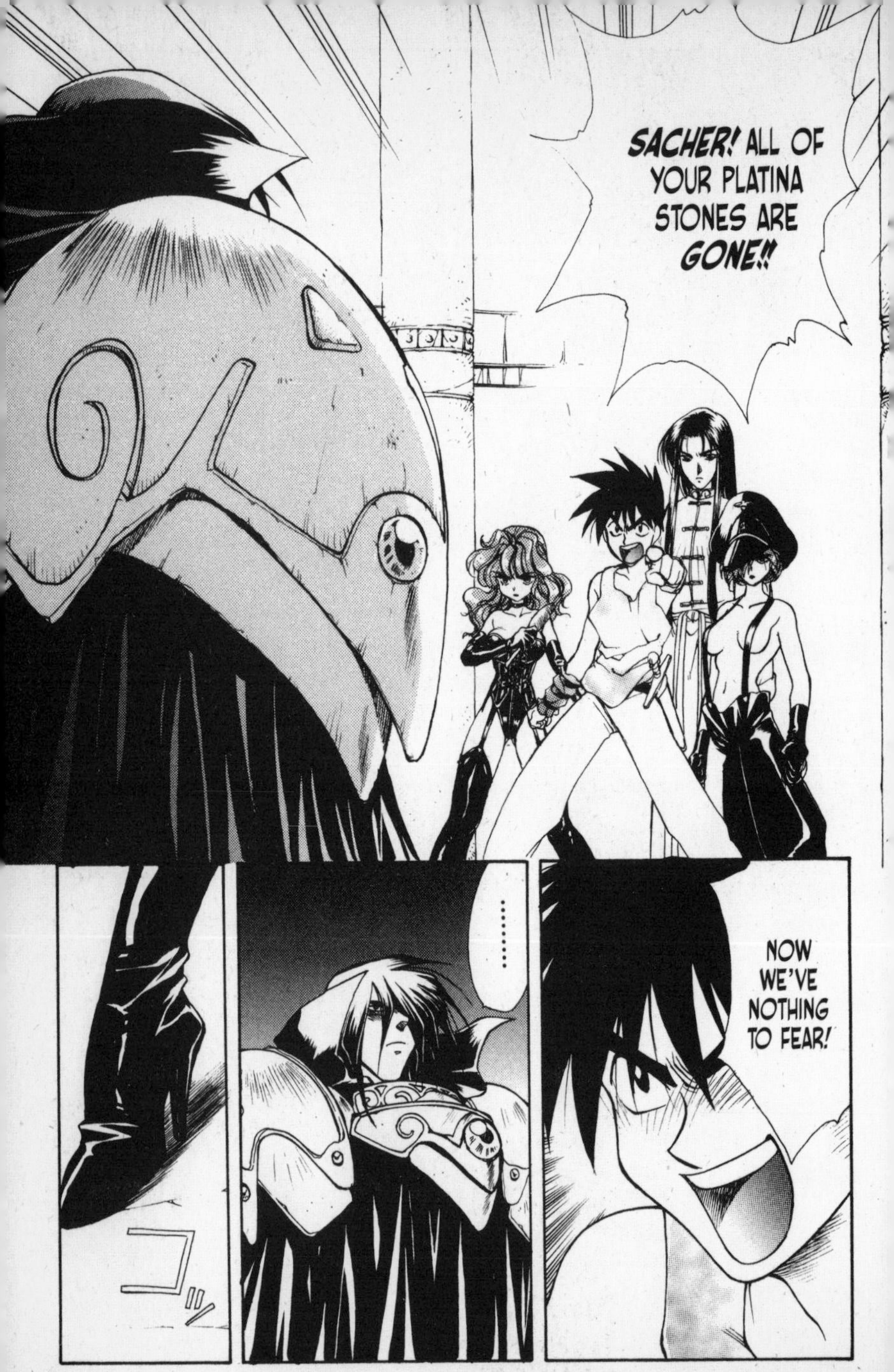
SACHER! ALL OF YOUR PLATINA STONES ARE GONE!!
NOW WE'VE NOTHING TO FEAR!
......

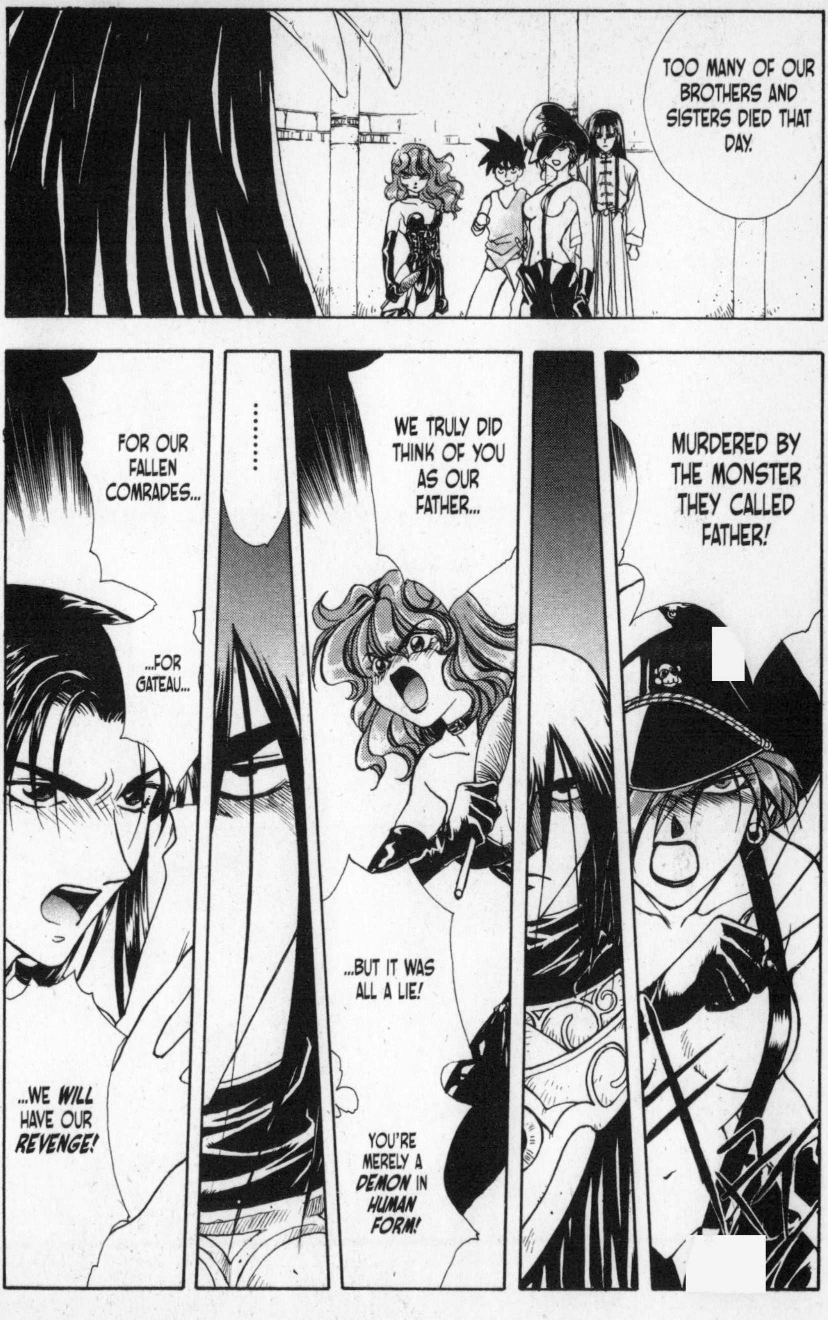
TOO MANY OF OUR BROTHERS AND SISTERS DIED THAT DAY.
MURDERED BY THE MONSTER THEY CALLED FATHER!
WE TRULY DID THINK OF YOU AS OUR FATHER...
...BUT IT WAS ALL A LIE!
YOU'RE MERELY A *DEMON* IN *HUMAN FORM!*
......
FOR OUR FALLEN COMRADES...
...FOR GATEAU...
...WE *WILL* HAVE OUR *REVENGE!*

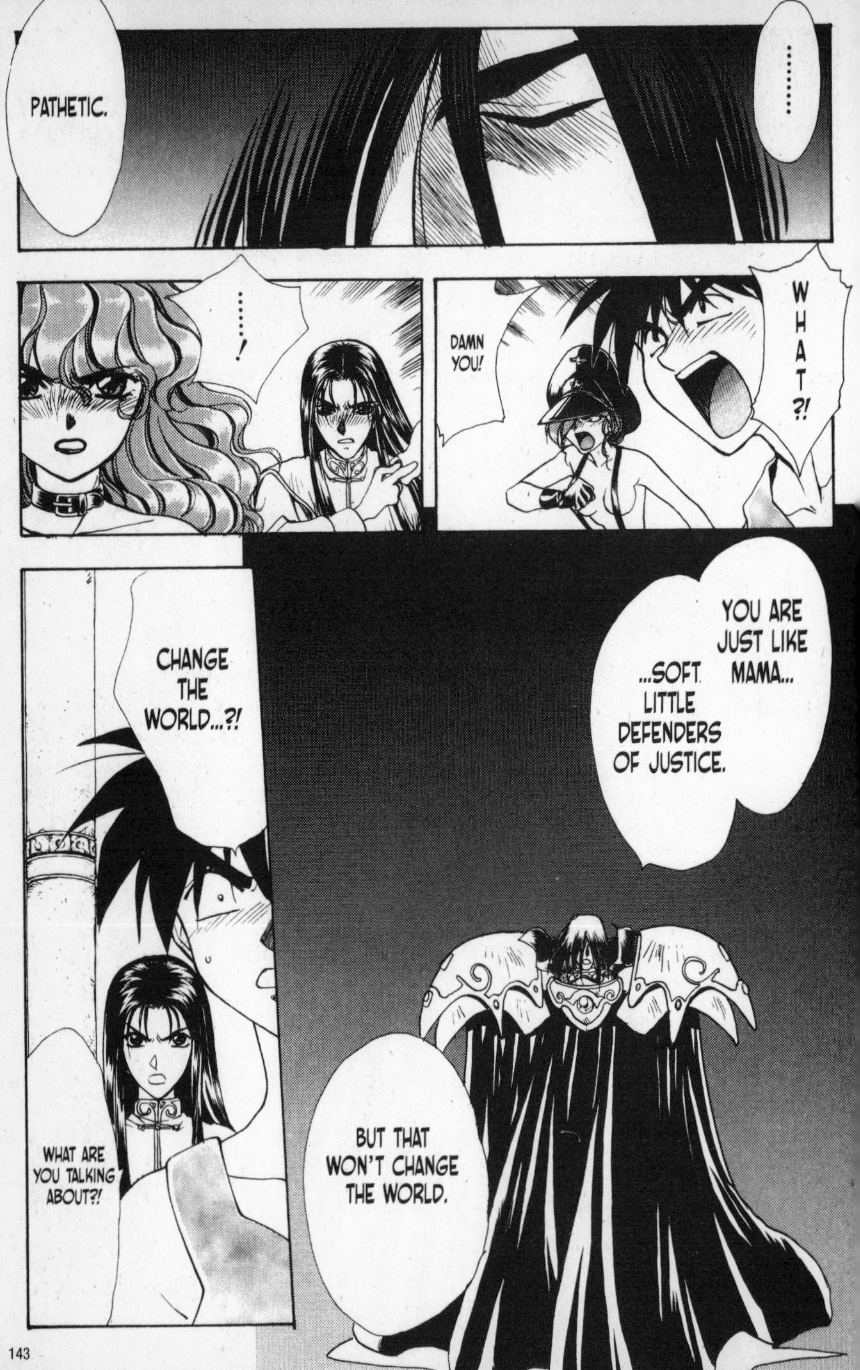
......
PATHETIC.
WHAT?!
DAMN YOU!
......!
YOU ARE JUST LIKE MAMA... ...SOFT LITTLE DEFENDERS OF JUSTICE.
BUT THAT WON'T CHANGE THE WORLD.
CHANGE THE WORLD...?!
WHAT ARE YOU TALKING ABOUT?!

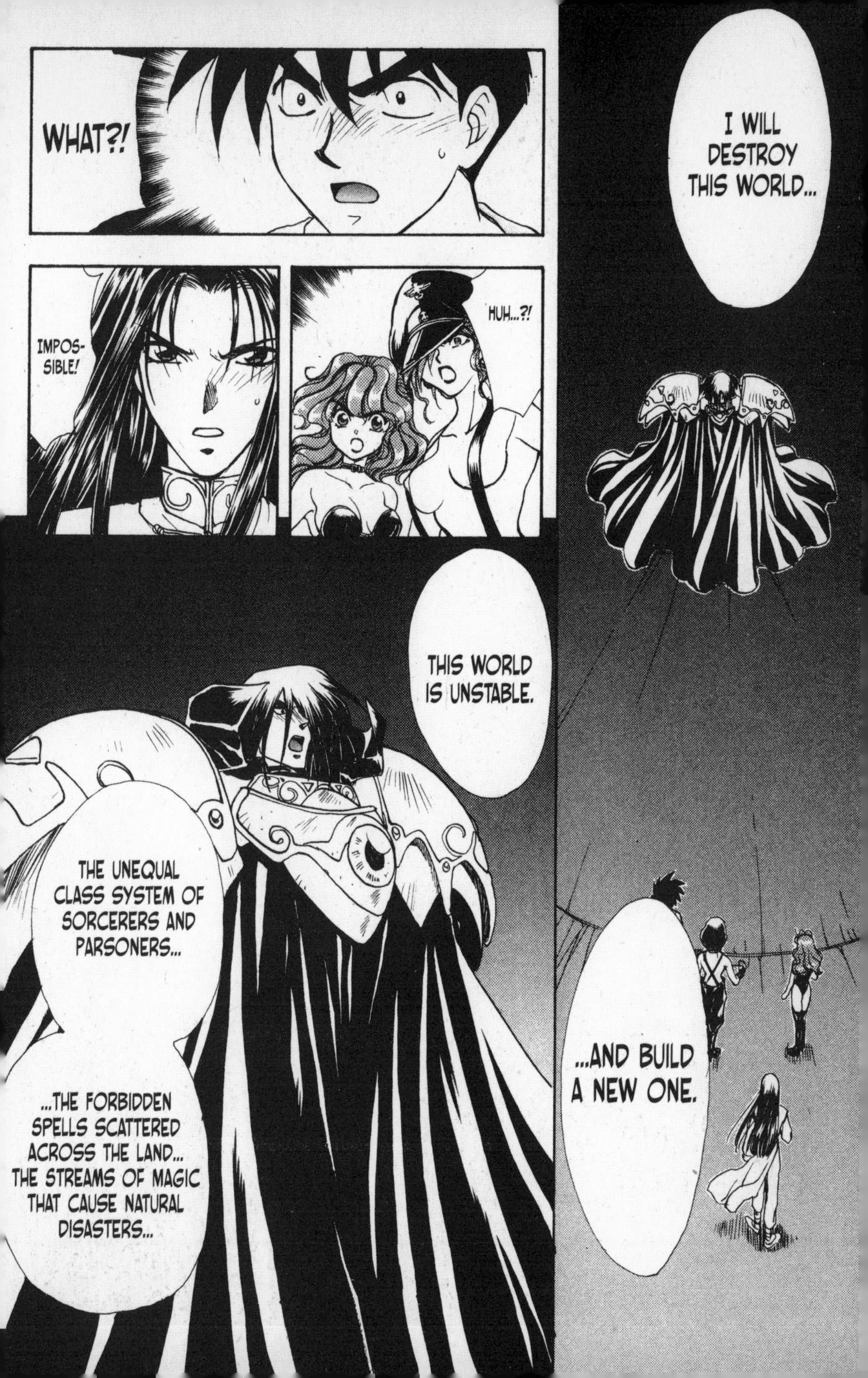
I WILL DESTROY THIS WORLD...
...AND BUILD A NEW ONE.
WHAT?!
HUH...?!
IMPOS-SIBLE!
THIS WORLD IS UNSTABLE.
THE UNEQUAL CLASS SYSTEM OF SORCERERS AND PARSONERS...
...THE FORBIDDEN SPELLS SCATTERED ACROSS THE LAND... THE STREAMS OF MAGIC THAT CAUSE NATURAL DISASTERS...

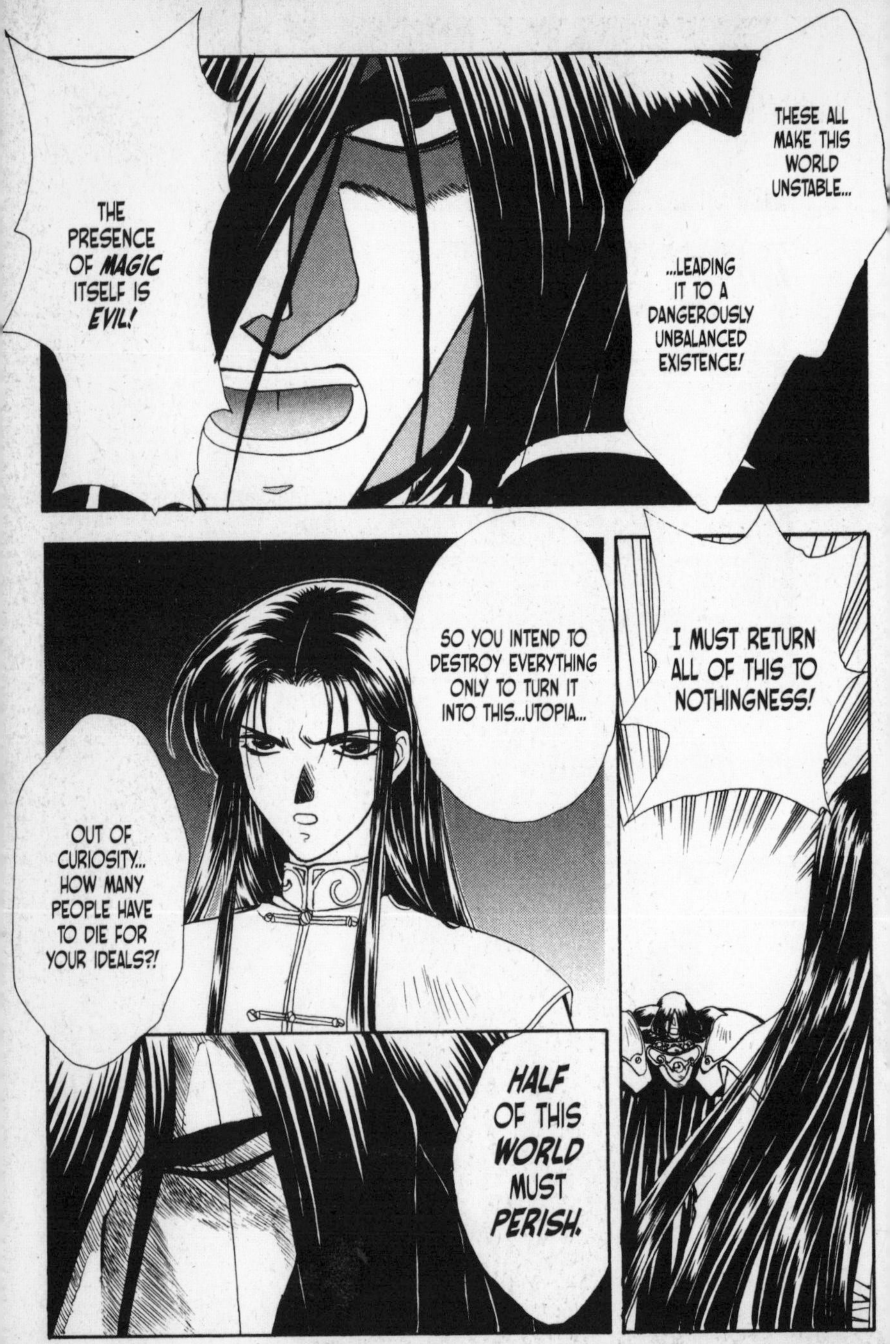
THESE ALL MAKE THIS WORLD UNSTABLE...
...LEADING IT TO A DANGEROUSLY UNBALANCED EXISTENCE!
THE PRESENCE OF MAGIC ITSELF IS EVIL!
I MUST RETURN ALL OF THIS TO NOTHINGNESS!
SO YOU INTEND TO DESTROY EVERYTHING ONLY TO TURN IT INTO THIS...UTOPIA...
OUT OF CURIOSITY... HOW MANY PEOPLE HAVE TO DIE FOR YOUR IDEALS?!
HALF OF THIS WORLD MUST PERISH.

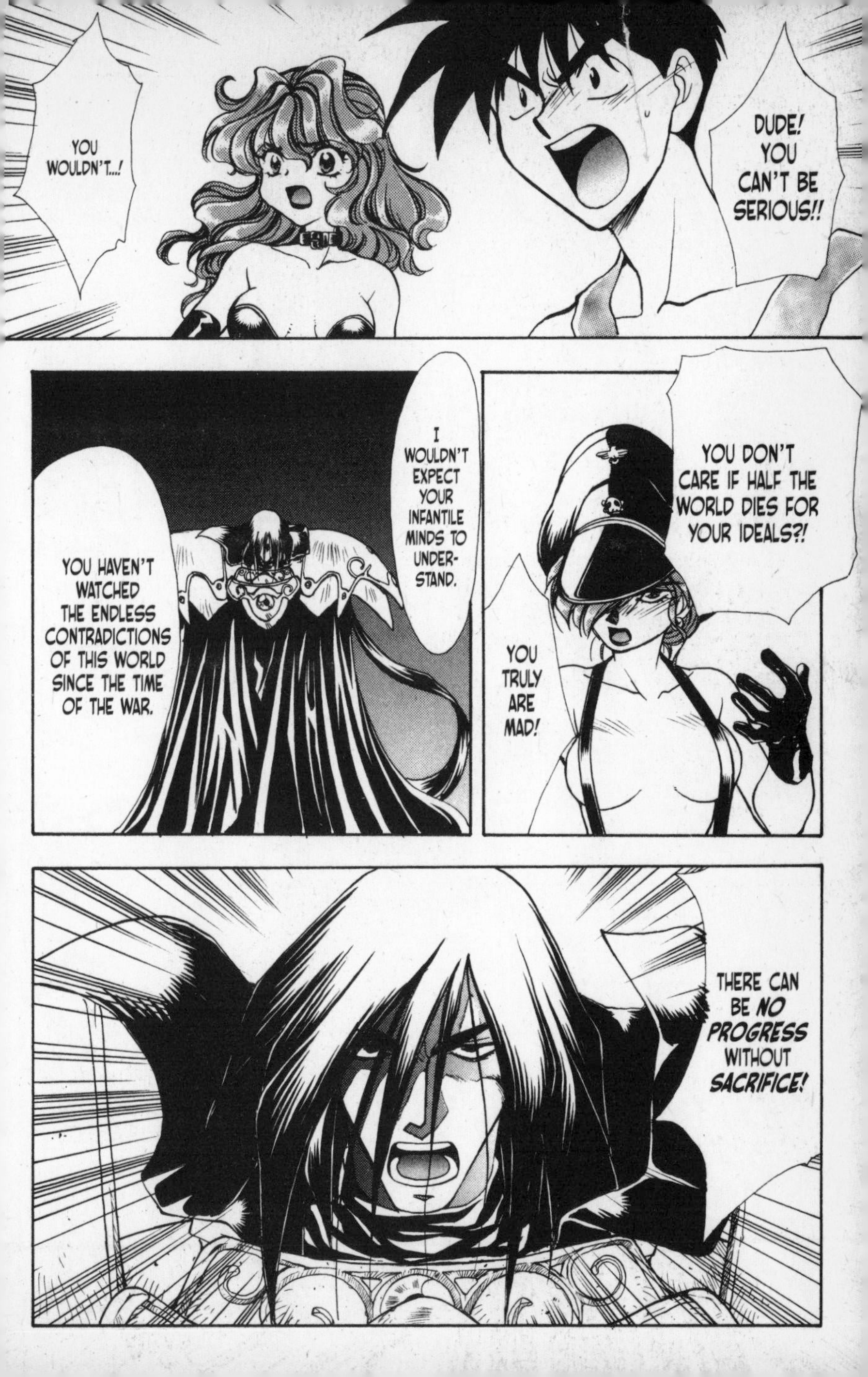
DUDE! YOU CAN'T BE SERIOUS!!
YOU WOULDN'T...!
YOU DON'T CARE IF HALF THE WORLD DIES FOR YOUR IDEALS?!
YOU TRULY ARE MAD!
I WOULDN'T EXPECT YOUR INFANTILE MINDS TO UNDER-STAND.
YOU HAVEN'T WATCHED THE ENDLESS CONTRADICTIONS OF THIS WORLD SINCE THE TIME OF THE WAR.
THERE CAN BE *NO PROGRESS* WITHOUT *SACRIFICE!*

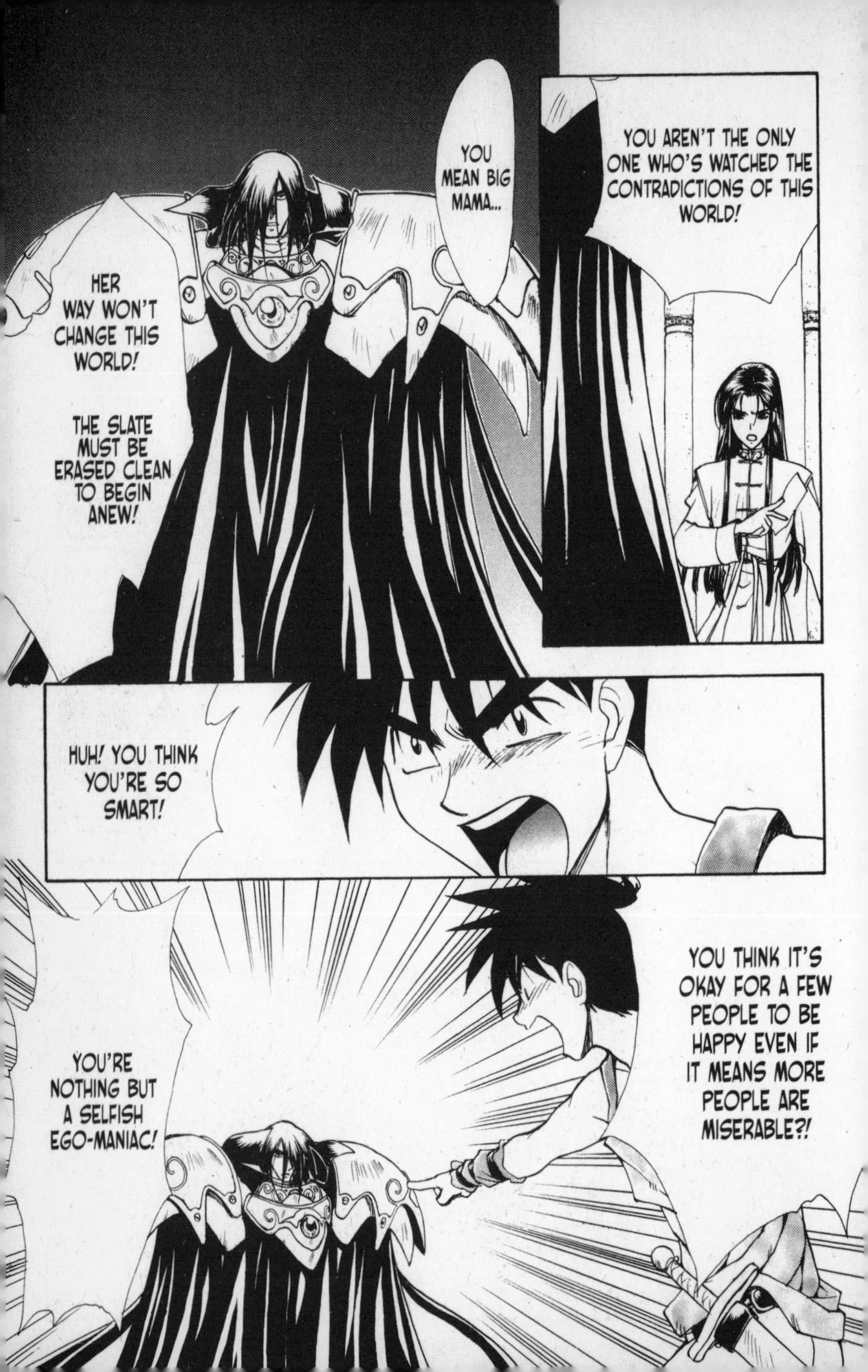
YOU AREN'T THE ONLY ONE WHO'S WATCHED THE CONTRADICTIONS OF THIS WORLD!
YOU MEAN BIG MAMA...
HER WAY WON'T CHANGE THIS WORLD!
THE SLATE MUST BE ERASED CLEAN TO BEGIN ANEW!
HUH! YOU THINK YOU'RE SO SMART!
YOU THINK IT'S OKAY FOR A FEW PEOPLE TO BE HAPPY EVEN IF IT MEANS MORE PEOPLE ARE MISERABLE?!
YOU'RE NOTHING BUT A SELFISH EGO-MANIAC!

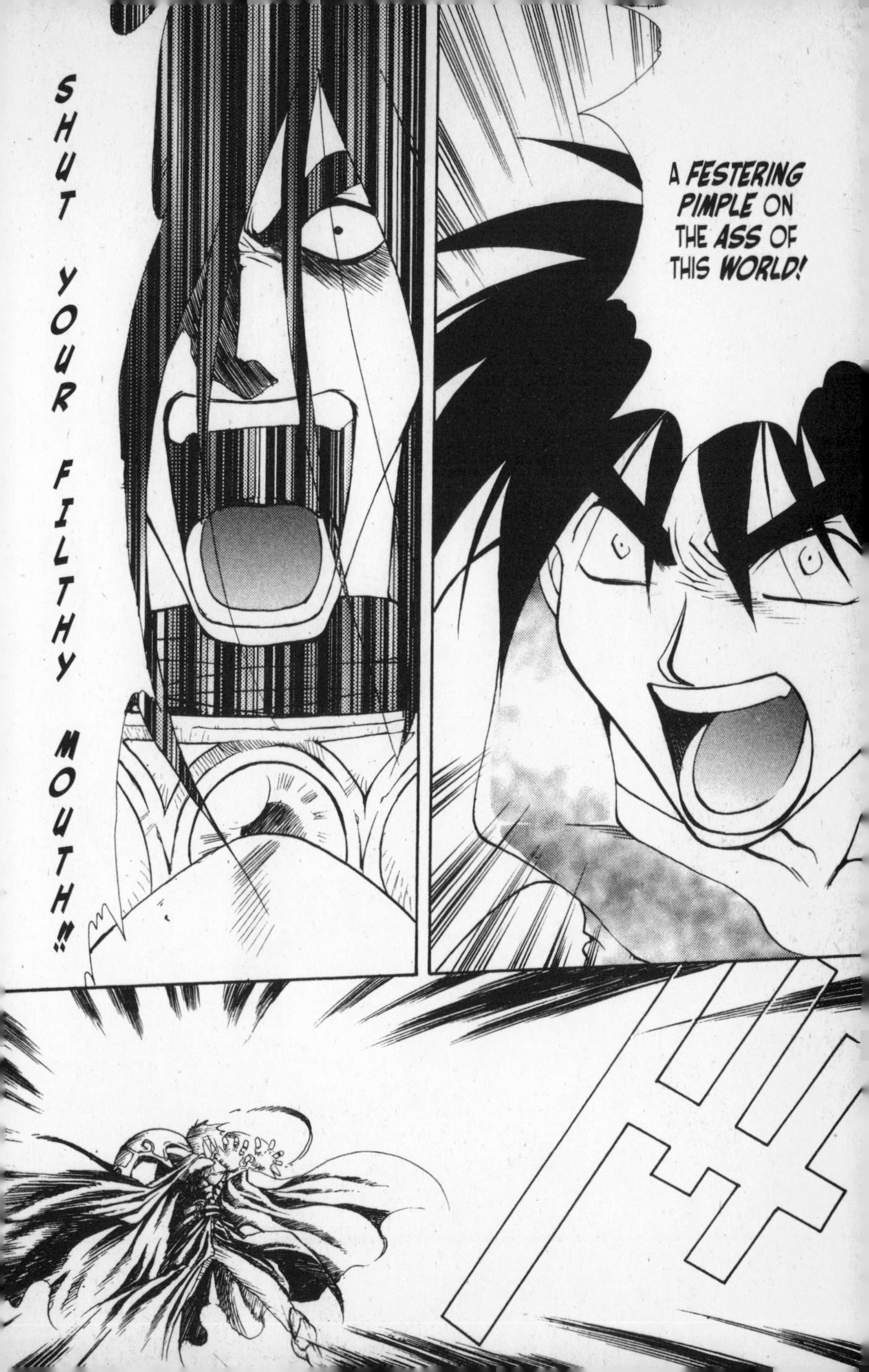
A FESTERING PIMPLE ON THE ASS OF THIS WORLD!
SHUT YOUR FILTHY MOUTH!!

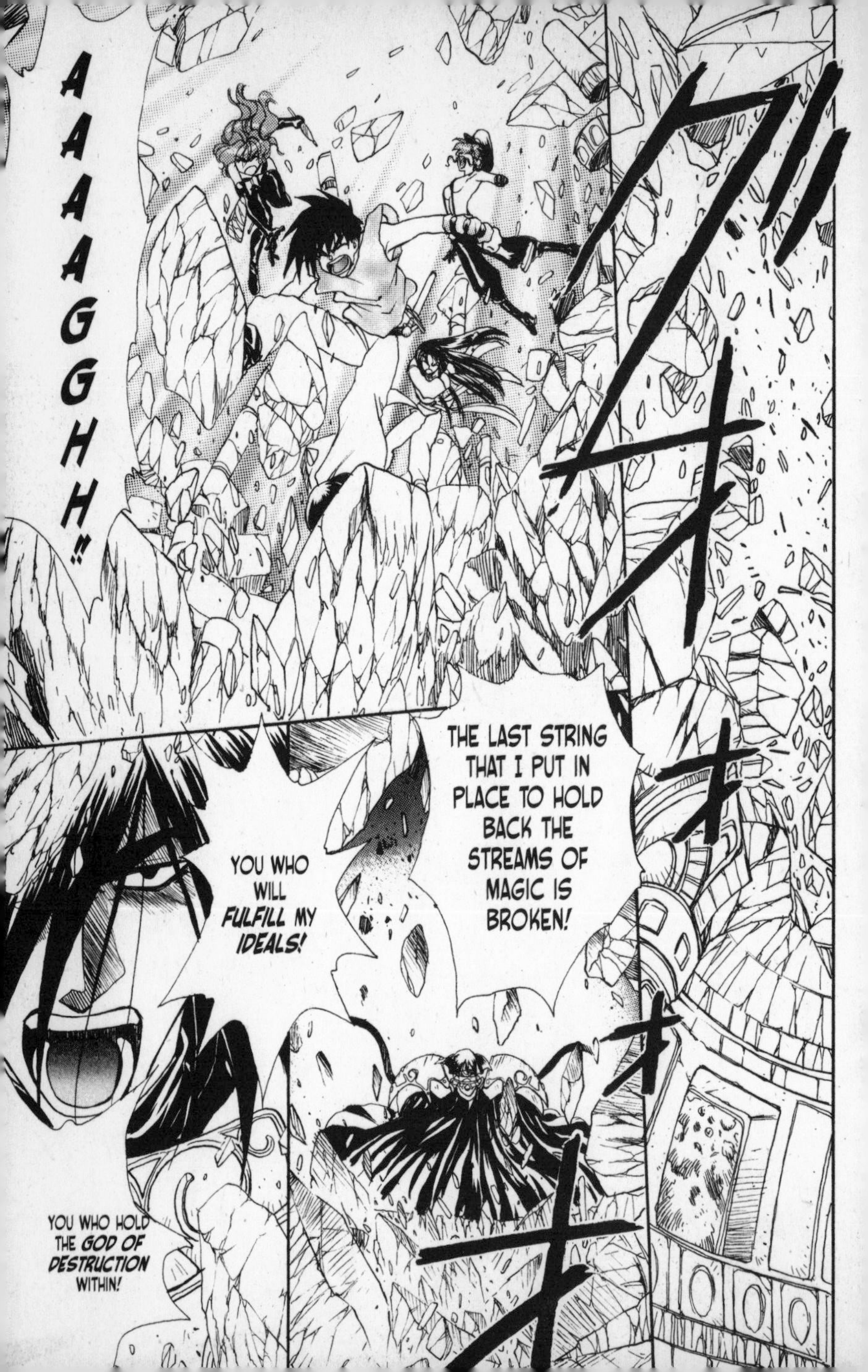
AAAAAGGHH!!
THE LAST STRING THAT I PUT IN PLACE TO HOLD BACK THE STREAMS OF MAGIC IS BROKEN!
YOU WHO WILL *FULFILL* MY *IDEALS!*
YOU WHO HOLD THE *GOD OF DESTRUCTION* WITHIN!

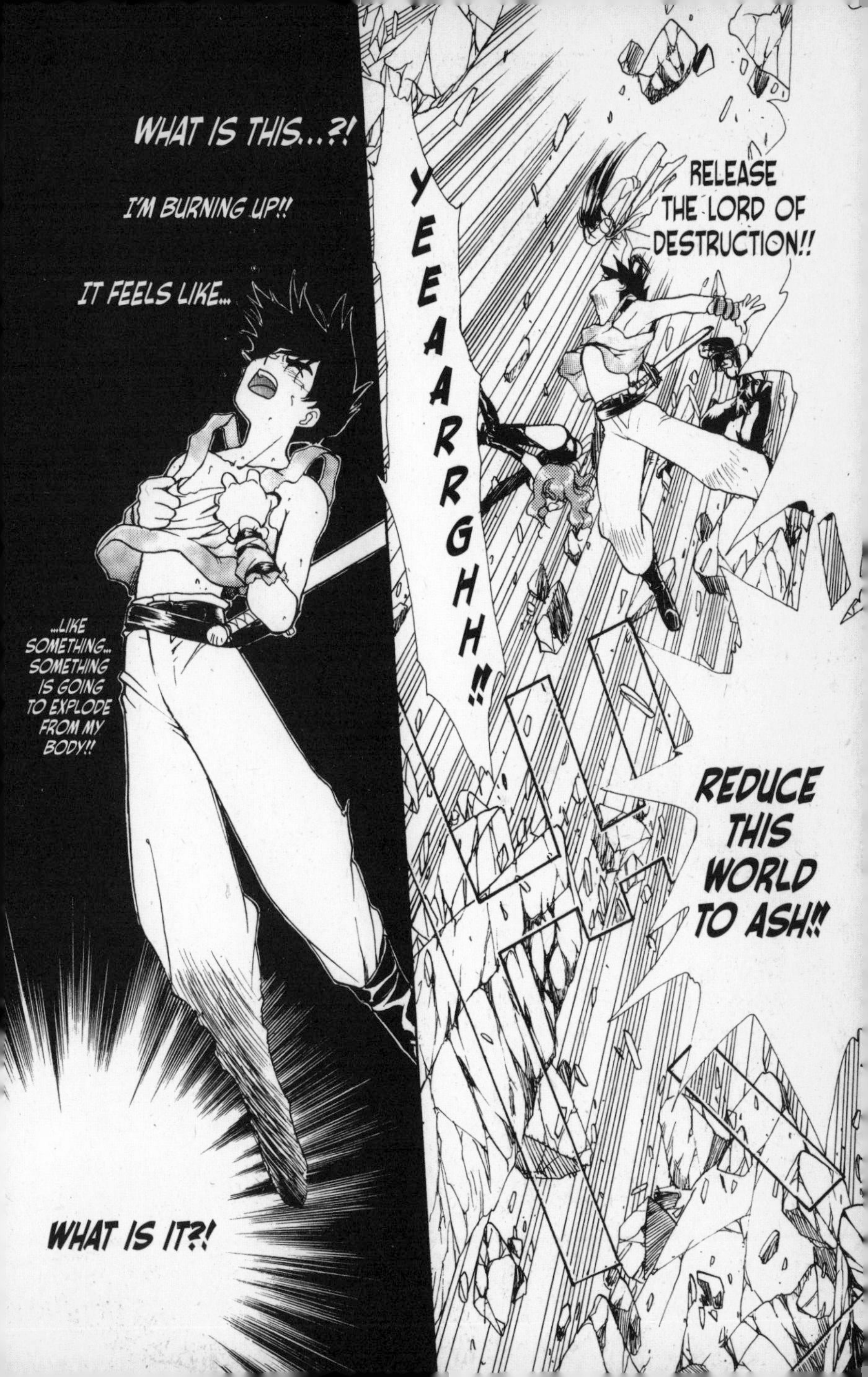
RELEASE THE LORD OF DESTRUCTION!!
YEEAARRGHH!!
REDUCE THIS WORLD TO ASH!!
WHAT IS THIS...?!
I'M BURNING UP!!
IT FEELS LIKE...
...LIKE SOMETHING... SOMETHING IS GOING TO EXPLODE FROM MY BODY!!
WHAT IS IT?!

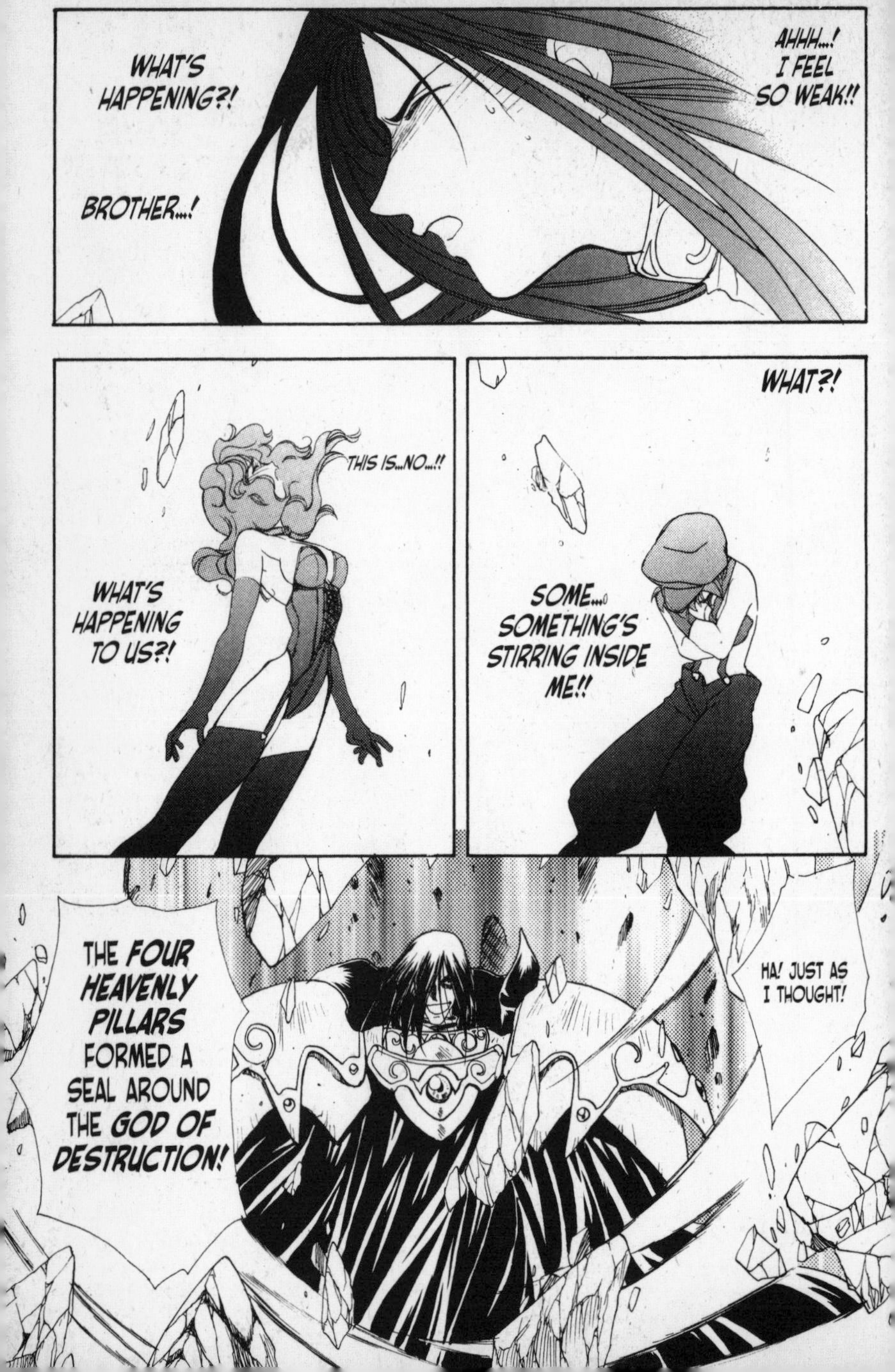
AHHH...! I FEEL SO WEAK!!
WHAT'S HAPPENING?!
BROTHER...!
WHAT?!
SOME... SOMETHING'S STIRRING INSIDE ME!!
THIS IS...NO...!!
WHAT'S HAPPENING TO US?!
HA! JUST AS I THOUGHT!
THE FOUR HEAVENLY PILLARS FORMED A SEAL AROUND THE GOD OF DESTRUCTION!

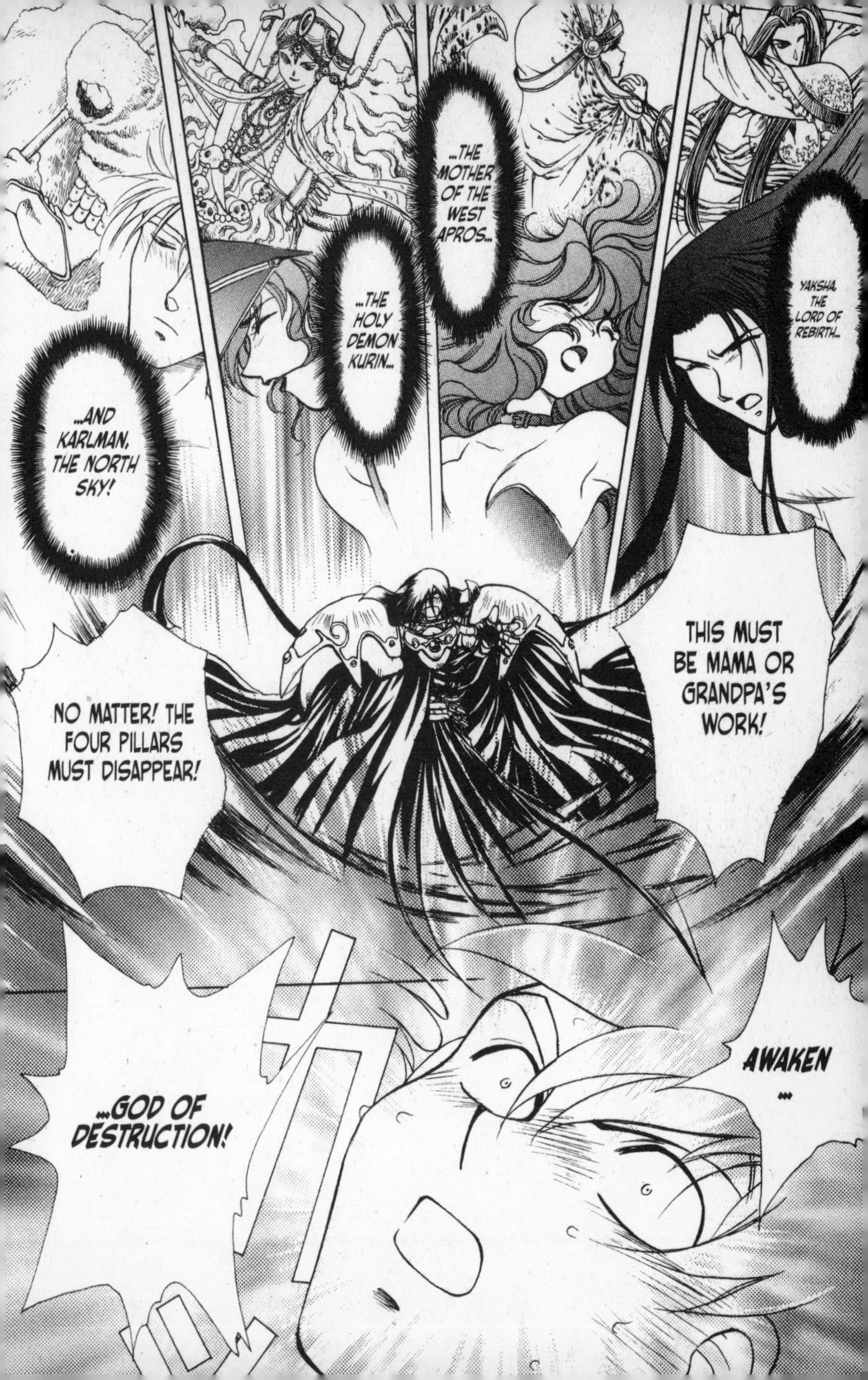
YAKSHA, THE LORD OF REBIRTH...
...THE MOTHER OF THE WEST APROS...
...THE HOLY DEMON KURIN...
...AND KARLMAN, THE NORTH SKY!
THIS MUST BE MAMA OR GRANDPA'S WORK!
NO MATTER! THE FOUR PILLARS MUST DISAPPEAR!
AWAKEN ...
...GOD OF DESTRUCTION!

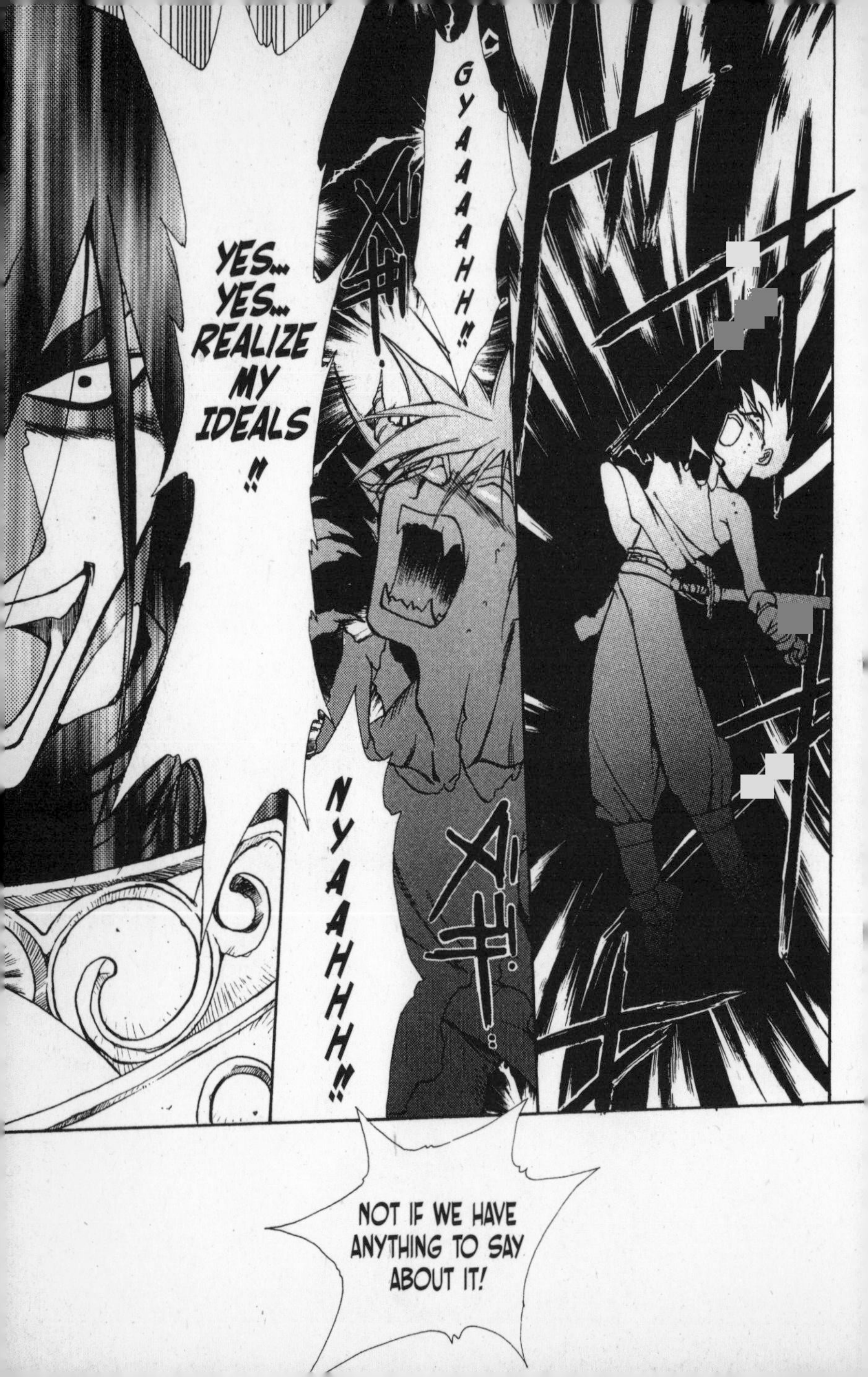
GYAAAAAHH!!
NYAAAHHHH!!
YES... YES... REALIZE MY IDEALS!!
NOT IF WE HAVE ANYTHING TO SAY ABOUT IT!

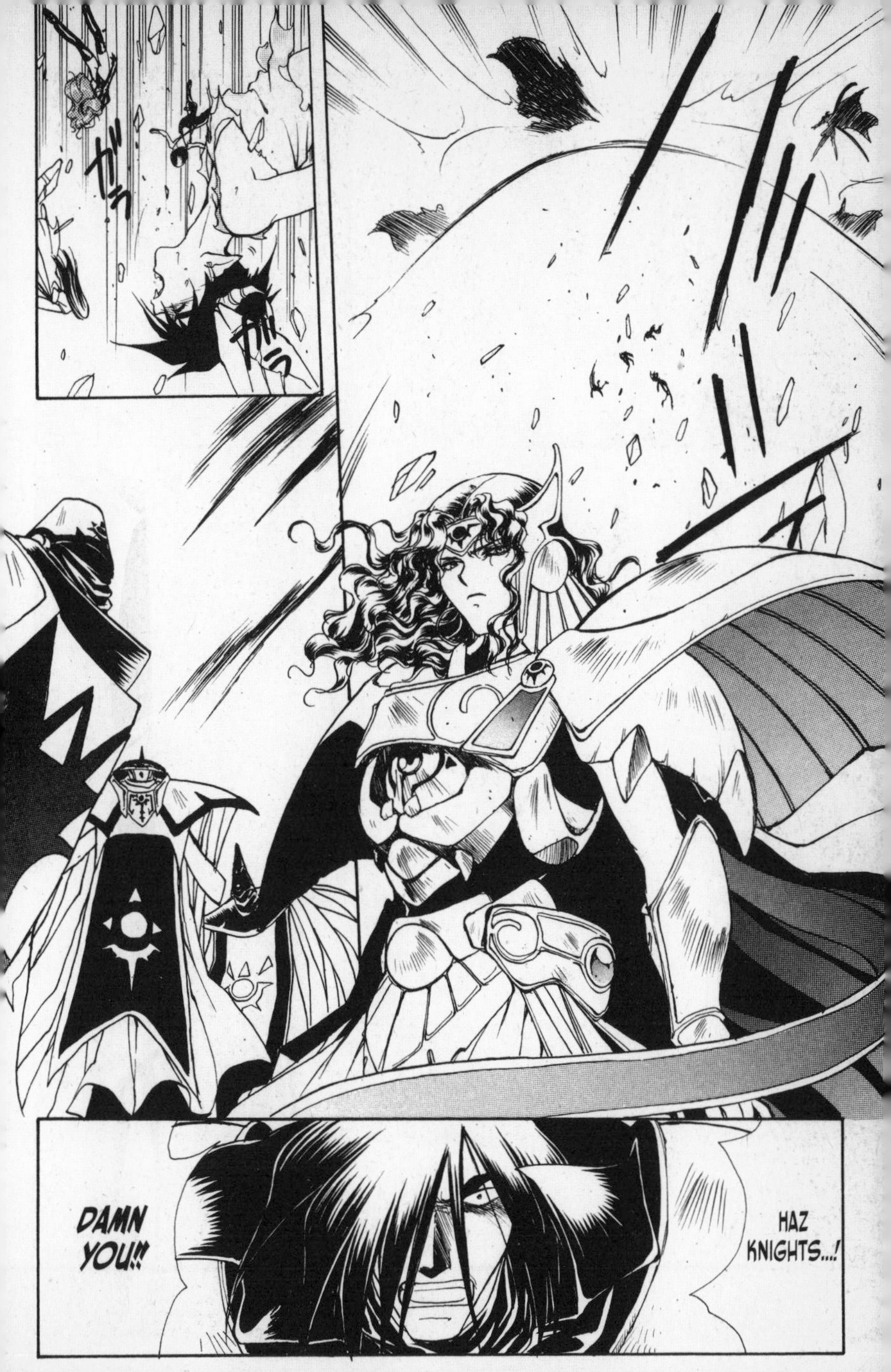
ガッ
ガラ
HAZ KNIGHTS...!
DAMN YOU!!

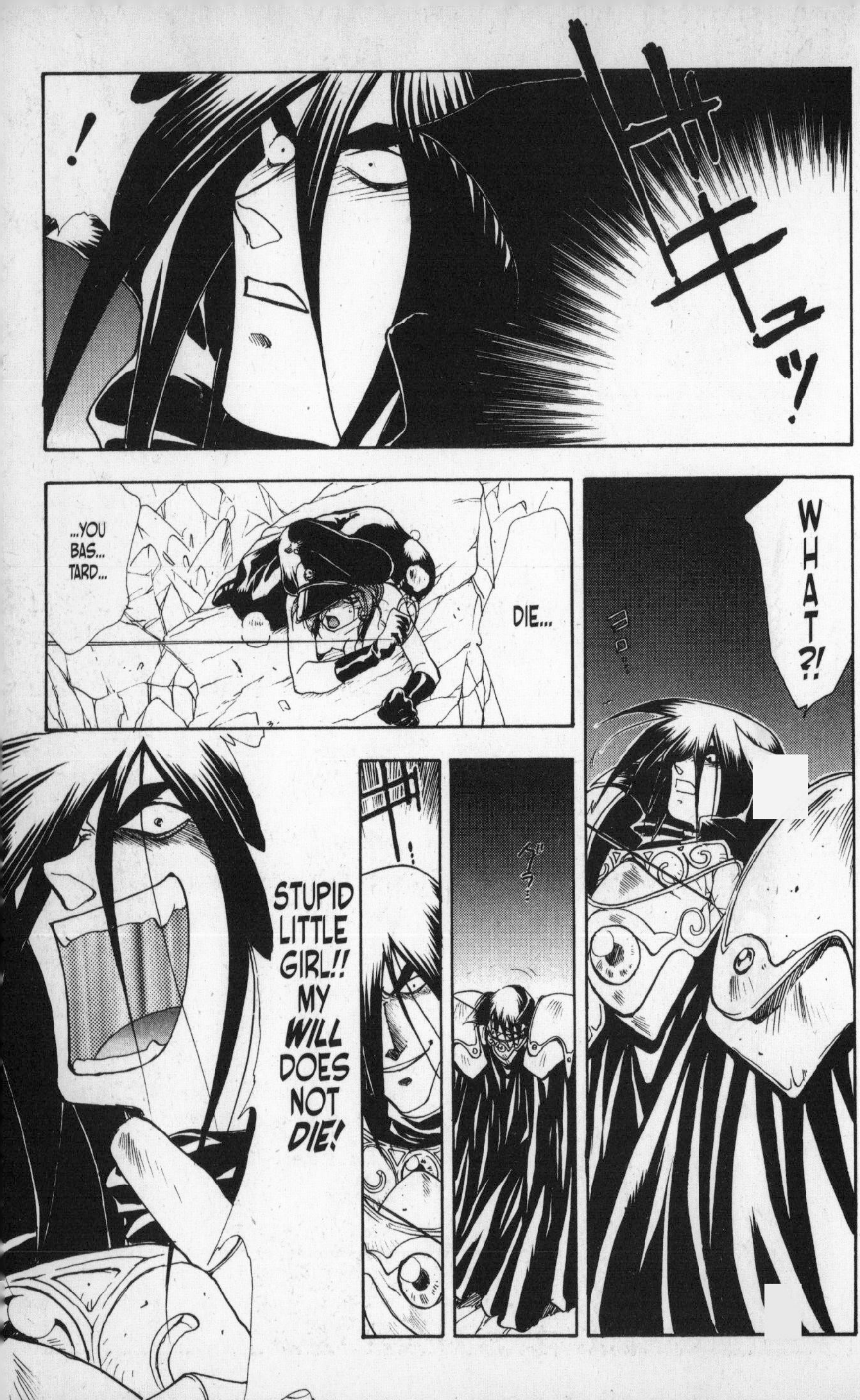
!
WHAT?!
...YOU BAS... TARD...
DIE...
STUPID LITTLE GIRL!! MY WILL DOES NOT DIE!

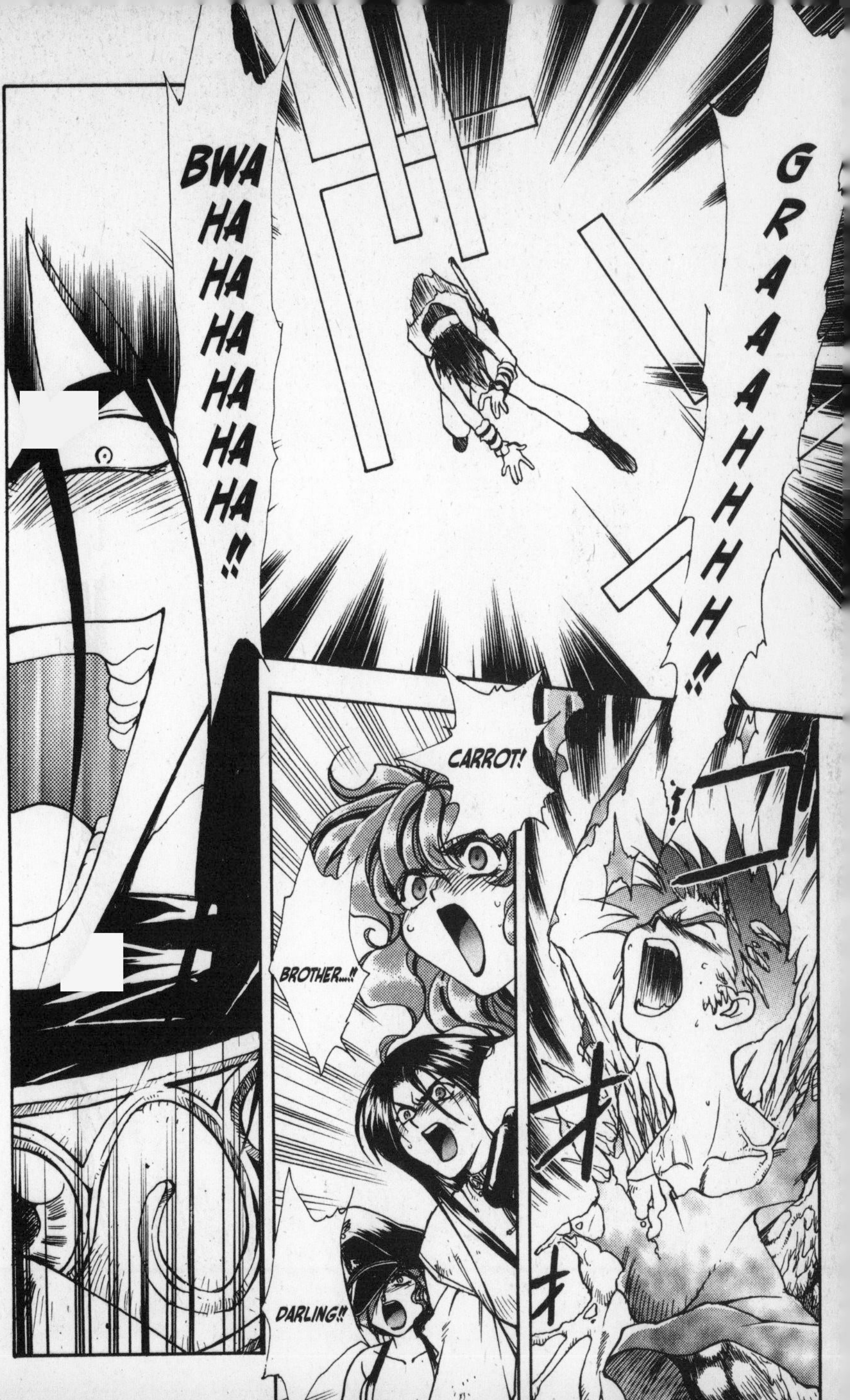
GRAAAHHHH!!
CARROT!
BROTHER...!!
DARLING!!
BWA HA HA HA HA HA HA HA!!

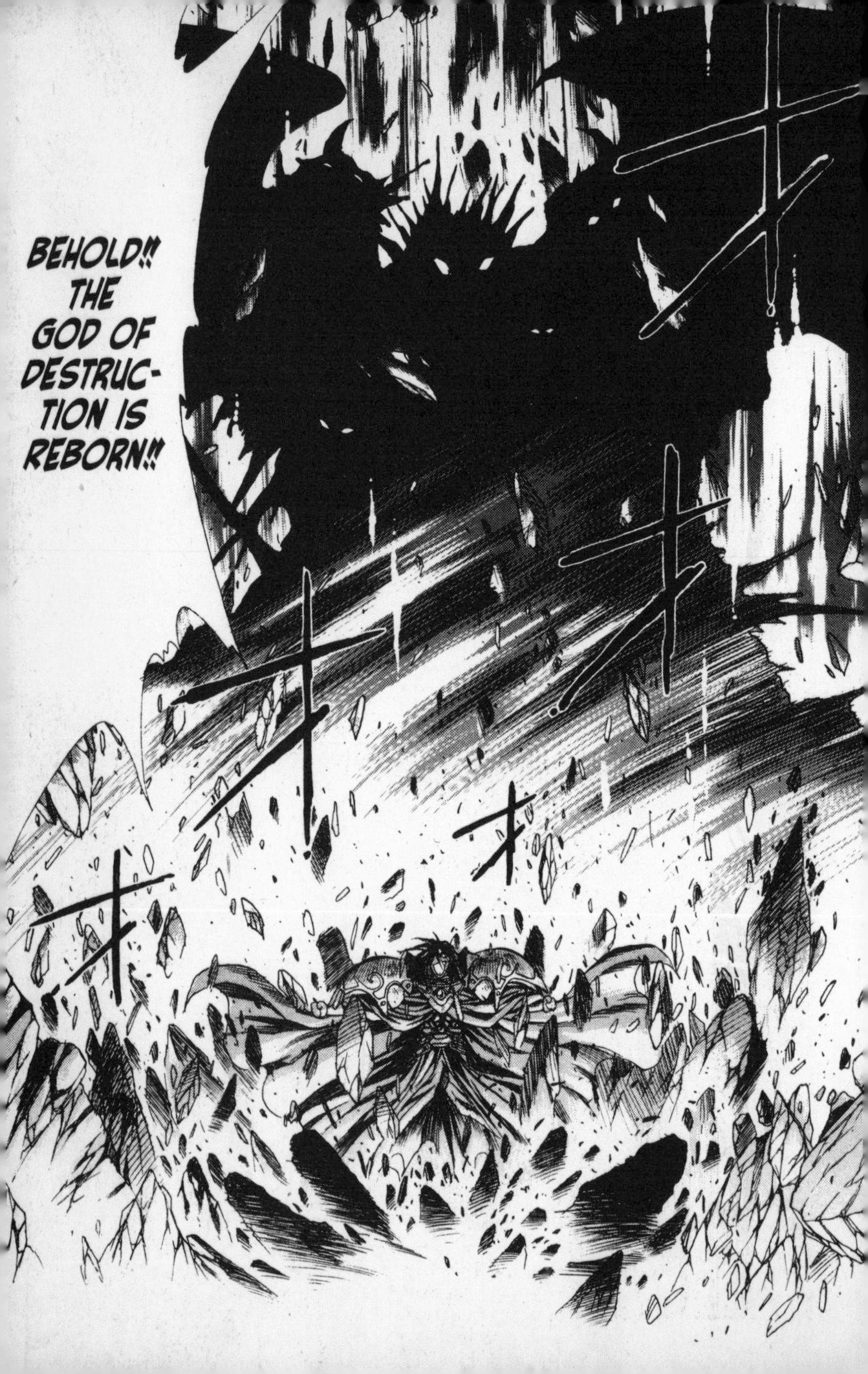
BEHOLD!! THE GOD OF DESTRUCTION IS REBORN!!

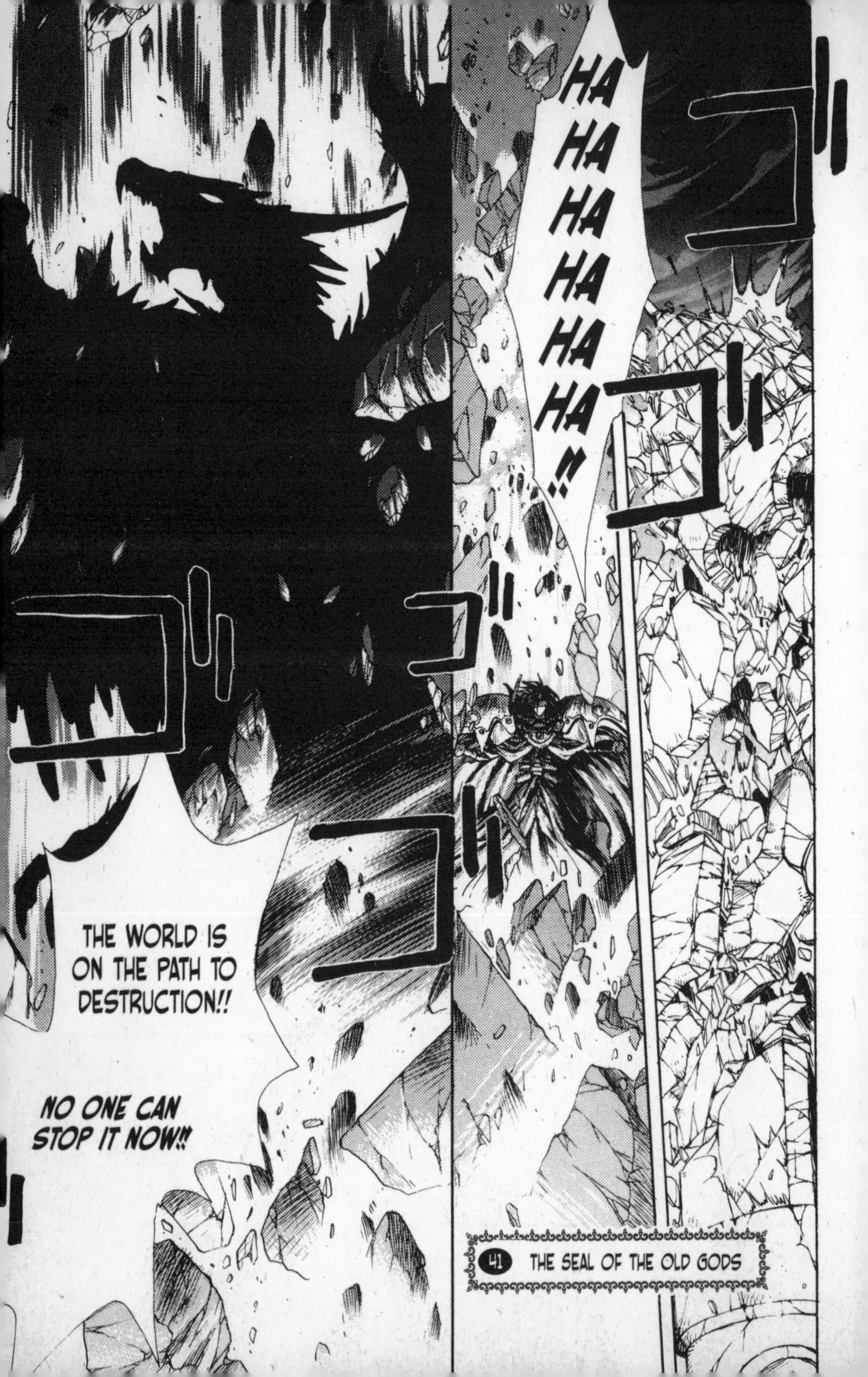
HA HA HA HA HA HA HA!!
41 THE SEAL OF THE OLD GODS
THE WORLD IS ON THE PATH TO DESTRUCTION!!
NO ONE CAN STOP IT NOW!!

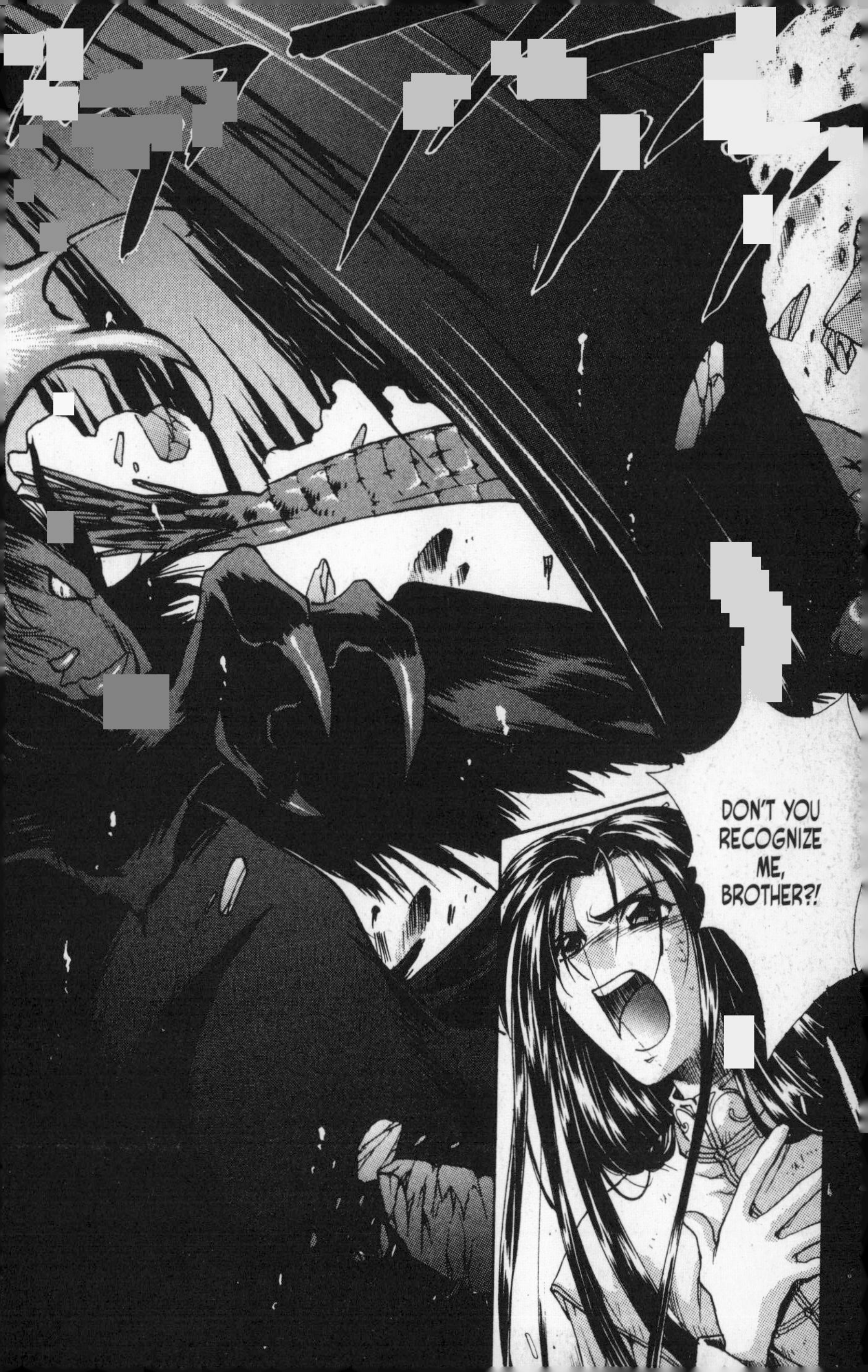
DON'T YOU RECOGNIZE ME, BROTHER?!

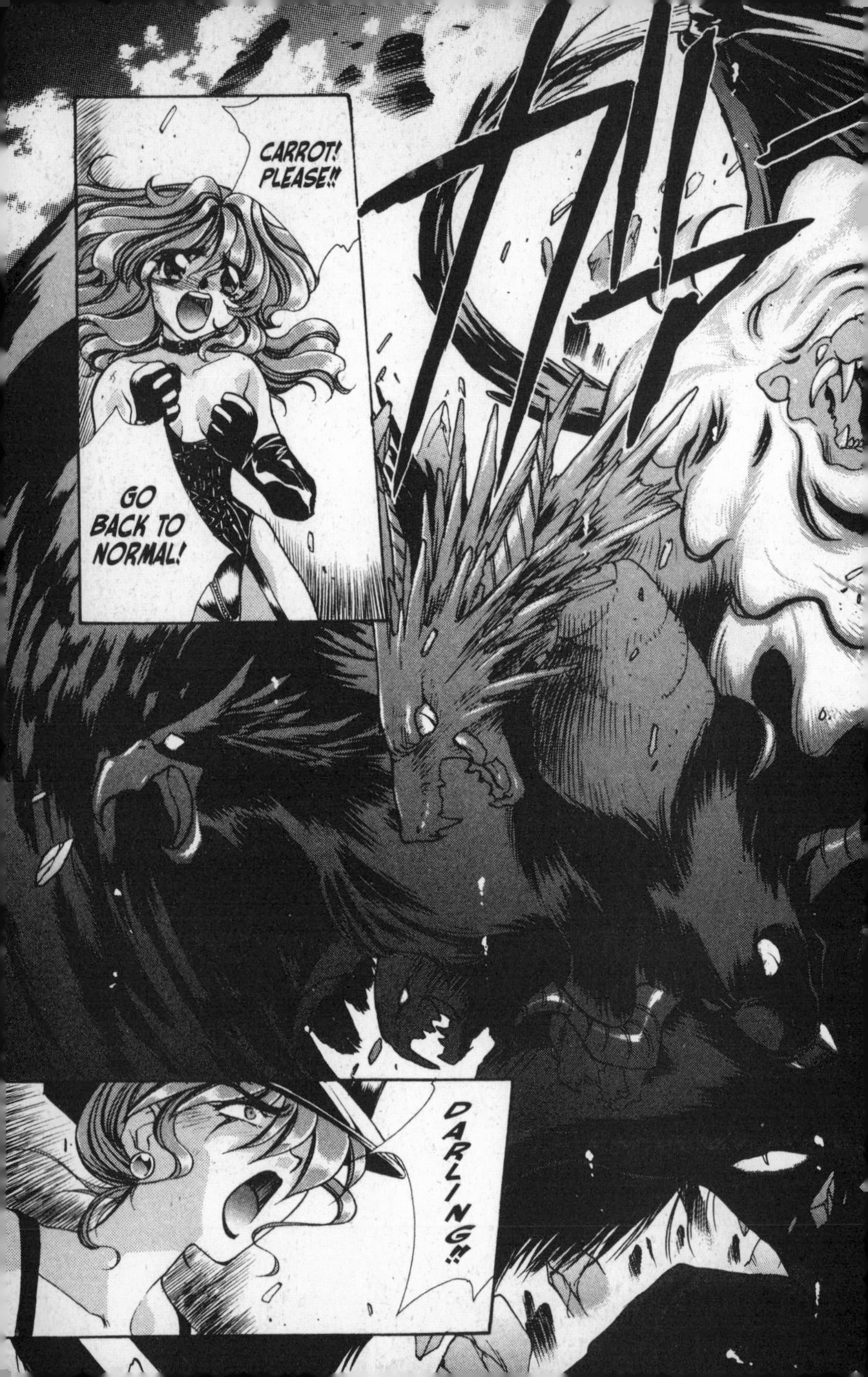
CARROT! PLEASE!!
GO BACK TO NORMAL!
DARLING!!

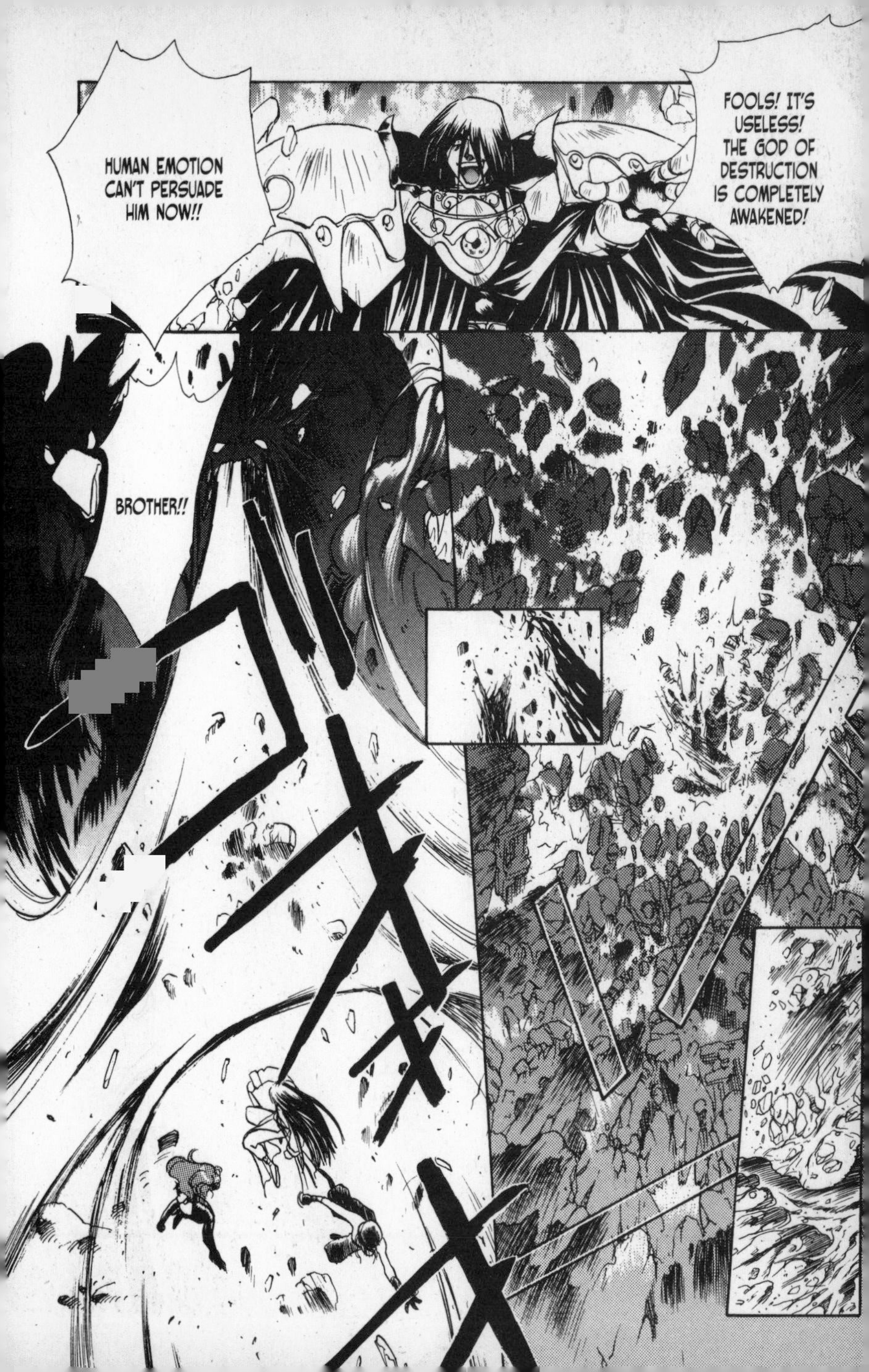
FOOLS! IT'S USELESS! THE GOD OF DESTRUCTION IS COMPLETELY AWAKENED!
HUMAN EMOTION CAN'T PERSUADE HIM NOW!!
BROTHER!!

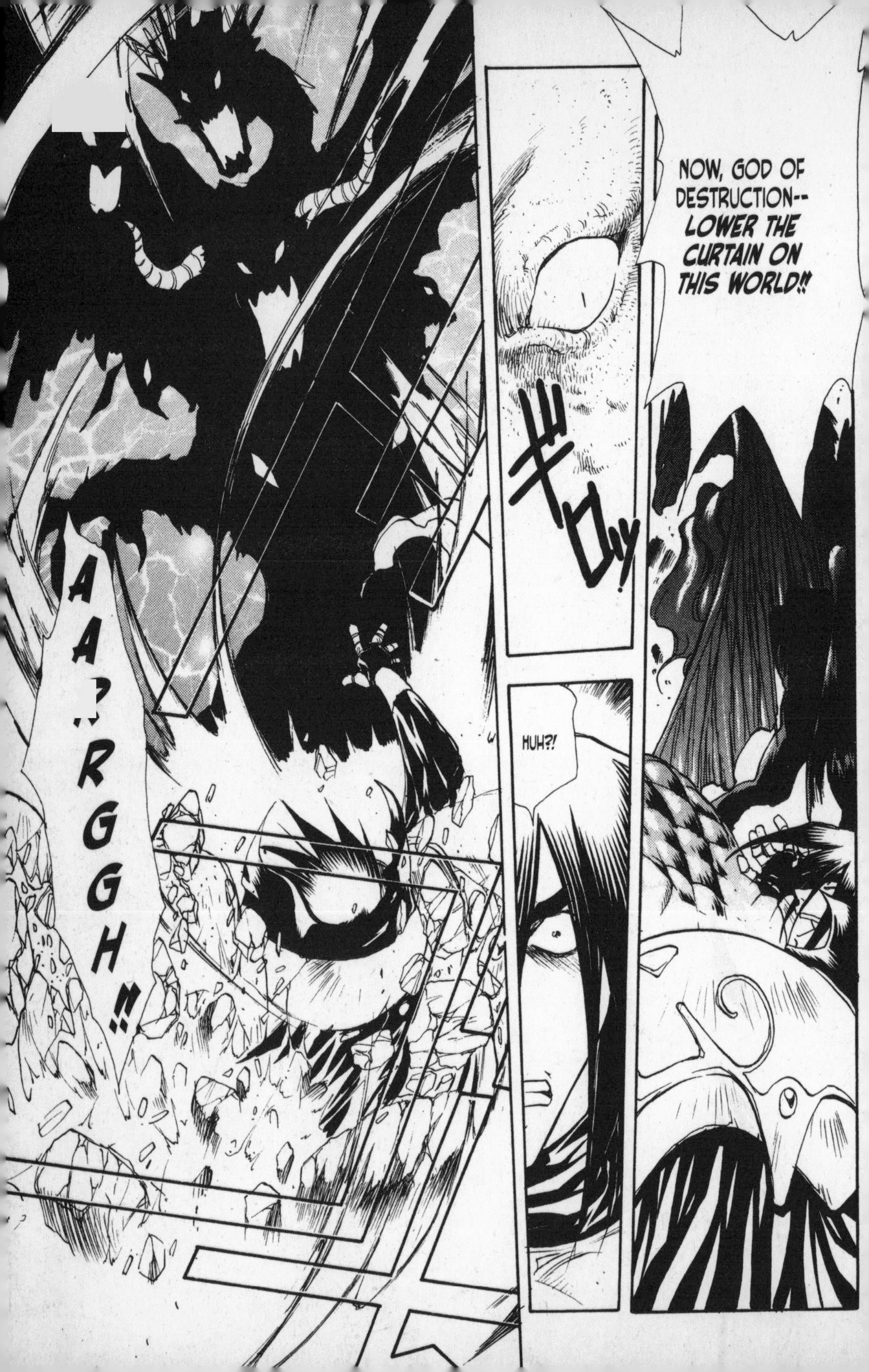
NOW, GOD OF DESTRUCTION-- LOWER THE CURTAIN ON THIS WORLD!!
ギロッ!
HUH?!
AARRGGH!!

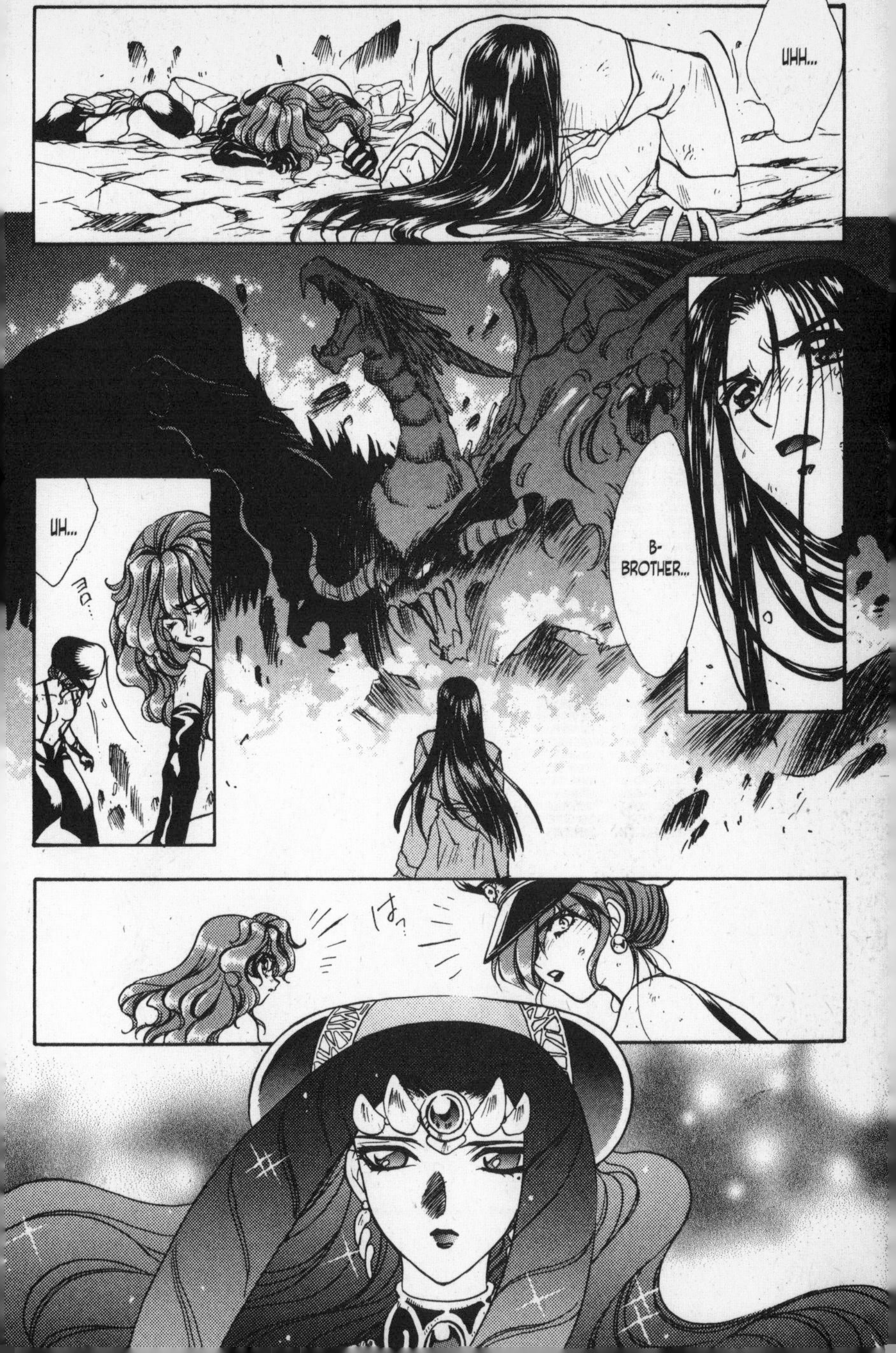
UHH...
B-
BROTHER...
UH...
ヨロ…
はっ

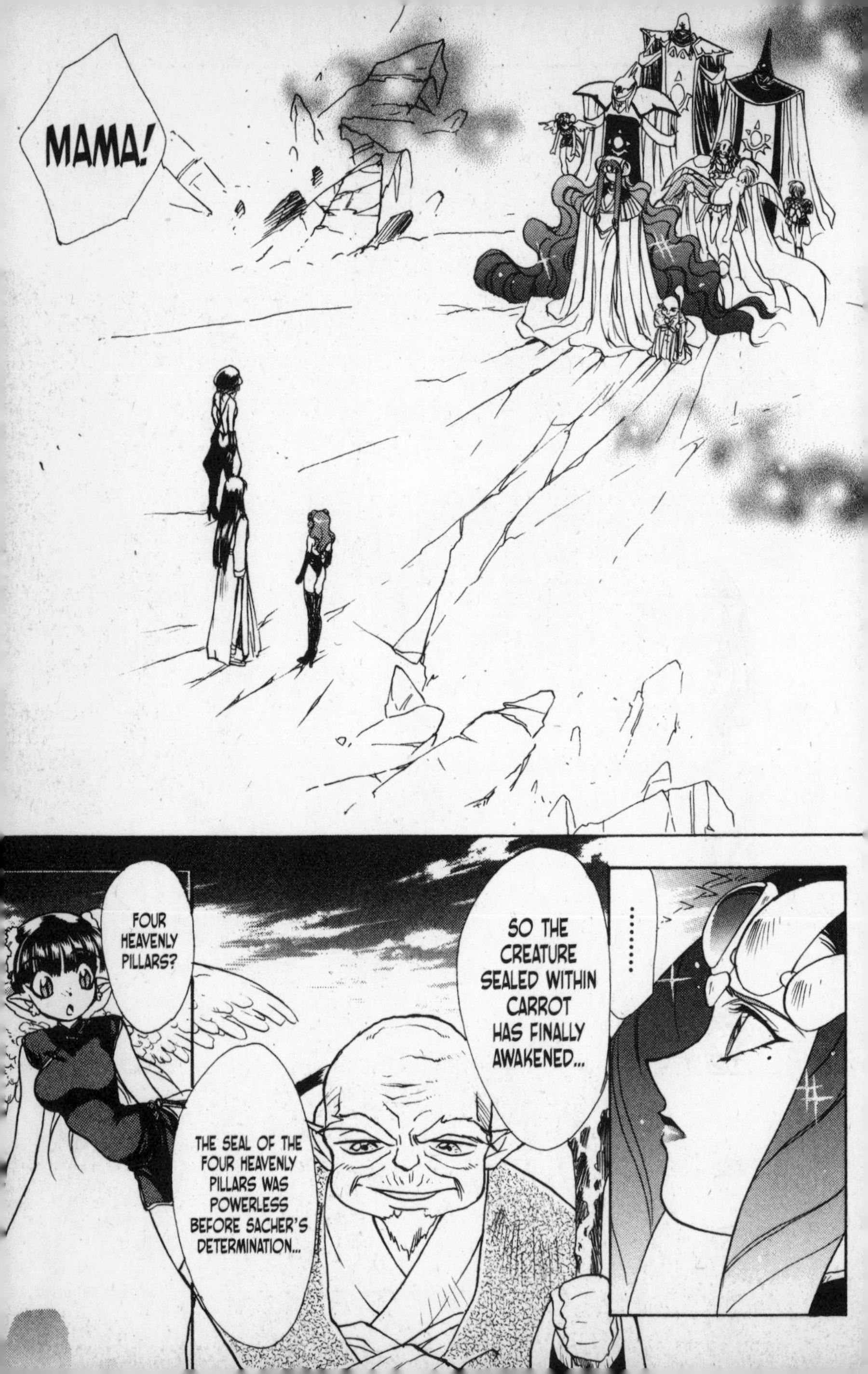
MAMA!
......
SO THE CREATURE SEALED WITHIN CARROT HAS FINALLY AWAKENED...
THE SEAL OF THE FOUR HEAVENLY PILLARS WAS POWERLESS BEFORE SACHER'S DETERMINATION...
FOUR HEAVENLY PILLARS?

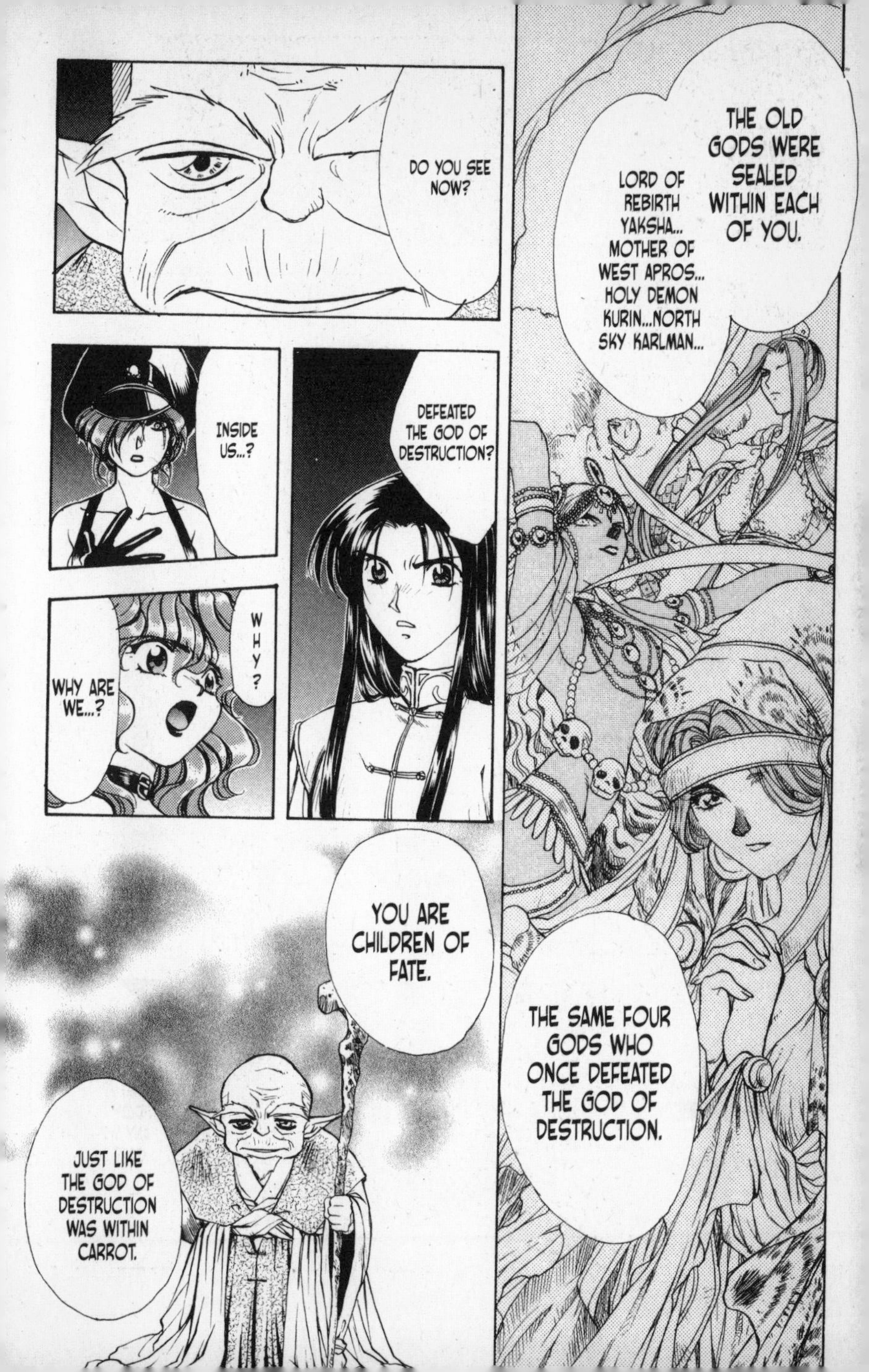
THE OLD GODS WERE SEALED WITHIN EACH OF YOU.
LORD OF REBIRTH YAKSHA... MOTHER OF WEST APROS... HOLY DEMON KURIN...NORTH SKY KARLMAN...
THE SAME FOUR GODS WHO ONCE DEFEATED THE GOD OF DESTRUCTION.
DO YOU SEE NOW?
DEFEATED THE GOD OF DESTRUCTION?
INSIDE US...?
WHY?
WHY ARE WE...?
YOU ARE CHILDREN OF FATE.
JUST LIKE THE GOD OF DESTRUCTION WAS WITHIN CARROT.

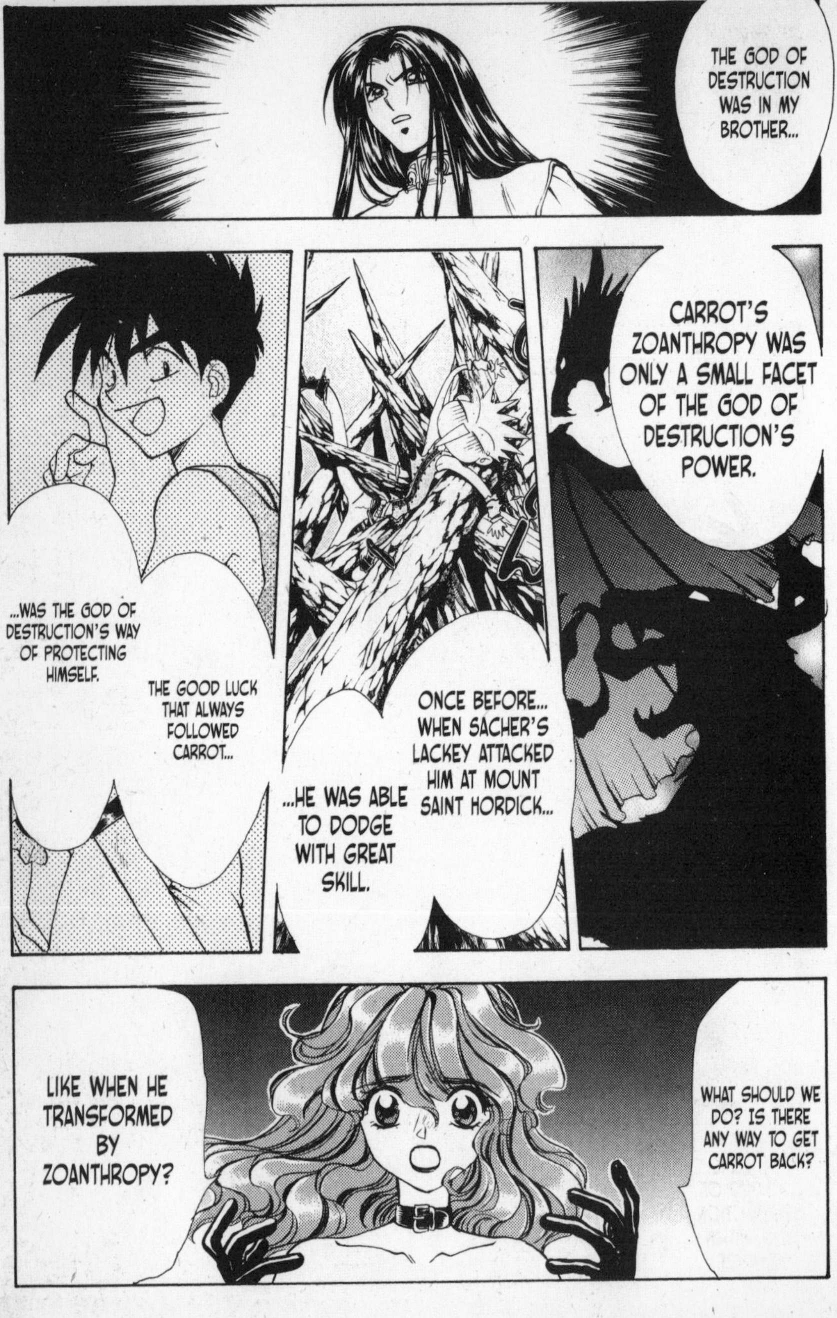
THE GOD OF DESTRUCTION WAS IN MY BROTHER...
CARROT'S ZOANTHROPY WAS ONLY A SMALL FACET OF THE GOD OF DESTRUCTION'S POWER.
ONCE BEFORE... WHEN SACHER'S LACKEY ATTACKED HIM AT MOUNT SAINT HORDICK...
...HE WAS ABLE TO DODGE WITH GREAT SKILL.
THE GOOD LUCK THAT ALWAYS FOLLOWED CARROT...
...WAS THE GOD OF DESTRUCTION'S WAY OF PROTECTING HIMSELF.
WHAT SHOULD WE DO? IS THERE ANY WAY TO GET CARROT BACK?
LIKE WHEN HE TRANSFORMED BY ZOANTHROPY?

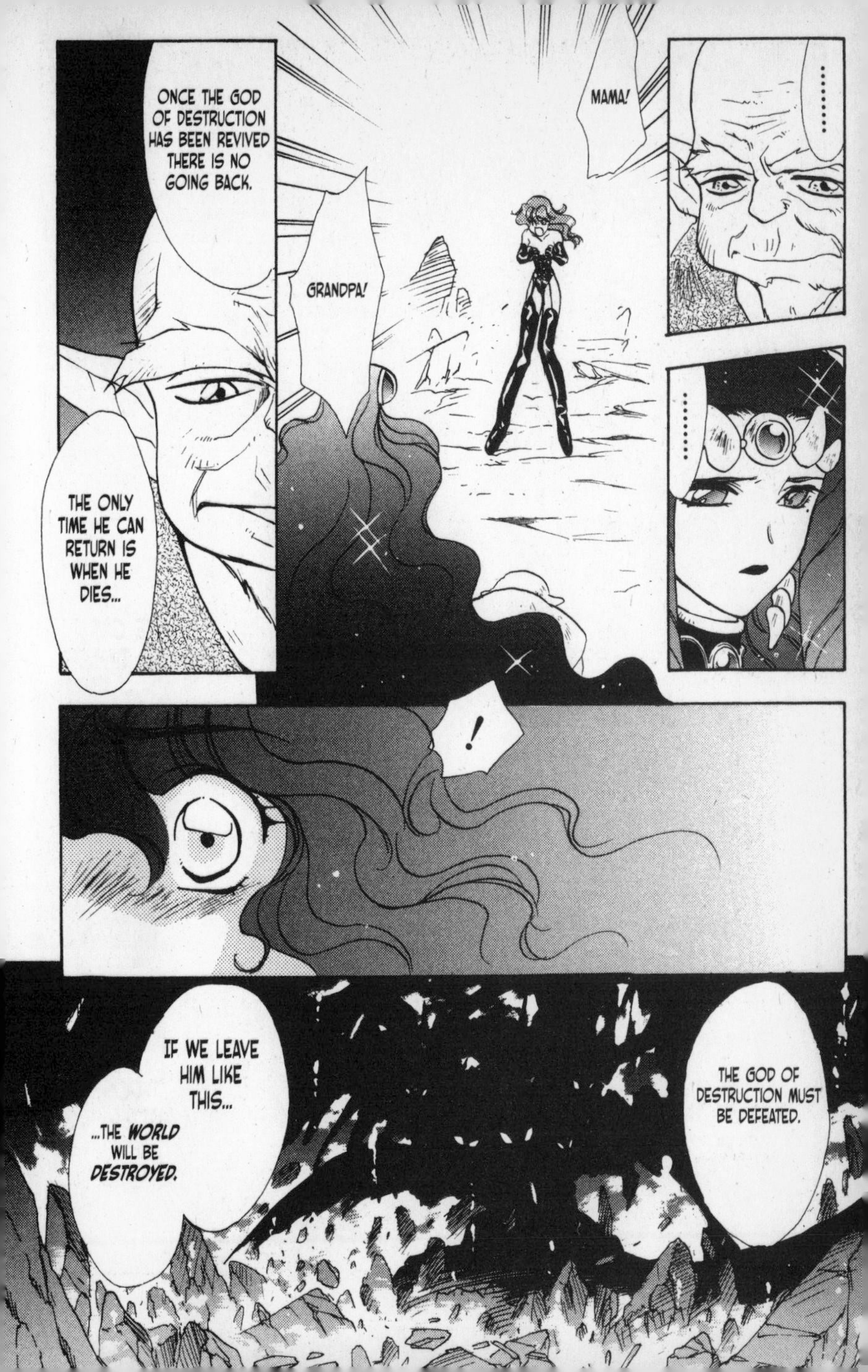
......
......
MAMA!
GRANDPA!
ONCE THE GOD OF DESTRUCTION HAS BEEN REVIVED THERE IS NO GOING BACK.
THE ONLY TIME HE CAN RETURN IS WHEN HE DIES...
!
THE GOD OF DESTRUCTION MUST BE DEFEATED.
IF WE LEAVE HIM LIKE THIS...
...THE *WORLD* WILL BE *DESTROYED.*

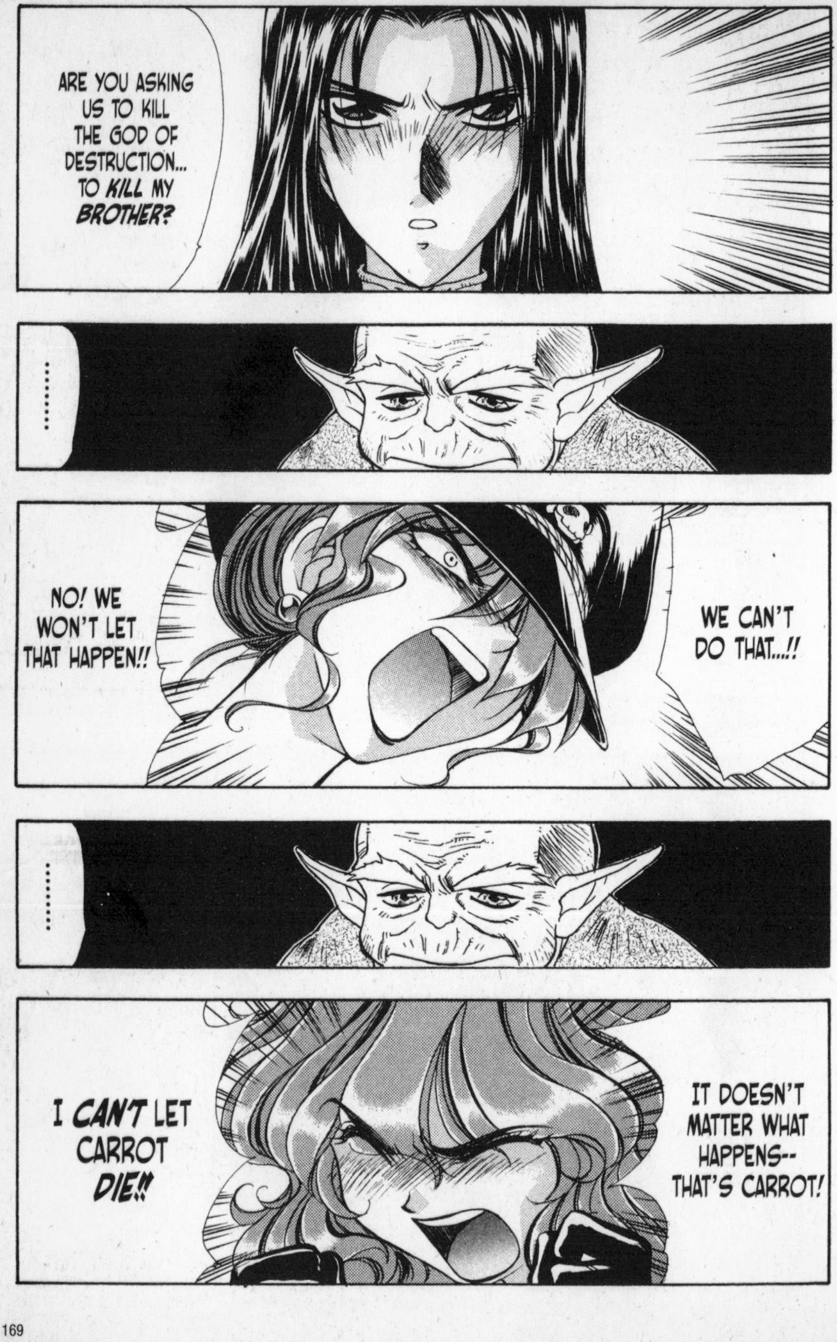
ARE YOU ASKING US TO KILL THE GOD OF DESTRUCTION... TO *KILL* MY *BROTHER?*
....
WE CAN'T DO THAT...!!
NO! WE WON'T LET THAT HAPPEN!!
....
IT DOESN'T MATTER WHAT HAPPENS-- THAT'S CARROT!
I *CAN'T* LET CARROT *DIE!!*

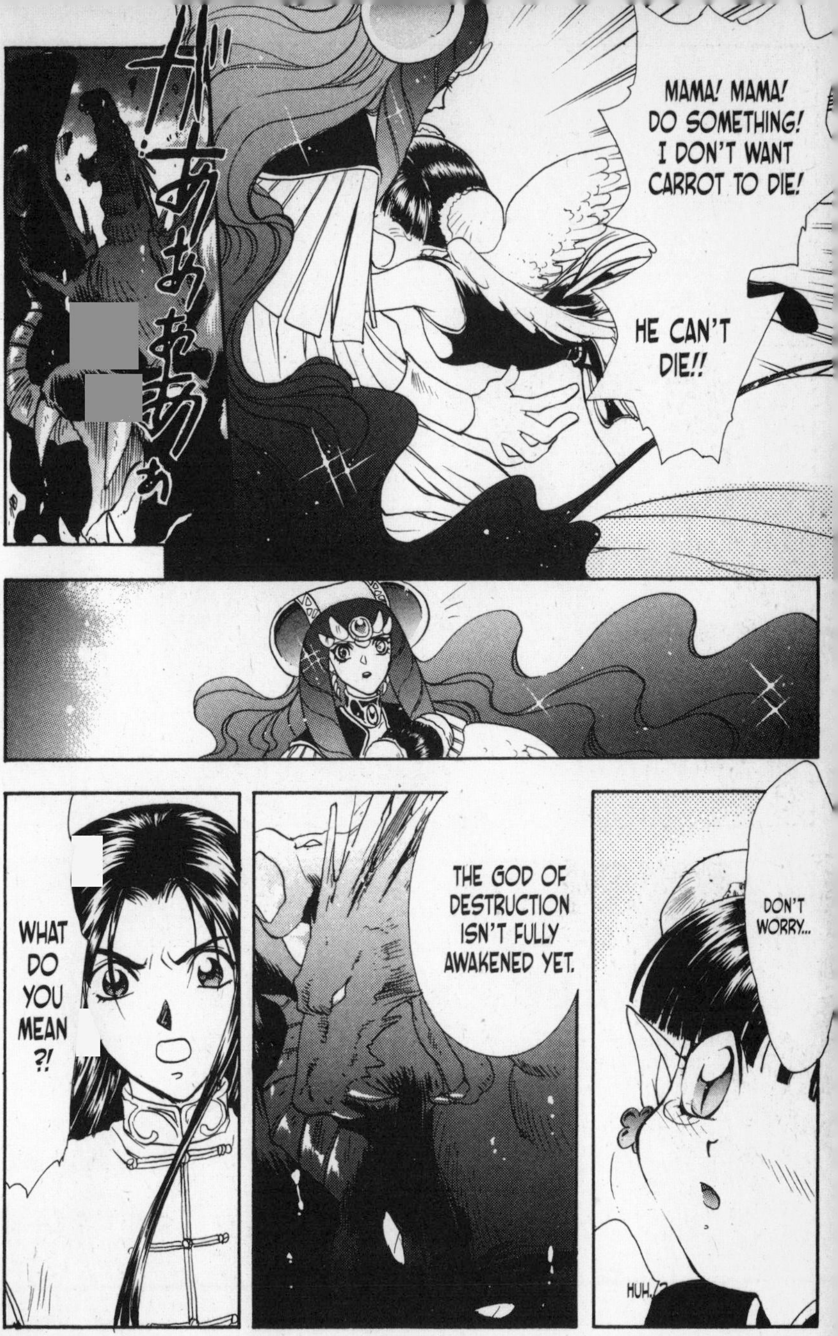
MAMA! MAMA! DO SOMETHING! I DON'T WANT CARROT TO DIE!
HE CAN'T DIE!!
DON'T WORRY...
HUH...?
THE GOD OF DESTRUCTION ISN'T FULLY AWAKENED YET.
WHAT DO YOU MEAN ?!

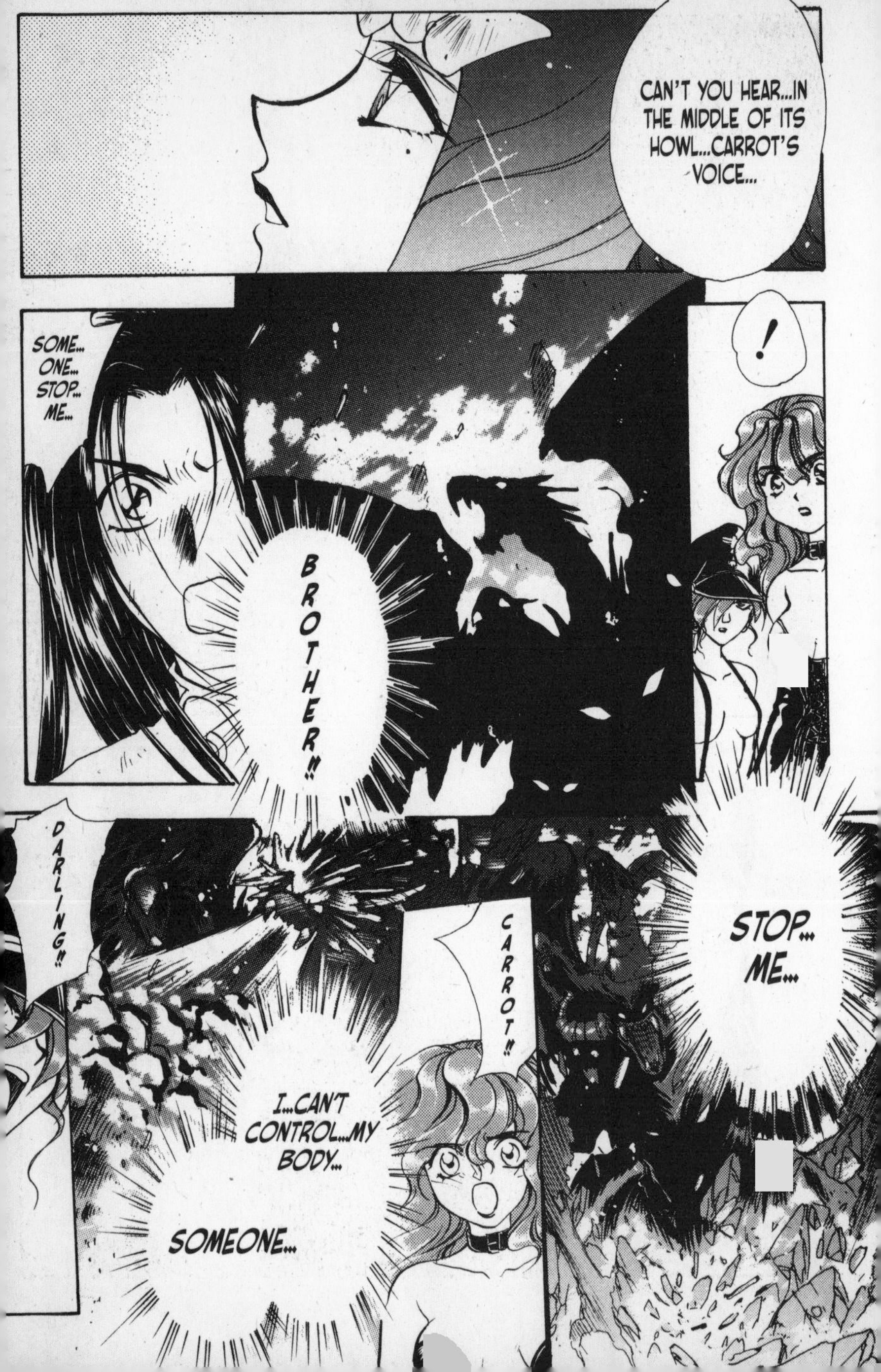
CAN'T YOU HEAR...IN THE MIDDLE OF ITS HOWL...CARROT'S VOICE...
!
BROTHER!!
SOME... ONE... STOP... ME...
STOP... ME...
CARROT!!
I...CAN'T CONTROL...MY BODY...
SOMEONE...
DARLING!!

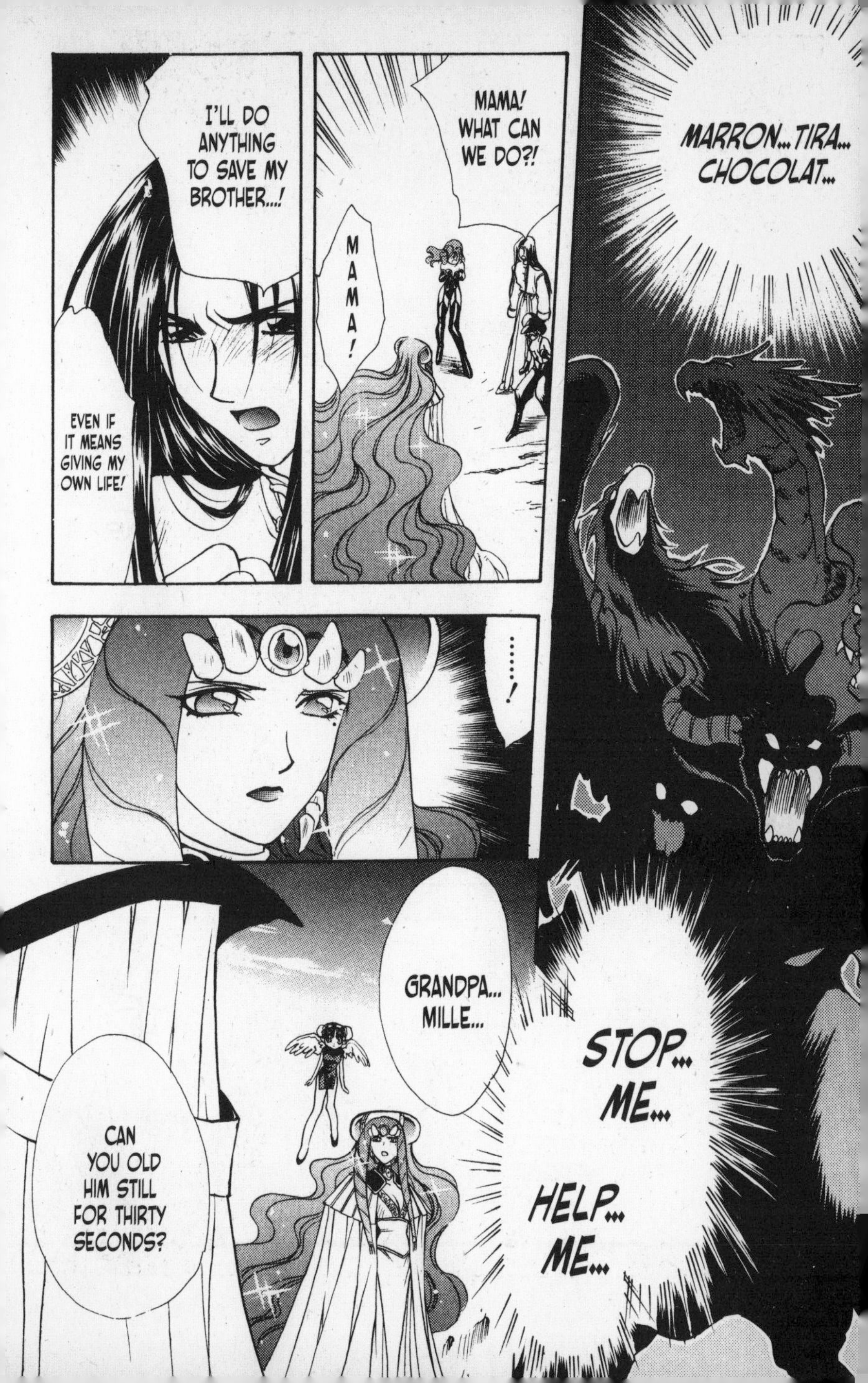
MARRON...TIRA... CHOCOLAT...
STOP... ME...
HELP... ME...
MAMA! WHAT CAN WE DO?!
MAMA!
I'LL DO ANYTHING TO SAVE MY BROTHER...!
EVEN IF IT MEANS GIVING MY OWN LIFE!
......!
GRANDPA... MILLE...
CAN YOU OLD HIM STILL FOR THIRTY SECONDS?

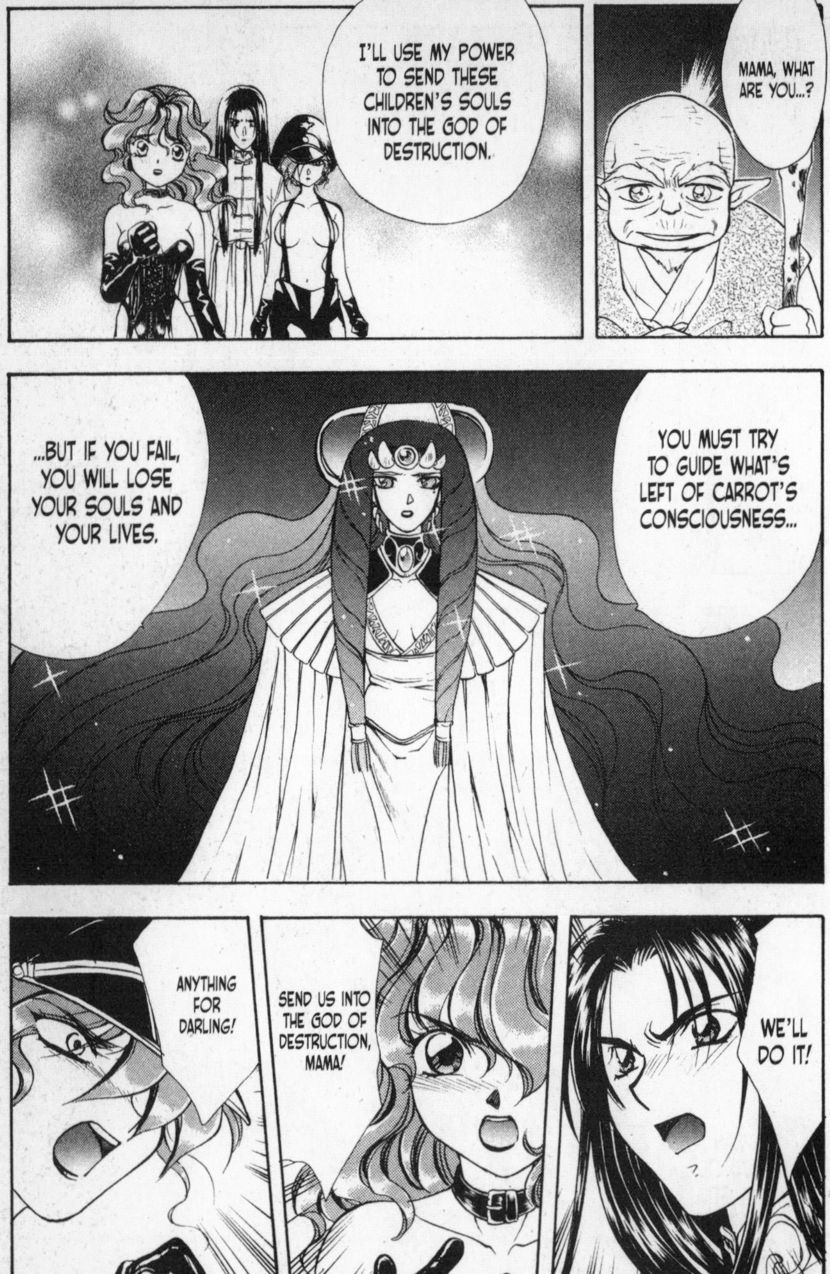
MAMA, WHAT ARE YOU...?
I'LL USE MY POWER TO SEND THESE CHILDREN'S SOULS INTO THE GOD OF DESTRUCTION.
YOU MUST TRY TO GUIDE WHAT'S LEFT OF CARROT'S CONSCIOUSNESS...
...BUT IF YOU FAIL, YOU WILL LOSE YOUR SOULS AND YOUR LIVES.
WE'LL DO IT!
SEND US INTO THE GOD OF DESTRUCTION, MAMA!
ANYTHING FOR DARLING!

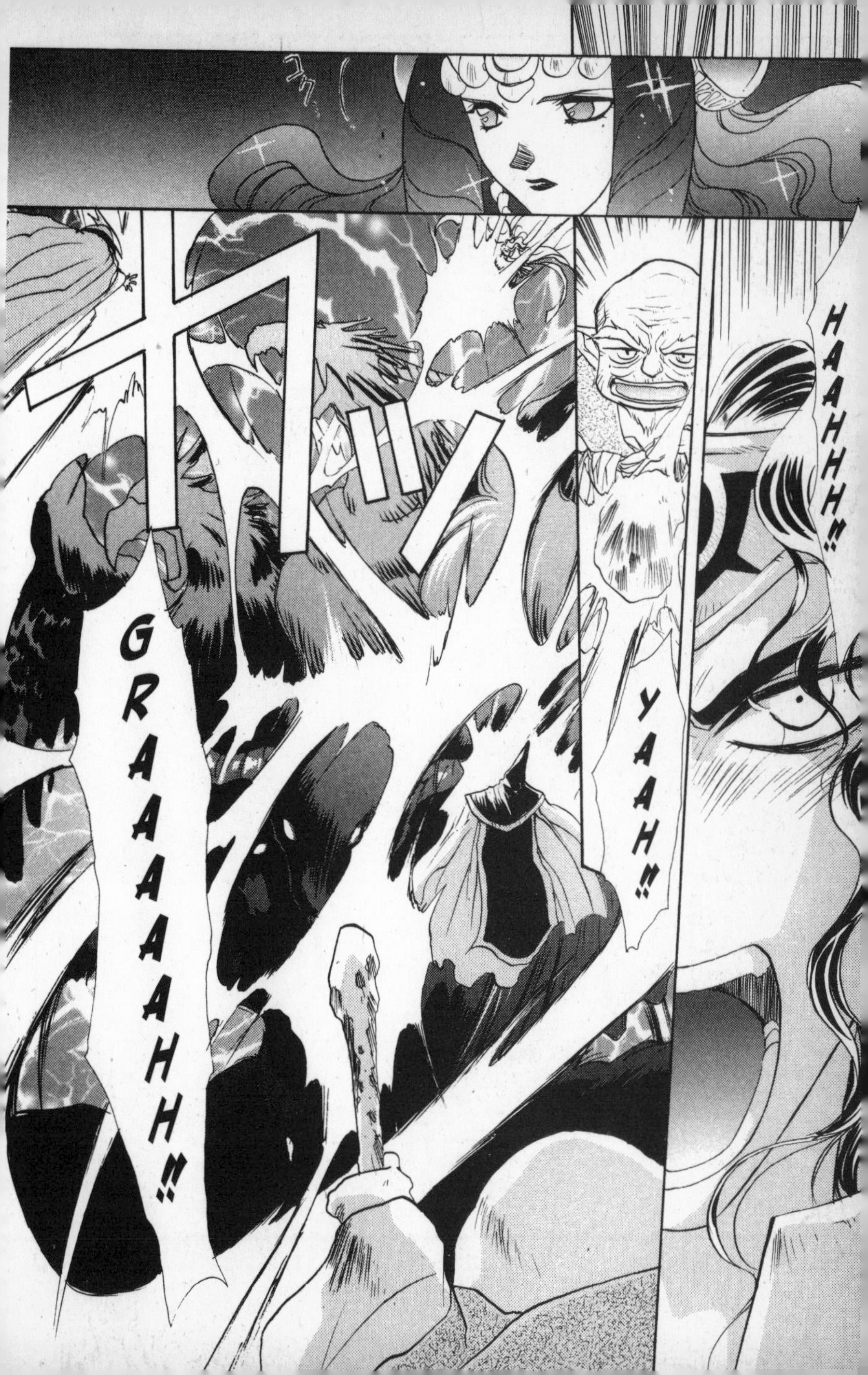
HAAAHHHH!!
YAAAH!!
GRAAAAAHH!!

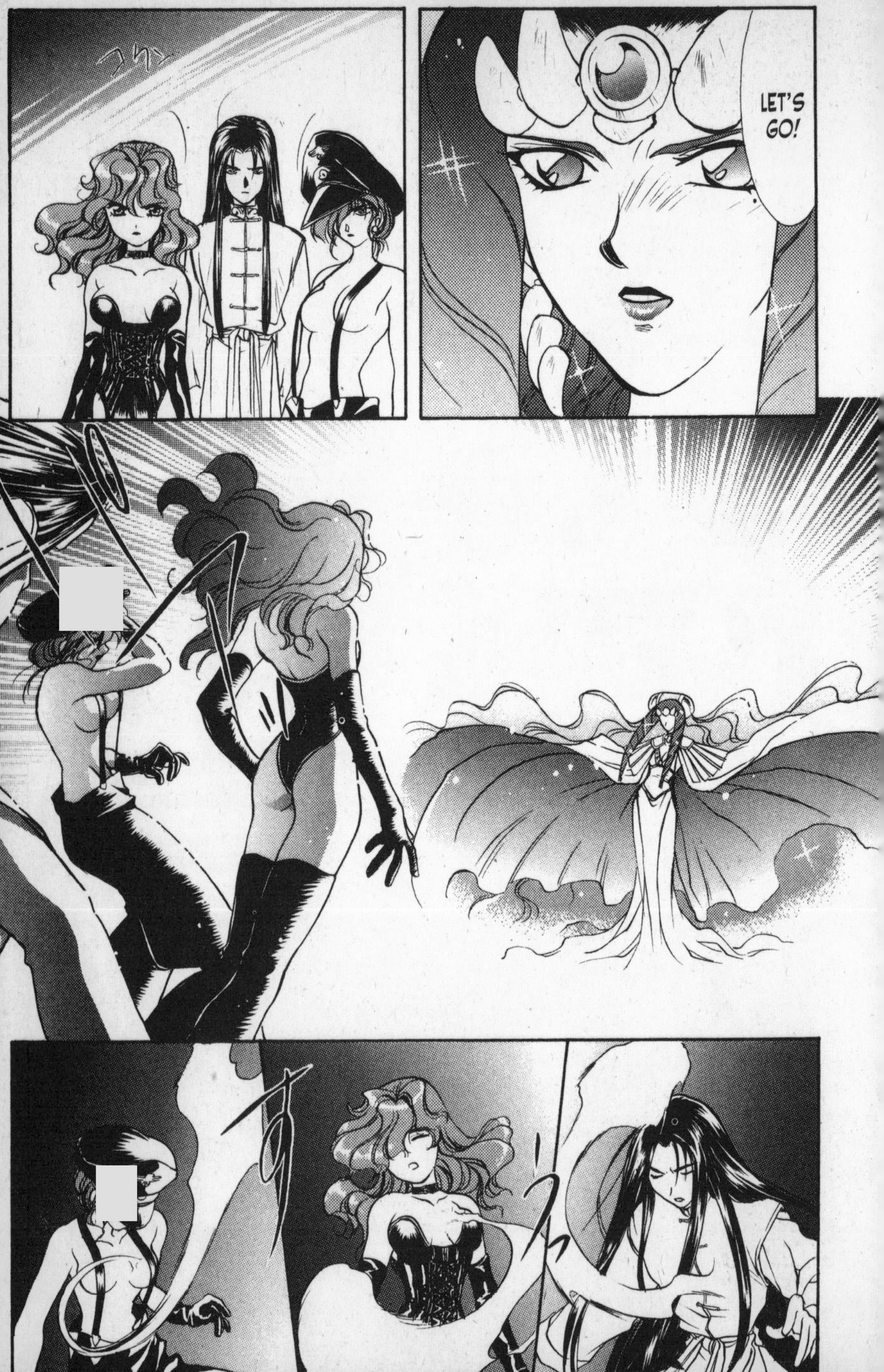
LET'S GO!

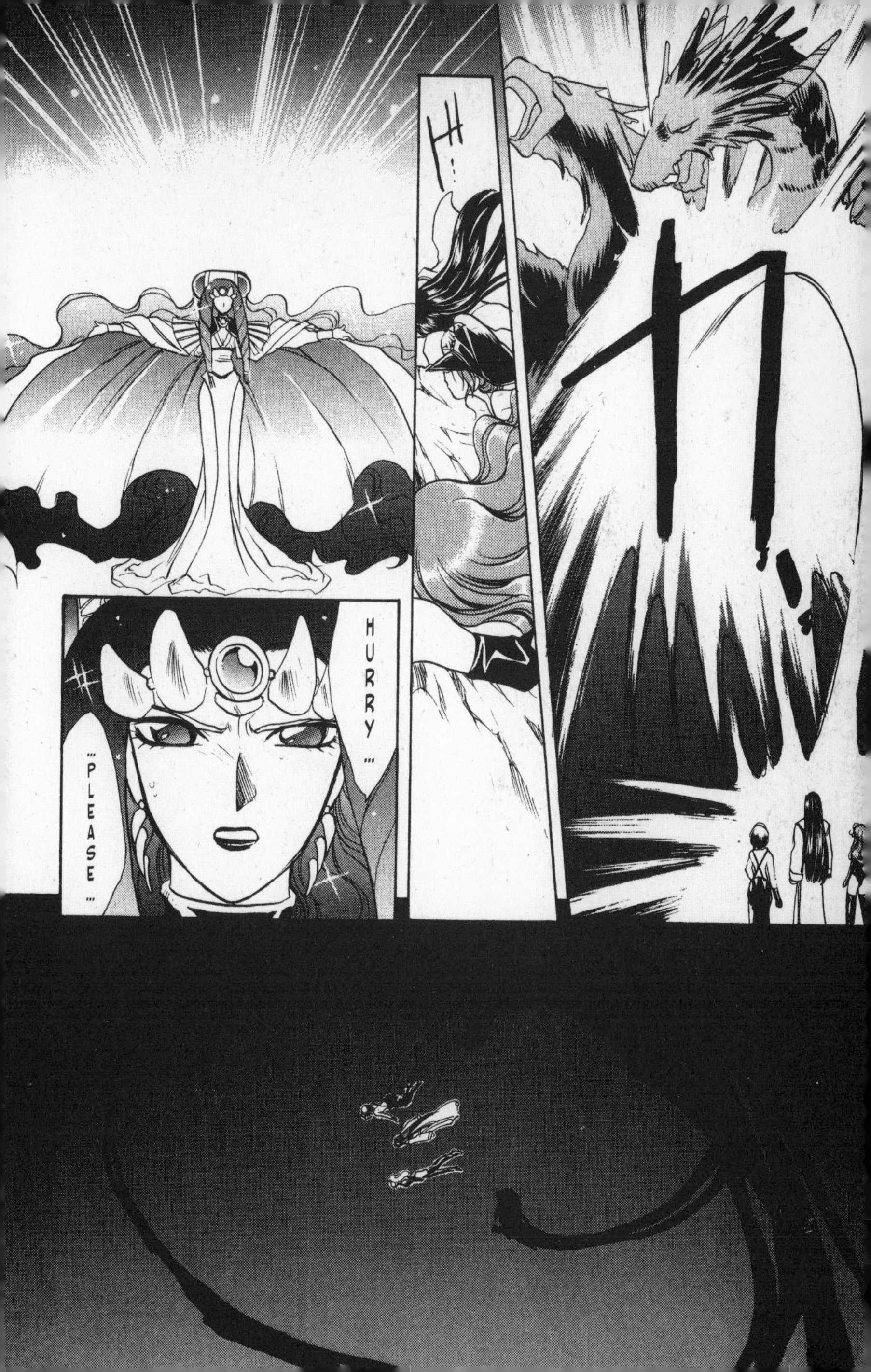
HURRY ...
...PLEASE ...

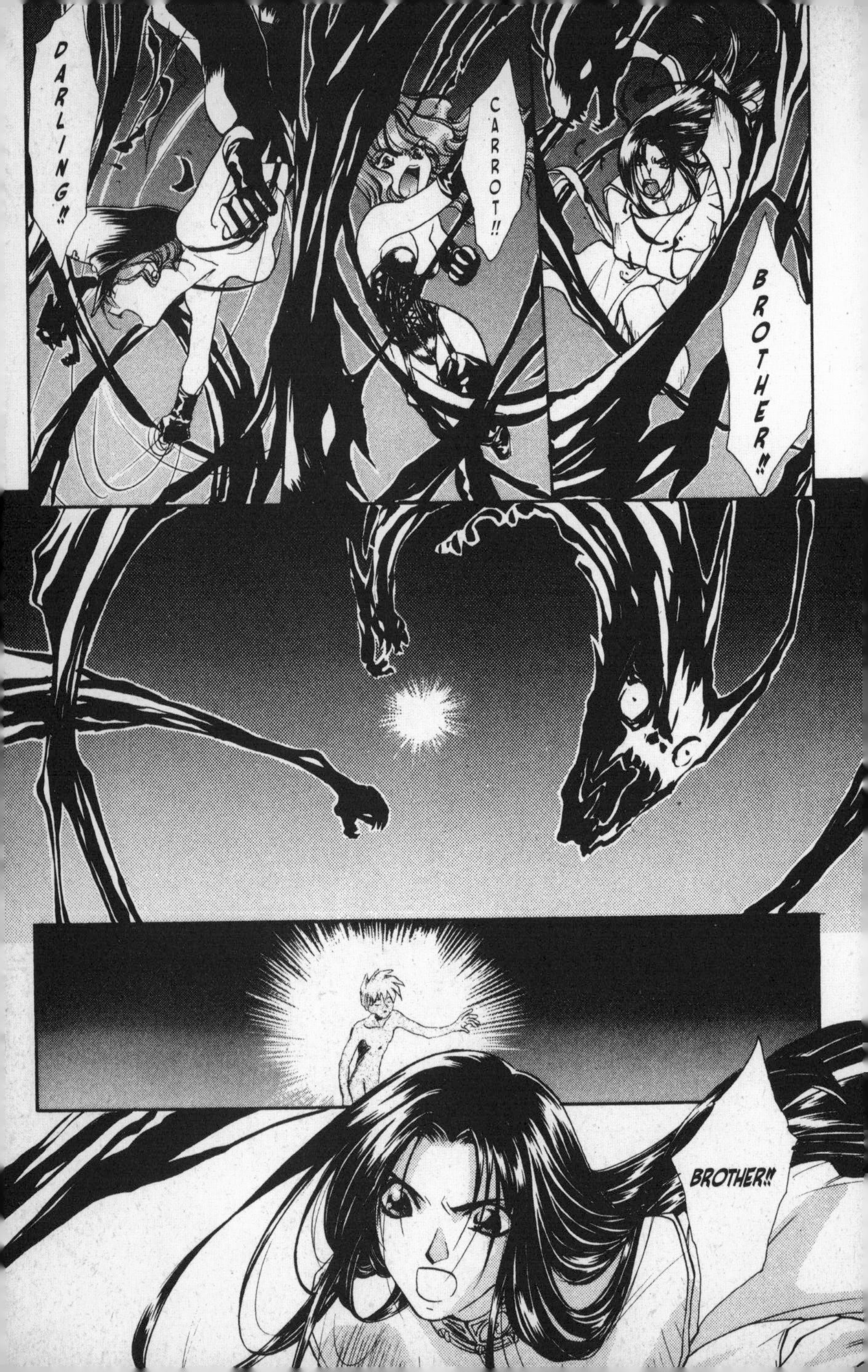
BROTHER!!
CARROT!!
DARLING!!
BROTHER!!

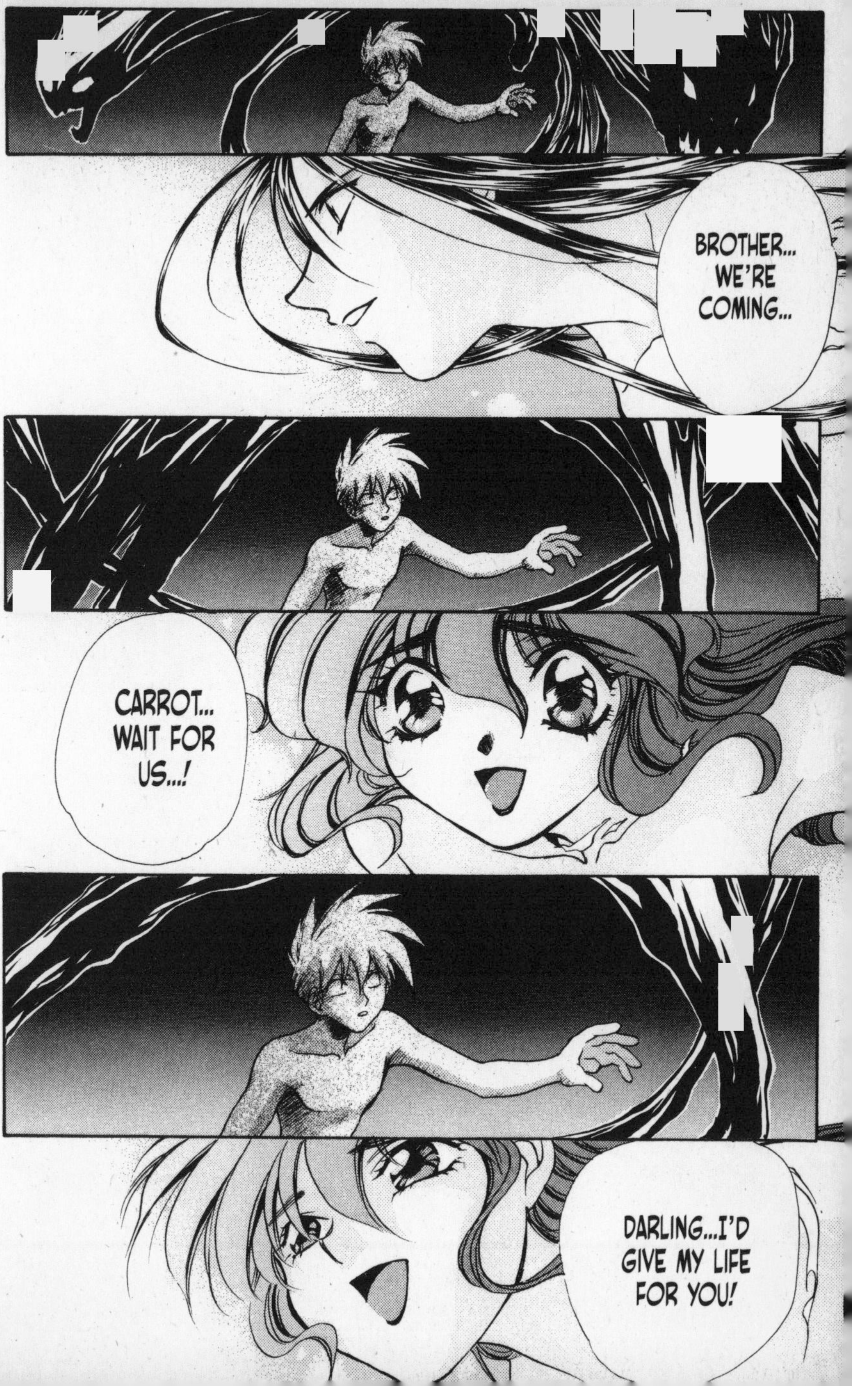
BROTHER... WE'RE COMING...
CARROT... WAIT FOR US...!
DARLING...I'D GIVE MY LIFE FOR YOU!

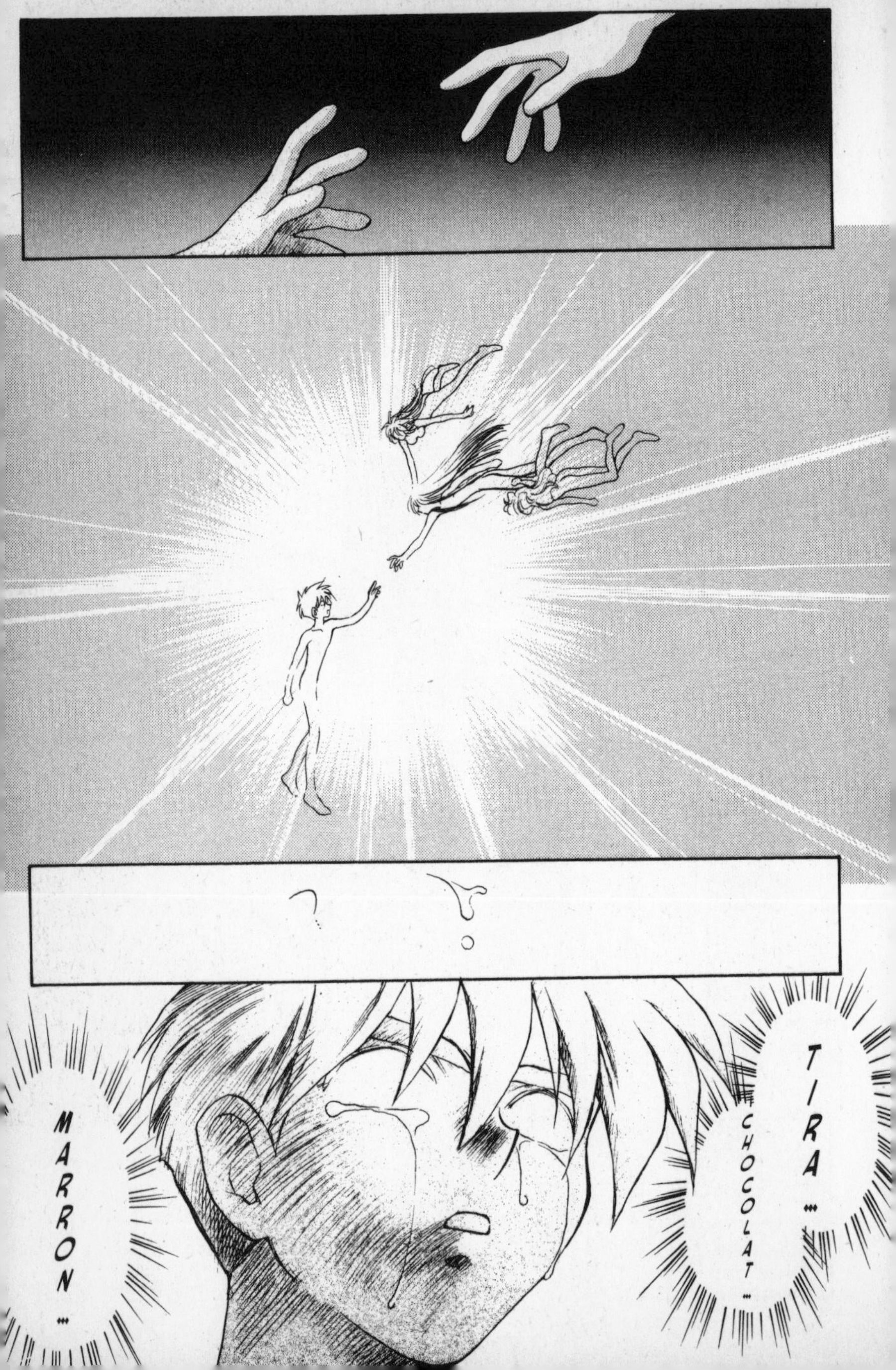
TIRA...
CHOCOLAT...
MARRON...

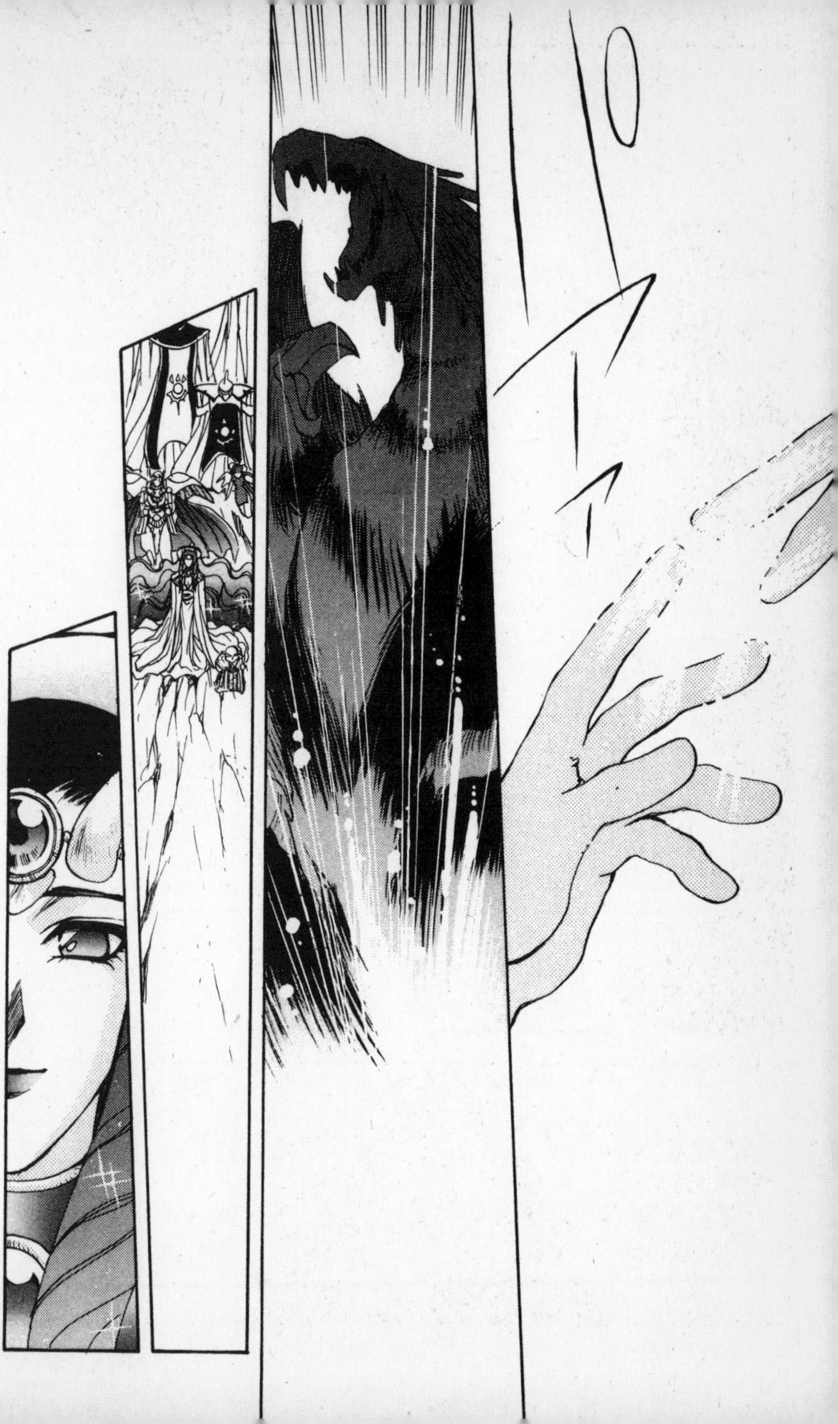

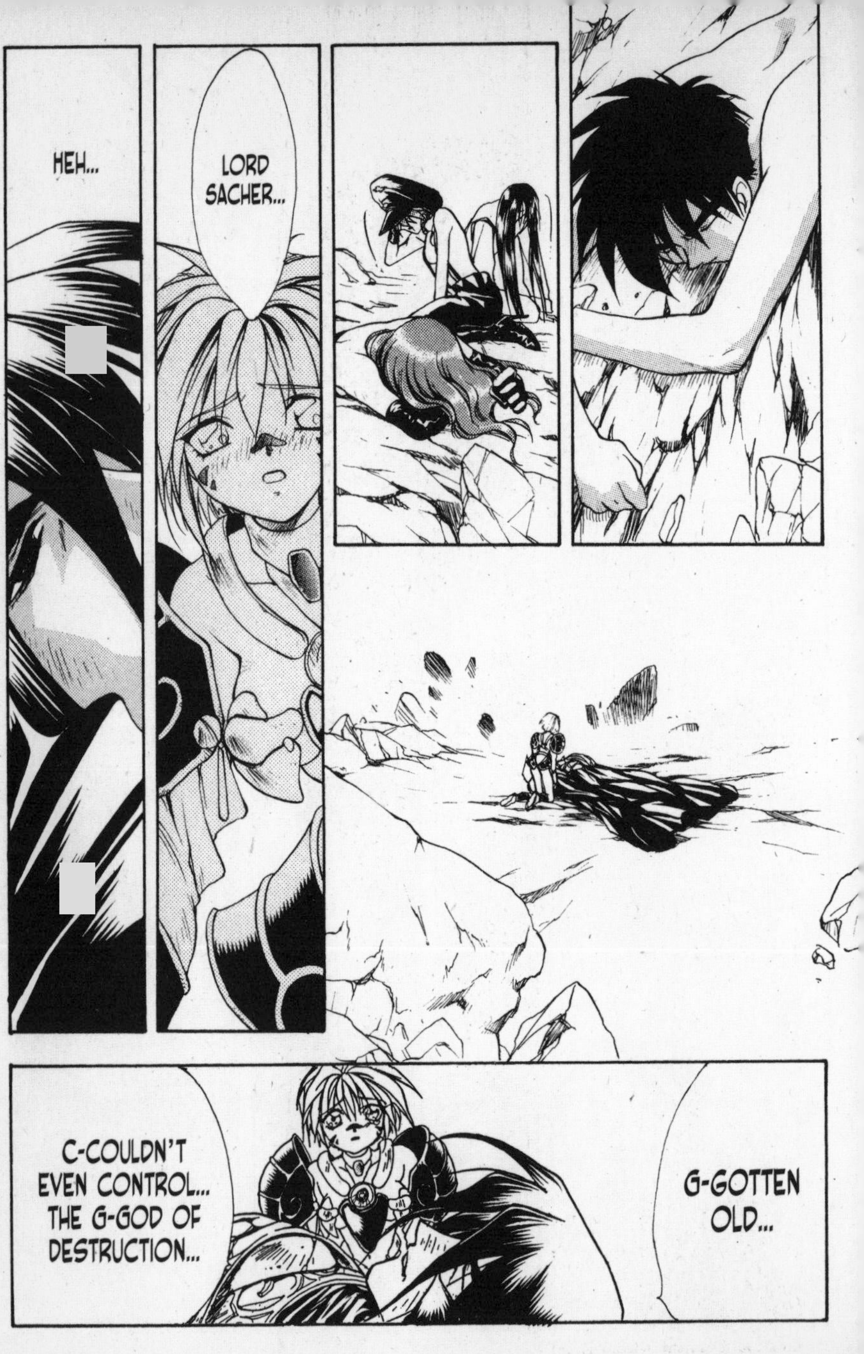
LORD SACHER...
HEH...
G-GOTTEN OLD...
C-COULDN'T EVEN CONTROL... THE G-GOD OF DESTRUCTION...

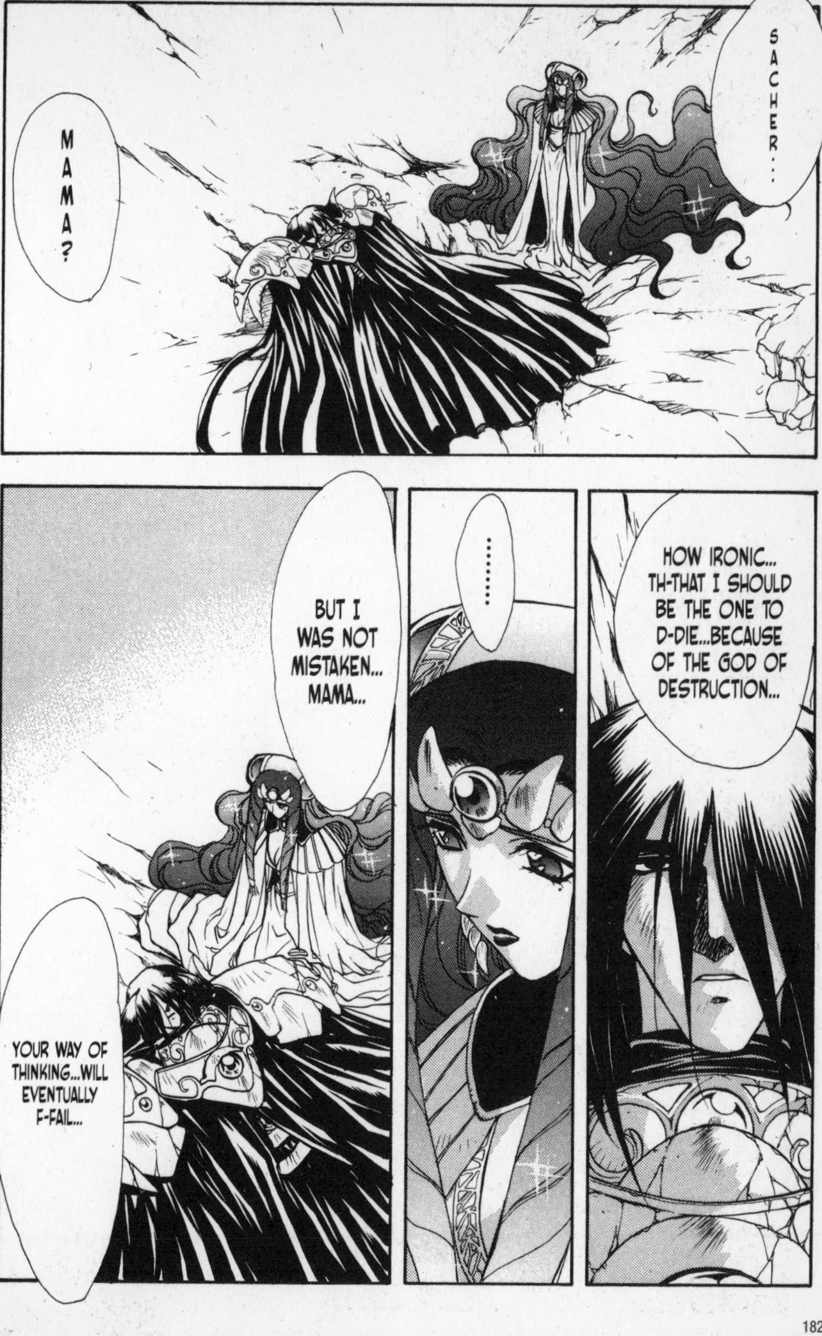
SACHER...
MAMA?
HOW IRONIC... TH-THAT I SHOULD BE THE ONE TO D-DIE...BECAUSE OF THE GOD OF DESTRUCTION...
....
BUT I WAS NOT MISTAKEN... MAMA...
YOUR WAY OF THINKING...WILL EVENTUALLY F-FAIL...

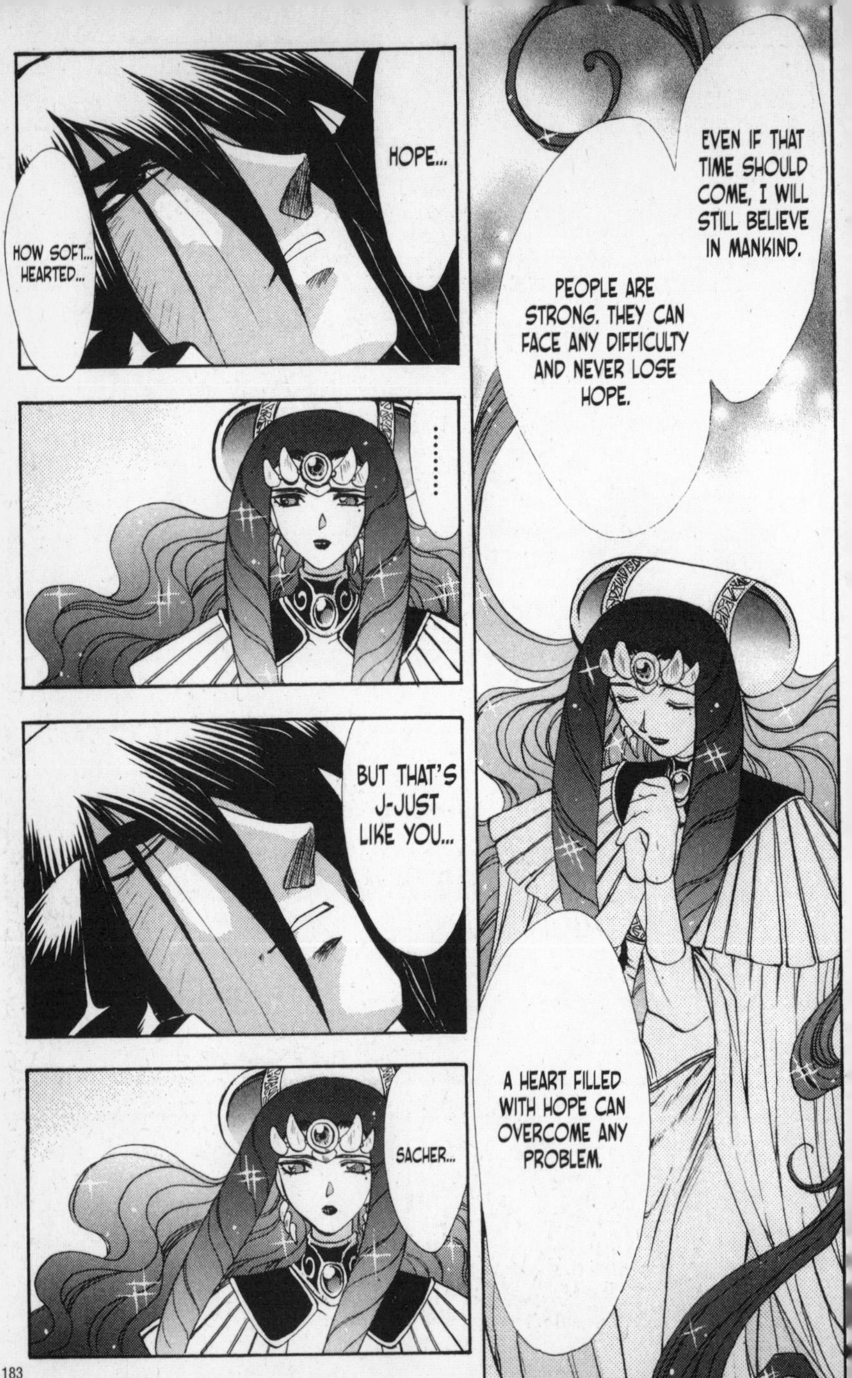
EVEN IF THAT TIME SHOULD COME, I WILL STILL BELIEVE IN MANKIND.
PEOPLE ARE STRONG. THEY CAN FACE ANY DIFFICULTY AND NEVER LOSE HOPE.
A HEART FILLED WITH HOPE CAN OVERCOME ANY PROBLEM.
HOPE...
HOW SOFT... HEARTED...
......
BUT THAT'S J-JUST LIKE YOU...
SACHER...

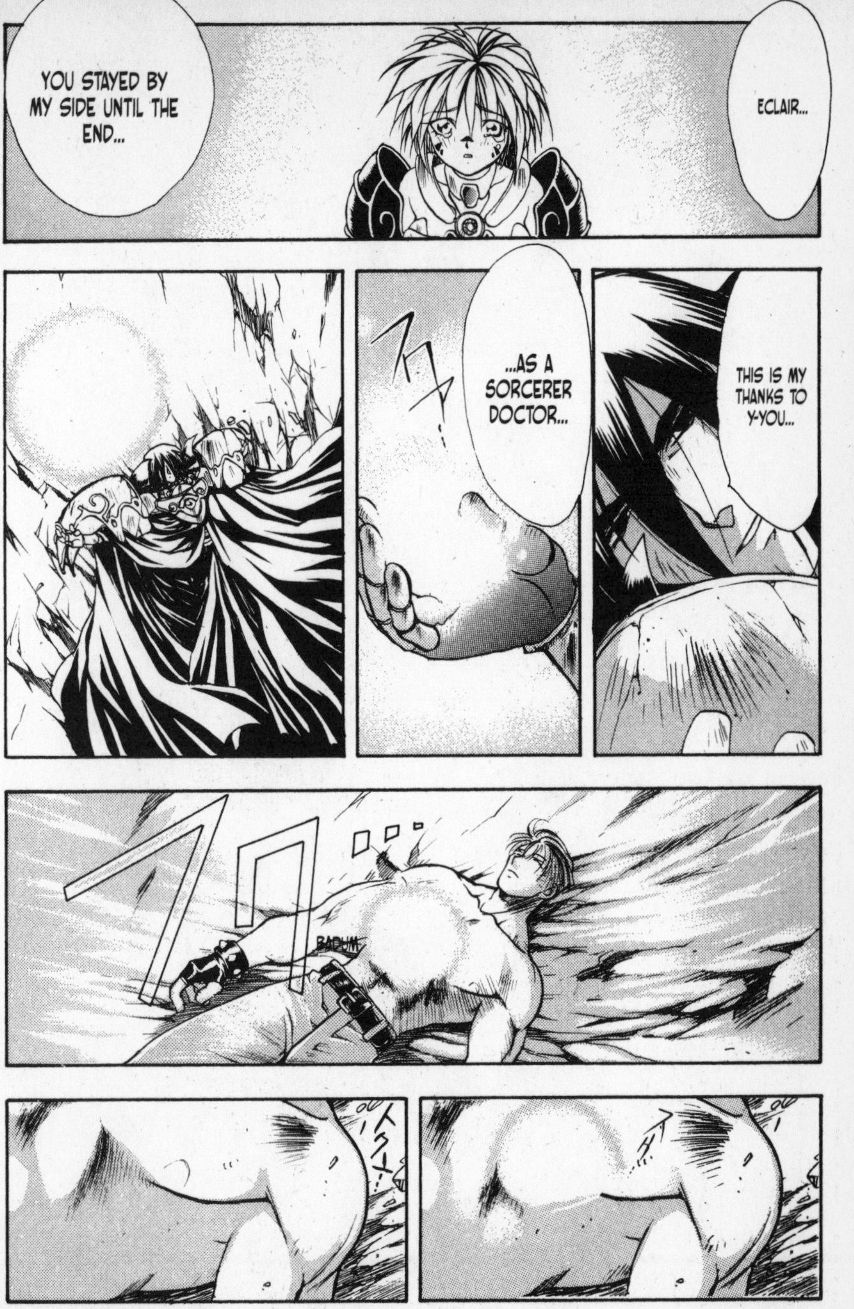
ECLAIR...
YOU STAYED BY MY SIDE UNTIL THE END...
THIS IS MY THANKS TO Y-YOU...
...AS A SORCERER DOCTOR...
BADUM

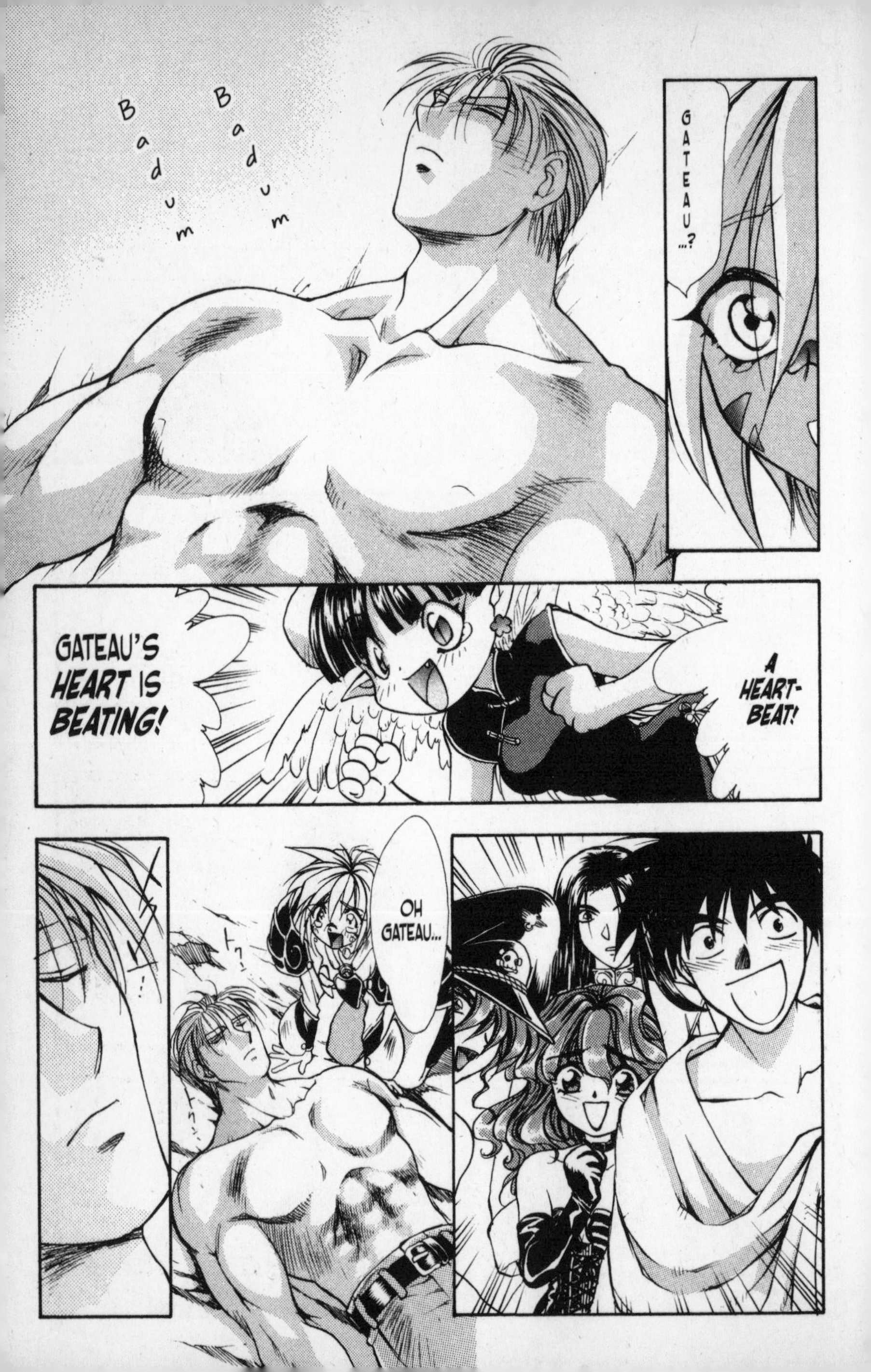
GATEAU...?
Badum
Badum
A HEART-BEAT!
GATEAU'S HEART IS BEATING!
OH GATEAU...

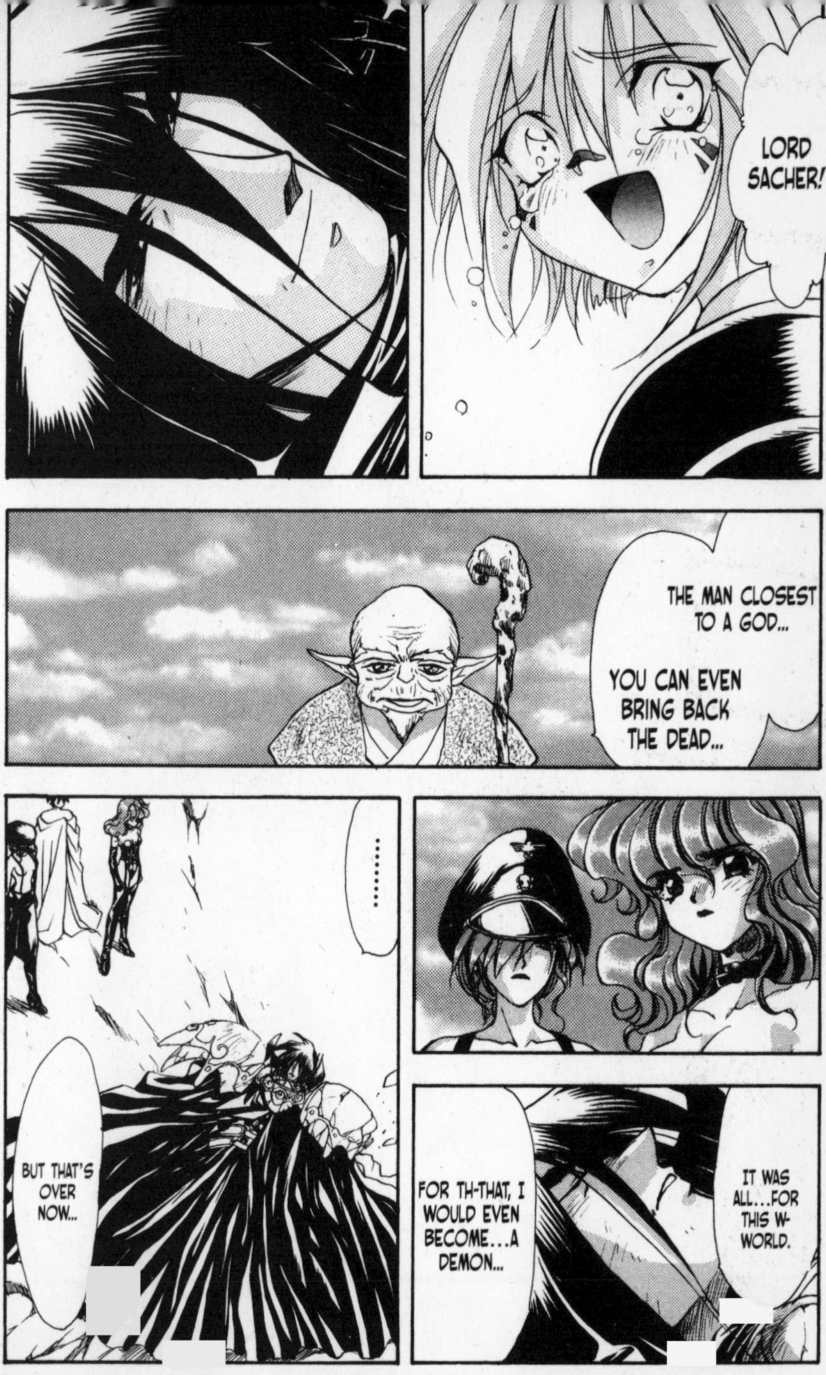
LORD SACHER!
THE MAN CLOSEST TO A GOD...
YOU CAN EVEN BRING BACK THE DEAD...
IT WAS ALL...FOR THIS W-WORLD.
FOR TH-THAT, I WOULD EVEN BECOME...A DEMON...
......
BUT THAT'S OVER NOW...

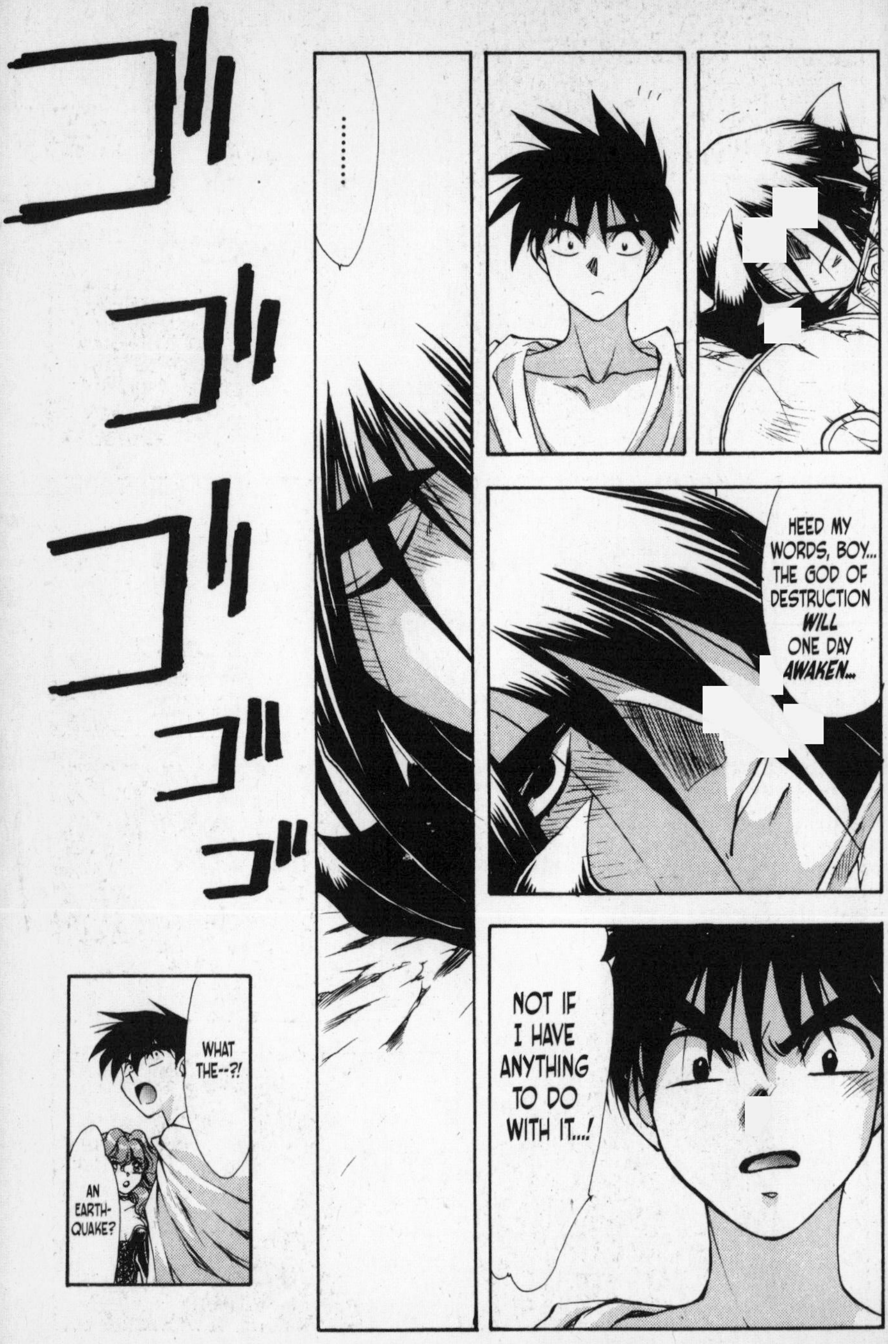
HEED MY WORDS, BOY... THE GOD OF DESTRUCTION *WILL* ONE DAY *AWAKEN...*
NOT IF I HAVE ANYTHING TO DO WITH IT...!
......
ゴゴゴゴゴ
WHAT THE--?!
AN EARTH-QUAKE?

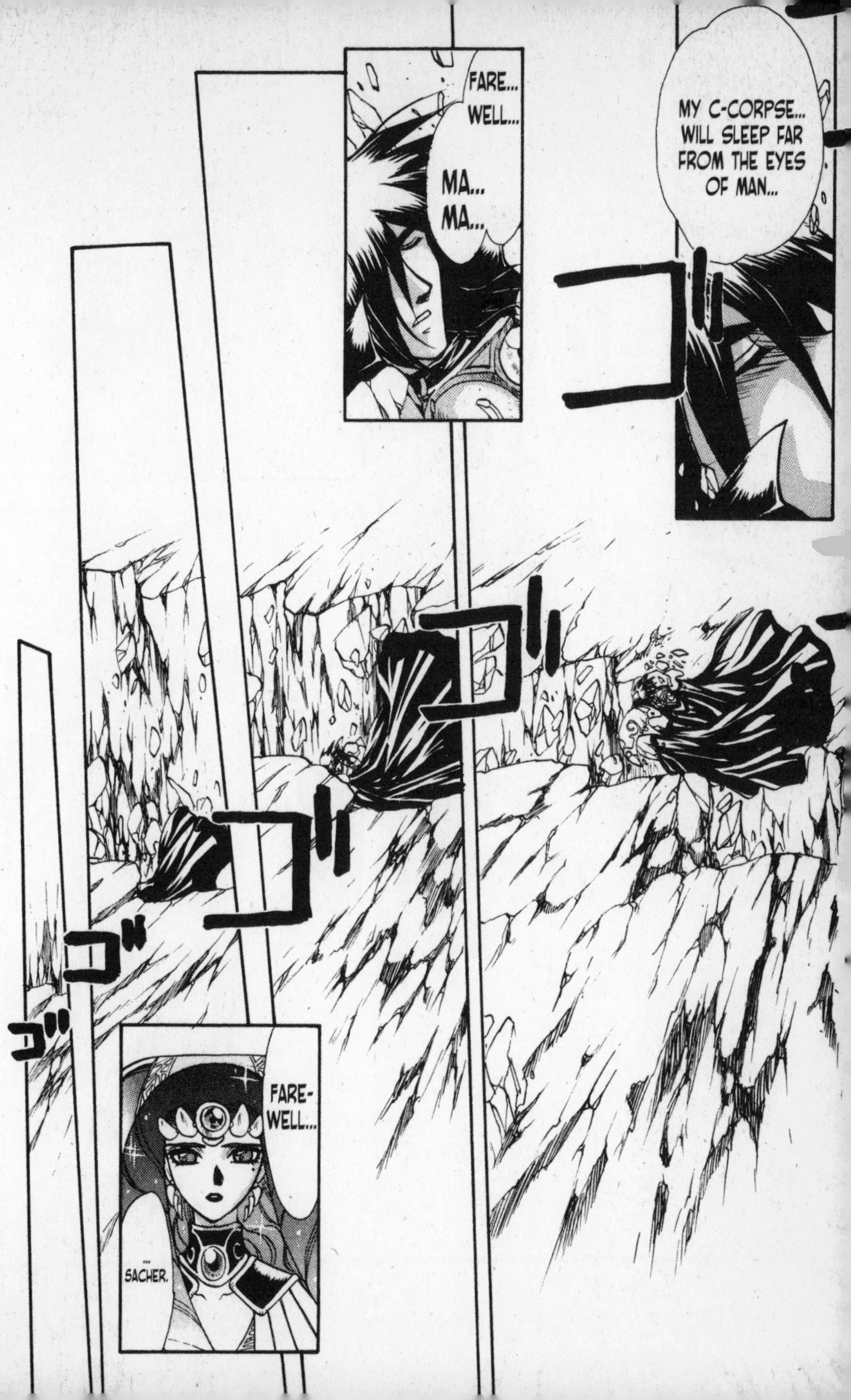
MY C-CORPSE... WILL SLEEP FAR FROM THE EYES OF MAN...
FARE... WELL...
MA... MA...
FARE-WELL...
...SACHER.

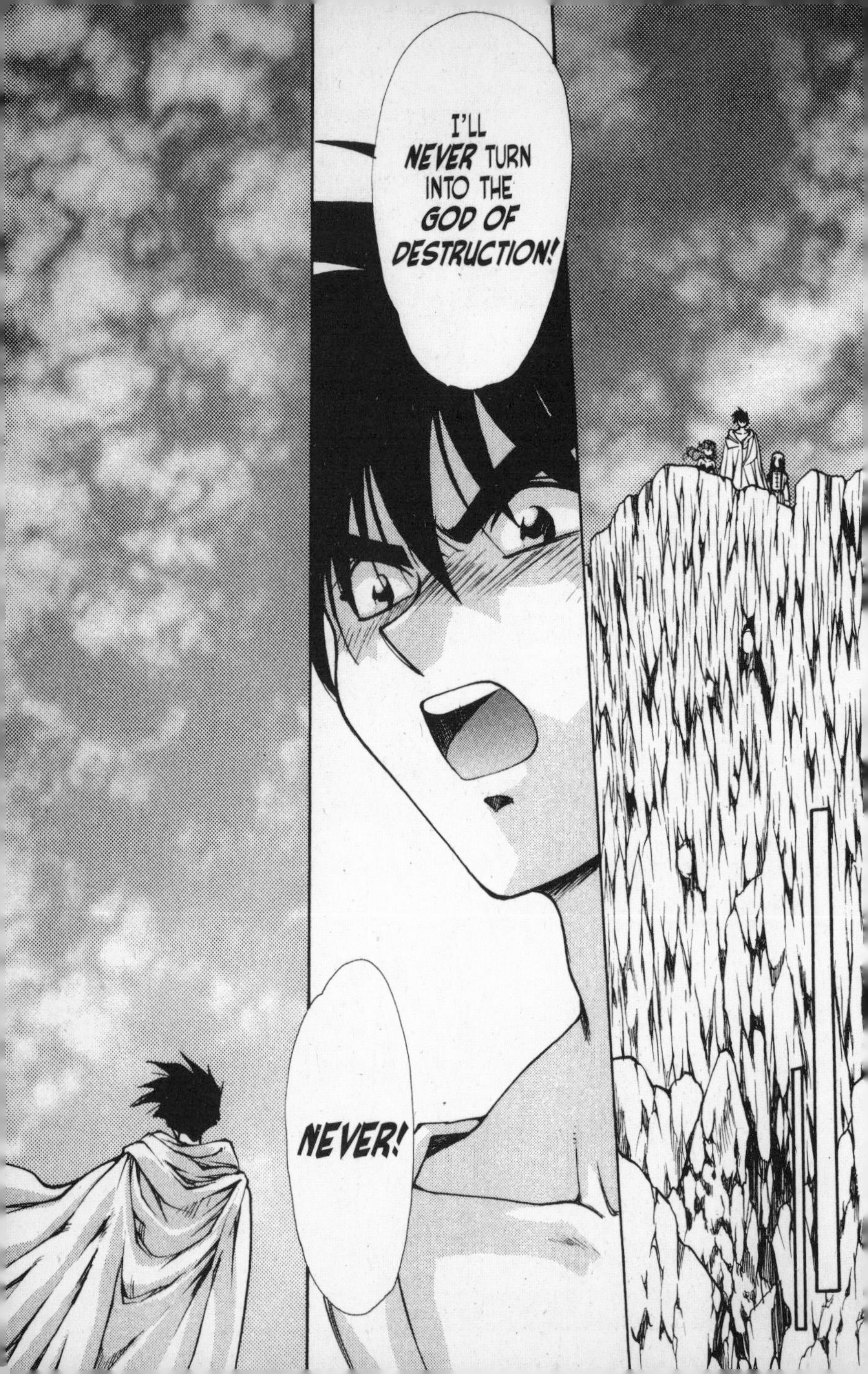
I'LL NEVER TURN INTO THE GOD OF DESTRUCTION!
NEVER!

P R E V I E W

WITH LORD SACHER OUT OF THE PICTURE, IT WOULD APPEAR THAT OUR HEROES' ADVENTURES ARE FINALLY OVER...NOT!! FOR THEIR NEXT ASSIGNMENT, CARROT AND THE OTHERS MUST TRACK DOWN A MAGIC CARPENTER WHOSE LATEST CREATION IS KILLING THE DENIZENS OF CRATER ISLAND. CAN THIS ABOMINABLE ABERRATION WITHSTAND THE LASHINGS OF TWO LEATHER-CLAD DOMINATRIX HEROINES?

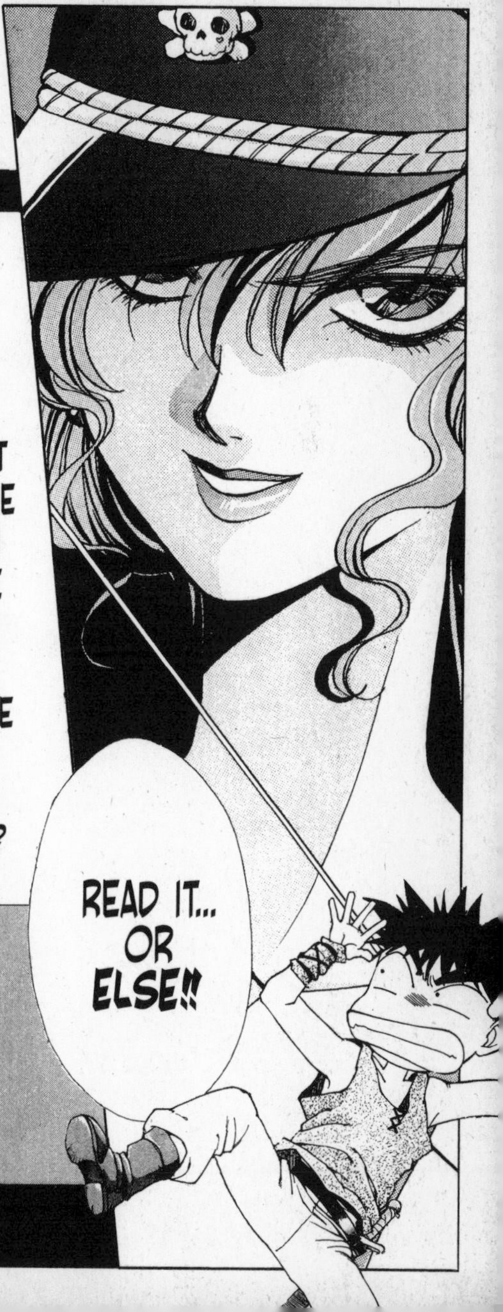
READ IT... OR ELSE!!

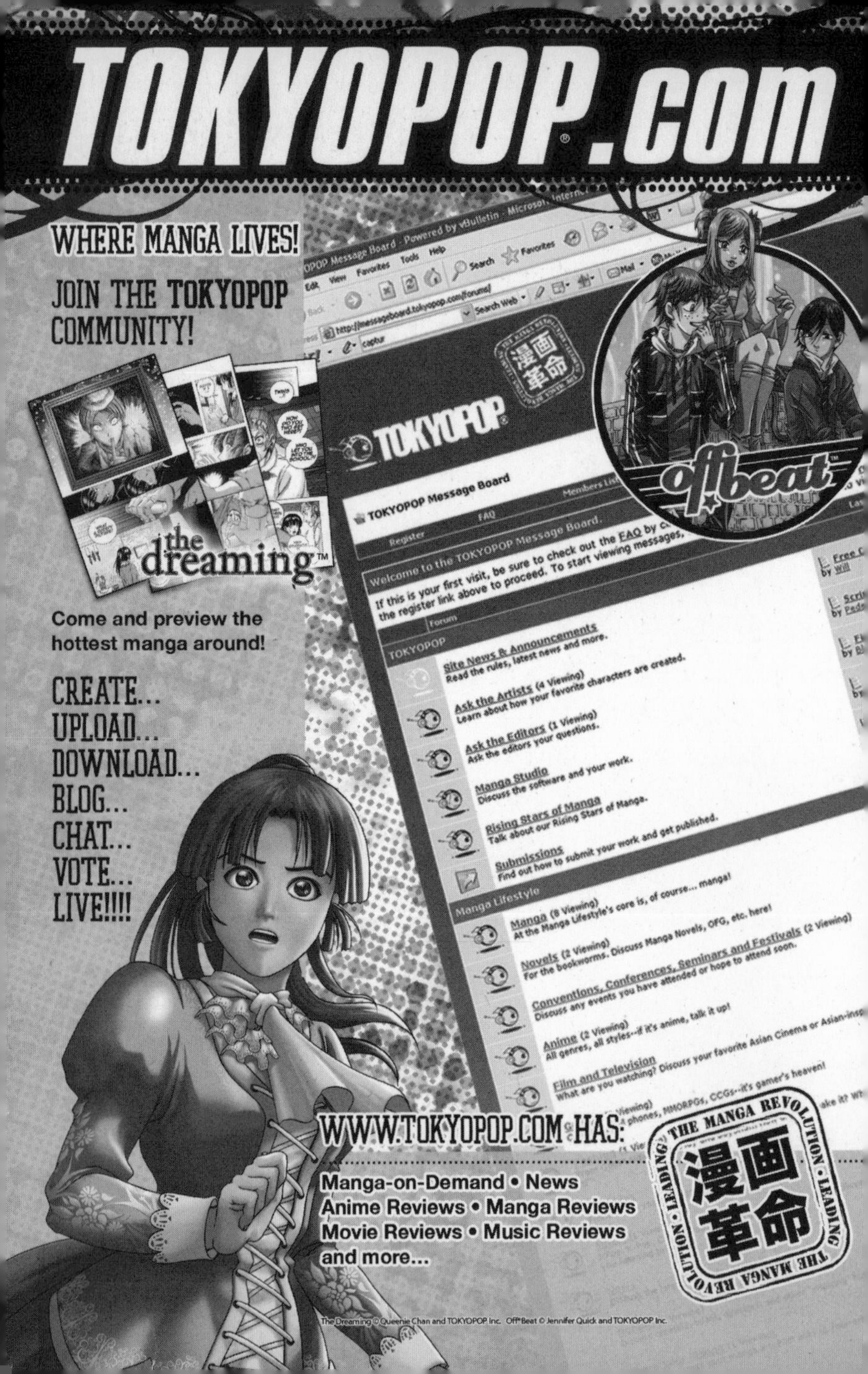
TOKYOPOP®.com
WHERE MANGA LIVES!
JOIN THE TOKYOPOP COMMUNITY!
the dreaming™
Come and preview the hottest manga around!
CREATE...
UPLOAD...
DOWNLOAD...
BLOG...
CHAT...
VOTE...
LIVE!!!!
TOKYOPOP
TOKYOPOP Message Board
offbeat™
WWW.TOKYOPOP.COM HAS:
Manga-on-Demand • News
Anime Reviews • Manga Reviews
Movie Reviews • Music Reviews
and more...
THE MANGA REVOLUTION • LEADING
漫画革命
The Dreaming © Queenie Chan and TOKYOPOP Inc. Off*Beat © Jennifer Quick and TOKYOPOP Inc.

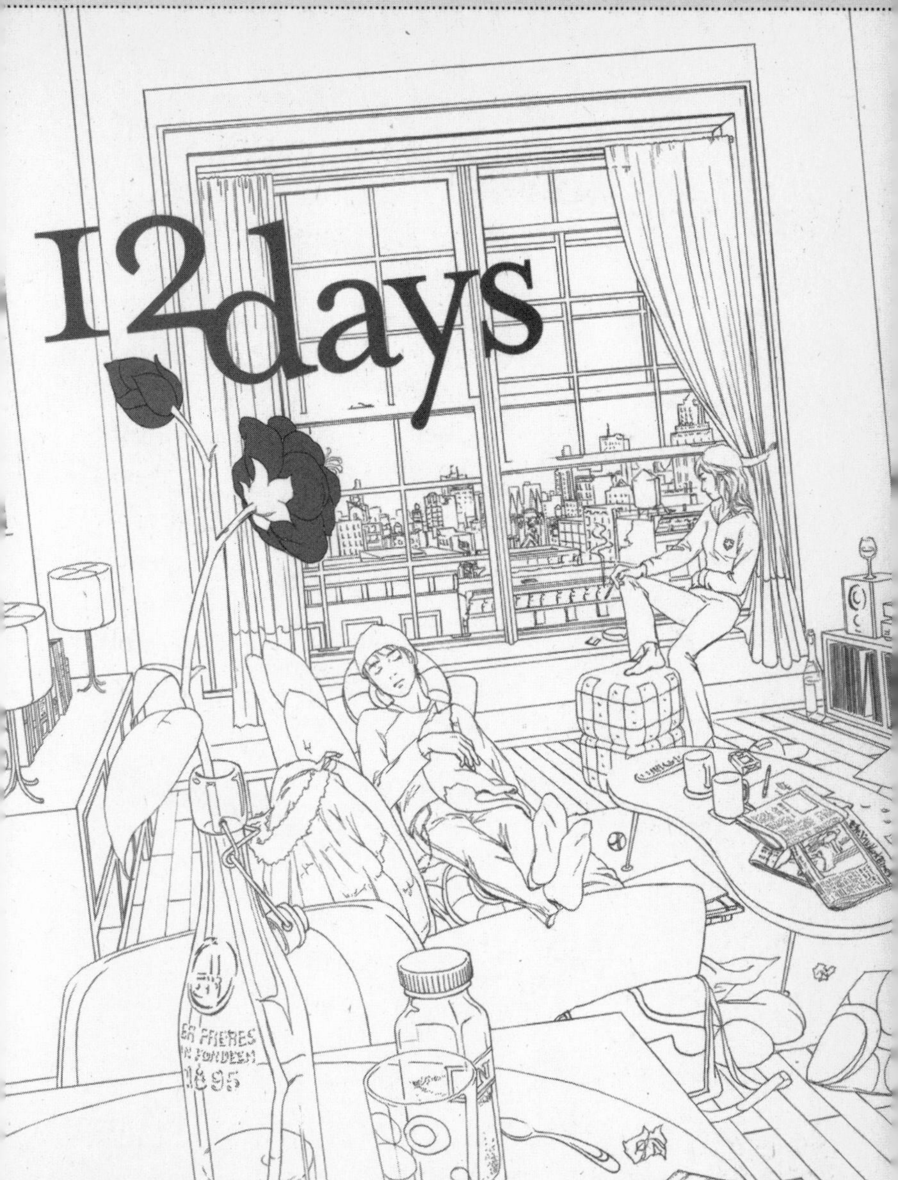
12days

How long would it take to get over...

losing the love of your life?

When Jackie's ex-lover Noah dies, she decides the quickest way to get over her is to hold a personal ritual with Noah's ashes. Jackie consumes the ashes in the form of smoothies for 12 days, hoping the pain will subside. But will that be enough?

From the internationally published illustrator June Kim.

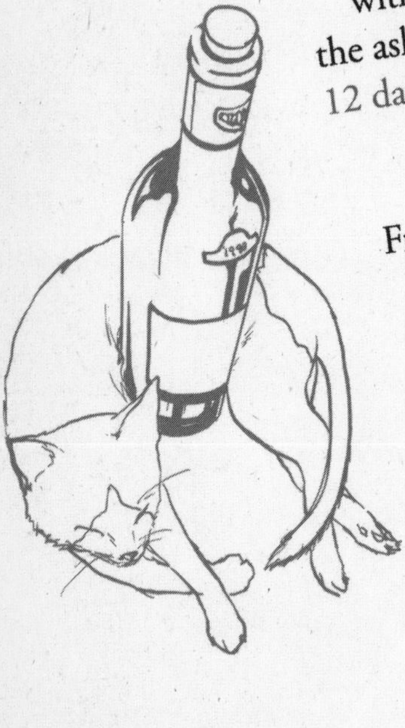

DRAMA

OT OLDER TEEN AGE 16+

FOR MORE INFORMATION VISIT:

ELEMENTAL GELADE VOL. 2
BY MAYUMI AZUMA

ELEMENTAL GELADE

A SKY PIRATE MANGA BOUND TO HOOK YOU!

Rookie sky pirate Coud Van Giruet discovers a most unusual bounty: a young girl named Ren who is an "Edel Raid"—a living weapon that lends extraordinary powers to humans. But just as he realizes Ren is a very valuable treasure, she is captured! Can Coud and Arc Aile join forces and rescue her without killing themselves…or each other?

THE MANGA THAT SPARKED THE HIT ANIME!!

ACTION

T
TEEN
AGE 13+

© MAYUMI AZUMA

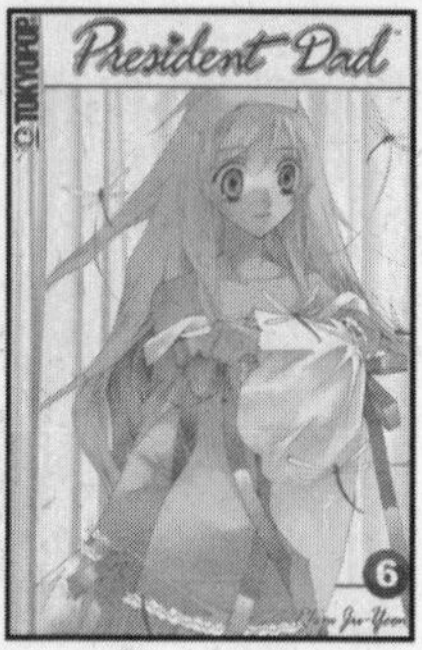
TOKYOPOP
President Dad
6

COMEDY TEEN AGE 13+

PRESIDENT DAD

BY JU-YEON RHIM

In spite of the kind of dorky title, this book is tremendously fun and stylish. The mix of romance and truly bizarre comedy won me over in a heartbeat. When young Ami's father becomes the new president of South Korea, suddenly she is forced into a limelight that she never looked for and isn't particularly excited about. She's got your typical teenage crushes on pop idols (and a mysterious boy from her past who may be a North Korean spy! Who'd have thought there'd be global politics thrown into a shojo series?!), and more than her fair share of crazy relatives, but now she's also got a super-tough bodyguard who can disguise himself as anyone you can possibly imagine, and the eyes of the nation are upon her! This underrated manhwa totally deserves a second look!

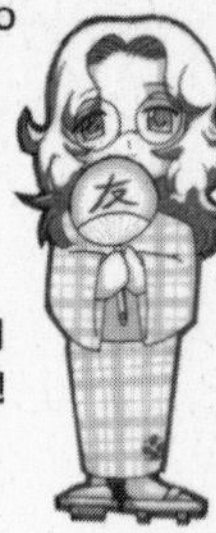

~Lillian Diaz-Pryzbyl, Editor

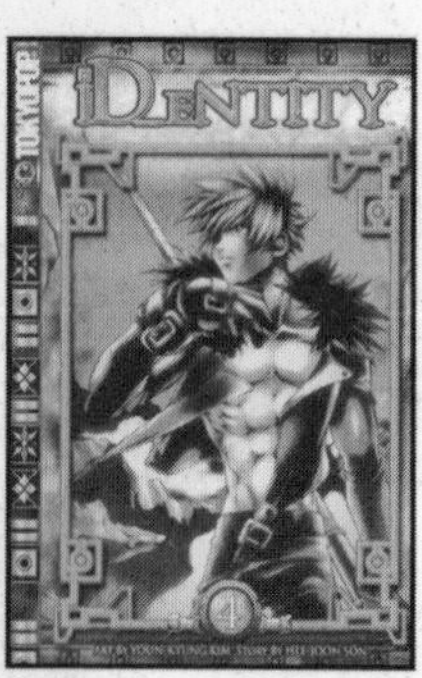
TOKYOPOP
iD_eNTITY
4

ACTION TEEN AGE 13+

ID_ENTITY

BY HEE-JOON SON AND YOUN-KYUNG KIM

As a fan of online gaming, I've really been enjoying *iD_eNTITY.* Packed with action, intrigue and loads of laughs, *iD_eNTITY* is a raucous romp through a virtual world that's obviously written and illustrated by fellow gamers. Hee-Joon Son and Youn-Kyung Kim utilize gaming's terms and conventions while keeping the story simple and entertaining enough for noobs (a glossary of gaming terms is included in the back). Anyone else out there who has already absorbed *.hack* and is looking for a new gaming adventure to go on would do well to start here.

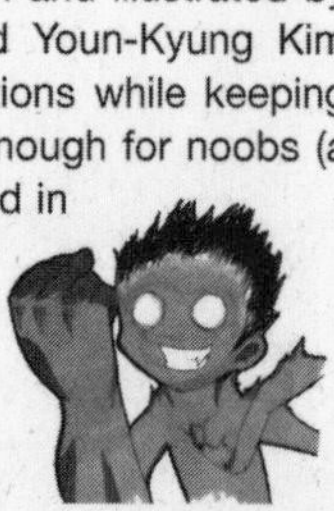

~Tim Beedle, Editor

TOKYOPOP MANGA SUPPLEMENT

From the creator of the bestselling manga *Kissxxxx!*

MAKI KUSUMOTO'S

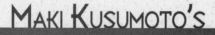

Dölis™

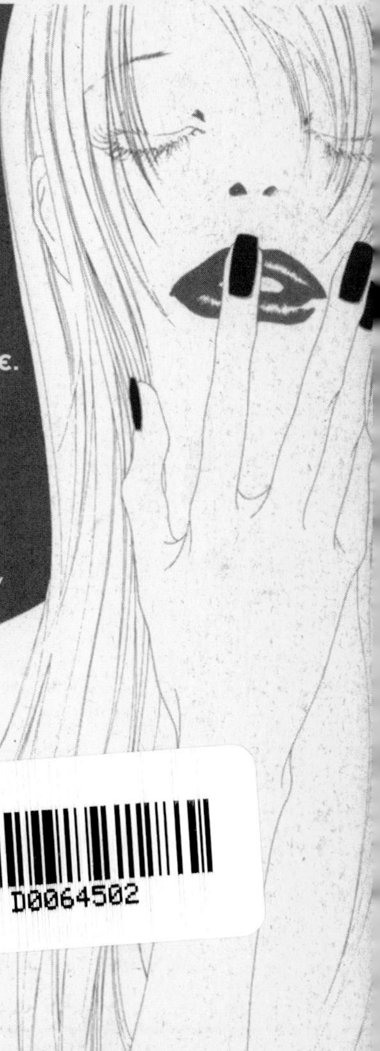

Two people that live their lives however they want to, but need each other to survive.

Mitsu has always been looked upon by men as the Dolis—the ideal girl, the eternal partner in any man's dream, the perfect lover... When Kishi falls head-over-heels in love with Mitsu, he soon discovers another side to this seemingly flawless woman. As the drama and romance between Mitsu and Kishi unfold, they take an extraordinary excursion into the uncharted arena where love and desire confront hope and survival.

D0064502

DRAMA

OT OLDER TEEN AGE 16+

FOR MORE INFORMATION VISIT: WWW.TOKYOPOP.COM